Rosetta. E. Hewinson.
June 1994.

An A–Z of Counselling Theory and Practice

An A–Z of Counselling Theory and Practice

William Stewart
Freelance Counsellor and Trainer
Eastleigh
Hampshire
UK

CHAPMAN & HALL
London · Glasgow · New York · Tokyo · Melbourne · Madras

**Published by Chapman & Hall, 2-6 Boundary Row,
London SE1 8HN, UK**

Chapman & Hall, 2-6 Boundary Row, London SE1 8HN, UK

Blackie Academic & Professional, Wester Cleddens Road,
Bishopbriggs, Glasgow G64 2NZ, UK

Chapman & Hall Japan, Thomson Publishing Japan, Hirakawacho
Nemoto Building, 6F, 1-7-11 Hirakawa-cho, Chiyoda-ku, Tokyo 102,
Japan

Chapman & Hall Australia, Thomas Nelson Australia, 102 Dodds
Street, South Melbourne, Victoria 3205, Australia

Chapman & Hall India, R. Seshadri, 32 Second Main Road, CIT East,
Madras 600 035, India

Distributed in the USA and Canada by Singular Publishing Group Inc.,
4284 41st Street, San Diego, California 92105

First edition 1992
Reprinted 1993

Typeset in 10/12 Palatino by Mews Photosetting, Beckenham, Kent

Printed in Great Britain by T.J. Press (Padstow) Ltd, Padstow,
Cornwall

ISBN 0 412 47430 1 1 56593 055 X USA

A catalogue record for this book is available from the British Library
Library of Congress Cataloging-in-Publication Data available

Contents

Preface

This A–Z of counselling theory and practice draws its inspiration from several years as a teacher of counselling skills and is an attempt to bring together in one volume many different ideas about counselling and many different approaches.

The number of topics covered is extensive, so it was a deliberate choice of what to include and what to leave out. Much more could have been added to many of the topics, and some readers will possibly be left with an impression of incompleteness. It is my hope that there is enough detail to provide an insight into the subjects and that the indexes will act as referral points for people wishing to study specific subjects in more depth. So it is both a reference and a source book.

There is an increasing awareness and interest in counselling as a discipline and in applying the principles to other types of work. Students of counselling, in whatever area, need a handy reference book. This is what I have set out to write. From this book people will be able to dip into theory and practice and taste what is there. I also hope that what they read will help them to explore what particular approach to counselling may best suit them.

The style is deliberately brief and to the point. I felt that long discussion would act as a deterrent, particularly for people who are having to fit counselling training around full-time occupation.

My thanks must go to the many authors whose works I have used and referred to in the bibliography. A second group of people who deserve thanks are the students and staff of St George's and Roehampton College of Health Studies, where I was student counsellor/lecturer for four years. They helped me to develop many of the ideas, principles, and skills I have included in this book.

My wife and family also deserve thanks. The 'project' has a tendency to take over, and there are times when my longsuffering wife has almost had to drag me away from the WP! Each of my children has inspired me in different ways, with their encouragement and helpful advice and support.

The writer's life can be a bit lonely at times; without the support of my family . . .

The real inspiration for this type of book (very different from my others) came from my son John, himself author of an encyclopaedia. His books are on different topics from mine, but the precise way he presents his data is an object-lesson in detail. Thank you, John.

Lastly, my thanks to the staff of St George's Medical Library, Southampton Medical Library, Winchester City Library, Eastleigh Town Library, and Southampton University Library. Tracking down some of the references meant going back into archives of ninety years. Finding this information was a splendid example of problem-solving at work.

Foreword by David Charles-Edwards

Counselling, which has frequently been confused with advice, has developed dramatically over the past 50 years, from an anonymous way of helping. After all, it is still the definition found in most dictionaries. Nevertheless, the confusion is slowly, if imperceptibly, beginning to abate as the hijack of the word from advice is consolidated in a successful way.

The British Association for Counselling, and other organizations, including the National Association for Citizens Advice Bureau, are making the *fait accompli* both respectable and well-known. The biggest counselling organization in the United Kingdom celebrated its 50th birthday recently by changing its name to Relate, and by losing the embarrassment of having the word guidance in its title.

Guidance and advice still have a significant and continuing role to play. The need is to clarify and understand the differences between the different modes of helping, so that we can make informed choices about what is more appropriate, if we are to seek or offer help competently. The skilled helper is not someone who has one way of helping to offer, but sells it hard to anyone who crosses his or her path.

The relative youth of counselling generates a creative but not always helpful confusion beyond the question of initial definition. The types of counselling, and the theories which explicitly or implicitly underpin the practice, are numerous. They have been estimated as over 200: a not-out double century! Many of these, however, are variations of one another, with fine-tuned differences of meaning or language. The latter is regarded as a marketing necessity by some, eager to offer a USP (unique selling point). For others, it is important – if we are to own what we do – to reword it in our own language. Before you know where you are, a new kind of counselling has apparently emerged.

Nevertheless, the range of concepts is considerable, and this A–Z is an important, intelligible and accessible contribution to helping you work your way through the maze.

David is a consultant in individual and organisational development and a counsellor. He co-edited the *Handbook of Counselling in Britain*, (with Windy Dryden and Ray Woolfe) Routledge 1989, and wrote *Death, Bereavement and Work*. CEPEC, 1992. A former Relate counsellor and NHS personnel manager, he managed the British Association for Counselling from 1982–1987. During those years he was also secretary of what is now the UK Standing Conference for Psychotherapy.

Biographical summary of author

William Stewart spent twenty years in the Royal Army Medical Corps and gained experience in general and psychiatric nursing in the UK and abroad. He was commissioned in 1968 as a specialist officer in mental health, and pioneered social work in the Armed Forces. Following his training as a Psychiatric Social Worker he established a private counselling and counselling training practice.

On retiring from the RAMC in 1974, he worked as Senior Nurse (Allocation) in the Southampton University Hospitals Combined School of Nursing until 1987.

In 1987 he was invited to set up the Student and Staff Counselling service (part-time Student Counsellor/Lecturer) at St George's and Roehampton College of Health Studies, and St George's School of Radiography, London. In addition to providing a counselling service for students and college staff, he taught a variety of interpersonal skills within the College.

Twenty years ago he was one of the early pioneers of counselling within the health care professions. He has been a member of the British Association for Counselling since its inception as the Standing Conference for the Advancement of Counselling.

His previous books are:

An Introduction to Counselling
A Guide to Counselling: every manager a counsellor
Health Service Counselling
Counselling for Nurses
Counselling in Rehabilitation.

He is the author of over thirty articles and case studies on counselling and related management topics and has conducted four major research projects.

Dedication

I have the privilege of dedicating this book to the memory of Colonel Richard Glanville (Dai) Davies Late RAMC. I twice served under his command at Royal Victoria Hospital, Netley, and he was my friend and mentor for many years. His own work as an army psychiatrist made him an ideal personal mentor and our sessions were precious to both of us. I learned from him, and I (as he so often said) kept him stimulated in his retirement. In the closing weeks of his life we both knew that he would not live to read this dedication. He had no regrets about dying, though he would like to have read this book. I publicly thank you, Dai, for your encouragement, love, wisdom and vision. You lived your life for the benefit of others. My desire is to show as much caring as you have shown to me and to return to others a little of what you have shared with me.

Dai, I salute you.

A

'A'-TYPE PERSONALITY

An ingrained pattern of behaviour observed in people who struggle to obtain something from their environment as quickly as possible. What they strive for is often not clear and may be in conflict with other things or persons.

PERSONALITY CHARACTERISTICS:

1. Extreme competitiveness;
2. striving for achievement;
3. aggressiveness (sometimes very repressed);
4. haste;
5. impatience;
6. restlessness;
7. hyperalertness;
8. explosiveness of speech;
9. tension in facial muscles;
10. feelings of being under pressure of time;
11. feelings of being under the challenge of responsibility;
12. deeply committed to their vocation or professions; other aspects of their lives may be neglected.

A high proportion of 'A'-type men develop coronary heart disease. The cardiovascular system seems particularly sensitive to 'A'-type behaviours.

ABRAHAM, KARL (1877–1925)

German psychoanalyst whose main contributions are on the role of infant sexuality in character development and mental illness. His ideas still stand in psychoanalysis.

His first psychoanalytic paper dealt with childhood sexual trauma related to later symptoms of schizophrenia. His pioneering work was the psychoanalytic treatment of psychoses, particularly manic depressive psychosis.

His work on myths and symbols enriched psychoanalytic theory. For example, his proposition that the spider represented the feared mother became widely accepted.

ABRAHAM'S STAGES OF LIBIDO DEVELOPMENT:

1. Earlier oral
2. oral–sadistic

3. anal expulsion
4. retentive
5. phallic
6. adult genital.

His thesis was that arrested development (non-gratification) results in fixation of libido at that level and gives rise to mental disorder.

Gratification at stage 1 is associated with the positive traits of curiosity, accessibility to new ideas, and sociability. Fixation at the anal stage results in the traits of reticence, moroseness, hesitation, procrastination, and inaccessibility to new ideas.

ABREACTION

(SYNONYMOUS WITH CATHARSIS)

The living again of painful emotional experiences in psychotherapy. Abreaction involves bringing repressed unconscious or preconscious material into conscious awareness.

ACCEPTANCE (*See also:* Relationship principles)

The feeling of being accepted as we really are, including our strengths and weaknesses, differences of opinions, and whatever, no matter how unpleasant or uncongenial, without censure. We do not feel accepted unless the very worst in us is accepted too. We never feel accepted when judgment is passed on us.

If we want to guide someone, even one step of the way, we must *feel* with that person's psyche. We may not put our judgments of other people into words; we may keep them to ourselves; this makes not the slightest difference. Judgment in the heart will be revealed.

We cannot change anything unless we accept it. Condemnation (which lies at the heart of rejection) does not liberate, it oppresses. We can only truly accept when we have already seen and accepted ourselves as we are.

In Person-centred therapy, the concept of acceptance enables the counsellor to distinguish between the client's 'self' and 'behaviour'. It means maintaining all the while a sense of the client's innate dignity and personal worth.

Rational emotive therapists practice unconditional acceptance by trying to show their clients that no matter how badly they act – toward the therapist or toward others – the therapist can still accept them and teach them to unconditionally accept themselves.

Acceptance does not mean approval of deviant attitudes of behaviour. The object of acceptance is not 'the good' but the 'real'.

Acceptance is not an all-or-nothing phenomenon, like perfect sight or total blindness. Rather, every counsellor has a certain degree of acceptance, which may vary from day to day or from client to client. No counsellor has, or is expected to have, perfect acceptance, for that would require a godlike wisdom and an immunity from human frailties.

ACKERMAN, NATHAN WARD (1908–1971)

Ackerman, a Soviet-born Jew, emigrated to the USA in 1912 and studied medicine and psychiatry. He was a founder member of the American Academy of Psychoanalysis and a pioneer of family therapy.

Ackerman's approach to psychoanalysis was creative and unorthodox. His belief in the influences of society and culture led him toward the treatment of the family as a group. He founded the Family Institute, New York, and co-founded the *Family Process* journal.

ACTING OUT – ACTING IN (*See also*: Defence mechanisms)

ACTING OUT

Where the individual expresses an unconscious wish or impulse through action, to avoid being conscious of the accompanying feeling.

Acting out behaviour is impulsive and gratifying, whereas control or inhibiting the impulse would provoke tension and anxiety.

Freud applied the term to transference and also to all breaking through behaviour within and outside of the therapeutic relationship.

Acting out takes the form of aggression or sexual responses that may be directed toward the therapist or toward others.

In pschyoanalytic terms, as acting out is a substitute for words, it is regarded as a resistance and a hindrance to therapy. It may be regarded as an inability to grieve appropriately for the past, and since the feelings cannot be expressed in healthy grieving, they are expressed in abnormal behaviour.

Examples of acting out:

1. Re-enactment of violence on others;
2. taking it out on our own children;
3. spontaneous age regression – temper tantrums;
4. inappropriate rebellion;
5. carrying on the rules of idealized parents;
6. child abuse;
7. pleasureless promiscuity.

Very often acting out is not accompanied by apparent guilt. Severe acting out invariably engenders fear in the observer. It seriously threatens the therapeutic relationship.

ACTING IN

Used in contrast to acting out; a midway stage between acting out and verbalization.

Acting in means directing inward the behaviours associated with acting out – punishing ourselves in the way we were punished as children. Unresolved emotions from the past are often turned against the self.

The child who is taught to be perfectly obedient, and that anger is 'sinful', may well turn that anger inward, to be expressed behaviourally as depression, apathy, ineptness, and powerlessness.

Physical problems – affecting any of the bodily systems – may also result from acting in. Accident proneness, for example, where one punishes oneself by accident, is another form of acting in.

ACTION PLANS (*See also*: Goals and goal-setting)

Stage 3 in the Egan model of counselling.

There is more to helping than talking and planning. If clients are to live more effectively they must act. When they fail to act, they fail to cope with problems in living or to exploit unused opportunities. Attaining goals cannot be left to chance.

THREE STEPS IN ACTION ARE:

1. Discovering strategies for action.
2. Choosing strategies and devising an action plan.
3. Implementing plans and achieving goals.

A goal is an *end*; a strategy is a *means* for achieving a goal.

Many people fail to achieve goals because they do not explore alternatives. Brainstorming ways of achieving a goal increase the probability that one of them, or a combination of several, will suit the resources of a particular client.

Planning helps to initiate, and give direction, to action.

Clients and the counsellors will know when the goal has been reached only when the clients feel sufficiently free from the forces that have been restraining them to take constructive action. The aim is to help the client discover, then harness, inner resources which have been locked in.

Increased self-awareness and insight are often the keys that will release these resources.

THE STAGES OF THE ACTION PLAN:

1. Thinking it through. Inadequate thinking through may spell disaster.
2. Carrying it out.

GOALS SHOULD BE:

1. Stated as accomplishments or outcomes rather than means or strategies;
2. clear and specific;
3. measurable or verifiable;
4. realistic;
5. genuine;
6. in keeping with the client's overall strategy and values;
7. set in a realistic time frame.

ADAPTATIONAL PSYCHODYNAMICS

Developed by Hungarian psychoanalyst Sandor Rado (1890–1970).

It is a unified, systematized theory of human behaviour. The individual's purpose is the fulfilment of pleasure (hedonism).

A psychologically healthy psyche has adapted effectively to the balance between pleasure and reality. Psychological ill-health is where the psyche has not adapted.

The factors that contribute to mental ill-health are:

1. learning
2. culture
3. discipline
4. biological.

LEVELS OF MENTAL INTEGRATION

1. Hedonic

Pain – moving away: reduces esteem
Pleasure – moving toward: enhances esteem.

2. Emotional

Emergency emotions – fear, rage, fight/flight response.
Welfare emotions – love, pride, clinging to, to possess.

Daily living is primarily at the hedonic and emotional levels. Fear and rage are stronger than the welfare emotions which stimulate:

trust
cooperation
exchange of affection.

3. Emotional thought

fantasies
dreams
prejudices
illusions
delusions
hallucinations.

Emotional thought is responsible for much of everyday thought. The principal characteristic of emotional thought is *justification* – reinforcement of the emotion from which the particular experience springs.

4. Unemotional thought which equates with Freud's *reality principle* allows the person to:

Postpone action and gratification; tolerate pain in order to:

forego pleasure in the present in favour of future pleasure;
gain control over emotional responses. The stages in the development of the person's concept of self:

1. All-powerful and magical;
2. realization that powers are limited;
3. magical powers are repressed;
4. power and magic delegated to powerful parents who use these to benefit the child;
5. perceives self as the provider of pleasure which is the basis of self-esteem or pride.

In therapy, the emotionally healthy person stimulates feelings of pleasure in others; this, in turn, stimulates one's own feelings of pleasure. The emergency responses are still present, but they find non-destructive outlets through activities and dreams.

THE AIM OF THERAPY IS TO:

1. Increase welfare emotions;
2. reduce emergency responses;
3. help the client relinquish dependency;
4. increase self-reliance.

Adaptational psychodynamics explores the past only to understand the present and the emphasis is on actual, observable behaviour.

There is a strong belief in the educational role of the therapist, with much less attention paid to developing and working through transference.

ADAPTED CHILD (*See also*: Transactional analysis)

A personality ego state whose functions are:

1. To conform.
2. To rebel to what another person wants.

The adapted child ego state is highly complex and contains one's life script. The basic need of the adapted child is for approval.

Some typical words

Can't; did I do all right?; do it for me; I didn't do it; it's all your fault; mine; nobody loves me.

Some typical gestures and postures

Batting eyelashes; dejected; nail-biting, obscene gestures; temper tantrums.

Some typical voice tones

Asking permission; annoying; spitefulness; sullen silence; swearing; whining.

Some typical facial expressions

Eyes directed upward/downward; helplessness; pouting; woebegone.

Life position	Behaviour
1. I'm not OK You're not OK	Sulking
2. I'm OK You're not OK	Complaining
3. I'm OK You're OK	Resilient
4. I'm not OK You're OK	Dependent

ADULT (*See also*: Transactional analysis)

An analytical, rational, and non-judgmental ego state.

The adult problem-solves and obtains information.

The basic need of the adult is *rationality*.

Some typical words

According to statistics; alternatives; check it out; have you tried this?; result; how?

Some typical gestures and postures

Active listening; checking for understanding; giving feedback; pointing something out.

Some typical voice tones

Calm; clear, with appropriate emotion; confident; informative; inquiring; straight.

Some typical facial expressions

Attentive; confident; eyes alert; direct eye contact; lively; responsive; thoughtful.

Life position	Behaviour
1. I'm not OK You're not OK	Cynical
2. I'm OK You're not OK	Task oriented
3. I'm OK You're OK	Problem-solving
4. I'm not OK You're OK	Helpless

ADVICE

Advice is opinion, judgment (as it appears to me), probability, careful thought, consideration, deliberation, recommendation regarding a course of conduct, information or notice given, or action to be taken.

Advice is generally considered inappropriate in person-centred therapy, and most humanistic and holistic approaches. It may be more appropriate and acceptable when working with the very young, or people who are disturbed or helpless, or in essentially practical issues.

Directive therapies – behaviour therapy, cognitive therapy, crisis intervention and brief therapy – rely on advice giving, though not in the lay understanding of the term.

The advice so given is aimed at helping the person deal with the problem, to achieve a goal.

It is useful to distinguish between advice on how the client's life should be lived, and instruction about specific aspects of the therapeutic process.

Counsellors who offer a lot of advice run the risk of increasing the dependency of the client. Advice should always be, 'this is what is possible', not, 'this is what you should do'. The stronger the emotional content of the issue, the less appropriate is advice.

IN ORDER TO GIVE ADVICE, COUNSELLORS MUST:

1. Be reasonably sure they know what is best for the client.
2. Be quite sure that the need for advice rests in the client and not in themselves.

3. Induce clients, whenever possible, to think things through for themselves.

There are occasions when counsellors put strength behind the advice; when they 'advocate' some course of action, for example, to seek medical opinion.

AGGRESSION

A variety of behaviour patterns in which (in human terms) a person shows a tendency to approach in attack, rather than flee from something perceived as a threat. It is almost impossible to arrive at a concise definition of aggression; there are more than 250 definitions.

AGGRESSION IS VIEWED AS:

1. A motivated state;
2. a personality characteristic;
3. a response to frustration;
4. an inherent drive;
5. the need to fulfil a socially learned role.

In everyday terms, aggression refers to acts of hostility and violence, and meets with disfavour, yet there are contradictions. We speak approvingly of an athlete running an *aggressive* race, or the successful entrepreneur who conducts an *aggressive* sales campaign.

Competition, dominance, rivalry and victory, all characterize aggression.

Many murders or serious violent assaults appear to be instances of hostile aggression or explosive outbursts resulting from an argument or perceived threat. The majority of people who commit aggressive acts, are more likely to commit them against people known to them, usually family members.

The clients to be wary of, when they express anger towards others, are:

1. Those who lack perspective – they may misinterpret events.
2. Those who want to hurt specific people, in unspecified ways.
3. Those who have a history of episodic aggression.
4. Those unable to express anger toward another person on whom they are dependent.

Hostile or destructive feelings and intentions may also be expressed through passive or submissive behaviour. *Passive aggressive* characters usually direct such behaviours toward others on whom they feel dependent or to whom they feel subordinate. Manifestations or passive aggression include:

1. Disinterest
2. withdrawal
3. negativism
4. obstructionism
5. insufficiency
6. procrastination
7. sabotage
8. perfunctory behaviour
9. errors of omission
10. indifference
11. foot-dragging
12. lack of initiative
13. literalness in compliant behaviour that frustrates the outcome
14. dumb insolence.

The individual denies any hostile or negative intent, although there may be periodic angry outbursts.

ALEXANDER, FRANZ G. (1891–1964)

Hungarian physician and psychoanalyst; the first enrolled student of the Berlin Psychoanalytic Institute (1919).

Alexander is often referred to as 'the father of psychosomatic medicine', because of his leading role in identifying the relationship between emotional tension and physical illness.

His success in applying psychoanalytic principles to the study and diagnosis of criminal personalities took him to America where he had a distinguished career in treating delinquency and psychosomatic conditions.

He contributed to psychotherapy in his study on the influence of the therapist's personality on the therapeutic process.

Although determinedly upholding most of the Freudian principles, he maintained that disturbed human relationships, rather than disturbed sexuality, was the main cause of neurotic behaviour.

ALIENATION (*See also*: Anomie, Existential therapy)

1. In Sociology, the condition of being an outsider; a state of isolation.
2. In Psychology, a state of estrangement between the self and the objective world, or between different parts of the personality.

Alienation is one of the most serious consequences of neurotic development.

Synonyms of alienation are: deflection, variance, separation, disaffection, coolness, withdrawal, estrangement, breach, rupture, weaning away, division, diverting.

The roots of the idea of alienation are found in philosophy and religion. Karl Marx adapted Hegel's idea to produce his theory of social change. For Marx, alienation centred on man's alienation to work by the capitalist system.

ALIENATION IS CHARACTERIZED BY:

1. Powerlessness

   The feeling that one's destiny is controlled by outside agencies such as luck and fate.

2. Meaninglessness

   Feelings of total lack of comprehension and purpose in all aspects of life.

3. Normlessness

   Does not share a commitment to social behaviour.

4. Cultural estrangement

   Removal from established values of society.

5. Social isolation

   Loneliness/exclusion in social relations.

6. Self-estrangement

   Where a person is out of touch with herself/himself.

Alienation results either from separateness from others and the world, or from an inability to choose and act in a relationship.

The central task of counselling is to enable clients who feel alienated to see themselves in a relationship to the world and to choose and act in accordance with what they see.

Alienation from self results from repeated, active denial and the repression of genuine feelings and impulses. As this process continues, such persons lose touch with the very core of their being, as well as the ability to determine and act on what is right for them.

People who experience alienation may be seized by weird and monstrous thoughts. The whole world seems changed. It is not a state of which one is conscious. It can only be recognized from outside the experience.

Whole groups experience alienation. But even the individual members are remote from one another. They feel that no one is close, or in touch, or can meaningfully share a feeling–life. To the existentialist therapist, alienation is the patient's core problem to be overcome.

ALTRUISM (*See also*: Equity theory)

In ethics, a theory of conduct that regards the good of others as the end of moral action. An altruistic act is where the donor promotes the fitness of the recipient at the donor's expense. Two basic types have been identified:

1. RECIPROCAL ALTRUISM

Where one person performs a service or makes a sacrifice for another person, to achieve some sort of balance between giver and recipient. Examples would be:

Helping in times of danger or distress;
Sharing food, tools, knowledge.

Reciprocal altruism may lead to 'cheating', if one person does not reciprocate, thus creating imbalance.

2. KIN ALTRUISM

This is achieved mainly through identification, coupled with some innate desire or disposition.

The socializing process within the family is the one most important influence.

The most potent example of kin altruism is in the upholding of the incest taboo, the breaking of which is the ultimate rejection of altruism.

EXAMPLES OF ALTRUISTIC BEHAVIOUR:

1. Blood donation
2. money donating
3. rendering assistance at an accident
4. volunteeering
5. challenging shoplifters.

The bystander effect has been studied relating to altruism, in which individuals are less likely to help when they are in the presence of others, than when they are alone.

The bystander response seems to be governed by:

1. Age;
2. sex and number of bystanders;
3. characteristics of the person in need;
4. the help given by others;
5. familiarity of the situation;
6. cultural norms.

STEPS IN THE PROCESS THAT LEADS TO ALTRUISM:

1. Notice that something is happening;
2. interpret that help is needed;
3. assume personal responsibility;
4. choice of a form of assistance;
5. implement the assistance.

ALTRUISM (Defence mechanism)

Through this defence mechanism (similar to reaction formation), the individual experiences inner satisfaction through unselfish service to others. It is different from **altruistic surrender**, where serving others is to the detriment of oneself and arises from an almost pathological feeling of self-worthlessness.

ANAL PHASE

A psychoanalytic term to describe the second stage of psychosexual (libidinal) development, postulated in Freud's instinct theory.

In the anal phase the anus and defaecation are the major sources of sensuous pleasure. This forms the centre of the infant's self-awareness.

This phase is also important in the development of ego, as the infant begins to exercise sphincter control, something so obviously important to the parents and which brings mutual pleasure.

ANALYTICAL PSYCHOLOGY (Carl G. Jung (1875–1961))

Jung, a renowned Swiss psychologist and psychiatrist was a contemporary of Freud. Jung had already formulated some of his major ideas before he came to know Freud. He used the term 'analytical psychology' to distinguish his method from psychoanalysis.

His work was influenced by religion, mysticism and parapsychology.

PRINCIPAL DIFFERENCES BETWEEN JUNG AND FREUD

1. Jung attached less importance to the role of sexuality in the neuroses.
2. He believed that the analysis of patients' immediate conflicts were more important than the uncovering of the conflicts of childhood.
3. He defined the unconscious as including both the individual's own unconscious and that which he inherited – the 'collective unconscious'.
4. His interpretation of dreams was less rigid.
5. His emphasis on the use of the phenomenon of transference.
6. The psychotherapeutic approach to the individual.

Analytical psychology does not possess a detailed personality theory.

In Analytical psychology, the psyche comprises several autonomous, yet interdependent subsystems:

1. Ego

The centre of consciousness.
The experiential being of the person.
The sum total of:

Thoughts
ideas
feelings
memories
sensory perceptions.

2. Personal unconscious

Consists of everything that has been repressed during one's development.
Contains elements easily available to consciousness.
Contains complexes – emotionally toned ideas and behavioural impulses, having an archetypal core.

3. Collective unconscious which includes:

Archetypes.
Persona – the archetype of adaptation.
Shadow– all we would not like to be.

The Animus and Anima. Two complimentary parts. Similar to the Yin – feminine principle, and Yang – masculine principle of Chinese philosophy.

Feminine principle

Nature, creation and life;
earthiness and concreteness;
receptivity and yielding;
dark and containing;
collective and undifferentiated;
the unconscious.

Masculine principle

Driving and energetic;
creative and initiating;
light and heat;
penetrating;
stimulating and dividing;
separation and differentiation;
restriction and discipline;
arousing and phallic;
aggression and enthusiasm;
spirit and heaven.

The self

An archetypal image of one's fullest potential and the unity of the personality as a whole. The self is our god within ourselves. The process by which we achieve the goal of realization of self is individuation.

The person who is all animus or all anima is like an egg without a yolk.

THE FOUR STAGES OF THERAPY

1. Confession
2 Elucidation
3. Education
4. Transformation.

The goal of therapy is:

To help the individual gain insight; to journey toward individuation; to facilitate greater integration of both conscious and unconscious components.

Jung, as did Freud, believed that disturbance in the psyche often manifests itself in physical symptoms. He used dream analysis to understand the person's current problems as well as to uncover past conflicts. He also used interpretation and free association, as did Freud, but advocated a more active relationship between therapist and patient.

THE JUNGIAN THERAPIST MAY:

1. Teach
2. suggest
3. cajole
4. give advice
5. reflect feelings
6. give support
7. interpret dreams.

In fact, Jung was quite an eclectic. Other concepts associated with Jung are:

1. Archetypes
2. Shadow
3. Persona
4. Collective unconscious
5. Psychological types.

ANIMA (The feeling function) (*See also*: Animus)

In analytical psychology, the feminine principle latent in every male; the internalized female shadow image a man carries. The young man has a maternal anima which is a personification of the heart rather than the head; the source of receptiveness and sensitivity.

The man cannot contract with his own unconscious (expressed in imaginative symbols) without some recognition of the feminine qualities within him.

Anima is one of the archetypes of the collective unconscious, which derives in part from the man's relationships with his mother and other significant females and from his father's attitudes towards women. In addition, he is influenced by the deeper racial archetypal images of woman.

Some anima archetypes:

1. Good mother
2. Harlot
3. Spiritual guide
4. Temptress
5. Vampire
6. Virgin
7. Witch.

A man's relationship with women, and his choice of mate, are influenced by the anima, whose influence may be negative or positive. The internalized image of the anima is influenced by cultural patterns and expectations of what a woman should be.

Part of the process of analytical therapy is helping the male client recognize and integrate the repressed anima. No man is so entirely masculine that he has nothing feminine in him. Men who ignore their anima function only on half their psyche. Ignored, the anima will rule without the man's knowledge.

When men understand the true nature of the anima they can express their feelings more appropriately.

ANIMUS (The thinking function) (*See also*: Anima)
In Analytical psychology, similar to the anima in males. The animus is the latent masculine principle present in every female. The anima is represented in dreams by a single figure; the animus by several or many figures. The animus can be negative and destructive but very positive when integrated.

The woman who refuses to use her thinking powers, relying only on feelings, deprives herself and others of something precious. On the other hand, too much attention by a woman to thinking may rob her of something equally precious.

Some animus archetypes:

1. Hero
2. Man of authority
3. Scholar
4. Spiritual guide
5. Dark or eclipsed sun
6. Giants
7. Satyrs, devils.

The animus in action:

1. The adolescent girl is likely to project the image of the hero upon the physically powerful man.
2. The over-feminine woman may be attracted to the man who has achieved success in the world.
3. The woman who doubts her own thinking may be attracted to a man of intellectual attainments.

ANOMIE (*See also:* Alienation, Suicide)

A concept, similar to alienation, popularized by Durkheim in his study of suicide. A state where norms or standards of behaviour are unclear, are absent, or are in conflict with each other.

Where a social system is in a state of anomie, common values and common meanings are no longer understood or accepted, and new values and meanings have not developed.

Anomie is characterized by a sense of futility, lack of purpose, and emotional emptiness and despair. Striving is considered useless, because there is no acceptable definition of what is desirable.

Delinquency, crime, and suicide are often quoted as being reactions to anomie. It is the state of mind of a person who has no sense of continuity or obligation, where all social bonds and standards of behaviour are absent, unclear, or in conflict with each other.

ANOREXIA NERVOSA

1. Anorexia nervosa is a refusal to eat, or an abnormality in eating pattern, not a loss of appetite.
2. It was named about 100 years ago, exists in many countries of the world, and occurs in about 1 in 100 females aged between 16 and 18 years. Especially at risk are dancers, fashion models and food workers.

PHYSICAL SYMPTOMS

1. Malnutrition, resulting in extreme body weight loss and emaciation.
2. Drastic fasting may be interspersed with eating sprees, usually at night, after which vomiting is induced.
3. Cessation of menstruation, and in males a drop in the levels of testosterone.

EMOTIONAL SYMPTOMS

1. These range from a neurotic preoccupation with reducing weight, to full-blown schizophrenic delusions.
2. There is often a history of relationship difficulties, and fear of meeting strangers.
3. Irritability and depression.
4. Extreme weight loss over prolonged periods results in impaired reasoning and logic.

POSSIBLE CAUSES

1. Biological

There is no known cause. A disorder of the hypothalamus in the brain is a theory. A function of the hypothalamus is the control of metabolism and intestinal activity.

2. Psychological

The major psychological factor appears to be inability to face womanhood.

Sexual maturity

This means accepting femininity with all its changes and responsibilities.

Characteristics of the anorexic's immediate family:

Dysfunctional communication; closed, indirect, veiled, defensive.
Parental overprotectiveness.
The anorexic person is over-concerned for and feels responsible for the well-being of others.
Intense relationships with excessive togetherness and sharing.
Rigidity with resistance to change.
Anorexics often feel that if they get well their parent's marriage will fail.
There is often a family history of eating or weight problems.
Anorexics are discouraged from developing personal autonomy and their own unique identity.

Anorexics have a self-esteem characterized by:

A pathological need for approval.
A stern disapproval of themselves.
A compelling striving for perfection.
Considering themselves unworthy.
Fixed, almost delusional, beliefs about being unattractive.
Overestimation of their body width.
Starving themselves to achieve a still smaller body-image.
Appearing unconcerned at their undernourished state.
A self-imposed social isolation, involving eating and drinking.

Sexual relationships

Extreme weight loss leads to reduced sexual interest and activity.
They fear taking on the sexual roles observed in their parents.
They feel they cannot love another, when they do not like themselves.
The slightly masculine look, which many adopt, warns males off.
The break up of a relationship may be the result of curing anorexia.
Pregnancy is unlikely because of the extreme and prolonged weight loss.

Achievement

Academic success is highly valued by anorexics and their families.
An extreme fear of failure pushes them on to constantly seek approval.
Anything less than a 100% pass is a failure.
Praise for achievement is almost impossible to accept.
Their weight is the only thing over which they feel they have control.
They must control the intake of food, and every function of the body, mind, and emotions.

Dieting and exercise

Obsessive rigidity and unbalanced diets characterize their goal of ever lower weight and slimmer figure.
So much has calorie-counting taken over that they no longer control the diet; it controls them.
Many engage in a killing schedule of exercises and sport.
There is a close parallel between anorexics and long-distance runners. Both are likely to be from fairly affluent backgrounds, introverted, with depressive tendencies, and high achievers, with an obsessive interest in keeping up physical appearances.

PHYSICAL TREATMENT

Hospital admission may be necessary, to restore correct dietary intake and a balanced blood chemistry.
Cooperation is vital, so undue pressure must be avoided.
Weight gain alone is not necessarily a cure.

EMOTIONAL TREATMENT

Anorexia can be totally reversed, without lasting effects.
Anorexics must want to be cured; and this means putting on weight.
Treatment started within one year of the onset of anorexia has a far greater chance of quick recovery.

TREATMENT MAY BE:

Personal counselling concentrating on adolescent conflict, interpersonal problems, and personal experiences of stress and failure.
Behaviour modification.
Trance therapy and hypnotherapy.
Group therapy.
Family counselling. One particular approach includes taking meals

with the family, to identify the mealtime dynamics.

Self-help groups such as Anorexic Aid offer help in much the same way as Alcoholics Anonymous.

EARLY WARNINGS

Becoming isolated in their rooms
Missing meals or making excuses of having eaten
Eating alone in room
Slimming and diet magazines
Scales in the bathroom
Reluctance to eat in public
Small amounts of food eaten
Bread, potatoes and carbohydrates avoided
Bulky, loose sweaters that disguise shape
Food thrown away
Ultra health conscious
Fail to put on weight
Preoccupation with calorie-counting
Excessive amounts of exercise
Poor sleep, restlessness, hyperactivity
Cessation of menstruation.

PREVENTION

Establish effective communication
Don't insist on increased intake
Encourage outside help
Don't pressure for weight gain
Encourage self-action and responsibility
Parents may need counselling themselves
Remove pressure to succeed
Encourage independence.

AFTER - WHAT?

Anorexics may lapse when under pressure.

Anorexia is like alcoholism in that the person always must be on guard. Joining a group of ex-anorexics may provide the support necessary to cope with living.

Forming relationships with the opposite sex is a huge hurdle for many ex-anorexics.

ANXIETY

Anxiety is a distressing feeling of uneasiness, apprehension, or dread. The fear may be rational, based on an actual event, or irrational, based on an anticipated event which may or may not take place.

A certain amount of unrealistic and irrational anxiety is part of most people's experience, and seems to be an unavoidable part of human personality.

Existentialists describe anxiety as a *fear of non-being*, which may be fear of death, but also a sense of meaninglessness and a powerful sense of guilt.

When anxiety is chronic, and not traceable to any specific cause, or when it interferes with normal activity, the sufferer is in need of expert help.

Anxious people are in suspense, waiting for something, they know not what. A main source of anxiety is the fear of being separated from other persons who are felt to provide security.

THE SUSPENSE OF ANXIOUS PEOPLE IS CHARACTERIZED BY:

Watchful alertness
Overreaction to noise or other stimuli
Helplessness in the face of danger, whether actual or imagined
Mood that alternates between hope and despair.

ANXIETY IS OFTEN ASSOCIATED WITH:

Tightness in the chest and throat

Sinking feelings in the abdomen
Dizziness, or light feelings in the head
Skin pallor
Sweating, or less often flushed
Increase in pulse rate
Mild exertion produces undue increase in heart rate
Muscle tension
Loss of sexual interest.

Free-floating anxiety is a condition of persistently anxious mood in which the cause of the condition is unknown, and a variety of thoughts and events can trigger the anxiety.

Anxiety frequently manifests itself as the result of opposing or conflicting wishes, desires, beliefs, life events, or strain resulting from conflict between roles.

The more desperate the feeling of helplessness and indecision, and the more difficult the decision between two opposing forces, the more severe the anxiety. Defence mechanisms do not abolish anxiety. They try to bind or keep it from awareness.

APPROVAL

Approval, a form of social control, relates in some ways to Carl Rogers 'unconditional positive regard', but only in the positive sense of approval. Some people will seem to go to extraordinary lengths to gain approval from significant others.

THE CONSEQUENCES OF SOCIAL APPROVAL:

1. Recognition which confirms our identity.
2. Approval:

   Legitimates our existence.
   Increases our status and affords recognition.
3. Approval is:

   Acceptance of what we have to offer.
   The security of not being rejected because of inadequacy in our:

   Abilities
   opinions
   what we think, feel, or do.
4. A bond is established between approver and approved.
5. Approval means that we feel able to exercise a degree of control over our environment.

ARCHETYPES

An archetype is a primeval image, character or pattern that recurs in literature and in thought consistently enough to be considered a universal concept.

An archetype is an inherited disposition to perceive and experience typical or nearly universal situations or patterns of behaviour.

Archetypes are the basis for Jung's 'collective unconscious'.

The symbolic forms of these archetypes are transmitted through myths, stories, and dreams.

EXAMPLES OF ARCHETYPES:

1. One. The origin, the essence of nature.
2. Twofold structure:

   Masculine/feminine; Animus and anima; Positive/negative; Light/-dark; Yin/yang; Inner/outer.
3. Fourfold structure:

   North, south, east, west
   Summer, autumn, winter, spring
   Childhood, youth, adult, old age
   Fire, water, air, earth
   Ego, shadow, animus/anima, self
   Thinking, feeling, sensation, intuition.

4. Other combinations:

   The *I Ching;*
   The Chakras
   The Kabbalah
   The planets of the zodiac
   Tarot
   Gods and goddesses.
5. The hero
6. Search for food and shelter
7. Daily rhythm of work and sleep
8. The search for a mate.

ASCETICISM

The practice of the denial of physical desires in order to attain a spiritual ideal or goal, is practised by all the major religions.

THE FORMS OF ASCETICISM INCLUDE:

1. Celibacy, temporary or total
2. Denial of material possessions
3. Abstinence and fasting
4. Absence of personal hygiene
5. Restriction of movement
6. Psychological and pain-producing and self-mortifying exercises.

ASCETICISM (Defence mechanism)

In this defence, any pleasure resulting from experiences is eliminated. To experience pleasure from some act or experience has a moral value attached to it which some people need to deny. Indirect gratification is derived from the renunciation of the pleasure that would be normal to enjoy from that experience.

ASSERTIVENESS

Assertiveness is a clear, appropriate response to another person that is neither passive nor aggressive. It is communication in which self-respect and respect for the other person are demonstrated.

Assertiveness is where one person's rights are not demanded at the expense of the rights of the other person.

Many interpersonal difficulties and difficult behaviours arise because of people's inability to express positive or negative feelings clearly.

ASSERTIVENESS TRAINING HELPS PEOPLE TO:

Gain and maintain respect for themselves and others
Keep lines of communication open
Achieve goals
Recognize and develop inner resources.

ASSERTIVENESS TRAINING USES:

1. Behavioural rehearsal
2. Cognitive exercises
3. Modelling
4. Relaxation training
5. Role play
6. Simulation of feared situations
7. Social skills training
8. Structured exercises
9. Systematic desensitization.

Assertive training seeks to help people become aware of:

1. Aggressive behaviour
2. Avoidance behaviour
3. Assertive behaviour
4. Accommodating behaviour.

1. AGGRESSIVE BEHAVIOUR

A fight response: the goal is conflict

1. Competitive, motivated by results, power and control.

2. Offensive, because it violates the rights of other people.
3. Subtle, because it is often indirect.
4. Invasive of other people's psychological and/or physical space.
5. Other people are usually left feeling resentful.
6. Aggressive people tend to get their own way by manipulating other people's feelings.
7. Aggressive people spend a lot of time trying to repair hurt feelings.
8. Aggression often shows when they stand up for their own rights.
9. Aggressive people are often pushy and critical.

2. AVOIDANCE BEHAVIOUR

A flight response: the goal is to ignore conflict

1. We don't tackle intrusions on our rights, even when we feel they have been violated.
2. We evade and avoid any honest confrontation by emotionally running away.
3. We back down in the face of opposition.
4. Other people easily invade our space.
5. We may be more concerned with the image we present than being our own self.

3. ASSERTIVE BEHAVIOUR

The goal is direct, honest, open and appropriate verbal and non-verbal behaviour

1. It means standing up for what we believe to be our personal rights.
2. It means not attacking other people's rights.
3. It means expressing our thoughts, feelings and beliefs in direct, honest, and appropriate ways.
4. It should nurture our esteem and the esteem of other people.
5. It should lead to better respect and understanding in relationships.
6. It should avoid the feeling of being constantly put down and frustrated.

4. ACCOMMODATING BEHAVIOUR

The goal is harmony at all costs

1. We often express our thoughts and feelings indirectly.
2. What we say can be disregarded because it is indirect.
3. We hope other people will be nicer to us.
4. We tend to shuffle problems around instead of dealing with them.
5. We let problems build up, then – wow!

Constant avoiding may mean that aggressive behaviour is just around the corner.

OBSTACLES TO ASSERTIVENESS:

1. Lack of awareness that we have the option of responding in an assertive manner.
2. Anxiety about expressing ourselves, even when we know what we want to say.
3. Negative self-talk inhibits self-assertion by what we tell ourselves.
4. Verbal poverty. A difficulty in finding the right words at the right time leads to self-consciousness and hesitancy.
5. Behavioural poverty. A non-assertive, non-verbal manner hinders all assertive expression.

EXPRESSING POSITIVE FEELINGS ASSERTIVELY

1. I really like the way you did that.
2. You look attractive tonight.
3. I wanted you to know how much I enjoyed the meeting.
4. Thank you for appreciating me as a person of worth.
5. I really enjoy being with you.
6. I like the way you handled that situation
7. I love you.

EXPRESSING NEGATIVE FEELINGS ASSERTIVELY

1. I resent your not showing up on time.
2. I don't agree with you.
3. I want you to stop doing ... I don't like what you're doing.
4. I feel put down by comments like that.
5. I was disappointed that we had a change of plans.
6. I'm not satisfied with the work done on my car. I would like you to correct it without charge.
7. I feel that I'm doing all the reaching out in our relationship.
8. I am unhappy that you give your secretary instructions through me.
9. I'm furious that you didn't call me.

Many of us fail to be assertive because of the negative labels we carry, or we feel constrained by conforming to stereotypes.

Assertiveness training works with non-verbal behaviour, paying particular attention to:

1. Eye contact
2. Facial expressions
3. Paralinguistics – voice tone, inflection, volume
4. Body stance
5. Non-words, including silences.

An important technique in assertiveness training is getting people to make positive self-statements, instead of negative ones.

Participants are encouraged to create assertive hierarchies, starting with an encounter that would be relatively easy to handle to the most difficult, then to rehearse them in the group.

One of the aims in assertive behaviour is to change from being indirect to being direct and from using generalizations to being specific.

Examples:

Generalized: You don't love me.

Specific: When you come home from work, I would like you to kiss me.

Generalized: You never think about anyone but yourself.

Specific: If you know you're going to be late 'phone me. I worry about you.

Generalized: You're a male chauvinist pig.

Specific: I want you to listen to me while I'm stating my opinions, even if you don't agree.

Generalized: All you ever do is work.

Specific: I would like us to go to the beach next week.

Generalized: You never talk to me any more.

Specific: I'd like us to sit down together – with no T.V. – and talk for a few minutes each night.

THE VALUES OF ASSERTIVE TRAINING

1. *Self-awareness*: Knowledge of one's goals and behaviours and the reasons for them.
2. *Self-acceptance*: Positive self-regard in the face of one's natural human weaknesses and mistakes.
3. *Honesty and Openness*: Congruent and truthful verbal and non-verbal expression of thoughts, feelings and intentions.
4. *Empathy*: Understanding and acceptance of others' experiences and feelings as valid from their frame of reference.
5. *Responsibility*: Assuming ownership of one's thoughts, feelings, desires, needs, and expectations as well as ownership of the consequences of one's actions.
6. *Mutuality*: Accepting another person as equal and demonstrating willingness to negotiate issues from a win-win stance.

SOME OF THE MOST COMMONLY TAUGHT ASSERTIVE TECHNIQUES

1. *'I' statements* express thoughts, feelings, impact, wants/needs, expectations, preferences, decisions, and consequences.

   'You' statements express empathy or understanding of the other person's situation or experience, grant the other person's position or truth, or describe the other person's behaviour.

   'We' statements express mutual options or alternatives, compromises, decisions or actions. They also affirm the relationship or, in question form, request mutual problem solving.
2. *Broken record*. 'I want my holiday dates when you promised them. Yes I hear you say that there are difficulties, but I want my holiday dates which you promised.' (Repeating a comment as often as necessary to obtain what is desired.)
3. *Fogging*. 'I can see how you might say that I was too direct with that customer'. (Defusing criticism by agreeing with the critic's perception of the facts, without accepting the judgment.)
4. *Negative assertion*. 'I did fail to get my report to you on time.' (Admitting behavioural mistake without conceding personality flaws or making excuses.)
5. *Negative enquiry*. 'Would you like to tell me what it is that you dislike about the way I do things?' (Asking a question to allow someone to vent negative feelings and doing so without taking it personally.)
6. *Free information*. 'You said that you left your last position because you didn't agree with the philosophy of the company; would you elaborate on that?' (Using a previous comment as a base for gathering more information.)
7. *Self-disclosure*. 'I feel excited about having the opportunity to work with you.' (Positive disclosure.)

Scripting is a way of helping people plan for an encounter.

SCRIPTS

Describe a behaviour
Express a feeling

Specify a desired change
Specify *consequences* if no change

People who respond aggressively may find it necessary to tone down their responses.

'I think I understand that you . . .'
'However, when you do that, I . . .'
'I feel . . .'
'I would prefer that you . . .'
'I am concerned because . . .'

Assertiveness is a dignified approach to human interaction that preserves the esteem of all parties, while at the same time accomplishing a particular objective.

ASSOCIATIVE LEARNING (*See also*: Classical conditioning, Operant learning)

The psychological general principle of association states that when any past event or experience is recalled, the act of recollection tends to bring again into use other events and experiences that have become related to this event one or more of certain specified ways.

The general principle has been expanded to cover almost everything that could happen in mental life, except original sensations.

The principle goes back to Aristotle, who proposed three forms of association: similarity contrast, and contiguity.

Two early British associationists were John Locke in *An Essay Concerning Human Understanding* (1690) and David Hume in *A Treatise of Human Nature* (1739).

According to the association theory, all knowledge is acquired through the five senses. Connections are made between new and the original sensory data and are revived when required as images or ideas that represent the original sensation.

The association theory was fiercely attacked during the later part of the nineteenth century by F.H. Bradley, James Ward, and G.F. Stout, who denied that knowledge was founded solely on sensations.

Conditioned reflex and behavioural theories developed from the work of Ivan Pavlov, Edward Thorndike, and B.F. Skinner to give two major approaches: Classical conditioning and Operant conditioning.

In Classical conditioning we learn that one event follows another. In Operant conditioning we learn that a response leads to a particular consequence.

The behaviouristic approach to conditioning makes the assumption that:.

1. Simple associations are the building blocks of all learning.
2. The laws of association are the same for everyone, in every situation.
3. Learning is best understood in terms of external causes, rather than internal ones.

The scientific study of animals challenges the behaviourist theory, that all species learn in the same way. The ethological theory is that all species are limited by their internal, genetically determined 'behavioural blueprint'.

A cognitive approach to learning also disputes the behavioural approach; not everything can be understood by considering only external or environmental factors. This theory says that intelligence is (in the case of humans) the person's ability to make mental representations of the world and to act upon those representations.

While the classical approach to association, in its original form, lacks credibility in the latter part of the twentieth century, it still remains an important and effective principle which influences all aspects of learning.

ATTACHMENT (*See also*: Bowlby, E. John M., Bonding)

A theory developed by Bowlby at the Tavistock Clinic, London. Attachment describes the relationship between an infant and its mother or mother substitute (care giver). This early relationship is the foundation for all later relationships.

Attachment behaviour is evident from six months onwards when the infant discriminates sharply between the care giver and other people. Early attachment influences adult behaviour, particularly during illness, distress or when afraid. The primary attachment figure represents security. For attachment to be satisfactory, one principal care giver needs to be identified.

Separation anxiety is experienced when attachment is interrupted and is characterized by protest, despair, and detachment. When the care giver returns, the child's behaviour may demonstrate avoidance, resistance, and over-attachment. It is as if trust, broken by the separation, has to be re-established.

The work of bonding and attachment has had significant practical implications for childbirth methods and how children's hospitals are run. The understanding of grief, bereavement, mourning, loss, and loneliness have all been enhanced by attachment theory.

ATTENDING

Attending refers to the ways in which we physically and psychologically demonstrate our availability to other people.

ATTENDING MEANS CONCENTRATING AND INVOLVES:

1. Body

   The way we sit:
   distance
   angle of chairs

   A naturally open posture.
   Demonstrating involvement and interest, by moving forward from time to time.
   Maintaining comfortable eye contact.
   Being aware of one's own facial expressions and body language.
   Being relaxed, without slouching.

2. Mind

   Thoughts uncluttered and focused
   Open attitude

3. Feelings

   Secure
   Calm
   Confident

A disturbed spirit conflicts with attending.

At some of the more dramatic moments of life just having another person with us helps to prevent psychological collapse. Our face shows where our heart is.

When (though not necessarily during) counselling, we should ask ourself:

1. Was I effectively present and in emotional contact with this client?
2. Did my non-verbal behaviour reinforce my internal attitudes?
3. In what ways was I distracted from giving my full attention to this client?
4. What can I do to handle these distractions?

ATTITUDE

A pattern of more or less stable mental views, opinions, or interests, established by experience over a period of time. Attitudes are likes and dislikes, affinities or aversion to objects, people, groups, situations and ideas.

In order to make sense of experiences, the mind classifies and groups experiences with their responses into what we call attitudes. They express feelings (affective component), influence what we do (behavioural component), and our thoughts (cognitive component).

While we can ask if judgments are true or false, correct or incorrect, accurate or inaccurate, we cannot ask that question of an attitude; we can only ask, are they logically consistent with one another, with their associated beliefs and actions.

Thus, there must be cognitive consistency, consistency among beliefs, consistency among attitudes, consistency between beliefs and attitudes, and consistency between attitudes and behaviour.

AUTHORITARIANISM

An ideology that embraces zealous obedience to a hierarchy of leaders and to those who are stronger.

Dictatorship is an extreme form of authoritarianism.

AUTHORITARIAN PERSONALITY
(*See also*: Open-mindedness)

A term developed by Adorno *et al.*, where the person is characterized by:

Respect (reverence) for power
Uncritical submission to the authority of dominant groups
Aggression toward subordinates
Lack of self-insight
Superstitiousness
Contempt for weakness
Close-mindedness
Intolerance of ambiguity
Prejudice
Needs strong external support systems
Dependence on conventional values
Sensitive to interpersonal status
Dominance
Rigidity of thinking
Cynicism
Tendency to use projection
Curiosity about sexual behaviour.

Adorno's work on the authoritarian personality is best known by his *ethnocentrism scale*: the tendency to hold prejudiced attitudes toward all groups different from one's own.

High scores on this scale show a general tendency to see the world in terms of noble *in-groups* which must be supported, and offensive *out-groups* which must be avoided or rejected and attacked when they become threatening. High scores on:

1. The Ethnocentrism Scale
2. The Anti-Semitism Scale
3. The Political Scale, and
4. The Fascism Scale identify an authoritarian personality.

Authoritarian personalities, because they see everything in 'either/or' terms, and cannot tolerate ambiguity and uncertainty, do not cope well with disability.

SOME OF THE STATEMENTS

1. Obedience and respect for authority are the most important values children should learn.
2. Young people sometimes get rebellious ideas, but as they grow up they ought to get over them and settle down.
3. Businessmen and manufacturers are more important to society than artists and academics.
4. When a person has problem or worry, it is best for him not to think about it, but to keep busy with more cheerful things.

AUTOGENIC TRAINING

Autogenic training has its source in hypnosis and was developed by Johannes Schultz, a Berlin neurologist, early in the 20th century.

It consists of a series of mental exercises designed to reduce the 'fight or flight' response, and switch on to rest, relaxation and recreation. The client is taught to control the autonomic nervous system by a self-induced hypnotic or meditative state, induced by breathing and relaxation exercises.

While in this state, exploration of the unconscious mind, either alone or with the aid of a therapist, is encouraged. The client carries out a question-and-answer dialogue with the unconscious mind and is asked to visualize problems and their solutions.

Autogenic training has been used successfully to treat a wide range of stress-related conditions, and some organic conditions such as cancer. Psychoses and heart conditions contraindicate its use.

AVOIDANCE (Defence mechanism)

Avoidance is thinking and acting in ways that evade dealing with reality. A wish to dwell on the past may be avoiding working in the present.

Avoidance acts powerfully against the implementation of programmes. Avoidance will take place if the rewards for not doing something are stronger than the rewards for doing it.

Avoidance is manifested in:

1. Procrastination.
2. Trading down; choosing an alternative that is more psychologically acceptable and attractive.
3. Devaluing the unchosen alternative.
4. Delegating the decision to someone – fate horoscope, dice, obeying rules.

B

BEHAVIOUR THERAPY (*See also*: Rational emotive therapy, Cognitive therapy, Systematic desensitization)

The applied use of behavioural psychology to bring about changes in behaviour, the central principle of which is that all behaviour is learned and maintained as a result of the person's interaction with the environment. Rewarded behaviour will tend to increase in frequency, while behaviour not so rewarded, or if it is punished, will tend to decline.

THE ROOTS OF BEHAVIOUR THERAPY:

1. Wolpe's work on experimental neuroses in cats, and the clinical work which developed from that research. The most important technique is *Systematic desensitization*
2. Skinner's contribution of Operant conditioning
3. Social learning theory.

Behaviour therapy is a major form of therapy practised by clinical psychologists.

THE MAIN FEATURES OF BEHAVIOUR THERAPY:

1. It concentrates on behaviour rather than on the underlying causes of the behaviour.
2. Behaviour is learned, and may be unlearned.
3. Behaviour is susceptible to change through psychological principles, especially learning methods.
4. The setting of clearly defined treatment goals.
5. Classical personality theories are rejected.
6. The therapist adapts methods to suit the client's needs.
7. The focus is on the 'here and now'.
8. A belief in obtaining research support for the methods used.

THE STAGES OF BEHAVIOUR THERAPY:

1. A detailed analysis of the client's problems and behavioural factors
2. Specific treatment goals
3. Treatment plan using appropriate behavioural techniques.

4. Implementation of the plan, including full discussion with the client.
5. Evaluation.

THERAPEUTIC TECHNIQUES USED:

1. Exposure

   The aim is to extinguish the anxiety and its associated behaviour by systematic exposure to the feared situation. This may include modelling – observing someone carrying out the desired behaviour before attempting it.

2. Contingency management

   This means reinforcing positive behaviour but not reinforcing negative behaviour. Rewards in the form of tokens is an example.

3. Cognitive behaviour therapy

   Concerned with thoughts and beliefs. (*See also*: Cognitive therapy).

4. Assertive and social skills training. (*See*: Assertiveness).

5. Self-control

   Behaviour therapy aims to teach people methods of self-control and self-help, to enable them to cope with situations they find difficult.

   For example, exposure to the feared situation – rehearse the difficult situation, and arrange for positive reinforcement when the task has been done.

6. Role play

   Clients may be asked either to replay an actual situation, or to imagine one.

7. Guided imagery

   Clients symbolically create or recreate a problematic life situation.

8. Physiological recording

9. Self-monitoring

   For example, recording daily calorie intake.

10. Behavioural observation

    Assessment of problem behaviour is more accurate when based on actual observation.

11. Psychological tests and questionnaires

    Behaviour therapists will not generally use tests based on psychodynamic theories.

    They will use tests that yield the information necessary for a functional analysis or for the development of an intervention strategy.

12. Stress management

    Particularly the use of progressive relaxation.

Behaviour therapy does not ignore the importance of the therapeutic relationship. The client who is in a trusting, supportive relationship will generally work conscientiously through the therapy.

Behaviour therapy is tailor-made to suit individual client's needs. Much of behaviour therapy is short-term – 25–50 sessions.

Behaviour therapy is applicable over a full range of problems, for example:

1. Anxiety disorders
2. Cardiovascular disease
3. Childhood disorders
4. Depression
5. Hypertension
6. Interpersonal/marital

7. Obesity
8. Sexual disorders
9. Speech difficulties
10. Stress management
11. Substance abuse
12. Tension headaches.

While behaviour therapy is generally considered to be unsuitable in psychotic conditions, it is used in the treatment of people with chronic mental illnesses.

BEREAVEMENT COUNSELLING

Bereavement is the process that includes grief and mourning, over the loss of a significant person or object. Ideally counselling is commenced before the loss. Anticipatory grief and mourning can then be worked through.

COUNSELLING GUIDELINES FOLLOWING A DEATH:

1. Support to help deal with the many practical issues surrounding the death.
2. Working with feelings and encouraging catharsis, but not to push the person too far, too fast, too soon.
3. Helpers need to be able to accept the bereaved person's feelings, whatever they are.
4. Feelings, however negative, are valid.
5. Repeated telling of the story with the feelings.
6. Encourage the acceptance of the finality of the loss.
7. Facilitate disengagement and establish separateness from the deceased.
8. Help the bereaved person to gain a positive but realistic memory of the deceased through repeated discussion.
9. Help the bereaved person to accept the changes in role, social situation and self-image in becoming a widow/widower, fatherless, childless, no longer pregnant, disabled.
10. Encourage the bereaved person to think about new relationships, activities, self-help groups.

BIBLIOTHERAPY

The Greek meaning is 'book-healing', the aim of which is to create a psychological interplay between the reader and the material, which may be literature or audiovisual.

The therapeutic relationship so formed may then be used to promote insight, personal awareness and growth and psychological healing. It achieves this through overcoming moralization, active involvement, and fostering competence.

Bibliotherapy is often used as an adjunct to other forms of therapy. It may be conducted in a one-to-one relationship or in a group. It is used with client groups of all ages.

People can be helped through a story, play, music, songs, to explore any major themes of life which are creating difficulties for them.

CLASSIFICATION

1. *Institutional*. With hospitalized, usually psychiatric, patients, where the objective is the dissemination of information.
2. *Clinical*. With people who have emotional or behavioural problems, where the objective is insight or behavioural change. The empathic or imaginative nature of the material would aim to produce catharsis.

3. *Crisis*. Used with people who, apart from passing through a crisis, are not psychiatrically disturbed. The goal is self-actualization and growth through using both imaginative and directive, factual material. The underlying rationale is that people are encouraged to deal with their own threatening emotions and behaviours by displacing them on to the story. Identification takes place with the characters which promotes change.

BINSWANGER, LUDWIG (1881–1966) (*See also*: Existential psychotherapy)

Swiss-born physician and psychoanalyst. Contemporary and friend of Carl Jung, whom he accompanied on his visit to meet Freud. He was strongly influenced by the existentialist philosophies.

BION, WILFRED R. (1897–1979) (*See also*: Tavistock method)

Born in India, educated in Britain. Experienced service in the First World War. Read Modern History at Oxford; studied medicine and psychoanalysis.

Bion worked at the Tavistock Centre until the Second World War and was instrumental in developing group work for the selection and training of army officers.

After the War he entered analysis with Melanie Klein and became a leading figure in the work of the Tavistock Centre and of the British School of Psychoanalysis.

Although Bion devoted most of his life to psychoanalysis, it is his group work for which he is mostly remembered.

BIRTH TRAUMA (*See also*: Rankian dialectic)

A concept first used by Otto Rank, in which he states that the trauma associated with birth forms the basis for all following anxiety. While Freud agreed in part with Rank, he rejected the notion that all neuroses are rooted in the birth trauma. Rank's thesis was that healing of neuroses lay in:

1. Recognizing birth symbols and images.
2. Transference as an attempt to re-establish oneness with the mother.
3. Acting out final separation from the womb.

Rank believed that therapy is complete when the universal neurotic desire to return to the womb is overcome. A more recent extension of Rank's is the natural childbirth work of Leboyer and the bonding of the newborn baby.

BLEULER, EUGENE (1857–1939)

Influential Swiss psychiatrist who was instrumental in applying Freud's ideas to psychiatry. He identified several forms of mental illness to which he applied the term 'schizophrenia'.

Contrary to the opinion of the day, he considered that schizophrenia was curable. His statements on the nature and symptoms of schizophrenia are still regarded as valid.

He coined the term 'ambivalent' which he defined as 'the presence within the psyche of mutually exclusive contradictions'.

His approach to therapy was psychological-humanistic. He also contributed the understanding of autism, and described it as withdrawal from reality. He established a link between autism and the development of paranoia.

BLOCKING (Defence mechanism) (*See also*: Resistance)

A temporary or fleeting restraint of thinking, feelings, or action, which resembles repression, but differs in that tension results from the inhibition.

Blocking may manifest itself at any time during counselling. It may become apparent in the way the client refuses to consider what is being said, or argues against it without consideration.

Blocking may be an indication of transference or counter-transference. The counsellor may have used words that trigger some half-forgotten memory to which the client feels unable to respond at that moment.

Feelings generated by interaction may also have their roots in past relationships which the client now cannot relate to and blocks the response.

BODY-CENTRED THERAPY (*See also*: Reich, Wilhelm)

A group of therapies whose common aim is the altering of self-image or personality through work on the physical body.

THE PRINCIPAL BODY THERAPIES:

1. Bioenergetics

   Originated in the work of Wilhelm Reich, a disciple of Freud. He evolved the theory that many disorders are caused by an inability to achieve satisfactory orgasm. The body needs real convulsions, a degree of loss of control, to be fully therapeutic.

   Alexander Lowen and John Pierrakos developed their own approach from Reich, now known as Bioenergetics. A system of techniques for mobilizing the energies of people who have become aware of some blockage or disturbance in expressing feelings.

   The method is based on the theory that character is intimately related to posture, structure, energy flow, and tensions. Therapy is directed toward releasing blocked tension by applying pressure, by palpating, or massaging.

2. Rolfing (Structured integration)

   A technique of connective tissue manipulation and stretching that seeks to liberate the physical structures so that they may realign and integrate themselves.

   Dr Ida Rolf, whose background was biological chemistry, based her theory on the premise that so long as the body is correctly aligned, all is well, but if any part is out of alignment, the structure becomes unstable. She also maintained that faulty posture leads to faulty emotions, and that as physical restructuring takes place, so emotions and traumatic events linked to posture, are released. A ten-session course is now accepted as standard.

3. Feldenkrais method (Functional integration)

   A system of body movements and retraining designed by Dr Moshe Feldenkrais, to improve posture and general health. It combines manipulation of the body with movement work within a group, carried out mostly on the floor.

Gentle movements are characteristic of this method. The aim is to help the person to become aware of corrected body image through realignment.

4. Body-centred psychotherapy

   Two principal therapies are:

   The Hakomi method
   Psychomotor therapy

   In both, the therapist combines discussion, action and awareness to tap into and work on important emotional material. Fantasy, psychodrama, movement, and touch are all used, either individually or in groups.

BODY-IMAGE (*See also*: Femininity/ Masculinity)

The perception, conscious, or unconscious, of one's own body, distortion of which occurs in personality and psychiatric disorders.

PRINCIPAL POINTS TO CONSIDER:

1. Regard

   Is it negative or positive?
   Do specific part or parts cause concern?
   Generally satisfied, or dissatisfied?
   What is the person's ideal?
   What body experiences make for pleasure or displeasure?

2. Size

   The way we judge the size of our body, or a part thereof, is influenced by emotions and attitudes toward ourself and our relationship to others. Men tend to overestimate, and women to underestimate body size.

3. Awareness

   Some people have a high awareness while others have a minimal awareness. Most people focus more of their attention on specific sectors, and less on others.

4. Boundary

   The demarcation between our body and the outside world, which includes other people.

5. Spatial

   How accurately we are able to judge body position. Spatial dimension is part of our ability to separate from our surroundings.

6. Anxiety

   Some people are very afraid of body damage, while others seem unconcerned about such a possibility.

7. Masculinity/Femininity

   A. People who do not want to affirm their masculinity or femininity are rare. Masculinity and femininity are not concerned only with feelings about one's genitals.
   B. Females are generally more dissatisfied than men about the lower parts of their bodies.
   C. Males who experience failure are more likely to relate this to sensations of diminished height.

BONDING

The relationship that one individual

maintains with either an inanimate object, for example, a bird to its nest, or to animate objects, such as a child to its care giver or adult to mate. Behaviour is directed exclusively toward the preferred object.

Bonding partners recognize each other as individuals. Bonding occurs rapidly between adults and their young. Bonded partners tend to defend each other.

The effectiveness of the therapeutic relationship, or alliance, has characteristics of bonding. The relationship is influenced by:

1. How the counsellor demonstrates the core conditions of:

   Empathy
   Genuineness
   Non-possessive warmth
   Unconditional positive regard.

2. The client's feelings toward the counsellor, which are influenced by:

   Trust in the counsellor
   Feeling safe in the relationship
   Having faith in the counsellor.

3. The style of interaction of both client and counsellor. This is influenced by the 'fit' between the counsellor's approach and the ability of the client to work within it and how far the counsellor is able to adapt to the client's particular abilities and preferences.
4. The way transference and countertransference are acknowledged and worked through. In very general (though not strictly in psychoanalytic) terms, transference and countertransference refer to the tendencies we all have to perceive, feel, and act toward other people in the present, based on previous experiences with significant others in our past lives.

Therapeutic bonding is generally strengthened when something within the relationship is challenged, and the potential conflict is dealt with constructively.

BOWLBY, E. JOHN M. (1907–1990)
(*See also*: Attachment)

Bowlby was a British psychoanalyst who had a long association with the Tavistock Clinic and the Tavistock Institute of Human Relations.

During the Second World War he was an army psychiatrist dealing with the selection of officers. He had a distinguished career and made valuable contributions to the study of child development.

BRAIN-STORMING

An established technique for creative problem-solving, usually undertaken by a small group of between two and six members.

One member of the group, or an outside adviser, acts as coordinator. The aim is to release the mind and increase the flow of creative ideas and to assist decision-making.

No discussion or evaluation is permitted, until all ideas have been generated. This ensures that creativity is not blocked. One person may build upon the idea of someone else. All ideas are reviewed and graded for their usefulness.

BREUER, JOSEF (1842–1925)

Austrian physician and physiologist, generally acknowledged to be the principal forerunner of psychoanalysis.

Working with hypnosis, in the classic case of 'Anna O', he relieved symptoms of hysteria after she was induced to recall unpleasant past experiences. The Breuer/Freud alliance was dissolved because of basic theoretical disagreements.

Although his contribution to the treatment of hysteria was considerable, his work in the field of physiology is worthy of note:

1. He described the Hering–Breuer reflex, the mechanism that controls inhalation and exhalation in normal breathing.
2. In 1873 he discovered the sensory function of the semicircular canals in the inner ear and their relation to balance.

BRIEF THERAPY (*See also*: Single-session therapy)

A range of planned, short-term therapies.

CHARACTERISTICS OF SHORT-TERM THERAPY:

1. *Time limits* with an average of six to ten single sessions.
2. *Limited goals* with the focus on specific areas.
3. *Current problems* are dealt with in the 'here and now'.
4. *Direction*. The therapist is more active than in some other approaches.
5. *Early assessment* is needed to establish treatment rapidly.
6. *Flexibility* of approach is emphasized, because of the time limit.
7. *Ventilation* of feelings is considered essential.
8. *Therapeutic relationship and contract* are stressed.
9. *Selection*. Brief therapy is more suitable with less disturbed clients.

BRIEF THERAPY MAY BENEFIT CLIENTS WHOSE:

1. Problem is acute, rather than chronic.
2. Previous adjustment was effective.
3. Ability to relate is adequate.
4. Motivation toward therapy is high.

The results of brief therapy are said to be comparable with long-term therapy.

BRITISH SCHOOL (OF PSYCHOANALYSIS)

The term distinguishes the British contribution to psychoanalysis, from the American, the English Kleinian school, and other contributions to psychoanalysis.

The work of the British School was fundamentally concerned with object relations and their contributions have influenced many areas of contemporary psychoanalytic thought.

The basic beliefs:

1. The therapeutic task is all-important.
2. The seeds of psychopathology are sown in the early failure of the relationship between mother and baby.
3. The environment is an integral part of the person's psyche.

BULIMIA NERVOSA (Binge-eating)

Russell first used the term in 1979 to describe a group of patients who feared putting on weight, yet had a compulsive urge to eat. It is most common in societies where slimness is considered desirable and attractive.

IMPORTANT POINTS ABOUT THE CONDITION

1. The excessive eating, which causes distress, is not within the person's control.
2. People who have also experienced anorexia are more prone to develop bulimia. This is thought to be when the iron-like control over not eating suddenly cracks and results in a binge. Guilt takes over, resulting in self-induced vomiting. The starvation and binge cycle starts all over again.
3. Bulimia never comes of its own accord, but follows a period of self-imposed starvation. The body revolts against this deprivation and the food gorged is what the body most needs, especially carbohydrates.
4. Binge-eating is accompanied by self-induced vomiting, or the abuse of purgatives, or both. Self-induced vomiting ensures a secret method of maintaining weight at a level that keeps other people satisfied.
5. Bulimia may start just as the anorexic is reaching optimum body weight.
6. Pressure may push the recovering anorexic into bulimia.
7. Not all bulimics have been anorexic, but they are just as fearful of putting on weight. They seem not to have the same iron control to do without food for such long periods.
8. Bulimics are thrown into panic when they feel that their body has taken control away from them.
9. Bulimics fear that if they start eating they will eat everything in sight.
10. The mind of the bulimic is constantly full of thoughts about food. They dream about it. This is similar to the experiences of POWs in concentration camps, whose daydreams were often about food.
11. Binge-eating is usually done in secret, and the buying of the food is so arranged that no one could be suspicious.
12. The person may resort to strenuous exercise and the use of stimulants or diuretics.
13. Bulimics often feel depressed, brought on by the feeling of having lost control and self-disgust. Sustained use of stimulants often brings depression in their wake. Deterioration of relationships is also a factor in this depression.
14. Constant vomiting is harmful because the body is deprived, not only of food, but of gastrointestinal juices essential for health. Juices that have their function in the stomach have a harmful effect on the upper parts of the alimentary tract. Continual loss of fluid often leads to dehydration.
15. People who cannot make themselves vomit, often resort to repeated purging, also damaging to health.
16. Bulimia is but one indication of lack of control; many also overspend and get into financial difficulty. So overpowering is the

desire for food that some will steal to get it. Relationships are also entered into in the same overboard way. Few succeed in a long-term lasting sexual relationship.

17. Most bulimics, male and female, have a low self-esteem and desperately seek approval.
18. There is some evidence to support the theory that female bulimics identify with their fathers, and males with their mothers.
19. The basic conflict is their need to be admired and desired by a member of the opposite sex on the one hand, and a fear that they are not good enough and will be rejected on the other.
20. Unlike anorexics, bulimics normally continue to menstruate. Some conceive and a few give birth. Many, however, are against the idea of becoming pregnant.
21. Because bulimics normally weigh more than anorexics, their eating habits may escape notice for years. Their preoccupation with weight and size equates to that of anorexics.
22. Bulimics generally feel afraid when they feel the desire to binge coming on, when they have successfully controlled it for a period.

TREATMENT

1. A normal eating pattern must be established. This is not easy, for the patterns of eating and vomiting are firmly established.
2. As bulimics are intent on keeping their weight down, co-operation is problematic, but essential if their programme is to work.
3. Hospital treatment where skilled help is available is desirable if the pattern of binge-eating and vomiting is to be interrupted.

   Hospital admission is essential if there are physical complications or if there is depression.
4. Repeated information-giving about the effects of binge-eating and persistent vomiting is a necessary part of treatment, supported by an equally forcible plugging of the physical and emotional advantages of a balanced eating programme.
5. Eating small amounts slowly in the company of others encourages a normal eating pattern. Water intake is restricted; too much water gives a sensation of fullness. No eating is allowed between meals.
6. Some effort is made to gradually increase the weight beyond what the client thinks to be desirable.
7. Those not in hospital are trusted to keep a daily journal of all food they eat as well as times they want to, or actually do vomit.
8. Supervision is likely to continue for months or even years.

(*See* Anorexia for related counselling.)

BURN OUT (*See also*: Stress management, Equity theory, Empathy)

A term used to describe the injurious effects of the stress of psychotherapy upon psychotherapists. Burn out, resulting in physical or psychological withdrawal, is characterized by:

1. Chronic low level of energy
2. Defensive behaviour
3. Emotional distancing from people.

Therapists often look forward to

sessions where there is progress, and dread sessions that don't go anywhere. Sessions that go badly have a debilitating effect on the therapist, because prolonged client resistance depletes energy.

Burn out may also be associated with the relationship in which there is a high level of empathy, and with the high level of concentration that goes with giving full attention.

C

CASTRATION COMPLEX

In psychoanalytic theory, castration is the unconscious fear of losing the male genital organs, or the feeling (in the female) that they have already been lost. Boys fear punishment by castration from their fathers because of their (unconscious) wish for a sexual relationship with their mothers.

Girls feel the punishment has already been carried out; that is why they do not have a penis. Girls, therefore, have a residual penis envy. Female analysts, however, pointed out that many males can be as envious of the reproductive power of females, as females are of the male's penis.

The concept of castration complex is controversial, especially outside of psychoanalysis. The question must also be asked; who is the castrator?

In the nineteenth century the threat of castration was often used as a deterrent against masturbation. Freud linked the castration complex with the incest taboo, for which it serves as a major prohibition.

People who constantly undermine the self-confidence of others are said to be castrating. It can apply to females who, because of penis envy, are constantly disparaging toward men and are aggressively competitive toward them.

The term also applies to men who undermine thier sons. An extension of the word is where men make a habit of putting women down and do their best to make them feel incompetent and second-rate.

CATHARSIS (*See also*: Abreaction)

A medical term used metaphorically by Aristotle to describe the effects of true tragedy on the spectator. Aristotle states that the purpose of tragedy is to arouse 'terror and pity' and thereby effect catharsis – purgation or purification of these emotions.

The term catharsis was introduced into psychiatry by Freud and Joseph Breuer, who used it to describe a method of treating hysterical patients under hypnosis. The patients relived, or at least remembered, the circumstances under which their symptoms originated. When the emotions accompanying those circumstances were expressed, the patient was thus relieved of the symptoms. People who block emotions may experience a great rush of feelings as the blockage is removed.

Abreaction, insight and working through are three main experiences in psychoanalysis.

Catharsis is a prime treatment tool of such approaches as Primal therapy, Re-birthing, Z-process attachment, and many of the newer therapies, such as Six-category intervention. (*see* entry).

CENSORSHIP (*See also*: Dream theories)

In psychoanalysis, the mechanism of the ego which functions as a barrier to protect the conscious from painful memories and potentially dangerous wishes, by refusing them access from either the preconscious or the unconscious. It is the agency responsible for repression and for distortion of dream material.

Dreams, according to Freud, are dramatized unconscious wishes, made possible through the relaxation in sleep of the control exercised by the conscious mind. In sleep the conscious mind is still able to exercise some restriction by way of the censor. In order to pass the controlling function of the censor, the contents of dreams are disguised so that the contents are acceptable to the conscious mind.

CHALLENGING

In counselling, the aim of a challenge is to help the client face reality, as it is seen through the eyes of the counsellor. The force of the challenge depends on the type of therapy. In some instances it is offered as an observation, in others it is very strong and confronting.

There are times when it is wiser to ignore than to comment. There are times, however, when it could be valuable for the client to know how the counsellor feels about something.

The client may benefit from being confronted with the possible outcome of her/his behaviour or some contemplated course of action.

Any challenge is best put in a tentative way, as a suggestion, rather than as a statement of fact and then only after careful deliberation. It should never be used as a retaliation. Challenges are best left until the counselling relationship is firmly established. Sometimes it is difficult to challenge without its being interpreted as a judgment.

THE MAIN AREAS OF CHALLENGE:

1. Discrepancies
2. Distortions
3. Self-defeating thought patterns
4. Self-defeating behaviours
5. Games, tricks, and smoke screens
6. Excuses:

   Complacency
   Rationalizations
   Procrastinations
   Buck-passing.

EXAMPLES OF CHALLENGES:

1. 'You say you're not bothered about what your colleagues think of you and yet you get very tense every time you are with them.'
2. 'You say that being rejected really hurts you, yet you smile as you talk about it.'

3. 'You say you feel really anxious, yet you laugh whenever you say that.'
4. 'You say your previous counsellor was always very gentle with you. I wonder if you're asking me to go easy on you too.'
5. 'You say you feel inadequate to handle this difficulty in your life. Yet you have a bag full of resources. You're intelligent and persistent and have coped well with other difficult situations in the past.'
6. 'You feel you're taking responsibility for your life and yet you blame your wife and daughter for everything that is wrong in your relationship with them.'

CHILD (Transactional analysis) (*See also*: Adapted child, Free child)

A basic ego state consisting of:

1. Feelings
2. Impulses
3. Spontaneous acts.

As a result of learning, the child ego state takes the form of the adapted child, or the natural child.

CLARIFICATION

A communication skill which helps the therapist understand the client's communications by using:

1. Paraphrasing
2. Reflecting
3. Open questions
4. Summarizing
5. Focusing.

An important part of clarification is listening to the client's feedback and then making adjustments accordingly. Clarification is used particularly in person-centred counselling to develop empathy. Effective clarification provides a model on which clients may model their communications.

CLASSICAL CONDITIONING (*See also*: Associative learning, Operant conditioning)

In behavioural terms, learning that takes place when a new stimulus paired with an existing stimulus produces the same response as the existing stimulus. It is one of two forms of associative learning; also referred to as respondent conditioning.

Classical conditioning has its origins with the Russian physiologist, Pavlov (1849–1936) and his experiments. While studying digestion of dogs, Pavlov observed that dogs began to salivate whenever they saw a food dish, an associated response.

He extended this reflex action to getting them to salivate to a stimulus of light and sound, without food. Salivation in response to such a stimulus is a 'conditioned response', in contrast to the 'unconditioned response' (salivation) to the 'unconditional stimulus' (food).

For classical conditioning to occur the conditioned stimulus must be a reliable predictor of the unconditioned stimulus. In other words, there must be a higher probability that the unconditioned response will occur when the conditioned response has been presented, than when it is not.

Classical conditioning plays an important role in the animal kingdom, but more important, in counselling, is a person's reactions to fear.

Fears acquired in childhood can be eradicated by the principles of classical conditioning. A fear of spiders, for example, may be overcome by repeated exposure to spiders, provided the client is able to contain the anxiety without it becoming crippling, which would be harmful and would reinforce the fear.

CO-DEPENDENCE

Co-dependent behaviour is often related to families where there is chemical addiction, but there are other situations in which co-dependence operates. Co-dependent behaviour is learned in dysfunctional families in which certain unwritten, and in many cases unspoken, rules prevail. The behaviour is reinforced within the culture. Many rules which do not produce wholly functional people are linked to sex roles.

EXAMPLES OF DYSFUNCTIONAL RULES:

'Men should be ... '
'Women should be ...'
'Always do ...'
'Never do ...'

The rules stem from avoidance of interpersonal issues and the need to protect oneself from others. People from dysfunctional families learn to be 'people-pleasers'.

EXAMPLES OF DYSFUNCTIONAL FAMILY RULES:

1. Never talk to others about your problems. 'Don't wash your dirty linen in public.'
2. Never express feelings openly.
3. Indirect communication is best.
4. We have to be perfect – always.

When we are ruled by 'shoulds' and 'oughts' the ground is fertile for shame, doubt, frustration, and anger when we fail to attain perfection. (*See* Horney, Karen).

5. Don't be selfish, ever. Other people must always come first.
6. Don't do as I do, do as I say.
7. Play and fun are irresponsible.
8. Whatever you do, don't rock the boat.

People who are the product of dysfunctional families tend to 'awfulize' events. Minor omissions are major transgressions. Dysfunctional behaviours become evident in people who do not know how to ask for help (asking for help implies an acceptance of vulnerabilty), or how to forgive themselves.

Co-dependents may become dependent on other people, substances, or behaviours.

EXAMPLES OF DYSFUNCTIONAL COPING:

Co-dependents:

1. May adopt compulsive, perfectionistic, approval-seeking or dependent behaviour.
2. May become 'doormat' co-dependents.
3. May suffer from physical exhaustion, depression, and hopelessness.
4. May abuse or neglect their children.
5. May become suicidal.
6. May become self-destructive through overwork, chemical, or any other form of dependency.

DEVELOPMENT OF CO-DEPENDENCE

1. Failure of the primary care-giver to allow the developing child to separate and establish her/his own boundaries.

2. Male children are more likely to be encouraged to separate than female children.
3. Masculinity is defined through separation from the primary care-giver, while femininity is defined through attachment.
4. Men, generally, are threatened by attachment, while women, generally, are threatened by separation.

The two most typical behaviours of co-dependence are:

1. Compulsive care-taking
2. Attempts to control others.

CHARACTERISTICS OF CO-DEPENDENTS

1. Difficulty in identifying their own feelings.
2. Difficulty in acknowledging and expressing their feelings.
3. Difficulty in forming or maintaining close relationships.
4. Being rigid or being stuck in attitudes or behaviours.
5. Perfectionism with 'all-or-nothing' thinking.
6. Difficulty coping with change.
7. Feeling overly responsible for the behaviour or feelings of other people.
8. Become so absorbed in other people's problems that they are unable to identify or solve their own.
9. Attempting to control the behaviour of others and the feeling that they must solve other people's problems.
10. Continually seeking approval from others, in order to feel good and accepted. Not being able to say 'No'. is an example.
11. Difficulty making decisions and often pushed by what other people want for them.
12. Feeling powerless over their life; an addiction to security.
13. A sense of shame and low self-esteem.
14. Weak personal boundaries. Co-dependents may not know where they, themselves end and other people begin.
15. Compulsive behaviour, excessive working, eating, dieting, spending, gambling.

COGNITIVE BEHAVIOUR MODIFICATION (*See also*: Rational emotive therapy, Systematic desensitization)

Cognitive behaviour modification (CMB) is an extension of behaviour therapy, closely associated with Aaron Beck, Albert Allis, and Donald Meichenbaum. CBM treats thoughts as behaviours that will respond to restructuring using behavioural principles.

It is a general term for treatment methods that use behaviour modification principles, but also incorporates procedures designed to change beliefs that create difficulties for the person.

The therapist attempts to help clients control disturbing emotional reactions, such as anxiety by teaching them different ways of thinking about their experiences. For example, people who are depressed tend to view experiences negatively and from a self-critical standpoint. They often expect to fail, and do themselves down on successes.

The therapist works with the client's distorted thinking patterns that always drive them deeper into difficulty.

The behavioural part of the therapy comes in when the therapist encourages the client to formulate different ways of looking at the situation. For example, a client will be asked to keep a record of moods, and the thoughts connected with them.

The therapist will then use this record to challenge the client's assumptions and false logic.

Alteration of faulty beliefs is important in order to effect change that will last. At the same time, proving to one's-self that it can be done is also essential, such as rehearsing, say, a speech, with a colleague. Performing something successfully gives one a sense of mastery, which is far more morale-boosting than watching others do the same thing, however helpful that might be.

A programme might include, for example:

1. Assertiveness training
2. Relaxation training
3. Self-talk
4. Social skills training
5. Systematic desensitization
6. Training in positive thinking
7. Visualization techniques.

COGNITIVE DISSONANCE THEORY

A theory developed by the social psychologist, Leon Festinger, which proposes that when a person's actions are inconsistent with his or her attitudes, the discomfort produced by this dissonance leads the person to bring the attitudes in line with the actions.

The theory also states that people will constantly strive to maintain a cognitive balance.

The mental conflict that occurs when beliefs or assumption are contradicted by new information; when the new information is perceived to be incompatible or inconsistent with what is already established.

Groups also strive to maintain the balance of their interpersonal relationships.

THE PRINCIPLES

1. Two thoughts, attitudes or beliefs are not in harmony.
2. Disharmony creates psychological discomfort.
3. Something must be done to reduce the discomfort.
4. Avoidance action is taken.

DEFENSIVE MANOEUVRES WHICH PEOPLE USE TO RELIEVE CONFLICT

1. Reject the new information.
2. Explain away the new information.
3. Avoid the new information.
4. Persuade themselves that there is no conflict.
5. Reconcile the difference.

Example 1

After careful consideration of the positive and negative features of two models of cars, a man buys one of them.

The prediction is that he will tend to look for adverts that praise the positive features of the model he bought, and ignore adverts that mention the negative features.

Example 2

Jean's religious and family upbringing has instilled in her that premarital sex is a sin.

In her first relationship with a boy she has sex with him, telling herself, 'This can't be sin, we are so in love, and we're going to get married anyway'.

COGNITIVE RESTRUCTURING

A Behaviour therapy and rational emotive therapy (RET) term. A hard-headed, practically oriented, rational, and non-magical approach to replace faulty thought patterns with more resourceful ones. It has similarities to Becks' Cognitive therapy approach, but the therapist is more direct and confrontive.

COGNITIVE THERAPY

Developed by Aaron Beck, who puts forward the view that behaviour is primarily determined by what that person thinks.

It is particularly relevant in treating depression, where thoughts of low self-worth and self-esteem are a common feature.

Cognitive therapy works on the premise that thoughts of low self-worth are incorrect and are due to faulty learning. Such thoughts often centre around:

'I haven't achieved anything'.
'I have nothing to offer'.
'I deserve to be criticized'.

The aim of therapy is to get rid of faulty concepts that influence negative thinking.

Karen Horney refers to the 'tyranny of the shoulds': should do this, should not do that. Cognitive therapists, likewise, challenge all these assumptions, as well as all self-evaluations that constantly put the person down. Such evaluations are cumulative.

THE PERSON NEEDS HELP TO:

1. Identify the internal rules of self-evaluation.
2. See how selt-evaluation influences feelings and behaviours.
3. See how realistic the internal rules are.
4. Discover the origin of the rule.
5. See how the rule is maintained.
6. Discover ways to get rid of redundant rules.
7. Think through what it would mean to get rid of redundant rules.

ATTRIBUTIONS (*See also*: Transactional analysis)

1. Are being told what we are, what we must do and how we must feel.
2. Are generally approving of obedience and disapproving of disobedience.

THE CLIENT IS HELPED TO EXPLORE:

1. Personal responsibility
2. Blame and self-blame
3. Whether active or passive in meeting needs
4. Attributions
5. Alternatives
6. Am I responsible for my behaviour?
7. Am I in control or am I controlled?
8. If I am controlled – by whom?

The challenge the client has to face is: To change or not to change?

The person is helped to replace 'tunnel thinking' with 'lateral, flexible thinking'.

COMMON THINKING DIFFICULTIES

1. Memory lapse
2. Concentration
3. Incoherence
4. Blocking
5. Scatter

6. Restrictive thinking, in 'either/or' terms.

Problem-solving involves being able to work with shades of grey. The therapist needs to question behaviour based on unproven inferences such as, 'If I blush, people will think I am . . .'

Clients often need to learn decision-making and problem-solving skills as part of the process of thinking rehabilitation. Faulty self-evaluations, attributions and anticipations may lead to restricted perceptions and to restricted ability to solve problems.

TO MAKE DECISIONS WE MUST:

1. Be aware of alternatives
2. Understand the factors which influence choice
3. Accept responsibility for the consequences
4. Understand why we want to make the decision and for whose benefit.

TO SOLVE PROBLEMS WE MUST:

1. Accept that problems are normal but can usually be coped with.
2. Either have, or can develop, the capacity to solve a particular problem.
3. Resist the impulse to act on the first solution.

TO CARRY OUT DECISIONS AND TO SOLVE PROBLEMS WE MUST:

1. Plan realistically.
2. Explore motivation.
3. Evaluate what we do.

COUNSELLING INTERVENTIONS

1. Giving appropriate information may clear up misinformation and facilitate movement.
2. Acceptance and empathic understanding.
3. Focused exploration.
4. Specificity – get away from generalizations. Insist on 'I' instead of 'you' and 'my' instead of 'we'.
5. Challenge the discrepancies between:

   Thoughts, feelings and behaviours within and outside of counselling
   What is said and left unsaid
   Attributions
   False logic
   Self-evaluations
   Responsibility
   Irrational beliefs.

6. Use disputation, a form of sustained challenging.

   'Why . . . ?'
   'Yes, but why . . . ?'
   'That's still not clear.'

7. Interpretation from the external frame of reference:

   'It seems, from my point of view . . .'

8. Teaching:

   The Transactional analysis Parent, Adult Child framework, for example
   Problem-solving skills.

9. Information-giving:

   Tasks
   Homework
   Questionnaires.

10. Direction:

    Persuasion
    Exhortation
    Advice
    Advocating
    Encouragement
    Reassurance.

11. Modelling:

    The counselling relationship
    Behaviour rehearsal
    Group counselling
    Observing tasks being carried out.

12. Role play:

    Psychodrama
    Dramatic enactment
    Behaviour rehearsal
    Imagery.

13. Encourage performance

    Anticipations about tasks are often more negative than results would warrant.

14. Skills training
15. Visual aids/homework.

SOME HAZARDS OF ALTERING THINKING

1. Control by the counsellor creating dependence.
2. Intellectualization by the client may be at the expense of feelings and may cause distancing.
3. Projection by the counsellor to cover up personal and professional inadequacies.
4. Timing and resistance.

   Interventions must be carefully timed. A challenge too soon may lose the client.
   Change in thinking may be indicated by the acceptance of a previously rejected challenge.

A POSITIVE INTERVENTION IS:

1. Accurate
2. Relevant
3. Well-expressed
4. Accurately timed.

A positive intervention develops rather than diminishes the client's ability to take direction of her/his own life.

QUESTIONS TO HELP CLIENTS WITH THINKING (*See also*: RET)

1. *Explore and list negative thoughts:*

   When do you think them?
   Is there a pattern?
   Do they occur all the time or only at specific times?
   Are they concerned with specific people or events?
   Do you always lose out? Come off worse?
2. *Use imagination*. Imagination is a powerful ally. Whenever a negative thought occurs, 'Imagine the situation, then change the scene into something positive.'
2. *Use 'thought stop'*. Every time a negative thought intrudes, say (aloud, if you are able) 'STOP!' If thoughts are particularly troublesome, wear a loose elastic band on your wrist, and when the thought comes, snap the elastic.
4. *Substitute* a positive thought to replace the invasive negative thought. Substitution, coupled with imagination, is a powerful way to change from negative to positive thinking.

   Positive thinking can become as much a habit as negative thinking has been.

HELPFUL QUOTES

1. It's not what you think you are, But what you think, you are.
2. An old Chinese proverb:

   You can't stop the birds flying over your head, but you can stop them nesting in your hair.

COLLECTIVE UNCONSCIOUS
(Racial unconscious)

Term introduced by Carl G. Jung to describe those aspects of the psyche that are common to humankind as a whole.

It is part of everyone's unconscious and is distinct from the personal unconscious, which arises from the experience of the individual.

The collective unconscious contains archetypes, which express themselves as universal primitive images, accumulated down the ages and across cultures. The archetype is to the collective unconscious what the complex is to the personal unconscious.

Because the material in the collective unconscious has never existed in the conscious, it has not been repressed. Jung's evidence of the collective unconscious is found in myths, legends, folk tales, fairy tales and dreams.

COLLUSION (*See also*: *Folie á deux*)

An unconscious process whereby two or more individuals create a partnership in which they defend a common need.

An example of collusion is where one parent fails to support the disciplining of a child, in order to undermine the authority of the other parent. This alliance is then used to attack the other parent.

Folie á deux – in functional psychosis – is a form of collusion, where two people with a long-term intimate association share the same delusions.

Collusion between counsellor and client occurs when the counsellor unconsciously avoids confronting the deepest and most disturbed aspects of the client's condition in order to keep the relationship safe.

The collusive relationship, therefore, meets the neurotic needs of both parties.

Collusion impedes growth and the development of insight.

In groups, group members collude with one another to avoid the task of the group.

COMMUNICATION (*See also*: Creativity, Feedback, Listening, Questions)

Communication occurs when what takes place in one person's mind so influences the mind of another person, that the resultant experience of both are reasonably alike.

Interpersonal communication may be analysed in 50 different ways that draw upon dozens of disciplines.

Communication is a sharing of:

1. Attitudes
2. Facts
3. Feelings
4. Information.

ONE (LINEAR) MODEL OF COMMUNICATION HAS THE FOLLOWING ELEMENTS:

1. Source – a person on the telephone
2. Encoder – the mouthpiece
3. Message – the words spoken
4. Channel – electrical impulses
5. Decoder – the earpiece at the other end
6. Receiver – the mind of the listener.

Communication is influenced by:

1. *Entropy*, which is auditory or visual static, that decreases the effectiveness of the communication.
2. *Negative entropy*, which functions when the receiver, in spite of

mixed, or blurred messages, interprets enough of the message to make it intelligible.
3. *Redundancy* is the repetition of parts of the message that ensure the message gets through. Redundancy works against entropy. Entropy distorts; negative entropy and redundancy clarify.

   To be fully functional, and not static, the messages need to be understood.
4. *Feedback* corrects the default between entropy, negative entropy and redundancy.

   Effective communication cannot take place without feedback. The term 'feedback' derives from cybernetic theory – a cybernetic example would be a room thermostat.

METHODS OF COMMUNICATING:

1. Words (10%)
2. Tones (40%)
3. Visual (50%)

STYLES OF COMMUNICATING:

1. Tell
2. Negotiate
3. Persuade
4. Listen
5. Counselling.

There is more of self and less of the other person in 'tell'; more of the other person and less of self in 'counselling'.

BARRIERS TO EFFECTIVE COMMUNICATION

1. Lack of trust
2. Misinterpretation
3. Stereotyped language
4. Semantics
5. Emotional
6. Intellectual
7. Conceptual
8. Cultural.

EFFECTIVE COMMUNICATION HINGES ON:

1. *Creating a conducive atmosphere* based on time and place, motivation, and preparation.
2. *Being clear about:* Why we want to communicate, what the listener expects, and how we can put the points over.
3. *Active reception of information which is influenced by the skills of:*

   Active listening
   Attending
   Paraphrasing
   Reflecting
   Open questions
   Summarizing
   Focusing
   Self-disclosure
   Challenging.

UNCLEAR RECEPTION OF INFORMATION MAY BE INFLUENCED BY:

1. Lack of self-awareness
2. Hidden agendas
3. Preconceived ideas
4. Arguing
5. Interrupting
6. Criticizing
7. Putting down
8. Not able to get into the internal frame of reference.

The aim of giving and receiving feedback is to make someone more aware of:

1. What (s)he does
2. How it is done
3. The feelings
4. The consequences.

Giving feedback requires:

1. Courage
2. Other-respect
3. Self-awareness
4. Self-respect
5. Skill
6. Understanding.

Feedback should focus on:

1. Behaviour that can be changed
2. Description
3. Exploring alternatives
4. Giving information
5. Observation
6. Sharing ideas.

Feedback should not focus on:

1. Personal qualities
2. Judgment
3. Providing answers
4. Giving advice
5. Inferences
6. Giving direction.

We should consider how much feedback to give and then evaluate how clear and how accurate the feedback was.

Effective communication leaves people feeling OK, and is therefore a basis for change.

DEFENSIVE AND SUPPORTIVE COMMUNICATION

Communication, in addition to the foregoing, also depends on climate. Climates may be supportive or defensive.

Supportive climates promote understanding and problem-solving and are characterized by:

1. Empathy (*see* entry)
2. Spontaneity and openness
3. Synergy – a new situation that satisfies all needs.

Defensive climates are motivated by control, recognized by persuasion, coercion, and convincing. The desire to control results in:

1. Evaluations – characterized by criticism and judgment.
2. Strategies – with the focus on winning.
3. Superiority. The person who feels superior views the other as unintelligent and inferior.
4. Certainty. Correctness with no room for negotiation.

BARRIERS TO SUPPORTIVE CLIMATES

These are cultural, time/energy, risk, emotional.

Culture. In some cultures competition, not co-operation, listening and understanding is emphasized.

Time/Energy. Creating a supportive climate takes time, energy, and commitment.

Risk. Every time we view the world through someone else's eyes, from another person's frame of reference, we run the risk of having to change something within ourselves.

Emotional. Hostile, angry feelings get in the way of offering support.

FACILITATING SUPPORTIVE COMMUNICATION

This depends on three things:

1. Being genuinely open. False openness will create alarm.
2. Active listening, which is grasping the facts and meaning of the message; clarifying and checking.
3. Feedback, which is sharing perspectives; moving from 'me versus

you' to 'you and me together' and thinking of the goal(s), then seeking solutions to reach it (them).

DIRECT AND INDIRECT COMMUNICATION

Indirect communication is pseudo-communication, carried out with the purpose of manipulating, control, avoiding risks, and self-protection.

CHARACTERISTICS OF INDIRECT COMMUNICATION

1. *Non-communication*. Attempting to get ungenuine support:

   'I think I speak for the whole group.'

2. *Non-genuine questions*. Questions are generally indirect communication and seek to direct the person toward a certain response.

   A. Limiting questions.

      'Don't you think that . . . ?'
      'Isn't it a fact that . . . ?'

   B. Punishing questions, where the motive is to expose the other person without appearing to do so, and so put the person on the spot.

   C. Hypothetical questions, which are often motivated by criticism.

      'If you were making that report, wouldn't you say it differently?
      Hypothetical questions typically begin with 'If', 'What if', 'How about'.

   D. Demand or command questions, where the motivation is to impress urgency or importance.

      'Have you done anything about . . .?'

   E. Screened questions. Here the motivation is to get the other person to make a decision that fits with the speaker's hidden wish. This type of question puts great pressure on the person being questioned, not being sure what answer is required.

      'Would you like to go to . . . ?'

   F. Leading questions. The motive here is to manoeuvre the other person into a vulnerable position. Leading questions are often used by lawyers in court to confuse the witness.

      'Is it fair to say that you . . .?'
      'Would you agree that . . .?'

   G. Rhetorical questions. The motive here is to forestall a response because the questioner fears it may not be a favourable one. The attempt is to secure a guaranteed agreement. No response is required.

      'I'm coming for the weekend, OK?'

   H. 'Now I've got you' question. The motive is to dig a trap for the other person to fall into.

      'Weren't you the one who . . .?'

3. *Clichés*. Here the motive is to appear to be communicating, without sharing anything significant. The frequent use of tired, worn-out phrases reduces the effectiveness of communication.

THE EFFECTS OF INDIRECT COMMUNICATION:

1. Guesswork. Without direct, open communication, people cannot get to know each other. What we do not know, we will make guesses about.
2. Inaccuracy. Guessing means making assumptions and often we get the wrong answers.
3. Inferences. When communication is not direct, we are forced to infer the other person's motives. Pseudo-questions and clichés hide motives.
4. Playing games. Indirect communication encourages game-playing, leading to deception and dishonesty.
5. Defensiveness. This is one of the surest effects of indirect communication. (*See also*: Defence mechanisms).

DIRECT COMMUNICATION IS CHARACTERIZED BY:

1. Being two-way, in which ideas, opinions, values, beliefs, and feelings flow freely.
2. Active listening. (*See also*: Listening).
3. Giving and receiving feedback (*See also*: Feedback).
4. Not being stressful.
5. Being clear and relatively free from ambiguity and mixed messages.

WE CAN FOSTER DIRECT COMMUNICATION BY:

1. Making direct statements. When we make statements, based on what we have heard, rather than ask questions, we are more likely to be communicating directly.
2. Actively listening.
3. Owning that what we say and what we feel really does belong to us.
4. Locating the context. This means that in order to make a genuine response we have to understand the context in which the statement is made. We must not make assumptions.
5. Sharing. All true communication is a sharing process. For communication to be effective, we must be prepared to take risks, and work toward a mutual understanding through genuine sharing of a common meaning.

COMPENSATION

Alfred Adler's term to describe the process we use to react to our inferiority complexes, and which we disguise from ourselves.

As infants, because of our initial helplessness, we feel inferior, and strive to overcome this feeling of incompleteness.

Striving to overcome inferiority is a powerful motivator.

An inferiority complex arises when we cannot achieve normal development, and manifests itself in ideas of personal worthlessness.

Compensation is the drive to challenge situations which will prove that the misgivings we have about ourselves are false.

If we do not achieve normal balance, there is the danger of overcompensation, where our striving for power and dominance become so exaggerated and intensified that it must be called pathological.

Overcompensation is characterized by pride, vanity, and the desire to conquer everyone at any price. These attitudes bring us into contact with the dark side of life and prevent us from experiencing the joy of living.

Adlerian therapy is concerned with the personal aspirations and goals of achievement, both conscious and unconscious, as applied to our social setting and total life situation.

The man who is crippled, yet becomes a mountaineer, is probably compensating. He would be over-compensating if he gloated over his achievements at the expense of other disabled people.

COMPENSATION (Defence mechanism)

The tendency to cover up a weakness or defect by exaggerating a more desirable characteristic. 'I'm the greatest.'

An example would be someone who feels inferior because of lack of height and compensates by becoming overbearing and bossy.

Jung's view is that compensation is an unconscious attempt to achieve psychological homeostasis of the contents of the conscious. Compensation means balancing, adjusting and supplementing.

Material repressed into the unconscious by the conscious develops so much energy that it eventually breaks through as dreams, spontaneous images or neurotic symptoms. Compensation, then, acts as a link between the conscious and the unconscious.

COMPLEXES (*See also*: Repression)

In Analytical (Adlerian) psychology, a group of associated ideas that have been partially or wholly repressed. These are usually outside of awareness, and evoke emotional forces that influence a person's behaviour.

Complexes are archetypal in character and have their origins in early relationships with parents and significant others and have a 'magnetic' quality that attracts associated ideas and memories to them.

A complex may arise either from the personal unconscious or from the collective unconscious, or both. They always contain the characteristics of a conflict – shock, upheaval, mental agony, inner strife.

Complexes are the 'sore spots', the 'skeletons in the cupboard', that come unbidden to terrorize us, and always contain memories, wishes, fears, duties, needs, or insights which somehow we can never really grapple with.

They constantly interfere with our conscious life in disturbing and usually harmful ways. The presence of complexes act as obstacles, and, therefore, as new possibilities of achievement of growth. They act as filters through which life is perceived.

CONCRETE THINKING

Refers to literal-mindedness which is strongly tied to immediate and tangible information. It means thinking in the 'here and now', accompanied by difficulty, or inability, to think in the abstract and to form concepts.

The shift from concrete thinking to thinking in the abstract takes place around adolescence.

Concrete thinking, and the absence of abstract thinking, is typically seen in organic mental disorders, and is frequently observed in people suffering from schizophrenia.

CONFLICT

A psychological state of indecision, where the person is faced simultaneously with two opposing forces of equal strength, that cannot be solved together.

TYPES OF CONFLICT:

1. Choice between positives both of which are desirable. Approach–approach where chance factors determine the outcome. For example, the choice between two attractive careers.
2. Choice between negatives where both are undesirable. Avoidance–avoidance. For example, a man may dislike his job intensely, but fears the threat of unemployment if he resigns.
3. Choice between negative and positive. Approach–avoidance creates great indecision, helplessness and anxiety. A child, dependent on his or her mother, also fears her because she is rejecting and punitive.

Conflicts are often unconscious, in the sense that the person cannot clearly identify the source of the distress. Many strong impulses, such as fear and hostility, are not approved of by society, so children soon learn not to acknowledge them, even to themselves. When such impulses are in conflict, we are anxious without knowing why.

Related concepts are Cognitive dissonance and Kurt Lewin's Field theory.

CONFLICTS MAY BE AVOIDED OR RESOLVED BY:

1. Active listening
2. Appropriate disclosure.

Conflicts, poorly handled, can result in negative behaviours such as:

Aggression
Defiance
Forming alliances
Gossiping
Physical and psychological withdrawal
Retaliation.

Conflict resolution is strongly influenced by feelings of self-worth. People with low self-worth expect to be treated badly; they expect the worst, invite it, and generally get it.

People who do not feel confident generally feel small, and therefore view others as threateningly larger.

THINKING ABOUT RESOLVING CONFLICT:

1. Identify the rules that encourage conflict.
2. How much autonomy do people have, and give?
3. How much do we control each other?
4. Identify 'musts', 'oughts' and 'shoulds'.
5. Examine attributions (*see* TA).
6. Who blames whom and for what?
7. What are the risks and gains of resolution?
8. Are there any possible compromises?
9. What roles sustain the conflict?
10. What 'games' do people play? (*see* TA)

HELPING PEOPLE CHANGE

1. Teach assertiveness
2. Use video feedback
3. Teach empathic listening
4. Develop open communication

5. Concentrate on changeable behaviour
6. Work at a time free from distractions
7. Teach how to give specific and non-evaluative feedback.
8. Encourage the giving of written contracts
9. Explore agreed areas
10. Be an example of an effective, caring communicator.

CONFLICT: A PROBLEM-SOLVING MODEL

Let each person:

1. Describe the situation as they see it
2. Describe what they feel about the conflict, and what personal meaning it has for them
3. Describe a desired situation
4. Identify changes necessary to achieve the desired situation
5. Outline a problem-solving agenda or plan of action.

CONSCIENCE - PHILOSOPHICAL

The ability to arrive at a view of what is morally right or wrong. There are two basic views:

1. *Rationalist* which says that conscience is the normal powers of reasoning, not a special faculty, that we apply to most matters, particularly to moral decisions. A view put forward by Aristotle and Thomas Aquinas.
2. *Intuitive* which says that conscience is a moral sense or sensibility, similar to our physical senses. Conscience grasps the moral quality of actions, or the truth of moral principles, directly and straight to the point. This view can be integrated within the Christian tradition that maintains that:

A. Conscience is authoritative, not because it always judges correctly, but because as rational beings we have no alternative but to do what, in our best judgment, we believe we ought to do.
B. Conscience is also authoritative because it is 'the voice of God within us', and as such our moral duty is made plain to us.

CONSCIENCE - PSYCHOANALYTIC (*See*: Superego)

CONSCIOUS

One of Freud's regions of the mind which, with the preconscious and the unconscious, make up the psyche. Freud described the conscious as the 'sense organ of the ego'. The conscious is open to immediate awareness, unlike the preconscious and the unconscious, which are not.

The functions of the ego - reality testing, perception, observation, and evaluation - are all at a conscious level. Some of the superego functions - criticism and conscience - are also mainly conscious. The defence mechanisms and censorship are not within the conscious.

Behavioural, humanistic and cognitive therapies all emphasize working directly with the conscious in the belief that only what is observable can be accurately interpreted.

CONSTRUCT (*See also*: Personal construct therapy)

A construct, like a concept, is a

person's interpretation of external reality. Constructs enable us to judge similarities and events, referred to as elements by Kelly in his Personal construct theory. Constructs are bipolar, for example, happy–sad, good–bad, caring–uncaring.

Core constructs, which are central to the person's identity, produce anxiety and fear if they are shaken. A construct is considered to be permeable when it is capable of encompassing other elements.

CONTRACT

A formal, explicit agreement between counsellor and client. A contract helps to ensure the professional nature of the relationship and may include:

1. Venue
2. Frequency of sessions
3. Boundaries of confidentiality
4. Broad requirements of the treatment
5. Duties and responsibilities of each party
6. Goals of therapy
7. Means by which the goals may be achieved
8. The provision and completion of 'homework'
9. The setting of boundaries and expectations
10. The terms of the therapeutic relationship
11. Time limits of sessions and of counselling
12. Provision for renegotiation of contract
13. Fees, if appropriate
14. How therapy will be evaluated
15. Process of referral if and when necessary
16. Supervision.

The contract may be written, signed by both therapist and client, or each person in a group. In family therapy, the children need to be included in the terms of the contract; how, and at what age, needs to be considered.

In group therapy, part of the contract would include a full and frank discussion on 'ground rules'.

CONTROLLING (Defence mechanism)

Excessive attempts to manage or regulate situations, objects and people in the environment, in order to minimize anxiety and to resolve inner conflicts.

CONVERSION (Defence mechanism)

In psychoanalytic terms, where repressed material, ideas, wishes, feelings are converted into physical manifestations, such as hysterical paralysis of a limb. The physical symptom symbolizes the original conflict.

Paralysis of a limb (properly, conversion hysteria) for example, would remove the person from a conflict at work, where work depended on using the limb.

The person who uses conversion hysteria often adopts a curiously indifferent or theatrical attitude toward the paralysis, which invariably does not stand up to neurological analysis.

COPING IMAGERY (*See also*: Multi-modal therapy)

A Multi-modal therapy technique which pairs relaxation with images of successful outcomes in situations that previously evoked extreme anxiety.

An example would be where a medical student has already failed his final surgical examination. Having produced in him a relaxed state, the therapist, over repeated sessions, would take the student through an imaginary lead-up to the exam, study and revision, recreation and relaxation. All the while the therapist is reinforcing the positive outcome.

The student would then be prepared for the actual day; getting up, feeling good, going to the exam room, feeling relaxed, sitting down to answer the paper, feeling confident. Being able to control feelings of anxiety and not letting them get out of control.

Adopting a positive attitude in imagery eventually settles down into the unconscious with beneficial results, because positive imagery replaces negative imagery.

COPING SKILLS INTERVENTION

A variety of techniques designed to help people develop effective coping mechanisms. The aim is to teach ways of coping with stress, not to avoid or extinguish it.

THE MAIN TECHNIQUES ARE:

1. Self-help procedures
2. Modelling
3. A modified systematic desensitization
4. Imagery
5. Relaxation training
6. Anxiety management training
7. Stress inoculation.

THE THERAPIST HELPS BY:

1. Teaching the client to rethink by monitoring self-statements.
2. Demonstrating how to change negative self-statements into positive self-statements.
3. Teaching problem-solving skills.
4. Working with the client through progressively difficult tasks.

CORE CONDITIONS

The relationship qualities embraced in most therapies, and considered to be crucial in person-centred therapy.

THE CORE CONDITIONS ARE:

1. Empathy
2. Non-possessive warmth
3. Unconditional positive regard
4. Genuineness or congruence.

When they are present, and appropriately expressed, a climate is created in which a positive therapeutic outcome is likely.

Criticism centres more around their efficiency than their necessity.

Some theorists argue that while the core conditions must be present, by themselves they are insufficient. Other interventions are necessary.

There is a body of opinion that neither a 'relationship' nor a 'skills' approach is sufficient. Both are needed. This would depend on the nature of the problem and the personality of both client and counsellor. Counsellors generally choose an approach or method that suits their personality.

CORONARY-PRONE BEHAVIOUR

(*See also*: 'A'-type personality)

Studies using the Minnesota Multiphasic Personality Inventory (MMPI) concluded that patients with coronary heart disease (CHD) differ from people who remain healthy. The scales with the major differences, the 'neurotic' triad, were:

1. Hypochondriasis
2. Hysteria
3. Depression.

Patients with fatal disease tended to show greater depression than those who incur and survive CHD. Other studies portray patients with CHD or related illness as emotionally unstable and introverted.

COUNSELLING PROCESS (*See also*: Relationship principles)

THE MAIN ASPECTS:

1. Getting on the client's wavelength
2. Active listening and appropriate responding
3. Remaining impartial and suspending judgment
4. Using the skills of:

   Attending
   Paraphrasing the content
   Reflecting feelings
   Open questions
   Summarizing
   Focusing
   Challenging
   Self-disclosure
   Immediacy
   Concreteness.

5. Waiting for a reply
6. The constructive use of silences
7. Keeping pace with the client
8. Reading between the lines
9. Demonstrating the principles of the counselling relationship:

   Individualization
   Feelings
   Involvement
   Self-determination
   Confidentiality
   Acceptance
   Non-judgment.

10. Expressing understanding of the client's feelings
11. Being able to enter the client's frame of reference
12. Demonstrating empathy
13. Expressing support
14. Keeping the interview moving forward
15. Keeping objective when planning action
16. Dealing with transference and counter-transference
17. Saying 'goodbye', constructively.

COUNTER-TRANSFERENCE (*See also*: Bonding, Transference)

Counter-transference refers to unconscious needs, wishes, or conflicts of the therapist evoked by the client, which are brought into therapy and influence the therapist's objective judgment and reason.

INDICATORS OF COUNTER-TRANSFERENCE:

1. Altering lengths of sessions, or forgetting sessions with certain clients
2. Being overly strict with certain clients and being lenient with others
3. Being preoccupied with certain clients
4. Developing fantasies toward the client
5. Dreaming about certain clients
6. Emotional withdrawal from the client
7. Experiencing unease during or following sessions
8. Feeling drowsy without cause
9. Needing the approval of certain clients
10. Not being willing to explore certain issues

11. Not wanting the client to terminate
12. Promising unrealistic rescue
13. Reappearance of immature character traits in the therapist
14. Using the client to impress someone.

THEORETICAL PERSPECTIVES:

1. *The classical viewpoint*

   The therapist displaces on to the client feelings that would be more appropriately directed at another person, either in the present or, more likely, in the past.

   Counter-transference feelings thus arise from the therapist's own needs, and are not directed to meet the needs of the client.

   Counter-transference interferes with therapist neutrality, and therefore has an adverse effect on therapy.

2. *An integrated viewpoint*

   Counter-transference is not pathological, but is inevitable and an integral part of the relationship. How the therapist uses feelings and thoughts all help to increase understanding within the relationship.

3. *A 'totalistic' viewpoint*

   All of the counsellor's thoughts, feelings, and behaviours are indicators of counter-transference.

4. *A realistic viewpoint*

   The counselling relationship possesses both positive (constructive) and negative (destructive) elements.

   Research supports the point of view that the client influences the therapist much more that the literature would suggest.

OVERIDENTIFICATION OR DISIDENTIFICATION

Counter-transference may be either overidentification or disidentification, and may be one of four forms:

1. *Overprotective* (overidentification), characterized by parent/child interaction, collusion (allowing the client to blame others), cushioning the client from pain.
2. *Benign* (overidentification), characterized by talk/talk, as friends where distance is closed.
3. *Rejecting* (disidentification), characterized by being cool/aloof with minimal involvement and increased distance, failure to intervene, allowing client to struggle and stumble. The counsellor fears demands and responsibility.
4. *Hostile* (disidentification), which arises from fear of contamination and is characterized by the counsellor being verbally abusive, curt, or blunt.

AIDS TO MANAGING THE TRANSFERENCE

1. Self-analysis
2. Personal therapy
3. Mentor/supervision
4. Genuineness and self-disclosure
5. Refer the client.

THE THERAPIST AND COUNTER-TRANSFERENCE

Working with clients who have deeply ingrained personality problems or those who display self-defeating behaviour, may provoke similar behaviour in the therapist.

Countertransference behaviour may take the form of:

1. Anger
2. Losing concentration
3. Wishing to control
4. Feeling defensive
5. Denying the truth.

Anticipation, understanding, and adequate supervision allow therapists to avoid becoming engulfed in counter-transference. Concern over counter-transference is especially warranted when dealing with people who are depressed or manic, and those contemplating suicide.

CREATIVITY

Most people are born with the ability to be creative, yet not everyone makes use of that potential. Conformity thwarts expression of creativity in the developing child. The spark of creativity will be extinguished if it is not given expression. Increasing personal effectiveness requires creativity, plus unlearning non-productive and self-defeating behaviours.

Creative people generally are:

1. Open to experience
2. Flexible in thinking
3. Able to deal with conflicting information
4. Not unduly swayed by criticism or praise.

Creativity develops within a psychologically safe environment in which there is acceptance, a non-judgmental attitude and freedom to think and feel.

BARRIERS TO DEVELOPING CREATIVITY

These are mental fogs that prevent us from perceiving a problem correctly, or conceiving possible solutions.

1. Perceptual. *How we see things.* These barriers are recognized by the following:

   A. Failure to use all the senses in observing
   B. Failure to investigate the obvious
   C. Inability to define terms
   D. Difficulty in seeing abstract relationships
   E. Failure to distinguish between cause and effect
   F. Failure to use the unconscious, such as not using visualization or fantasy
   G. Inability to use the conscious mind, such as inability to organize data.

2. Cultural. *How we ought to do things.* These barriers are recognized by the following:

   A. A need to conform
   B. An overemphasis on competition or on co-operation.
   C. A drive to be practical and economical at all costs
   D. Belief that fantasy is time-wasting
   E. Too much faith in reason and logic
   F. A deep-seated need to find the proper setting, and to give oneself every advantage
   G. A work-orientated need to keep trying and to be always prepared and ready.

3. Emotional. *How we feel about things.*

These barriers are recognized by the following:

A. Fear of making mistakes
B. Fear and distrust of others
C. Grabbing the first idea
D. Personal feelings of insecurity, such as low self-esteem
E. Feelings of anxiety, fear of criticism, fear of failure, or lack of curiosity
F. Need for security, such as lack of risk-taking, or of not trying new things.

CREDIBILITY

The perceived ability of the counsellor to possess the knowledge and skill required by the client together with the willingness to use them on behalf of the client.

THE ESSENTIAL ELEMENTS OF CREDIBILITY:

1. Effective communication
2. Empathy and warmth
3. Expertness - qualifications and experience
4. Reliability
5. Reputation
6. Trustworthiness.

CRISIS THERAPY

A crisis is a limited period of acute psychological and emotional disorganization, brought about by a challenging or hazardous event.

Crisis therapy is a brief form of social and/or psychological treatment offered to people who are experiencing a personal crisis, whose usual methods of coping have proved ineffective.

TYPES OF CRISIS INTERVENTION:

1. Appropriate social and material assistance.
2. Emotional 'first aid' - supportive therapy, containment of the crisis and care, particularly during the early days following the event.
3. Crises, such as bereavement, have a similar meaning and effect upon individuals, regardless of their personalities and can usually be approached in the same way .
4. A dynamic approach that helps the client understand current reactions to previous crises.

The objective of all crisis intervention is the restoration of psychological balance to at least what it was prior to the crisis.

Dealing with crises usually means, initially, that a more directive approach is appropriate, because the person's inner resources have been paralysed. After the acute stage has passed, therapy should be directed toward:

1. Catharsis and ventilation of feelings
2. Helping the person to talk
3. Nurturing self-esteem
4. Developing problem-solving behaviour.

CRITICAL INCIDENTS

Planning for crises can reduce anxiety when they do occur. Dealing with a crisis demands fast decision-making and action, clear lines of communication, and easy access to all available information. What is not always appreciated is that people who are in the front line of coping with the crisis need support and personal supervision during and following the incident.

Suffering can be intensified by official obstruction and insensitivity.

Grief is a natural reaction to most traumatic events, particularly where there is loss of life. Relatives who have an opportunity to see the dead body usually grieve more constructively.

A proactive approach, reaching out to people to offer help, is often more helpful than waiting for people to ask for it. Offering help, however well-meaning the motive, does not guarantee acceptance of the offer. But it does show caring.

Early intervention, and opportunity to talk through their experiences and their feelings is important, before defences start building up.

CRITICAL INCIDENT STRESS DEBRIEFING

Debriefing should, ideally, take place on day 2, 3 or 4 following the incident. Day one is too soon. After day 4, perceptions, feelings and reactions begin to harden and the debriefing begins to have less healing value.

Debriefing should be conducted by an experienced group facilitator within a confidential environment.

Staff who provide support to traumatized and bereaved people need recognition, support, stress relief, adequate supervision, and the chance to record their experience, and to properly round off their participation when the time is right.

CRITICAL PARENT (EGO STATE)

(*See also*: Transactional analysis, Nurturing parent)

The critical parent ego state criticizes and finds fault, and is contrasted with the nurturing parent. The critical parent may also be assertive and self-sufficient. The basic need of the critical parent is power.

Some typical words:

Because I said so, brat, childish, naughty, now what, ought to, what will the neighbours say.

Some typical gestures and postures:

Eyes rolling up in disgust, finger-pointing, folded arms, tapping of feet in impatience.

Some typical voice tones:

Condescending, punishing, sneering.

Some typical facial expressions:

Angry frown, disapproving, furrowed brow, hostile, pursed lips, scowl, set jaw.

Life position	Behaviour
1. I'm not OK You're not OK	Traditional
2. I'm OK You're not OK	Prescriptive
3. I'm OK You're OK	Middle of the road
4. I'm not OK You're OK	Indifferent

D

DEFENCE MECHANISMS

Unconscious mental processes which enable us to reach compromise solutions to problems we are unable to resolve any other way. These internal drives, or feelings, that threaten to lower our self-esteem or to provoke anxiety, are concealed from our conscious mind.

Freud claimed that these unconscious drives are in conflict with one another and are the cause of mental disorders.

Defence mechanisms are developed unconsciously to ward off internal and external dangers, and to protect the individual from being annihilated. Their purpose is thus to protect the ego and maintain the *status quo* by diverting anxiety away from consciousness.

The functioning of the adult should be controlled by the perceptive and intelligent ego, and action by the ego ideally should satisfy the demands of id, superego, and reality.

Defences are not necessarily pathological, even though the ego may not function adequately. They become pathological when they fail to ward off anxiety and when more defences have to be used to control the ego. Neurotic symptoms are then formed which interfere with pursuing a satisfactory way of living. Psychoses is where there is a complete breakdown of the defence system.

THE PRINCIPAL DEFENCE MECHANISMS ARE:

1. Compensation
2. Denial
3. Displacement
4. Projection
5. Rationalization
6. Reaction formation
7. Regression
8. Repression
9. Sublimation.

Avoidance as a defence in therapy is characterized by:

1. Externalization. The fault is outside me.
2. Blind spots. If I don't look, it will go away.
3. Excessive self-control. I won't let anything upset me.

4. Being right. My mind is made up, don't confuse me with facts.
5. Elusiveness and confusion. Don't pin me down.
6. Self-disparagement. I'm always wrong.
7. Playing the martyr role. My suffering controls other people.

The goal of therapy is to modify the ego's defences but to keep anxiety within manageable bounds. This is done by developing the client's problem-solving skills and integrating the fantasy life into reality.

DEFINITION

The British Association for Counselling definition is:

1. People become engaged in counselling when a person, occupying regularly or temporarily the role of counsellor offers or agrees to offer time, attention and respect to another person or persons temporarily in the role of client.
2. The task of counselling is to give the client an opportunity to explore, discover and clarify ways of living more resourcefully and towards greater well-being.

EXPANSION

1. Not every person who uses counselling skills is designated as 'counsellor'. Many people use counselling as one of their repertoire of skills. They would be 'temporarily in the role'.
2. Most people enter into counselling of their own volition and it is something agreed between client and counsellor. Sometimes, particularly where counselling is part of another job, the need for counselling may be perceived and suggested.
   In any case, counselling should not be entered into without agreement from both parties. The relationship should be made explicit, and the roles clearly defined.
3. People who engage in counselling make a contract where one of the boundaries is time; number and length of sessions.
   Giving total, undivided attention means being able to free oneself from external and internal distractions.
4. One of the aspects of respect is that we recognize and accept the uniqueness of each and every person, while at the same time taking account of shared similarities.
   Many people who have difficulties – in whatever area of life, be it work, or at a personal level – suffer from a damaged self esteem. The counselling relationship encourages people to repair their damaged self-esteem for it is here, where free from judgment and criticism, they are able to start to respect themselves. It is almost as if the damaged self-esteem devalues all they are and what they do. Respect should be total; for the person and for what transpires during counselling.
5. People are not clients for life. The counselling relationship is only one of many, and much happens and takes place for one hour out of the 168 hours in the week.
6. Counselling helps clients make some sense out of confusion; choice from conflict and sense out of nonsense.
   Counselling helps clients discover resources hitherto not recognized and helps them put those resources to work on their behalf.

DEJA VU (French 'already seen')

Familiarity with what one has experienced in what one knows to be a new situation. *Dèjá* experiences have been recognized throughout history and have been thought by some people to be evidence of a previous existence.

The discrepancy between 'knowing', and the feeling of having experienced it before, can be a challenge to one's sense of reality.

One explanation is that the current situation has triggered off something that occurred in a dream.

Dèjá experiences are frequently reported by patients suffering from temporal lobe brain dysfunction.

DELUSIONS

In psychiatry a delusion is defined as a persistent false belief which is both untrue and cannot be shaken by reason or contradictory evidence, and which is inconsistent with the person's knowledge or culture.

Primary delusions appear suddenly and fully formed. Secondary delusions are derived from hallucinations or other psychotic states.

Delusions are most often seen in schizophrenia, severe affective disorders and organic mental states.

The most common are delusions of persecution and grandeur. Delusions of grandeur (also called megalomania, a psychotic conviction or one's greatness or goodness) occur in schizophrenia and paranoia. Others include delusions of disease (hypochondriasis), sin, guilt, and erotic delusions, e.g., that one is loved by some famous (often royal) person.

Delusions of guilt are often associated with depression.

DEMORALIZATION

A fundamental quality in all psychic disturbance. Symptoms are both the means of expressing the state of demoralization and the attempts to cope with that state.

CATEGORIES OF DEMORALIZATION:

1. Discontent
2. Neuroses
3. Psychoses
4. The shaken
5. The unruly.

CHARACTERISTICS OF DEMORALIZATION:

1. Alienation
2. Resentment
3. Guilt
4. Loss of control
5. Depression and anxiety, arising from a loss of belief in one's own significance, in the purpose of life and the ability to love and to be loved.

DENIAL (Defence mechanism)

'It hasn't happened.'
'It's not really happening.'

Employed to avoid becoming consciously aware of some painful thought, feeling or experience or event or part of self. The existence of facts cannot be tolerated in the conscious mind. It is not deliberate lying; the person fails to perceive the facts.

Freud maintained that denial of painful experiences is governed by the pleasure-principle and that the denial is part of a hallucinatory wish-fulfilment.

There may be massive denial of a particular idea, experience, the event itself, its memory, or only the associated affect. Complete denial is seldom encountered.

Denial is a frequently used defence mechanism in personality disorders. It is commonly employed in crises, and serves to protect the ego. It is the scar of the psychic traumas experienced by the individual but it does not make the traumatic experiences disappear. The excessive use of denial may precipitate a psychosis, and the denied reality may be replaced by a fantasy or delusion.

An example would be the man who refuses to accept that his leg has been amputated.

DEREFLECTION (*See also*: Logotherapy)

A technique in which the client is encouraged to divert attention from the anxiety-provoking symptom. Refocusing attention allows the client to live a more satisfying life in spite of the symptom.

DEVALUATION (Defence mechanism) (*See also*: Narcissism)

Often present in people with narcissistic tendencies.

CHARACTERISTICS OF DEVALUATION:

1. A poor self-esteem is bolstered by seeing themselves as powerful and all important.
2. They severely devalue other people.

THEIR BEHAVIOUR MAY BE LABELLED:

1. Vain
2. Grandiose
3. Clamouring for recognition
4. Narcissistic.

DIRECTION (*See also*: Self-determination)

A therapeutic skill in which the therapist tells the client what to do, mainly between sessions, in the form of advice and homework.

This approach would be more likely to be used in behavioural or cognitive therapy.

Existential, humanistic, person-centred, and psychoanalytic therapists use directives sparingly.

Direction may conflict with one of the basic relationship principles, self-determination.

DISCOVERY LEARNING

Discovery learning is closely identified with the work of Piaget and liberal educationalists such as Montessori and Froebel. It is an instructional approach that encourages students to arrive at their own conclusions. The process of discovery takes precedence over the acquisition of knowledge.

Proceeding from broad general principles to specifics, the method emphasizes problem-solving with minimal guidance from the teacher and maximum opportunity for exploration by the student. Learning by personal experience and experiment is thought to make memory more vivid, and helps to transfer knowledge to new situations.

The aim is to train children to have inquiring minds, so sensitive to the specific characteristics of things about them, and so expert in classifying, that everything would possess interest and value for them.

The teacher retains an important guidance role in trying to achieve a compromise between the ideal, which is time-consuming, and what is practical, yet still leaving the child with a sense of having 'discovered'.

DISPLACEMENT (Defence mechanism)

'She's to blame, not me.'

The shifting of affect from one mental image to another to which it does not really belong, in order to avoid anxiety.

It can be used to protect a valued object by channelling negative feelings on to a substitute that closely resembles the original.

An example would be the man who comes home in a temper because of a row with his boss, and verbally attacks his wife.

DISSOCIATION (Defence mechanism)

A temporary but extreme change in a person's character or personal identity in order to avoid emotional distress. It is the separating off of thoughts, feelings, and fantasies from conscious awareness. The term was used by Freud but he later dropped it in favour of the 'repression'.

Although the mental contents are disowned and separated from the rest of the personality, they are not repressed or projected on to someone else.

The term is often associated with aggressive and sexual impulses, fantasies, and theatrical behaviour.

In amnesia, the memory is dissociated. The fugue state is a major dissociation, characterized by loss of memory and by flight from one's usual environment.

Those who employ dissociation like to associate with people who lead dangerous or exciting lives and they often twist the truth.

When clients have an opportunity to ventilate their anxieties, they often 'remember' what they 'forgot'.

DISTANCING (*See also*: Individual (Adlerian) psychology)

A term used by Adler in which the person tries to preserve self-esteem by placing distance between him- or herself and some perceived threat.

It is also used to describe how close people allow themselves to come to others in relationships.

In psychoanalysis, the term refers to psychic detachment, or extreme reserve, of attitude or emotions, characteristic of certain psychoneurotic conditions.

DISTORTION (Defence mechanism)

Where external reality is grossly restructured to preserve the person's inner world. Its function in dreams is to make acceptable the content that otherwise would be unacceptable.

EXAMPLES OF DISTORTION:

1. Hallucinations
2. Wish-fulfilling delusions
3. Fantasies of power
4. Delusions of superiority.

DOUBLE BIND

Gregory Bateson's description of the contradiction experienced by people who receive contradictory messages from someone more powerful. It means that the person is placed in a situation in which there is no winning, no matter what is said or done.

The term evolved from the study of the nature of schizophrenic communication. Now it is applied to a wide range of interpersonal communications. Only repeated exposure within a survival relationship produces severe pathology.

It is likely to arise in a family where one or both parents, who cannot express affection, respond coldly to the advances of the child. When the child withdraws, confused, they respond in simulated love, coupled with accusations such as, 'you don't love your mother, after all she's done for you'.

As relationships are mutual, both parties become 'victims' of the double bind. It is experienced by people suffering from schizophrenia, who, whatever they do, will be labelled either 'mad' or 'bad'.

THE ESSENTIAL ELEMENTS:

1. Two or more people involved.
2. The 'victim' repeatedly experiences the double bind.
3. Threat of punishment or withdrawal of approval.
4. Statements that conflict with the threat: 'I only want what is good for you'.
5. Escape is impossible; the relationship has survival value for the 'victim'.

DREAM THEORIES

An Australian aboriginal expression says 'He who has no dreaming is lost'.

Dreams are hallucinatory experiences that occur during sleep. People have had experiences where complex problems have been solved in dreams. So dreams can aid creativity.

VIEWS ON THE NATURE OF DREAMS:

1. Dreams reflect reality:

   A. The Eskimo of Hudson Bay believe that a person's soul leaves the body during sleep, to live in a special dream world, and that the soul of a person awakened from dreaming is in danger of being lost.

   B. In Borneo, if a man dreams that his wife has been unfaithful, her father must take her back.

   C. In the Soviet culture of Kamchatka, if a man dreams of sex with a girl, she owes him sexual favours.

2. Dreams as a source of divination:

   A. Writings from ancient Egypt, of Homer, and from India, all support the belief that dreams predict the future.

   B. A Babylonian 'dream guide' was discovered in the ruins of Ninevah (circa 668–627 BC).

   C. The Bible has many examples of the belief in dreams.

   D. Dream interpretation was forbidden by Muhammad, the founder of Islam.

3. Dreams as curative:

   A. In classical Greece, dreams became directly associated with healing.

   B. Over 600 temples, dedicated to Asklepios (Aesculapius – Latin), drew suffering people to offer sacrifices and to sleep in his presence and receive healing through dreams.

4. Dreams as extensions of the waking state:

   A. For Aristotle, dreams were acted upon by the emotional state of the dreamer.

   B. In the 1850s, the French physician Alfred Maury, who studied more than 3000 dreams, concluded that dreams arise from external stimuli.

C. Anecdotal evidence abounds that dreams are stimulated by prior thinking or events. Coleridge, in writing 'Kubla Khan'; Robert Louis Stevenson's Dr Jekyll and Mr Hyde; the discovery of the benzene molecule by F.A. Kekulé von Stradonits are examples.

5. Psychoanalytic interpretations:

   A. Freud referred to dreams as 'the royal road to the unconscious'. He believed that dreams reflect waking experience. He developed a highly systematized approach to interpret and use dreams in therapy.
   B. Thinking during sleep is primitive and dips into repressed material.
   C. Dreaming is a mechanism for maintaining sleep and fulfilling wishes.

WISH FULFILMENT

In dreams, wishes and desires are disguised to keep us from waking and being confronted by repressed material too difficult to handle. This is all the more important if a frank expression of those wishes would be in conflict with our moral or social values and standards.

The original wish or desire corresponds directly to the dream's latent content. The meaning of any dream lies in the latent content.

The transformation of 'latent' into 'manifest' content is done by 'dream-work', initiated by the 'dream-censor'.

The latent material has been suppressed because of its sexual, aggressive, or otherwise frightening nature.

We employ mechanisms of symbolic imagery to deal with the repressed material:

1. *Condensation*. In which we combine certain elements within the dream into a single image.
2. *Displacement*. In which we shift an impulse from one object to another.
3. *Secondary elaboration*. The process of imposing structure to increase the coherence and logic of the dream.

   Therapy aims to retrace the dream-work and understand it by interpretation. The analyst does not interpret by referring to a dream guide in the manner of the ancients, but by understanding the general principles of transformation on which we all create our own highly personalized dream language.

ANALYTICAL INTERPRETATIONS

Jung's theories are different from those of Freud. For Jung, dreams are forward-looking, creative, instructive and, to some extent, prophetic.

1. Dreams draw on the collective unconscious.
2. Archetypes are the common symbols, which enshrine universal, even mystical perceptions and images.
3. Dreams serve to enlarge our insight into our own resources, and contain hints on how to solve our own problems.

Research into dreaming and cognitive functioning shows the following:

1. People with right-brain orientation, divergence, and creativity, find it easy to recall their dreams.

2. People with left-brain orientation, verbal, analytical, recall dreams less easily.

Problem-solving and creative dreams occur because one's habitual thought patterns are relaxed in sleep.

Dreams may be attempts to clear pathways and resolve cognitive conflicts due to blockages and dissonances within the system.

Recent research suggests that sleep may be dreamless or dream sleep. Dreams are likely to occur in all extended periods of sleep and their function seems to be to process sensory inputs throughout periods of wakefulness.

DYING – STAGES OF (Kubler-Ross)

1. Shock and denial

   Shock
   Dazed
   Disbelief
   Seek confirmation.

2. Anger

   Frustrated, irritated, angry
   'Why me?'
   Anger may be displaced
   May alienate friends and carers.

3. Bargaining

   Attempt to negotiate with God, friends, doctor, for a cure, or more time.
   'I promise . . .'

4. Depression

   Which may be due to the illness itself or its effects, or to work, economic hardship, isolation
   Anticipation of the loss of life shortly to occur
   Withdrawal
   Psychomotor retardation
   Sleep disturbances
   Hopelessness
   Possible thoughts of suicide.

5. Acceptance

   Death is inevitable
   Ideally the person is able to talk about facing the unknown.

Fear not death; remember those who have gone before, and those who will follow after.

E

EGO (*See also*: Ego psychology, Defence mechanisms)

Literally, 'I'. In psychoanalytic personality theory, the system of rational and realistic functioning of the personality.

The ego is one's perception of self. The part that is in touch with reality, influenced by the external world and dealing with simulation arising from without and within the individual.

THE CHARACTERISTICS OF THE EGO:

1. It has the task of self-preservation, which it achieves by developing defence mechanisms.
2. It gains control over the primitive demands of the id.
3. The ego remembers, evaluates, plans and interacts with the physical and social world around.
4. It gives continuity and consistency of behaviour.
5. It is separate from both personality and body.
6. It is capable of change throughout life.

The new-born infant has only the most rudimentary ego.

The ego influences the id by what happens in the external world, and replaces the pleasure principle with the reality principle.

Ego-strength and ego-control can be assessed by psychological measurement.

EGO-STRENGTH IS CHARACTERIZED BY:

1. Objective appraisal of the world and one's place in it
2. Self-knowledge (insight)
3. Ability to plan and organize
4. Ability to choose between alternatives
5. Not being overwhelmed by needs and desires
6. Ability to pursue a chosen course.

Ego-psychologists are those who give greater weight to ego processes, such as reality-perception, conscious learning and voluntary control.

EGO STAGES (LOEVINGER)

LEVEL 1 – IMPULSIVE

1. Does not recognize rules

2. Sees action as bad only when punished
3. Impulsive
4. Afraid of retaliation
5. Has temper tantrums.

LEVEL 2 - SELF-PROTECTIVE

1. Recognizes rules, but obeys for immediate advantage
2. Has expedient morality: action becomes bad if one is caught
3. Blames others; does not see self as responsible for failure or trouble.

LEVEL 3 - CONFORMIST

1. Partially internalizes rules; obeys without question
2. Feels shame for consequences
3. Concerned with 'shoulds' and 'oughts'
4. Morality condemns others' views
5. Denies sexual and aggressive feelings.

LEVEL 4 - CONSCIENTIOUS

1. Self-evaluated standards: morality is internalized
2. Self-critical: tendency to be hyper-critical
3. Feels guilt for consequences.

LEVEL 5 - AUTONOMOUS

1. Add to the previous level: plus
2. Behaviour as an expression of moral principle
3. Tolerates multiplicity of viewpoints
4. Concerned with conflicting duties, roles and principles.

LEVEL 6 - INTEGRATED

1. Add to the previous level: plus
2. Reconciles inner conflicts and conflicting external demands
3. Recognizes the unattainable
4. Concerned with justice
5. Spontaneous, creative.

EGO STATES (Transactional analysis) (*See also*: Parent, Adult, Child)

Three distinct and independent ego states or levels of psychological functioning:

Parent, Adult, Child.

The terms are capitalized - PAC - to distinguish them from parent, adult and child.

EGOCENTRISM

Self-centred, interested primarily in self and one's own concerns, and indifferent to the concerns of others.

Term first proposed by Piaget. Said to be typical of childish thought, it can also be evident in adult life.

An example of egocentric speech would be a lecturer who is so taken up with his own specialized knowledge that he fails to read the signs that the students have not understood a word of what he has said.

ELECTRA COMPLEX (*See also*: Oedipus complex)

In mythology, the daughter of Greek leader, Agamemnon, and Clytaemnestra. Electra saved the life of her brother, Orestes, by sending him away when their father was murdered.

Later, when he returned, she helped him avenge their father's death by slaying their mother and her lover, by whom Agamemnon had been killed.

Freud adopted the term as the female equivalent to the Oedipus complex, though it is rarely used in modern psychoanalysis.

It is where the female child has an erotic attraction to her father, accompanied by hostility toward her mother.

EMPATHY (*See also*: Identification, Frames of reference)

The ability of one person to step into the inner world of another person and to step out of it again, without becoming that other person. An example is of the singer or actor who genuinely feels the part she or he is performing.

It means trying to understand the thoughts, feelings, behaviours and personal meanings from the other's internal frame of reference.

For empathy to mean anything, we have to respond in such a way that the other person feels that understanding has been reached, or is being striven for.

Empathy is to feel 'with'
Sympathy is to feel 'like'
Pity is to feel 'for'

Empathy is not a state that one reaches, nor a qualification that one is awarded. It is a transient thing. We can move into it and lose it again very quickly. Literally, it means getting 'alongside'.

Empathy is the central core condition of the person-centred approach, though therapists from a wide range of approaches rank empathy as being one of the highest qualities a therapist can demonstrate.

Levels of empathy are related to the degree to which the client is able to explore and reach self-understanding. It can be taught within an empathic climate.

The difference between empathy and identification is that in identification the 'as if' quality is absent. We have become the other person.

Some client statements about empathy:

1. Helps me to learn a lot about myself
2. Understands how I see things
3. Understands me
4. Can read me like a book
5. Is able to put my feelings into words
6. Knows what it's like to feel ill.

ENCOUNTER GROUPS (*See also*: Marathon groups)

Encounter groups developed as part of the 1960s human potential movement, influenced by sensitivity training groups.

The focus is on individual awareness and growth, the removal of psychological barriers and defences, achieving openness, honesty and the willingness to confront the difficulties of expressing emotions.

It is therefore an intense experience which helps group members to get more in touch with themselves and with one another in the 'here-and-now'. More emphasis is placed on activities and non-verbal encounters than verbal interactions.

THE FUNDAMENTAL VALUES

1. A belief in holism
2. A belief that healthy relationships with significant people are dependent on openness
3. We all have the power to choose what happens to us
4. We have to take responsibility for what happens to us
5. Encounter is a way of life, not a therapeutic technique.

RECOMMENDED GROUP STRUCTURE:

1. Size – between eight to fifteen
2. Setting – normally residential
3. Frequency – several times over a period of a week.

One of the principal dangers of this type of experience is the lack of follow-up.

ENVY

In general envy is classified as a special form of anxiety, based on an overpowering desire to possess what someone else has.

Kleinian theory relates envy to the conflict between love and hate. The developing infant may experience hate toward the good objects. This love/hate relationship may be seen in adult life where something is hated because of its goodness.

Schizophrenic states have been attributed to prolonged and early envy, with continued confusion between love and hate.

For Adler, envy is present wherever there is a striving for power and domination. The person who is consumed by envy has a low self-evaluation, and is constantly dissatisfied with life.

Envious people act as if they want to have everything. The universality of the feeling of envy causes a universal dislike of it.

People who envy someone else's achievements, tend to blame others for their own lack of success.

Envious people tend to be aggressive, obstructive and officious, with no great love for relationships, and with little understanding of human nature.

Envy may go so far as to lead a person to feel pleasure in someone else's suffering and pain. Working to raise self-esteem may help to reduce envy.

EQUITY THEORY

A theory of social behaviour in which we attempt to establish what we perceive to be equality between input and output.

Intimate and long-term relationships and groups seem to be governed by the principle of equity.

Carers need to receive some psychological reward if they are to continue in the role. One way of doing this is to find meaning in caring.

Withdrawing from a relationship is one way of altering the inputs and so restoring equity.

ERIKSON, ERIK H. (1902–) (*See also*: Lifespan psychology)

Erikson was born in Germany of Danish parents. His work as a psychoanalyst has had a profound influence, particularly in child development. He conducted major studies of American Indian children.

He was one of the first specialists in child psychoanalysis in the USA. While his theory of the crisis of youth and adolescence is central to his thinking, he has given insight into understanding the problems of women, minorities, and authority conflicts.

EROS (*See also*: Instincts, Thanatos)

In Greek mythology, the god of sexual love, passion and fertility. He was the son of Aphrodite, and brother of Anteros, the god of mutual love.

His chief associates were Pothos (longing) and Himeros (desire). He is also described as the fertilizing force that united Heaven and Earth and produced the world out of original Chaos.

Eros was involved in the stealing of the Golden Fleece, for it was one of his arrows that smote Medea with an overwhelming passion for Jason, with whom she fled to Corinth.

Freud used the Eros myth to describe the life-giving, life-preserving instinct. This instinct is fuelled by energy from the libido and is opposed by Thanatos, the death instinct.

Freud's use of Eros is apt, for Eros was the secret love of Psyche, and he brings harmony to chaos.

ETHICS

Counselling and psychotherapy have incurred criticism because of the lack of a common frame of reference for practitioners.

Some of the following guidelines may require adapting, to fit the requirements of individual agencies, and/or different approaches to therapy.

THE PRINCIPAL AREAS:

1. The therapeutic relationship
   - A. Contracting should be clear
   - B. Is non-exploitative
   - C. Does not encourage dependency
   - D. Encourage personal autonomy
   - E. Is not collusive
   - F. Is not sexually exploitative
   - G. The counsellor handles transference and counter-transference to the benefit of both parties
   - H. Does not enforce value or attitude change
   - I. Ensures physical and psychological safety
   - J. There is no intrusion, coercion or persuasion
   - K. Confidentiality to third parties should be made explicit to the client, for example, to the Courts, to other agencies, records – handwritten and computer, case conferences.
2. Competence of therapists
   - A. They should work within limits of competency.
   - B. Their own needs should be recognized.
   - C. They should update knowledge and experience and technical skill.
   - D. The need for supervision should be discussed at the contract stage.
   - F. The therapist should build up an effective referral network.
3. Therapists have a responsibility to:
   - A. The client
   - B. Self, to stay fresh, and to protect private and social life
   - C. Colleagues
   - D. The wider community
   - E. The law of the land.
4. Other issues
   - A. Advertising and announcements should be accurate.
   - B. Research material and writing should ensure the anonymity of clients.
   - C. Ethical conflicts should be resolved through discussion.

EVALUATION

INDIVIDUAL COUNSELLING SESSIONS

By evaluating or analysing counselling sessions, counsellors will continue to make progress. Evaluation encourages the growth of both client and counsellor.

If counsellor and client are active partners in the evaluation process, they can learn from each other.

On-going evaluation gives both partners an opportunity to explore their feelings about what is happening and also to appraise constructively what should next be done.

1. WHAT HAPPENED WITHIN THE COUNSELLOR?

   Was the counsellor:

   A. Fully attentive
   B. Listening actively
   C. Asking too many questions
   D. Leading the client
   E. Open or closed
   F. Afraid to challenge
   G. Insensitively challenging
   H. Able to empathize
   I. Relaxed or tense
   J. Friendly or aloof
   K. Anxious or at ease
   L. Quiet or talkative
   M. Interested or bored.

2. WHAT HAPPENED WITHIN THE CLIENT?

   Was the client:

   A. Fully present
   B. Responding to the counsellor
   C. Showing evidence of blocking
   D. Open with feelings
   E. Prepared to explore
   F. Waiting for answers
   G. An active partner

3. WHAT HAPPENED BETWEEN THEM?

   Was there:

   A. Participation
   B. Involvement or over-involvement
   C. Argument
   D. Persuasion
   E. Feeling versus intellect
   F. Reassurance versus exploration
   G. Tolerance
   H. Achievement of insight.

4. WAS THE FOLLOWING BEHAVIOUR EXHIBITED: IF SO, BY WHOM?

   A. Tension release
   B. Support
   C. Caring
   D. Aggression
   E. Hostility
   F. Manipulation
   G. Rejection.

5. BODY LANGUAGE AND ITS SIGNIFICANCE?

   A. Physical contact
   B. Proximity and position
   C. Gestures
   D. Facial expressions
   E. Eye contact.

6. ATMOSPHERE?

   A. Formal/informal
   B. Competitive/Co-operative
   C. Hostile
   D. Supportive
   E. Inhibited/permissive
   F. Harmonious/destructive.

ON TERMINATION OF COUNSELLING

A terminal evaluation gives both client and counsellor a feeling of completeness. It gives the counsellor an opportunity to look at some of those things that did not go according to plan, as well as those that did.

A well carried out evaluation not only looks backward, it also looks forward. A final evaluation provides the client with something positive to carry into the future.

Termination should be well planned and worked through. Abrupt termination can be very traumatic to both client and counsellor. It should be approached with as much sensitivity and caring as any stage in the counselling.

When counselling has taken place over a long period, the original reason(s) may have faded into insignificance. Counselling is like taking a journey; we know from where we have come, and roughly the route taken, but looking back, the starting point has become obscured, partly through distance, but also through time.

Unlike a journey, it is necessary for both counsellor and client to look back in order to firmly establish the final position.

Looking back to where and why the journey began may prove difficult; feelings, as well as memories, fade with time. Looking back is not always comfortable. It may reveal obstacles not previously recognized.

EVALUATION SHOULD IDENTIFY:

1. The different problems and how these were tackled.
2. The goals and how they have been achieved.
3. Areas of growth and insights.

The relationship between counsellor and client is not an end in itself. Evaluation helps to establish just how the client has been able to transfer the learning into relationships outside of counselling.

Evaluation helps the client to realize and acknowledge personal gains. The counsellor, in return, receives something from every counselling relationship.

Success in counselling is not easily measured, however.

1. Clients who have succeeded in climbing a few hills are more likely to want to tackle mountains, and, emotionally, are more equipped to.
2. Counsellors who have helped create an atmosphere of trust and respect, and have helped a client travel a little way along the road of self-discovery, are entitled to share the success the client feels.

The feeling of failure in counselling is difficult to handle. Blame should not be attributed to either counsellor or client. Both (if possible; if not, the counsellor alone) should examine what did happen rather than what did not happen.

If counselling goes full term it is unlikely to be a failure. The feeling of failure and consequent blame, is more likely when the client terminates prematurely.

If counsellors have created a conducive climate, and clients are unable to travel their own road toward self-discovery, then the responsibility for not travelling that road must rest with them. We can only take people along the road of self-discovery who are willing to travel with us. We can only travel at their pace. Unless two (or a group) are in agreement, the journey toward self-discovery will be fraught with impossibilities.

SOME INDICATORS OF IMPENDING TERMINATION

1. Abandonment
2. Acting out
3. Apathy
4. Decrease in intensity
5. Denial
6. Expressions of anger
7. Feelings of separation and loss
8. Futility
9. Impotence

10. Inadequacy
11. Intellectualizing
12. Joking
13. Lateness
14. Missed appointments
15. Mourning
16. Regression
17. Withdrawal

EXISTENTIAL THERAPY (*See also*: Existentialism)

A psychodynamic approach within psychotherapy, influenced by existentialism. Enshrined in this approach is a belief in the individual's capacity to transcend self through self-consciousness and self-reflection.

The principal existential psychotherapists are Binswanger, Boss, May, and Laing.

Existentially oriented psychotherapists concern themselves with how the client experiences life, rather than with diagnosis and cause. Psychoanalysis, conversely, concentrates on cause and effect and on trying to reduce complicated patterns to individual parts.

IMPORTANT PRINCIPLES:

1. The immediate moment of experience
2. Conscious, personal identity
3. Unity of the person
4. The search for the meaning of life
5. Pathology arises from the need to defend against alienation from self and others and the anxiety generated by the threat of the immediate experience.
6. Alienation from self leads to rigid, restrictive behaviour, a clinging to the past, and a desire to impose a false order on the present and future.

Existential therapists engage in a dialogue within an authentic and equal relationship, in which the therapist is totally present.

THE AIMS OF THERAPY:

1. To help people take responsibility for their own being in the world.
2. To become independent and self-governing.
3. To move beyond self into full fellowship with others.
4. To exercise conscious intention.
5. To make ethical choices.
6. To accept high ideals.
7. To engage in loving relationships.
8. To help clients confront normal anxiety, an unavoidable part of being human.
9. To help clients confront and reduce anxiety that is related to fear. Anxiety is more basic than fear.
10. To help people live without neurotic anxiety, but to be able to tolerate normal existential anxiety.

The cost of change may mean having to deal with anxiety and inner crises. The person's only authentic response to the contribution of the family and other social institutions may be to choose madness.

Existentialism is similar to humanistic therapies, although it may be more confronting. On a dimension, it is the opposite to the more technical, behavioural, and strategy-dominated therapies.

It is an attempt to grapple with the meaninglessness and extinction that threaten present-day societies.

BASIC CONCEPTS

1. The 'I AM' experience

   A. The 'I AM' experience is known as an 'ontological' experience, which translated from the Greek means 'the science of being'.
   B. The realization of one's being, and the choice one has of saying, 'I am the one living, experiencing. I choose my own being.'
   C. Being is not tied to status or what one does, occupation, or the life one leads.
   D. When everything else is stripped away, one can still say, 'I AM'.
   E. The experience of being also points to the experience of non-being, or nothingness.
   F. Examples of non-being would be the threat of death, destruction, severe and crippling anxiety or sickness.
   G. The threat of non-being is ever present, for example in the remark by someone that puts us down.

2. Normal and neurotic anxiety

   A. In existential terms anxiety arises from our personal need to survive, to preserve, and to assert our being. It is the threat to our existence, or to values we identify with our existence.
   B. The characteristics of normal existential anxiety are that it is proportionate to the situation, it does not require to be repressed, it can be used constructively, for example, to discover the underlying dilemma that created the anxiety.
   C. The characteristics of neurotic anxiety are that it is not appropriate to the situation, it is repressed, it is destructive and paralysing, not constructive and stimulating.

3. Guilt feelings

   A. *Neurotic guilt* feelings usually arise out of fantasized transgressions.
   B. *Normal guilt* feelings make us sensitive to social and ethical aspects of behaviour.
   C. *Existential guilt* feelings arise from locking up our potentialities.

4. The world

   A. The world includes all past events and influences which condition our existence.
   B. The way one relates to these events and influences is what holds meaning.
   C. The three forms of world:
      The 'world around' (environment): the world of objects, the natural world, biological drives.
      'Own world' (relationship to self): self-awareness, self-relatedness, grasping the meaning of something in the world.
      'With-world' (fellow humans): interpersonal relationships and love. To truly love, one must have become truly individual and sufficient unto oneself. The 'with world' is empty of vitality if 'own world' is lacking.

5. The significance of time

   Time is considered to be the heart of existence.

A. Experiences such as anxiety, depression, and joy, are usually related to time.
B. People who cannot relate to time, who cannot hope for the future, who view each day as an island with no past and no future, are seriously disturbed.
C. The ability to relate to time is one of the characteristics of being human.
D. Time fixes us in the here and now and prevents us from being lost in space.
E. Some experiences, such as the development of life, cannot be measured by time.
F. Experiencing in the 'now' breaks through time.
G. Insight is not time-controlled; it comes complete.
H. When one's past does not come alive, it is probably because one's future has no attraction.
I. Being able to change something, however small, in the present, gives hope to work toward a future.

6. The capacity to transcend the immediate

A. Existing means a continual going beyond the past and present to reach out to the future.
B. Transcendence means being able to think in terms of 'the possible'.
C. People who are unable to think in terms of the possible, feel threatened by the lack of specific boundaries. It is as if they already perceive themselves 'lost in space'.
D. People who are unable to think of the possible experience a world that has shrunk around them, with consequent loss of freedom.

The existential model of personality postulates that the basic conflict is between the individual and the 'givens' (or ultimate concerns) of existence.

1. DEATH

This is a core conflict which exists between one's awareness of death and the concurrent wish to continue living.

It is an emotional disturbance which is often the result of inadequate death transcendence, which then leads to terror of death.

2. FREEDOM

In existential terms, freedom is bound to dread. Inherent in freedom is self-responsibility, for life design and its consequences. Responsibility for one's situation is bound to the principle of 'willing', which consists of wishing and then deciding.

Many people cannot wish, because they cannot feel. When we fully experience a wish, we are then faced with a decision. Some people experience 'decisional panic', and try to pass the decision-making on to others.

3. ISOLATION

A. *Interpersonal isolation* is the separation of oneself from others which results from either a deficiency in social skill, or a pathological fear of intimacy.

B. *Intrapersonal isolation* is where we have dissociated parts of ourselves – experiences, desires, feelings – out of awareness.
C. *Existential isolation* is a fundamental isolation, from people and from the world.

There is always a gap that cannot be bridged. The personal dilemma is that no matter how intimate the relationship, there is always a part that we will never be able to share.

This has been referred to as 'the fundamental loneliness'. The most poignant example of the fundamental loneliness is the experience of death.

The fear of death, and of isolation, keep many people from entering relationships of any depth and intimacy. Some people doubt their own existence so much that they only feel they exist in the presence of another.

Many undergo a 'fusion' with others, so that 'I' becomes 'we', resulting in the safety of conformity.

Compulsive sexuality is a common antidote to the terrifying prospect of isolation. The sexually compulsive person relates only to part of the other, not to the whole.

4. MEANINGLESSNESS often revolves around questions such as:

A. What possible meaning can life have?
B. Why do we live?
C. How shall we live?
D. Is my self-created meaning of life strong enough to bear my life?
E. In the same way as we need to organize random events into something we can understand, so we deal with the existential situation.

   Were we not able to find some meaning, we would be desperately unsettled.
F. From a sense of the meaning of life, we generate values, that provide a master-plan for life conduct. Values not only tell us why we live, but how to live.
G. The dilemma of existential meaninglessness then, is how do I find meaning in a universe that has no meaning?

To an existentialist therapist, anxiety results from confrontation with death, freedom, isolation, and meaninglessness.

TWO DEFENCE MECHANISMS ENSUE:

1. Specialness

A. In which one has a deep, powerful belief that one cannot be destroyed, is totally invulnerable, and will never die.
B. The person believes that the laws of biology do not apply.
C. These beliefs (of delusional quality) give rise to narcissism, search for glory, search for power, suspicious behaviour.
D. Such people often seek therapy when their defence of specialness no longer holds up, and they are hit by anxiety.

2. An ultimate rescuer

A. The belief in an omnipotent protector who will always snatch us from the deepest hell.
B. These beliefs (of delusional quality) give rise to passivity, dependency, servile behaviour.

C. Such people often dedicate themselves to living for the 'dominant other', which is fertile ground for depression.

Existential therapy is not a system of psychotherapy, it is a frame of reference, a pattern for understanding a client's suffering in a distinctive manner.

EXISTENTIALISM

A body of ethical, philosophical thought, influenced mainly by Jaspers, Kierkegaard, Nietzsche, Husserl, Heidegger, and Sartre.

The various principal tenets of existentialism are:

1. The uniqueness and isolation of individual experience in a universe indifferent or even hostile to humankind.
2. Human existence is unexplainable.
3. Humans are responsible for the consequences of their own acts, toward themselves and toward others.
4. We are real only to ourselves, and are our own judgments.
5. The rejection of the philosophy of first principles and ultimate reality.
6. Objectivity is an illusion.
7. Truth is a personal realization, unique to each person, and cannot be hardened into dogma.
8. To be able to grasp what is not the case, as well as what is, is the basis of possibility.
9. To claim that one is bound to do something or could not help it, is self-deception.
10. We all choose our own morality.
11. Personal relations can never be other than a struggle for power.
12. Some existentialists believe that we are free to be reconciled to God.

EXTERNALIZATION (Defence mechanism)

This refers to the tendency to perceive in the outside world elements of our own:

1. Thoughts
2. Feelings
3. Impulses
4. Conflicts
5. Moods
6. Attitudes
7. Styles of thinking
8. Personality.

EXTRAVERSION (*See also*: Myers–Briggs type indicator)

One of Jung's personality types, characterized by:

1. Outgoing in attention and interests
2. Responsiveness to external stimuli, especially other people.
3. Impulsiveness.

Extraversion is the opposite of introversion. An extreme extravert may become aggressive and over-dependent on group acceptance, and may lose independence in actions and thoughts.

Research has placed most people between the two types. Very few people can be accurately described as being wholly extravert or wholly introvert.

People who are more extravert than introvert:

1. Are social beings and relate to the people and things around them.
2. Endeavour to make their decisions in agreement with the demands and expectations of others.
3. Are outgoing.
4. Are socially free.
5. Are interested in variety and in working with people.

The extravert may become impatient with long, slow tasks and does not mind being interrupted by people. A typical extravert dreads isolation, while the typical introvert abhors communal living.

F

FAMILY THERAPY

The focus of therapy is on the whole family (the system) as the client.

The task is to so change relationships between family members that dysfunctional behavioural symptoms disappear.

A system has in common:

1. Interconnected and interdependent parts.
2. Every part is consistently related to the other over a period of time. Systems may be closed (house heating) or open (the family).

PROPERTIES OF AN OPEN SYSTEM

1. Wholeness
   - A. The sum of the parts plus the interaction.
   - B. One part cannot be understood unless its relationship to the other parts is also understood.
   - C. Wholeness is a Getstalten; the interdependence between parts.
   - D. The family consists of the members and the relationships between them.
2. Relationship
   - A. Considers the 'what' rather than the 'why' of what is happening.
   - B. The shift is from what is happening within the members to what is happening between them.
3. Equifinality (Self-perpetuation)
   - A. When interventions are made in the 'here and now', changes are produced in the family open system.
   - B. Concentrating on the here and now, and not becoming involved in blaming the past, is valid, because a system has no memory.

The building blocks of the family system are a series of interlocking triangles, the function of which is to reduce or increase the emotional intensity within the family.

The man in a partnership that is shaky, who becomes a workaholic could be seen as creating a triangle to reduce tension.

The prime therapeutic task is to analyse the various triangles in a family, and make interventions to change the system.

The family system school of thought considers triangles over three generations.

The structuralist school of thought is more concerned with triangles within the nuclear family.

Feedback, the mechanism by which the system is constantly being adjusted, and equilibrium restored, is an important concept and function in systems theory. Positive feedback forces change on the system, by not allowing it to return to its former state.

MAIN SCHOOLS

1. Object relations family therapy – where the identified 'patient' is often seen as the one who carries the split-off and, therefore, unacceptable, impulses of the other family members.
2. Family systems therapy – works with eight concepts:

    A. Triangles.
    B. Differentiation of self; which measures the amount of fusion between members.
    C. The emotional system of the family.
    D. Family projection process; how a family selects the identified patient.
    E. Emotional cut-off; the extent to which one member relates to the others.
    F. Transmission; the mechanism by which pathology is passed through generations.
    G. Sibling position; determines one's existential view of the world.
    H. Societal regression; patterns that occur in the family are also found in society. Families are taught not to react but to respond. Reacting means acting only on the basis of feeling, and ignoring the needs of other people.

    Responding is making a rational, not a purely emotional, choice, and taking into account the needs of others. Family members learn to be both 'self' and a member of the system.

3. Structural family therapy views pathology as either 'enmeshed' or 'disengaged'. In an enmeshed structure, the therapist works on loosening the boundaries. In a disengaged structure, the therapist works toward establishing or strengthening the boundaries.
4. Strategic intervention family therapy views therapy as a power struggle between client and therapist. In family therapy, the identified 'patient' is the controller who makes the others feel helpless. The role of the therapist is to restructure the system by re-establishing family boundaries, and changing the balance of power.

Family therapy seeks to answer three questions:

1. *What is a family?* A family has physical and emotional needs and the basic emotional needs are intimacy, self-expression and meaning.
2. *What is a 'dysfunctional family'?* A family where there is an inability of the family to meet basic emotional needs.

    In family systems therapy, all members are an essential part of the therapeutic process.

The functional family will work to solve conflicts, while the dysfunctional family will not.

3. *Why must a family change*? In order to be functional, families must become 'we', as well as retaining their individual 'I'. Feedback, possible with adults, is entirely different with children, and is not immediate. The birth(s) of subsequent siblings changes the system.

   Entry to school admits others into the system, so forcing further change. Children with school phobia may be responding to the family's inability to widen the boundaries.

   Adolescence, with its need for greater freedom, is a potential for dysfunction, as parents experience loss of meaning. The 'empty nest syndrome' is often experienced by parents when children leave home. Dramatic change may allow marital differences to surface.

THREE FAMILY DIMENSIONS

1. Marital subsystem

   A. Two people become a couple.
   B. 'Fusion' or 'enmeshment' is where one or both are unable to separate from their family of origin. The boundaries of the new relationship are thus blurred.
   C. The ability to close a door and shut out others (symbolically) is important in the development of a functional family system.
   D. In functional families, it is spouse first and others next.
   E. Children-oriented marriages are invariably dysfunctional, because the children are needed to give meaning to the marriage.
   F. A firm alliance between parents prevents a child from forming an alliance with one or other of the parents.

2. Sibling subsystem

   A. The alliance between parents forces children into forming their own subsystems with brothers and sisters or others of their own generation.
   B. The sibling subsystem has its own boundaries.

Questions to ask:

(a) Are parents clearly separated from children?
(b) Is the difference between children clear?
(c) Are older children treated differently from younger ones?
(d) What levels of responsibility?
(e) What are the levels of respect for their uniqueness, privacy, common courtesies, freedom?
(f) What is the influence of the neighbourhood culture? The school culture? Peer group pressure?

3. Homeostasis

   This is the balance between marital and sibling subsystems. If disrupted limits cannot be corrected, homeostasis is upset and the system will eventually disintegrate.

   Homeostasis is threatened, for example, when a family moves to a new neighbourhood or culture. 'Destructive behaviour' may be an attempt to restore homeostasis.

GOALS OF THERAPY

A primary goal in family therapy is to produce visible change in behaviour, even though family members may not be totally aware of what is happening.

Insight, helpful for the therapist, is not considered important for the family; getting them to be aware of the interactions is the important factor.

The history of the family is important for object relations and family systems therapists; less important for structural and strategic intervention therapists, for whom the present is what is relevant. Family therapists are less concerned than are traditional therapists with arriving at a correct diagnosis.

Feelings, which are thought to arise from behaviours, are not given first place, due possibly to the emphasis on the 'system'.

Learning and teaching form an essential part of the therapies of Schools 1 and 2, but less so in 3 and 4.

Transference, and working through it, does not form an explicit part of family therapy; the concentration is on the family interaction, not on the relationship between individual and therapist.

The therapist is viewed as a model, a change agent, or teacher, who helps the family develop problem-solving skills.

Therapists are active; they are not 'blank screens'.

TECHNIQUES

1. *Re-enactment*. Instead of 'talking about', the family are encouraged to 'talk' and interact; sometimes called 'psychodrama *in situ*.
2. *Homework*. To build bridges between the sessions and interaction in the home.
3. *Family sculpting* (*see* Psychodrama).
4. *Genogram*. A three-generational diagram that graphically illustrates family relationships.
5. *Behaviour modification*. (*see* Behaviour therapy)
6. *Multiple family therapy*. Some of the advantages of involving several families at the same time are:

   A. Pointing out similarities, and differences in interactions.
   B. Permits the family members to act in a co-counselling role.
   C. Loosens the authority of the therapist.
   D. Helps to hasten the formation of the therapeutic alliance.

Family therapy does produce change, though it is not clear how that is accomplished, or why one approach may work with one family and not with another.

FANTASY (Defence mechanism) (*See also*: Imagery)

Also known as autistic or schizoid fantasy. Characteristics of people most likely to make use of this are:

1. Lonely and frightened
2. Eccentric and those labelled schizoid
3. Aloof and unsociable
4. Fear of intimacy.

They seek comfort in their own world, by creating an imaginary life, especially imaginary friends. Acceptance of them, just as they are, is essential, without pressure to change.

FEEDBACK (*See also*: Johari Window)

Feedback is a term borrowed from rocket engineering by Kurt Lewin and gives one person the opportunity to be open to the perceptions of others.

Feedback is an essential mechanism in any interpersonal communication, particularly in group work. An example of social feedback is returning a smile.

Giving feedback is both a verbal and a non-verbal process where people let others know their perceptions of our behaviour.

GUIDELINES FOR GIVING FEEDBACK

1. Your intention must be to help.
2. If the person has not asked for feedback, check whether he/she is open to it.
3. Deal only with observable behaviour.
4. Deal only with modifiable behaviour.
5. Describe specifics, not generalities.
6. Describe behaviours.
7. Do not judge the person.
8. Do not make assumptions or interpret.
9. Let the person know the impact the behaviour has on you.
10. Check that the message has been received and understood.
11. Suggest, rather than prescribe means for improvement.
12. Should be directed toward meeting the need of the other person, not designed to punish.
13. Encourage the person to check out your feedback with other people.
14. Feedback, if well-timed and accurate, enhances the relationship.

GUIDELINES FOR RECEIVING FEEDBACK

1. When you ask for feedback, be specific in describing the behaviour about which you want feedback.
2. Try not to act defensively.
3. Try not to rationalize the behaviour.
4. Summarize your understanding.
5. Share your thoughts and feelings.
6. Accept the responsibility for the behaviour.
7. Try to see things through the other's eyes.
8. Explore the feedback, don't use it as an excuse to attack.
9. Don't brush it off with misplaced humour or sarcasm.
10. Don't put yourself down, assuming that everyone else is correct.
11. Plan how you could use the feedback.
12. If it is hard to take, remember, you did ask!

EXAMPLES OF FEEDBACK

1. *Direct expression of feelings* 'I like you.'
2. *Descriptive feedback* 'Your fists are clenched.'
3. *Non-evaluative feedback* 'You are angry, and that's OK.'
4. *Specific feedback* 'When you shouted, I felt anxious.'
5. *Freedom of choice to change* 'When you called me "son", I felt put down and small.'
6. *Immediate feedback* 'I'm feeling angry at what I consider to be a sexist remark.'
7. *Group-shared feedback* 'Does this group see me as being supportive?'

FEMININITY/MASCULINITY (*See also*: Anima, Animus, Myers–Briggs type indicator, Self-esteem, Shadow)

Femininity/masculinity generally refers to gender, those personal characteristics that are believed to differentiate one sex from another. Gender is more than the manifest biological differences.

Family patterns and wider cultural behaviours exert a powerful influence on the development and acceptance of what is 'feminine' or 'masculine'. It can be said (in Freudian terms) that men adopt the masculine role and women accept the feminine role, and only do so when they have renounced the penis. This view has been seriously criticized by female psychoanalysts.

Gender difficulties occur when people feel pressured into denying attributes they feel are vital to their identity and which other people feel are inappropriate.

Females, generally, want to tell you they feel feminine, and males want to tell you they feel masculine. Girls more than boys seem to be concerned about distortion of the legs.

Women seem more dissatisfied than men about the lower parts of their bodies. Males who experience failure are more likely to relate this to sensations of diminished height: 'It makes me feel small'.

Generally speaking, women are less able to tolerate disfigurement than men; while men are less able to tolerate disability than women.

Many children are brought up to believe that femininity is characterized by:

1. A mentality that is underdeveloped, childlike or primitive
2. A thirst for curiosity
3. Prejudice
4. Feeling, imagination or dreaming
5. Wishful
6. Solving riddles
7. Faith or superstitions or makes assumptions
8. Rule by heart. All 'tender' feelings are, therefore, more appropriate to females
9. Caring.

Many children are brought up to believe that masculinity, conversely, is characterized by:

1. A mentality that is highly developed, and, by implication, superior
2. A thirst for knowledge
3. Judgment
4. Thinking
5. Will
6. Problem-solving
7. Knowledge and understanding
8. Rule by head, reason and logic
9. Providing.

Emma Jung observed these differences and while she did not imply that the one group was superior to the other, society seems to have done so. 'Feminine' traits are still thought to be inferior to 'male' traits.

FEMINIST ISSUES

The feminist issue has to be addressed in counselling, for there is a whole ideology – assumptions, ways of thinking, attitudes, values and beliefs – that need to be examined.

Two important polarities are Feeling/thinking and Intuition/sensing.

FEELING/THINKING

Women are more likely to make heart judgments, with feeling and sympathy. Men are more likely to make head judgments governed by logic and reason. Most of us, women and men, function to some degree in both modes, but are more comfortable in one.

Women are more likely to value co-operation, caring and nurturing, while men seem to be more attracted to competition, goals, and goal-setting. Women are more likely to be feeling types and men thinking types.

INTUITION/SENSING

Women generally use their intuition more than men, make connections between possibilities, see the 'big picture', what might be, rather than what is, and like working with opposites. Men are more likely to feel comfortable with sensing, and want to categorize, delineate, and make decisions based on carefully worked-out, detailed plans.

Women are more likely to be intuitive types and men sensing types.

Neither feeling nor thinking, intuition nor sensing, is better than the other. They are different. In each pair, the one is as closely related to the other as two faces on a coin.

The word 'different' is important in counselling. The words 'superior' and 'inferior' carry connotations of competition, win–lose, hierarchy, strong–weak, capable–incapable.

Alfred Adler (*See* Individual psychology) speaks of the difference between 'horizontal' and 'vertical' relationships. A hierarchy is a vertical relationship which does not respect differences, but places people in superior/inferior positions.

Many of the differences will disappear and true equality (not uniformity) will be established when we relate to men and women in horizontal, not vertical relationships.

In order for men to truly accept women, and women to accept men as equals they must accept the male or female within themselves which is so often our 'shadow' side. An acceptance of our shadow brings wholeness and a richness hitherto seen only through darkened glass.

Female clients are more likely to respond to warmth and empathy, to use their intuition, to work with dreams, and to use symbols and imagery. These are the fundamentals of the person-centred approach, and the humanistic and transpersonal psychologies.

Men often prefer to work at a cognitive, and factual level, which is more suited to psychoanalysis and cognitive or behaviourally-based therapies. This does not mean that men do not relate to a feelings approach, but as a general rule they do not respond so readily.

On the other hand, a woman who is (in Jungian terms) animus ridden (whose masculine principle is in control), who perceives through the senses, and who makes judgments with the head, may find a cognitive approach easier to cope with.

Thinking and sensing women and men are in danger of relegating their feeling and intuition to the shadow, and may need to be led gently into an exploration of feelings.

Feeling and intuitive women and men may ignore their thinking and sensing, and be just as incomplete as thinking/sensing people.

Counselling, of whomsoever, is about wholeness and integration. Counsellors who ignore the fact that for centuries women have been put down and made second-class citizens (and in some respects, still are), will never be able to make effective contact with female clients which is essential if integration and wholeness is to take place.

Likewise, we need to recognize when the feminine side of male clients is being repressed and help them work toward liberation, integration and wholeness so that they, too, can become wholly alive.

Women and men have to believe that they are both equal to and different from the other sex and that their unique differences are valuable to each other.

However much women tell other women this, the greatest change will come when men start valuing women for themselves. It is not what men say but what they do that will convince women that their uniqueness is respected for what it is.

CROSS-GENDER COUNSELLING

Many cultures in the world are still very male dominated and this is reflected in the way women relate to men and is demonstrated in the way power is shared.

Men have assumed, and women for centuries have colluded with them, that their role is to do, and the role of women is to provide. Male counsellors (the archetypal 'doctors'), may (unconsciously) reinforce this power difference.

The female client who is compliant, and submissive and does not argue openly, may well be caught in this power trap.

The reverse may be true. A male client with a female counsellor may feel uncomfortable with what he (consciously or unconsciously) perceives as a reversal of roles, and attempt to dominate the session.

Cross-gender counselling may also create difficulties where the subject is a delicate one. Just as some prefer same-sex doctors, so with counselling. However, there are many issues where same-sex counselling is more appealing than with someone of the opposite sex.

Some women may prefer to talk with a female counsellor about, for example, the problems associated with pre-menstrual tension, rape, or abortion. Likewise, some men would probably find it easier to talk with another man about sexual impotence.

Another area of potential difficulty in cross-gender counselling is sexual attraction, and, in some instances, sexual harassment.

While there are many jokes about clients 'falling in love' with therapists, (of either gender) the reality of it is far from humorous.

The possibility of it should always be hovering in the wings of the counselling room. Apart from any overt involvement, these transference feelings (*see* entry) may cause the relationship to flounder unless recognized and dealt with.

Another potential difficulty is in expressing an opinion. Two people of the same sex can express an identical opinion and both parties will generally be able to discuss and argue it through.

When the same statement is made from the person of one gender to a person of the other, the statement is filtered through gender values. What is said by a man to a woman may be interpreted as a pronouncement, rather than a suggestion, or a possibility. What was acceptable in one situation could be perceived as patronizing or domineering in another.

Cross-gender counselling can also produce problems in the counselling process. While women are generally able to express tender feelings, expressing anger verbally may be a problem. The anger of women very often turns to tears.

Men, on the other hand, very often strive to control their tender feelings, even when in a climate of trust and openness.

The tears they feel are often turned into anger, an emotion many find easier to express.

A woman crying in front of a male counsellor, or a male client becoming angry in front of a female counsellor, serves to reinforce (unconsciously) male and female stereotyping.

In same-gender counselling, it is possible that there would be more intuitive awareness of the feelings that could result from either the crying or the anger, rather than embarrassment.

Cross-gender counselling can add a great deal to the counselling process. The female client with a male counsellor who demonstrates total respect for the client as a person, and who does not relate only the stereotype, will gain a fuller understanding of her feelings. She can know the reality of being in a relationship of equals; an experience she can then use constructively in other relationships with men.

Counsellors, of whichever gender, and of whatever professional persuasion, will never fully understand femininity or masculinity unless they are willing to enter the other's frame of reference. Only as we risk leaving our own frame of reference will any of us be able to understand anyone else's personal meanings.

The more one person can work with, and understand someone's personal meanings, the more that person will understand her or himself, and each will have achieved new insights into themselves.

Entering the client's frame of reference in cross-gender counselling will mean confronting our own hidden anima or animus. When we accept the challenge of integrating our shadow, our personality will be more complete, and our counselling will be richer.

FERENCZI, SANDOR (1873–1933)

Hungarian psychoanalyst, a member of Freud's 'inner circle', noted for his fundamentalism and also for experimenting with new therapeutic techniques.

He believed that understanding the history of the person's symptoms was not enough to bring about desired personality changes.

His approach was to encourage patients to perform actions usually avoided because of their unconscious, symbolic meaning.

Ferenczi's more controversial ideas:

1. That modification of neurotic behaviour is not necessarily dependent upon the recollection of problem-related memories.
2. That the wish to return to the womb symbolizes a wish to return to the origin of life, the sea.
3. Ferenczi favoured a relaxed therapeutic atmosphere and a flexible approach.

FIGHT/FLIGHT RESPONSE (*See also*: Stress management)

The effect of a stressor is to mobilize the body's fight/flight system to combat a perceived enemy. Stress stimulates chemical, physical and psychological changes to prepare the body to cope with a potentially life-threatening situation. The process is controlled by the autonomic nervous system and the endocrine system. The process is:

1. The liver releases extra sugar to fuel the muscles.
2. Hormones are released that stimulate the conversion of fats and proteins to sugar.
3. The body's metabolism increases in preparation for increased activity.
4. Certain unessential activities, such as digestion, are slowed up.
5. Saliva and mucus dry up, so increasing the size of the air passages to the lungs and giving rise to the early sign of stress, a dry mouth.
6. Endorphins, the body's natural painkillers, are secreted.
7. The surface blood vessels constrict to reduce bleeding in case of injury.
8. The spleen releases more red blood cells to help carry oxygen, and the bone marrow produces more white cells to help fight infection.

The autonomic nervous system, regulated by the hypothalamus (the stress centre), with the pituitary, is responsible for releasing more than 30 hormones that control these physiological responses to an emergency.

When neither response is appropriate – to fight or to run away – the biochemical changes have already been aroused, and the body takes time to return to normal. It is the continued presence of the hormones that give rise to the prolongation of the bodily symptoms described above. When appropriate action is taken, the chemicals are used up and the body returns to normal functioning.

People who experience stress live in a state of constant readiness to respond to fight or flight.

FIGHT/FLIGHT DEFENCES IN COUNSELLING

In addition to the listed defence mechanisms, various manoeuvres by the client (and sometimes by the counsellor) may be included in this section on the fight/flight response.

FIGHT MANOEUVRES

These are based on the premise that the best defence is a good attack.

1. *Competing with the counsellor*. The client who struggles to control the counsellor is very likely doing so to avoid dealing with some hidden agenda.
2. *Cynicism*. This is characterized by frequent challenge to the counsellor's role and method of working, questioning genuine behaviour in a sceptical way.
3. *Interrogation*. Where the client cross-examines the counsellor, 'to gain helpful information and understanding.'

FLIGHT MANOEUVRES

1. *Intellectualization*. A deliberate avoidance of dealing with feelings by filtering and analysing everything through head logic.
2. *Generalization*. This is a refusal to get to grips with specifics, and applying to someone else what we ourselves are experiencing.
3. *Rationalization*. An attempt to justify certain behaviour by substituting 'good' behaviour for the real ones. An example would be, 'I would be able to look at my feelings if I had a different counsellor.'
4. *Projection*. Where the client attributes to other people the traits of his/her own personality.
5. *Withdrawal*. This may vary from boredom to actual physical removal from the session. The tendency to avoid dealing with the

'here-and-now' is also a flight response.

FLOODING (Also known as *Implosion therapy*)

A behavioural technique, the aim of which is the extinction of some undesired behaviour by exposing the client to massive doses of anxiety-provoking stimuli.

In contrast to systematic desensitization, the client is exposed repeatedly to high arousal until extinction occurs.

Bombarding the client with particular kinds of experiences results in either building up a distinct aversion to the experience or to a numbing so that there is no longer a response.

The method has been used successfully to treat people with phobic and obsessional conditions. Flooding is often combined with drugs that reduce anxiety and with cognitive therapy.

For example, smoking continuously, one after another, makes one feel sick. A second example would be a client with a phobia, who is presented repeatedly with the situation, the result of which is that anxiety is no longer evoked.

FOCUSING

Focusing has two meanings:

1. A body-centred therapy technique
2. As applied in counselling.

1. GENDLIN'S BODY-CENTRED THERAPY

   A. Focusing helps the client get to grips with a complex problem, with its feelings, by examining the problem in stages.
   B. Specific instructions concentrate attention on what is happening in the body.

Examples of focusing

A. How does the body feel inside?
B. What feelings are being experienced?
C. Allow a problem to emerge and gain a sense of it as a whole.
D. Pay attention to the most powerful feeling.
E. Allow the feeling to change.
F. Put an image to the feeling.
G. Watch the image change.
H. Relax and reflect on the changes.

Focusing tries to address the client's problems directly, rather than just by talking about them. It is also used in existential and humanistic therapies.

2. FOCUSING IN COUNSELLING

   A. Focusing helps the client get to grips with a complex situation, by teasing out details and exploring specific parts in depth.
   B. Focusing helps the client look beyond the problem to possible solutions or alternatives.
   C. Focusing helps both client and counsellor not to get lost.
   D. Focusing involves a certain degree of direction and control by the counsellor, which has to be carefully used.

Principles of focusing

A. Help the client deal with the immediate crisis.

B. Focus on issues important to the client.
C. Begin with a problem that causes pain.
D. Deal with issues the client is willing to work on.
E. Work on manageable parts of a larger problem.
F. Work for something with quick success.
G. Work from the simple to the complex.

Underlying focusing is clients' need to feel some reward and some hope.

Focusing implies a certain degree of direction and guidance of the exploration and not everything can be worked out at once.

Focusing uses specific questions to tease out detail and to explore particular topics in depth. There needs to be a focus in the helping process, around which the resources of the client can be mobilized. Focusing helps client and counsellor to find out where to start, or having started, in which direction to continue.

Points to bear in mind

1. If there is a crisis, first help the client to manage the crisis.
2. Focus on issues that the client sees as important.
3. Begin with a problem that seems to be causing the client pain.
4. Focus on an issue that the client is willing to work on, even if it does not seem important to you.
5. Begin with some manageable part of the problem.
6. Begin with a problem that can be managed relatively easily.
7. When possible, move from less severe to more severe problems.
8. Focus on a problem where the benefits will outweigh the costs.
9. Make the initial experience of counselling rewarding as an incentive to continue.

Example

'I've heard what you've been saying, and there is a lot there. It seems as if the main strands are .... Which do you think is the most urgent issue to explore first?'

Some useful focusing guidelines

1. Does the problem use a lot of energy?
2. Is the problem of high, moderate, or low significance?
3. What priority would the client give to this problem?
4. Could it be managed if it was broken down?
5. If it is resolved, would it influence other issues?
6. Small issues resolved give a boost.
7. Is it within the client's direct control?
8. In cost terms, how important is it? In other words, would the client be spending 80% of time to get 20% result?
9. Is the client open to explore this issue?
10. Does it need more time than is available now?

FOLIE Á DEUX (*See also*: Collusion) (French for insanity in pairs)

A rare functional psychosis in which two persons with a long intimate association come to share the same delusion or delusional system.

One of the two, the inductor, is usually suffering from paranoia, or some other paranoid disorder.

The other, the inductee, generally a woman or a passive male, seems to accept the delusional attitudes of the dominant person.

When the passive person is removed from the relationship, the symptoms are likely to disappear, but for the dominant person, the psychosis remains.

FORCE FIELD ANALYSIS (*See also*: Goals and goal-setting)

A decision-making technique developed from Lewin's field theory, designed to help people understand the various internal and external forces that influence the way they make decisions.

For most of the time these forces are in relative balance, but when something disturbs the balance, decisions are more difficult to make.

When the forces are identified, counsellor and client work on strategies to help the client reach the desired goal.

STAGES

1. What is the goal to be achieved?
2. Identify restraining forces
3. Identify facilitating forces
4. Work out how either the strength of some of the restraining forces can be reduced, or how the strength of some of the facilitating forces can be increased
5. Use imagery to picture moving toward the desired goal and achieving it.

Forces may be external or internal.

Examples of internal forces:

1. Type of personality
2. Age
3. Health
4. Previous experience.

Examples of external forces:

1. Family
2. Friends
3. Locality
4. Job and career
5. Finance
6. Mobility
7. Commitments
8. Hobbies.

The underlying principle is that by strengthening the facilitating forces and diminishing the restraining forces, a decision will be easier to make, because energy, trapped by the restraining forces, has been released.

FOULKES, SIGMUND H.
(1898–1976)

German-born pioneer of group psychotherapy and group analysis. He settled in London in 1933, at the invitation of Ernst Jones, and became a naturalized British subject.

His group work methods were developed at the Northfield Military Hospital, Birmingham, where he transferred the hospital into a therapeutic community. He was founder member of the Group Analytic Society (London).

FRAMES OF REFERENCE (*See also*: Person-centred therapy)

A two-part concept which is emphasized in Person-centred therapy.

INTERNAL FRAME OF REFERENCE
(The inner world of the client)

Examples:

Behaviours
Cultural influences
Experiences
Feelings
Meanings

Memories
Perceptions
Sensations
Thoughts
Values and beliefs.

EXTERNAL FRAME OF REFERENCE
(The inner world of the counsellor)

The contents of the counsellor's frame is similar to the client's frame, and therein lies a danger. When the experiences of one person are similar to someone else, it is tempting to 'know' how the other person feels. This knowing cannot come from experience. It can only resonate within us as we listen to what it means to the other person.

The external frame of reference is when we perceive only from our own subjective frame of reference and when there is no accurate, empathic understanding of the subjective world of the other person.

Evaluating another person through the values of our external frame of reference will ensure lack of understanding.

When we view another person within the internal frame of reference, that person's behaviour makes more sense.

The principal limitation is that we can then deal only with what is within the consciousness of the other person. That which is unconscious lies outside the frame of reference.

For person A to understand the frame of reference of person B, person A needs to:

1. Build a bridge of empathy in order to enter the other person's world.
2. Help the other person to communicate.
3. Understand the personal meanings of B.
4. Communicate that understanding to B.

The bridge of empathy is built upon the foundations of self-awareness. Lack of self-awareness acts as an obstruction to being able to enter someone else's frame of reference.

The more we feel able to express ourselves freely to another person, without feeling on trial, the more of the contents of our frame of reference will be communicated.

Communicating with another person's frame of reference depends on:

1. Careful listening to the other person's total communication – words, non-verbal messages, voice-related cues.
2. Trying to identify the feelings that are being expressed, and the experiences and behaviours that give rise to those feelings.
3. Trying to communicate an understanding of what the person seems to be feeling and of the sources of those feelings.
4. Responding by showing understanding, not by evaluating what has been said.

FREE ASSOCIATION

Free association is a technique developed by Freud from Jung's word association. It describes the mode of thinking in psychoanalysis, whereby the patient reports spontaneous thoughts, ideas, or words, without reservation. There should be no attempt to concentrate or analyse during the process.

By saying whatever comes to mind, without any attempt to control or censor it, the unconscious mind is tapped. The analyst refrains from any prompt that might influence the patient's selection of material.

Free association is not normal communication. The patient is required to give the first word evoked by the trigger word.

FREE CHILD

A transactional analysis term, to describe the spontaneous, eager, and playful part of the personality. Also called 'natural child'.

People whose free child is too dominant generally lack self-control.

The basic need of the free child is creativity.

Some typical words

Eek! gee whiz, gosh, I'm scared, let's play, look at me now, wow!

Some typical gestures and postures

Joyful, skipping, curling up, pretending.

Some typical voice tones

Belly laughing, excited, giggling, gurgling, whistling, singing.

Some typical facial expressions

Admiration, wide-eyed and curious, excited, flirty.

	Life position	Behaviour
1.	I'm not OK You're not OK	Humorous
2.	I'm OK You're not OK	Unconventional
3.	I'm OK You're OK	Innovative
4.	I'm not OK You're OK	Satirical

FREUD, ANNA (1895–1982)

Youngest daughter of Sigmund. One of the founders of child psychoanalysis and one of its foremost practitioners.

She contributed to the understanding of how the ego functions in averting painful ideas, impulses and feelings.

Her work on defence mechanisms is profound and her contribution to adolescent psychology of great significance.

She, with Sigmund, settled in London in 1938, where she became an influential figure at the Hampstead Child Therapy Clinic, and founded the London Child Therapy Course.

She worked closely with parents, and believed that therapy should have an educational value for the child. Her view of play was that while it was the child's way of adapting to reality, it did not necessarily reveal unconscious conflicts.

FREUD, SIGMUND (1856–1939) (*See also*: Instincts, Psychoanalysis)

Moravian-born founder of psychoanalysis who studied medicine in Vienna, which became his home until 1938, when with his daughter Anna he went to live in London.

He developed his psychoanalytic method and the technique of free association during the years 1892–1895.

His basic theory was that neuroses are rooted in suppressed sexual desires and sexual experiences in childhood. He analysed dreams in terms of unconscious desires.

He maintained that many of the impulses forbidden or punished by parents are derived from innate instincts.

Forbidding expression to these instincts merely drives them out of awareness into the unconscious.

There they reside to affect dreams, slips of speech or mannerisms and may also manifest themselves through symptoms of mental illness.

Freud's view – that the conscious and the unconscious are sharply divided and that access to the unconscious is denied except by psychoanalysis – does not meet with universal acceptance. Rather, many believe that there are but various layers of awareness.

In summary, Freud's view was that humans are driven by sex and aggression, the same basic instincts as animals. Society is in constant struggle against any expression of these.

Freud's Psychological Wednesday Circle – the 'inner circle' – was formed by invitation from him to several like-minded people to discuss psychoanalytic matters and later became the Vienna Psychoanalytic Society.

FROMM, ERICH (1900–1980)

Born in Germany and trained in psychoanalysis at Munich and Berlin. Settled in the United States in 1934.

His belief that economic and social factors exert a profound influence upon human behaviour modified his psychoanalytic approach, particularly related to unconscious drives.

Fromm's unconventional approach to psychoanalysis, expressed in his books, brought him into conflict with traditionalists. One of Fromm's concerns was international harmony, in an age threatened by nuclear disaster.

G

GAMES (*See also*: Adult, Child, Parent, Transactional analysis)

Games describe unconscious, stereotyped and predictable behaviours. When games are conscious, it is manipulation. The transactions in games are partially ulterior, and result in negative payoffs for the players.

Games are classified as first-, second- or third-degree depending on the seriousness of the consequences. They allow the player to collect 'stamps'. Stamps are stored up feelings, positive or negative. When we have stored up enough stamps we may cash them in for a 'prize': letting fly at someone with whom we have been really tolerant over a long period; allowing oneself a period of relaxation, for example.

Brown stamps are for negative feelings; gold stamps are for positive feelings.

Stamp collecting is a way of trying to help the Child to feel OK.

A game consists of:

1. An apparent (conscious) transaction (usually Adult–Adult)
2. A hidden (unconscious) transaction (usually Parent–Child or Child–Child)
3. A sudden and unpleasant reaction (a stamp).

Over 90 games have been described. The most common are:

'If it weren't for you.'
'Kick me.'
'I'm only trying to help.'

Rackets are habitual ways of feeling bad that we have learned from our parents, or significant others. They belong to our parents, not to us, but we act as if they do.

Rackets and stamp collecting originate from the Not OK Child of our parents and our own Child uses these as an excuse for not taking constructive action.

GENITAL STAGE

A psychoanalytic term to describe the final stage of psychosexual (libidinal) development, usually around late adolesence.

The previous stages:

1. Oral
2. Anal
3. Phallic
4. Latency.

Sexual gratification is no longer limited to specific body areas but is achieved through sexual intercourse.

GENUINENESS (CONGRUENCE)

(*See also*: Core conditions, Empathy, Unconditional positive regard, Self-disclosure)

The degree to which we are freely and deeply ourselves, and are able to relate to people in a sincere and undefensive manner.

Also referred to as authenticity, congruence, truth, it is the precondition for empathy and unconditional positive regard.

Effective therapy depends wholly on the degree to which the therapist is integrated and genuine. In Person-centred therapy skill and technique play a much less important role than relating to the client authentically. Genuineness encourages client self-disclosure.

Appropriate therapist disclosure enhances genuineness. The genuine therapist does not feel under any compulsion to disclose, either about events, situations, or feeling aroused within the counselling relationship.

Some client statements about therapist's genuineness:

1. What she says never conflicts with what she feels.
2. She is herself in our relationship.
3. I don't think she hides anything from herself that she feels with me.
4. She doesn't avoid anything that is important for our relationship.
5. I feel I can trust her to be honest with me.
6. She is secure in our relationship.
7. She doesn't try to mislead me about her own thoughts or feelings.
8. She is impatient with me at times.
9. Is sometimes upset by what I say.
10. Sometimes looks as worried as I feel.
11. Treats me with obvious concern.

GESTALT THERAPY

A German word which when translated loosely means 'pattern' or 'form'. When the pattern, or 'gestalten', is incomplete, we talk of 'unfinished business'.

The chief tenet of gestalt psychology is that analysis of parts, however thorough, cannot provide an understanding of the whole.

Parts are not understood when analysed in isolation. Mental processes and behaviours come complete.

An example is that we hear a melody as a whole, and not merely as a collection of individual notes.

Gestalt psychology sprang out of dissatisfaction over the inability of both psychoanalysis and behaviourism to deal with the whole person.

Gestalt therapy, developed by Fritz Perls, aims to help the person to be self-supportive and self-responsible, through awareness of what is going on within the self at any given moment, the 'here-and-now'. Gestalt therapy is heavily influenced by existentialism, psychodrama and body therapies.

THE AIM OF GESTALT THERAPY IS:

1. Change through activity
2. The central meaning of present experience

3. The importance of fantasy and creative experimentation
4. The significance of language.

The therapist draws attention to:

1. What the client says
2. How it is said
3. The client's behaviour
4. Non-verbal communication
5. Breathing pattern
6. Tensions within the session.

Clients are encouraged to act out various roles in life which they and others have played or are currently playing, and to take responsibility for their own conflicts.

GESTALT THERAPISTS BELIEVE:

1. That human beings are responsible for themselves, for their lives and for living.
2. That the important question about human experience and behaviour is not 'why' but 'how'.
3. That each person functions as a whole, not as separate parts.
4. In the philosophy of holism.
5. In the principles of homeostasis – a state of equilibrium produced by a balance of functions within an organism.
6. That the past exists only within a faulty memory. The future exists only in present expectations and anticipations. The past affects the individual and persists as unfinished business.

Perls rejected the dualities of:

1. Mind–body
2. Body–soul
3. Thinking–feeling
4. Thinking–action
5. Feeling–action.

THE GOALS OF THERAPY

1. To re-establish contact and normal interaction; the restoration of ego function, and the restoration of the whole.
2. To foster:

   Maturation and growth
   Independence
   Self-support
   Awareness.
3. To help the client:

   Deal with unfinished business
   Learn to live in the 'here and now'.

THE PROCESS OF THERAPY

Clients are asked, and sometimes actively encouraged, to experience as much of themselves as possible – gestures, breathing, voice, and so on. In so doing they become aware of the relationship between feelings and behaviours, and are thus able to:

1. Integrate their dissociated parts.
2. Establish an adequate balance and appropriate boundaries between self and the environment.

Unfinished business must be concentrated on and re-experienced, not just talked about, in order to be resolved in the here and now.

As each piece of unfinished business is resolved, a gestalten is completed, and the way is thus prepared for the client to move onto the next unfinished business.

Clients are constantly required to repeat, and complete, the basic sentence, 'Now I am aware ...' and its variations:

1. 'What are you aware of now?'
2. 'Where are you now?'
3. 'What are you seeing ... Feeling?'

4. 'What is your hand, foot doing?'
5. 'What do you want?'
6. 'What do you expect?'

Therapists make clients take responsibility by getting them to use 'I' not 'it' when referring to their body. Any statement or behaviour that does not represent self is challenged.

CONFUSION

Confusion is unpleasant and clients will attempt to get rid of it by:

1. Avoidance
2. Blanking out
3. Verbalism
4. Fantasy.

When confusion is not avoided or interrupted, when it is allowed to develop, it will be transformed into a feeling that can be experienced and can result in appropriate action.

DREAMS

1. Dreams are the royal road to integration.
2. Dreams are existential messages.
3. Dreams contain everything we need, if all the parts are understood.
4. Dreams reveal missing personality parts.
5. Clients are encouraged to relive the dream in the present and to act it out.
6. Interpretations are left to the client.
7. The more the counsellor refrains from telling the client, the more the client is encouraged to travel the road to self-discovery and self-responsibility.

Integration means:

1. Owning disowned parts of oneself.
2. Being responsible for ones' own life goals.
3. Expressing everything that is felt in the body.
4. Expressing the vague feelings associated with shame and embarrassment at expressing certain thoughts and feelings. Shame and embarrassment are the prime tools of the defence mechanism of repression. Endurance of embarrassment brings repressed material to the surface.

TECHNIQUES:

1. *The 'chair'*. Clients move forward and backward from one chair to another and engage in dialogue between parts of themselves, between other people, or between dream objects.
2. *Skilful frustration*. In this the therapist:
   A. Repeatedly frustrates clients' avoidance of uncomfortable situations, until they show willingness to try and cope.
   B. Helps clients to identify the characteristics they project on to others that are most missing in themselves.
   C. Helps clients express and understand resentment, in the belief that the expression of resentment is one of the most important ways of helping people make life a little easier.

   Gestalt theory proposes that behind every resentment there is a demand, and that expressing the demand is essential for real change.
3. *Monotherapy* – where the client creates and acts every part of the production.

4. *Fantasy* – through the use of symbols. Fantasy can be verbalized, written, or acted.
5. *Shuttle* – directing the client's attention back and forth from one activity or experience to another.
6. *Topdog–Underdog*

   A. *Topdog* represents the 'shoulds' which the person has introjected. Topdog is righteous, perfectionist, authoritarian, bullying, and punishing.
   B. *Underdog* is primitive, evasive, 'yes but', excusing, passively sabotaging the demands of topdog. The client enters into a dialogue and alternately takes the part of both topdog and underdog.

Disowned parts of the personality are integrated into the whole, to complete that person's 'Gestalten'. When a need is satisfied, the situation is changed and the need fades into the background. If a need is not fulfilled – if a 'gestalten' is not completed – it may produce a conflict which is distracting and draining of psychic energy.

The awareness of, and the ability to endure, unwanted emotions, is the precondition of a successful outcome. It is this process and not the process of remembering, that is the royal road to health.

Critics of gestalt therapy say that it may help clients get in touch with their needs, but does not necessarily teach them the skills or wisdom to deal with those needs.

GOALS AND GOAL-SETTING (*See also*: Action plans)

Many people become clients because they feel stuck in situations from which they can see no way out. Counselling can help them to develop a sense of direction which often accompanies hope.

Direction. In order to move from:

1. *Point A* (the now), to
2. *Point B* (the desired outcome): counsellor and client need to explore:

   A. Feelings
   B. Thoughts
   C. Behaviours. In order to develop a new perspective, and work through hindrances.

EXAMPLE

Point A Tom is dissatisfied with work.
Point B Tom to look for satisfying job.

Perspective

There is no reason why Tom should stay in an unsatisfying job.

Hindrances

1. Tom's self-defeating beliefs and attitudes.
2. Tom's misplaced loyalty.
3. Tom prefers the comfort zone.

Problem-solving counselling is successful only if it results in problem-handling action.

Listening, as part of problem-solving, is effective only if it helps clients to become more intentional and leads to realistic goal-setting.

Intentional people:

1. Are in charge of their own lives.
2. Do not waste time and energy blaming other people or circumstances for their problems.
3. Refuse to capitulate to unfavourable odds.

4. Have a sense of direction in their lives, characterized by:
   A. Having a purpose
   B. Feeling they are going somewhere
   C. Engaging in self-enhancing activities
   D. Focusing on outcomes and accomplishments
   E. Not mistaking aimless actions for accomplishments
   F. Setting goals and objectives
   G. Having a defined lifestyle
   H. Not indulging in wishful thinking.
5. Are versatile – thinking about and creating options.
6. Become involved in:
   A. The world of other people
   B. Social settings.
7. Evaluate their goals against the needs and wants of others.
8. Are ready to work for win–win rather than win–lose situations.

ADVANTAGES OF GOAL-SETTING

1. Focuses attention and action
2. Mobilizes energy and effort
3. Increases persistence
4. Strategy oriented.

THE GOAL-SETTING MODEL OF GERARD EGAN

Stage 1 – The present scenario

The aim of stage one is to help clients:

1. Understand themselves
2. Understand the problem
3. Set goals
4. Take action.

The client's goal is self-exploration.
The counsellor's goal is responding.

The counsellor helps clients to:

1. Tell their story
2. Focus
3. Develop insight and new perspectives.

Stage 2 – Creating new scenarios and setting goals

The aim of stage two is to help clients:

1. Examine their problem
2. Think how it could be handled differently
3. Develop their powers of imagination.

The client's goal is self-understanding.
The counsellor's goal is to integrate understanding.

The counsellor helps clients to:

1. Create new scenarios
2. Evaluate possible scenarios
3. Develop choice and commitment to change.

Stage 3 – Helping clients act

The client's goal is action.
The counsellor's goal is to facilitate action.

The counsellor helps clients to:

1. Identify and assess action strategies
2. Formulate plans
3. Implement plans.

Some useful questions for clients to ask – what:

1. Would this situation look like if I managed it better?
2. Changes would there be in my lifestyle?
3. Would I do differently with the people in my life?
4. Behaviours would I get rid of?
5. New behaviours would there be?
6. Would exist that doesn't exist now?

7. Would be happening that isn't happening now?
8. Would I have that I don't have now?
9. Decisions would I have made?
10. Would I have accomplished?

GRIEF (*See also*: Mourning, Dying – stages of)

A normal reaction of intense sorrow, following the loss of:

1. An emotionally significant person
2. A material object or objects
3. A part of the self
4. A previous stage of the life-cycle.

The psychoanalytic view is that grief allows ties with the lost object to be broken through the withdrawal of libido.

Freud identified a period of between one to two years as the normal period for accomplishing 'grief work', with improvement after about six months.

For Bowlby, grief is an attempt to re-establish ties rather than a withdrawing of them.

Grief can also be viewed as the working out of conflicting impulses.

Grief is the price we pay for loving.

TYPES OF GRIEF

1. Anticipatory grief ends when the actual loss takes place.
2. Acute grief, substages:
   Shock where the focus is on the past, is characterized by alarm and denial.

   Realization where the focus is on the present, is characterized by:

   A. Intermittent denial
   B. Searching behaviour
   C. Preoccupation and identification with the lost object.
   D. Idealization
   E. Regression
   F. Crying
   G. Bodily symptoms
   H. Depression/helplessness
   I. Guilt, anger, shame.

   Integration where the focus is on the future, and is characterized by acceptance and a return to physical, social and psychological well-being.
3. Morbid or pathological grief may be:

   A. *Inhibited*, where reactions are absent or distorted.
   B. *Chronic*, where severe reactions are prolonged.
   C. *Delayed*, where severe reactions occur later.

PATHOLOGICAL GRIEF IS MORE LIKELY TO OCCUR FOLLOWING:

A. Experience of loss or separation in childhood
B. Lack of effective support
C. Sudden or violent death
D. The loss of a child.

SOME HELPFUL COUNSELLING AIDS

1. *Journals and diaries*. Writing letters of what is happening, including feelings and thoughts can be very therapeutic. Some people feel able to burn the writings at some stage, thus signifying a letting go.
2. *Pictures*. These need not be 'artistic'. What is important is what the person includes, as well as what is left out. The picture can then be used as a talking point, not as something to be 'interpreted'. This method is superb when dealing with children. Children's drawings may take

the form of fantasy, with monsters and other frightening figures.
3. *Photographs*. Family snapshots provide a focus for communication. The person in a photograph always has a certain substance. The viewer often has to contain the 'then' within the reality and pain of the 'now'.
4. *Scrapbooks*. As with photographs, collecting material to paste into a scrapbook may be painful. The therapeutic benefit of having put together a memorial in this way, as something to look back on, is of inestimable value.
5. *A family tree*. A family tree is a visual record of one's heritage and should include those dead as well as those still alive. It is an ideal medium for the grieving person to talk about the interaction between various people on the tree.

   A related technique is family sculpting, where shapes can be used to represent members of the family. (*See also*: Sociogram.)
6. *Bibliotherapy*. (*See* main entry).
7. *Relaxation*. (*See* Autogenic training).

GROUP THERAPY (*See also*: Tavistock method)

The use of group discussion and other group activities to treat psychological disorders.

The large number of servicemen requiring psychotherapy following the Second World War encouraged the development of group therapy.

The aim is to create an atmosphere conducive to increased self-understanding and personal development. Members learn to recognize, understand, and handle feelings and behaviours of one another.

Membership of such a group can increase the sense of support and readiness to accept others and be accepted by them.

The size of the group varies, but eight to twelve is normal, usually with two facilitators.

The role of the facilitators, not leaders, varies according to style. Some observe and interpret, others are participators.

Therapy groups may be divided into:

1. *Psychoanalytic*, where the focus is on individual people in turn.
2. *Action-based*, which include:
   A. Encounter groups
   B. Transactional analysis
   C. Gestalt therapy
   D. Sensitivity groups
   E. Psychodrama
   F. Support groups.

GROUP TRAINING

Kurt Lewin, in the USA, and Bion at the Tavistock Institute, introduced experiential methods of group training, based on the assumptions that:

1. People learn best from analysing their immediate psychological experiences.
2. Facts, feelings, reactions and observations are often withheld in normal interaction.
3. A safe climate makes immediate exploration less difficult.
4. Cultural attitudes influence the way people react and respond in groups.

Experiential learning is widely used to improve:

1. Self-awareness
2. Effectiveness within groups
3. Relationships within the family
4. Relationships at work.

GUILT AND SHAME

Objectively, guilt is a fact or state attributed to a person who violates the will of God and/or some moral or penal code. Subjectively, guilt is awareness of having violated personal norms, or the norms of family, religion or society. The offence may be real or imaginary.

Shame is a complex, painful feeling resulting from a strong sense of guilt, unworthiness, or disgrace. We feel shame when we are faced with something that draws attention to a discrepancy between what we are and what, ideally, we would like to be.

The feeling of guilt may or may not be proportional to the nature of the offence. Guilt is often experienced as an alienation from relationship with God, others, or self. The act that causes shame is often inconsequential, but the self feels attacked.

'False guilt' is usually associated with sexuality, self-assertion, self-love, and putting oneself first, sometimes. A distinction needs to be made about 'having' desires to do 'wrong' and acting upon such desires.

Guilt about having wrong desires often wreaks havoc with the psyche, producing severe neuroses and sometimes, psychoses. Guilt and shame are both concerned with internalized standards of conduct. Guilt is more abstract and judgmental than shame.

It is possible to say one feels guilty without experiencing it; one cannot be ashamed without feeling it. Shame is more tied to threat of exposure than is guilt. Shame is the more fundamental of the two feelings.

Psychoanalytic theory regards guilt as internalization of prohibitions and is not so concerned with the fact of guilt, as with the sense of guilt. Psychoanalysis distinguishes 'normal' guilt (remorse) which would respond to 'confession' from 'pathological' guilt for which therapy would be more appropriate.

Behaviourists regard guilt as a conditioned response to past actions which has involved punishment.

It is said that men may be more prone to experience guilt, while women may be more prone to experience shame. One view of guilt is that it is anger turned inward.

A total absence of guilt is one of the features of 'character disorder'. Dealing with guilt is difficult. Working at it indirectly by tackling the underlying feelings that support the guilt may be more productive.

SOME EXPRESSIONS OF GUILT

1. 'I feel I've let someone down so badly, I deserve to be punished.'
2. 'I've done something wrong against someone.'
3. 'I've not done anything wrong, but I feel I've left something undone I should have done.'
4. 'I feel caught beween what's realistic and the selfish desires of other people.'
5. 'I've made a mistake and can't live with it.'
6. 'I can't forgive myself and I'm being punished.'
7. 'I can't help people making me feel guilty.'
8. 'I need to get a balance between guilt and what I've done, or feel I've done.'
9. 'I feel guilty because other people make demands on me that I can't meet, and I feel I should.'
10. 'My burden of guilt robs me

of any self-esteem and makes me feel so unworthy.'

POINTS TO REMEMBER ABOUT GUILT:

1. Guilt may be anger turned inward. Work, therefore, with the anger.
2. Guilt often has delusional qualities, in that it cannot be shaken by reason or logic.

   Sometimes there is the feeling of being excommunicated, even though the person may not be 'religious'.
3. No one can make us feel guilty (or feel anything else) if we do not want to. When we say 'That person makes me feel ...,' we pass on to that person the responsibility for how we feel. We have chosen to take on board something someone else wants to offload onto us.
4. In all work with guilt, there is an urgent need to help the person balance conscience with responsibility.

Authentic awareness of guilt seems to be a necessary aspect of healthy human beings. It is a warning system that we are at odds with God or with the structures, values, and truths to which we subscribe.

H

HARTMANN, HEINZ (1894–1970)

Viennese-born physician and psychoanalyst who fled Austria in 1938. He became a leading figure in the USA, where his contribution was mainly the field of ego psychology.

With Anna Freud and Ernst Kris he founded and edited the *Psychoanalytic Study of the Child*.

HERE AND NOW (IMMEDIACY)

Where the counsellor helps the client to look at the interaction within the relationship, as it is happening.

There is often a natural tendency to talk about feelings in the past (the then and there), rather than in the 'now'. People who rarely talk in the present, often dilute the interaction by the use of 'You' instead of 'I',

They may be helped to feel the immediacy of the statement when 'I' is used.

Example 1

'I find it difficult, listening to you, to know how you really feel right now. Everything seems so remote and distant.'

When delivered in a caring way, it has the effect of challenging the client to identify how he/she does feel.

Example 2

'When you talk about your wife, you sound as if you're talking about a little child. Just now you used the same tone with me. I felt really very small.'

HIERARCHY OF HUMAN NEEDS

(*See also*: Maslow, A.)

Maslow's theory was that experienced needs are the primary influences on behaviour. When a particular need emerges, it determines behaviour in terms of motivations, priorities, and actions.

Motivated behaviour thus results from tension when a need presents itself, whether the tension is pleasant or unpleasant. The goal of behaviour is the reduction of tension.

Maslow identified five levels of human needs. In order to progress upward, the person must have experienced secure footing on the first rung in order to proceed to the next.

Inability to fulfil a lower-order need may create locked-in, immature behaviour patterns.

Maslow did not say that all needs of a certain level must be fulfilled before progress upward was possible. It is a question of how much energy is being used up at a lower level.

THE HIERARCHY

1. Basic

   Physiological and survival needs: met by food, shelter, clothing, sex.

2. Safety

   Security, orderliness, protective rules, and risk avoidance – met by salary, insurance policies, alarm systems.

3. Belongingness

   The need of relationship with others, to be appreciated and accepted – met through family ties and membership of groups.

4. Ego-status

   Related to status within a group, ambition and a desire to excel. The Ego-status needs will motivate the person to display competence in an effort to gain social and professional rewards. Meeting status needs depends on the willingness and ability of other people to respond appropriately.

5. Self-actualization

   The level of personal growth, which may be met through the challenge of creativity, or demanding greater achievement. Self-actualizing behaviours include risk-taking, seeking autonomy, and freedom to act.

HOPE

Hope is to entertain a wish for something with confidence and expectation of fulfilment. Although the future cannot be known, we imagine the outcome. Sometimes the imagined prospect is terrifying. When we are convinced that the future is totally empty or bleak, we may lose our will to endure even the present.

HOPE IS ESSENTIAL FOR PERSEVERANCE

Pain and suffering are often endured in the present in the hope that the future will be better, and it is therefore worth struggling through. It is therefore the ability to rise above the limitations of the present, and be open to new possibilities.

While hope is essential for effective living, living in false hope – which resembles wishful thinking – is symptomatic of a dysfunctional psyche that functions in the realm of illusion. Authentic hope is founded on being realistic about the way things are.

Some people attempt to counsel with the hard face of reality, believing in the 'short, sharp shock'. This, in the early stages, is likely to lead to despair and hopelessness. Hope, founded on evasion does nothing to reassure, but coating reality with hope does not mean living in a world of unreality.

Acceptance does not mean banishing hope.

HORNEY, KAREN (1885–1952)

Born in Germany, worked for the last 20 years of her psychoanalytic career in America. She disagreed with many of Freud's tenets, and became known as one of the Neo-Freudians. Horney, with Alfred Adler, Erich Fromm and Harry Stack Sullivan are the best known of this group of psychoanalysts who modified Freud's original theories.

HORNEY'S PSYCHOANALYTIC THEORY OF PERSONALITY:

1. We are continually striving to evolve toward self-realization.
2. Our real self, which never changes, and which helps us to make choices and to accept responsibility for those choices, is characterized by energy, aliveness, and spontaneity.
3. Self-realization

    A. Is perceived as a natural unfolding of potential that finds its expression in relationships and healthy activities.
    B. Means that we are able to express love and trust, and opposition in order to master our environment.
    C. Means that at the same time, we are able to move away from others enough to become self-sufficient.

4. Neurosis develops when children are not provided with the warmth and acceptance necessary for healthy growth. Children deprived of warmth and acceptance are anxious, and direct their psychic energies toward survival, not growth.
5. Horney's belief, that women are not biologically predestined to submissiveness and suffering, was an issue that drew her into dispute with traditional psychoanalysts. She believed that much of the 'typical' female behaviour is culturally determined.

HORNEY'S THEORY OF NEUROSIS

Neurosis is a disturbance in the relationship between self and others. Feelings of helplessness and despair drive us into making decisions that are not fulfilling and which leave us feeling dissatisfied. Such feelings (formed early in childhood into defensive patterns) are self-perpetuating strategies against anxiety.

Three strategies are available to the child in its search for safety:

1. Moving toward others, seeking affection and approval. This 'moving toward' only emphasizes helplessness.
2. Moving against others, and in so doing accepts a hostile environment.
3. Moving away from others and in so doing accepts the difficulty of relating to people at an intimate level.

Behaviour, then, is influenced by whichever one of these strategies is found to bring the greatest rewards. Only one strategy is used, therefore the child does not explore the feelings and impulses of the other two. A deep sense of instability is thus created, which leads to ever greater restriction and repression of genuine feelings. Feelings are mistrusted and projected onto the outside world, where they develop into neurotic trends.

HORNEY'S NEUROTIC CHARACTER TYPES

1. Compliant, self-effacing – moving toward, characterized by:

    A. Seeking constant approval
    B. Dependent

C. Ultra-sensitive to others' needs
D. Constantly subordinating themselves
E. Unassertive
F. Value goodness, sympathy, and ultra-unselfishness
G. Panic at first hint of rejection.

2. Aggressive, expansive – moving against, characterized by:

A. Motivated by power and mastery
B. Need to control everyone and everything
C. Superiority over success
D. Exploit the vulnerability of others
E. Fiercely competitive
F. Toughness is valued
G. Tenderness is considered a weakness
H. Love of others is less important than their admiration and submission.

3. Detached, resigned – moving away from, characterized by:

A. Avoidance of conflict at all costs
B. Very private people
C. Hypersensitive to involvement
D. The typical 'onlooker'
E. Avoid any hint of competition
F. Deny any need for others
G. Feel uniquely superior
H. Self-sufficiency is a virtue.

The basic conflict results from the submerged and restricted impulses of the other two styles and leads to:

1. Auxiliary strategies to relieve inner tension.
2. Idealized image of self which glosses over contradictory impulses.
3. Claims. The demands made on other people to support the idealized self.
4. Shoulds, which become tyrannical, are perfections aimed at the self. People who use shoulds expect other people to comply with them and are very critical when they don't.
5. Self-hatred is brought about by the prospect of failing to meet the demands of the shoulds.

Neurotic pride is a substitute for healthy self-confidence, and when it is hurt, the response is outrage coupled with a desire to punish. Neurotic pride supports and protects the idealized self.

The central inner conflict is the battle between neurotic pride and healthy self-realization. Conflict also exists between upholding the idealized self and dealing with the shoulds that attack the idealized self.

When we repeatedly deny and repress genuine feelings and impulses, we lose touch with the very core of our being and experience alienation. We can then no longer determine what is right or wrong for us. We feel lost, uncertain and confused. In extreme alienation, we may feel deadened and empty inside. (*See also* Alienation).

In therapy the focus is on the present, not on recovering or reliving childhood memories.

Transference and counter-transference feelings must be recognized and worked through constructively.

Therapy is a co-operative venture, enabling clients to move from their neurotic character structure toward creative self-realization by the removal of blockages.

The disillusioning process uncovers, identifies and clarifies:

1. Protective blockages

   Used to ward off anxiety:

   A. Attacking the therapist's value
   B. Cancellation of sessions
   C. Lateness
   D. Pseudo compliance
   E. Resorting to unprescribed medication
   F. Self-accusation
   G. Silence

2. Positive-value blockages

   Used to prevent self-awareness 'I'm alright'
   Blockages reinforce and support the idealized self and need to be confronted with great care.

Horney believed that for behaviour change to last, an attitude change has to take place within an environment where underlying values and goals are openly explored.

Dreams play an important part in this therapy, and highlight the struggle between the pride system and the real self.

This central inner conflict produces psychic tumult, pain, and hate. Successful resolution means that we can move toward the discovery and creative use of our spontaneous, real, inner self.

HUMANISTIC PSYCHOLOGY

Its roots are in humanism, a philosophy attaching importance to humankind and human values.

Often described as the 'third force' in modern psychology.

It derives much of its impact from the 'growth movement' of the 1960s.

The main streams of humanistic psychology:

1. Mind-expanding drugs
2. Group dynamics, particularly T-groups
3. Laing's and Perls' interpretation of existentialism
4. Peak experiences
5. Roger's person-centred approach
6. Assagioli's psychosynthesis
7. Reichian emphasis on the body
8. Maslow's doctrine of 'self-actualization'
9. Taoism – centring and yin–yang polar unit
10. Tantra, the body as an energy system
11. Zen Buddhism – the concept of 'letting go'.

Although fundamentally eclectic, there are common themes in humanistic psychology:

1. Personal growth, human potential, responsibility, and self-direction
2. Lifelong education
3. Full emotional functioning
4. The need to learn, or to re-learn, what play and joy are about
5. Recognition of a person's spirituality, with an acknowledgment of human capacity for altered states of consciousness.

Humanistic psychology is a way of dealing with problems related to the following beliefs:

1. Intense personal experiences radically alter attitudes to self and others.
2. Unity of the human and natural worlds achieved through 'peak experiences'
3. Existential experiences lead to being completely independent and totally responsible for one's thoughts and actions.

EXAMPLES OF HUMANISTIC INTERVENTIONS:

1. Body methods:
   - A. Alexander technique
   - B. Bioenergetics
   - C. Feldenkrais method
   - D. Holistic health
   - E. Reichian therapy
   - F. Rebirthing
   - G. Rolfing
   - H. Sensory awareness.
2. Feeling methods:
   - A. Co-counselling
   - B. Encounter groups
   - C. Gestalt
   - D. Person-centred counselling
   - E. Primal integration
   - F. Psychodrama.
3. Thinking methods:
   - A. Family therapy
   - B. Neuro-linguistic programming
   - C. Personal constructing
   - D. Rational–emotive therapy
   - E. Transactional analysis.
4. Spiritual methods:
   - A. Dream work
   - B. Dynamic meditation
   - C. Enlightenment workshops
   - D. Psychosynthesis
   - E. Sand play
   - F. Transpersonal counselling

THE KEY CONCEPTS

1. The real self is hidden behind roles and masks.
2. Subpersonalities. (*See also*: Psychosynthesis.) Each of us is a crowd and every single one in that crowd can be at odds with every one else.
3. Abundance motivation

   There is more to life than simply maintaining the status quo. Motivation cannot be inferred from performance; it is known only to the actor.
4. Self-interest

   Attention to one's own states and motives makes self-deception possible.

HUMOUR

Humour is defined simply as a type of stimulation that tends to elicit the laughter reflex. The co-ordinated contraction of 15 facial muscles, accompanied by altered breathing, combine to produce a conventional pattern we call smiling or laughter.

The only biological function of laughter is to provide relief from tension. It is the only form of communication in which a complex stimulus produces a predictable, physiological response.

Humour, then, can be applied to a stimulus, a response, or a disposition.

Humour is also regarded as a form of play involving symbols, images, and ideas. Through laughter and smiling, it serves a variety of social functions:

1. Assists interaction
2. Reveals attitudes
3. Engenders fellow feeling
4. Aids understanding
5. Raises esteem
6. Confirms the standing of relationships.

Humour is different from wit which involves distraction from the feelings associated with the issue.

The emotion discharged in laughter often, though not always, contains an element of aggression. Malice may be combined with affection in friendly teasing, and the aggressive component in civilized humour may no longer be conscious.

There is often a relationship between laughter and ugliness, deformity, and cruelty; delight in suffering and contempt for the unfamiliar.

HUMOUR AS A DEFENCE MECHANISM:

1. Is an antidote to sympathy.
2. Is a protection from the shortcomings of others.
3. Is a defence against showing true feelings.
4. Allows the individual to focus on something, in a way that makes bearable what, in reality, is too terrible to be borne.

Freud regarded jokes and parapraxes as revelations of the unconscious.

Humour in therapy needs to be distinguished between that which is used to attack, and humour as a shared response. Appropriate humour may aid therapy where it lowers anxiety, reduces distance, focuses attention on the material being discussed, assists in building the relationship, and promotes catharis.

HYPOCHONDRIASIS (Defence mechanism)

Excessive preoccupation with bodily symptoms (especially pain), often accompanied by fears of serious physical illness, such as cancer or heart disease.

Hypochondrial people are typically concerned with the 'vital functions' – head, heart, lungs, abdominal, bladder functions and reproduction. The appearance of the occasional pimple or spot is interpreted as heralding a more serious complaint. These are the people who shop around for sympathetic doctors: reassurances are futile.

Hypochondriasis is linked with borderline, dependent or passive–aggressive traits.

THE HYPOCHONDRIACAL PERSON

1. Is a help-rejecting complainer
2. Resists complaints being relieved
3. Induces guilt, anger and rejection in those who try to help
4. Uses self-reproach
5. Sufferer of pain
6. Is prone to somatic illness
7. Often has suicidal ideas
8. Is reproachful of others.

Hypochondriasis often conceals bereavement, loneliness and unacceptable aggressive impulses.

THREE USEFUL GUIDES IN THERAPY:

1. *Amplification*. Overstating the severity often leads the client to minimize the complaint.
2. *Dependency*. Make some symbolic effort to meet the client's overall need for dependency, rather than attacking the presenting symptom.
3. *Respond, don't react*. A careful history-taking, accompanied by active listening and trying to work within the client's frame of reference, is more reassuring than any attempt to argue against the symptoms.

I

ID

A psychoanalytic term to describe one of the three parts of the psyche; a completely chaotic, primitive reservoir of energy, derived from the instincts which demand immediate satisfaction.

The id is not synonymous with the unconscious, although it represents a major portion of it. Freud proposed that at birth the neonate is endowed with an id with instinctual drives seeking gratification.

It is entirely self-contained and isolated from the world about it and is bent on achieving its own aims.

CHARACTERISTICS OF THE ID:

1. It contains the psychic content related to the primitive instincts of the body, notably sex and aggression, as well as all material inherited and present at birth.
2. It is oblivious of the external world and unaware of the passage of time.
3. It functions entirely on the pleasure–pain principle.
4. It supplies the energy for the development and continued functioning of mental life.

The task of psychoanalysis is to make the ego function more effectively at the expense of the id. Totally effective functioning is never totally achieved, or even desirable, for the id provides the creative energy to sustain the ego and superego. The aim should be to integrate the id, not to overpower it.

IDEALIZATION (Defence mechanism)

Where the person, as a defence against guilt, attributes exaggerated positive qualities to self or others, in order to deal with emotional conflicts and internal or external stressors.

Idealization views external objects, as 'all good', or 'all bad', and endows them with great power. Most commonly, the 'all good' object, the 'ideal', is seen as possessing god-like power, while the badness in the 'all bad' object is greatly exaggerated.

In psychoanalytic psychology, idealization refers to the overvaluing of the sexual drive.

IDENTIFICATION (Defence mechanism)

Identification is the process by which we model aspects of ourselves upon other people.

We behave, or imagine ourselves behaving, as if we were the person with whom we have a strong emotional tie, and take on the attitudes, patterns of behaviour and emotions of that person.

The psychoanalytic view is that it is an important means by which the ego and superego are developed. Empathy depends, to some extent, upon the therapist's ability to identify with the client's feelings.

Freud's theory was that a child's conscience is formed by incorporating parental standards of conduct. The child acts in accordance with these standards, even when the parent is absent, and experiences guilt when those standards are violated.

For Jung, identification is an alienation of people from themselves, for the sake of some object in which they are, so to speak, disguised.

Adler goes so far as to say that it is impossible to undersand people if at the same time we do not identify with them. Therapists need to be aware of the danger of 'overidentification'.

An inability to identify with another person is as much a defence mechanism as identification is. Imitation and modelling depend on the extent of identification achieved. Identification is unconscious; imitation is conscious.

Identification is useful until it gets in the way of the subject's becoming a separate person.

It is important in the development of the child; maturity, conversely, is marked by separateness.

For the behavioural therapists, identification is continuous throughout life.

Identification is a major link between the psychoanalytic and social learning theories of development and it is a powerful influence in the socialization process.

PSYCHOANALYTIC PROCESSES OF IDENTIFICATION

1. Symptom formation

   A symptom is the means by which we reject a feeling, wish or behaviour, and desire the opposite. In the process we develop a symptom that most symbolizes the changed orientation. For example, a man's sexual impotence may preserve his self-image of his being a non-aggressive non-penetrating male figure.

2. Narcissism (*see* entry)

   Identification between people in an intimate relationship occurs as a defence against handling differences.

3. Bereavement

   Where the one who is left tries to become like the lost one, in order to lessen the feelings of loss and the anxiety of separation.

4. Authority figures

   Identification with parents and others, is based on a mixture of love and fear.

Projective identification is where I (the subject) attribute unwanted aspects of myself to another person (the object). I imagine myself to be inside that other person. This creates an illusion of control over the subject and I gain some satisfaction from the achievements of the object.

IMAGERY (*See also*: Psychosynthesis)

This article draws together imagination, guided fantasy, directed daydream and Guided affective imagery (GAI).

Imagery. The inner representation of objects and events created at will by the conscious mind.

Fantasy. Imaginary activities that are produced spontaneously (as in daydreams) or as a requested response to stimuli such as inkblots or ambiguous pictures.

Imagination. Expresses repressed parts of personality.

Imagery has an obvious and a hidden meaning:

1. The obvious is conscious and concrete.
2. The hidden is unconscious and implied, and takes the form of symbols. Understanding the fantasy means working with the symbols.

IMAGERY – GUIDED (Also referred to as 'symboldrama')

A form of creative imagination, facilitated by the therapist, who prompts, encourages, develops and brings the fantasy experience to a close. The material may then be analysed in terms of its meaning and symbolism – similar to dream analysis. Symbols, which may conceal or reveal, always derive from archetypes.

Symbols have four meanings:

1. Literal
2. Allegorical
3. Moral
4. Mystical.

Kinds of symbols:

1. Nature
2. Animal
3. Human
4. Man-made
5. Religious
6. Mythological
7. Abstract
8. Individual/spontaneous.

Guided imagery is used in one form or another in many different therapies. It may also be used in groups, either for individuals or for the whole group. The fundamental truth of therapeutic imagery is that the psyche always strives to represent itself in fantasy using images.

PRINCIPLES OF GUIDED IMAGERY THERAPY

1. The principle of symbol confrontation

   The client is encouraged to be courageous and to confront images (usually a part of self) that cause anxiety. Successful confrontation causes transformation and removal of anxiety.

2. The principle of feeding

   Where confrontation is inappropriate, or unacceptable – the challenge may be too great – the therapist may suggest that the client feeds the frightening figure, to make it lazy and sleepy.

3. The principle of transformation

   While transformation may take place in confrontation, sometimes the transformation has to be more clearly directed if it doesn't occur spontaneously. Changing the feared object into something more acceptable is not just a way of coping; the new object often reveals significant psychological growth.

4. The principle of reconciliation

   This is where the client makes friends with a hostile symbolic figure, by addressing and touching it.

5. The principle of the magic fluid

   The brook or stream represents the flow of psychic energy and the potential for emotional development. Bathing in the stream, or drinking from it, may prove therapeutic.

   Bathing in the sea can be very revealing, from what is felt and from what one discovers in the depths.

6. The principle of exhausting and killing

   Should only be used by an experienced therapist, because it is very often an attack against the client's self.

PRINCIPAL MOTIFS

1. Meadow
2. Brook
3. Mountain
4. House
5. Edge of woods
6. Animals
7. Rosebush
8. Lion/dragon
9. Significant person
10. Cave
11. Swamp
12. Volcano
13. Book
14. Sword
15. Container
16. Witch/sorceress/wizard/magician
17. Sleeping Beauty
18. Wise person – guide.

PRINCIPAL GROUPS OF SYMBOLS

1. Introversion, or interiorization

   The external life must be counterbalanced by an adequate inner life. The task is to discover our centre.

2. Deepening – descent

   The exploration of the unconscious. To become aware of, and incorporate, one's 'shadow' – the lower parts of one's personality.

3. Elevation – ascent

   The mountain-top, sky, or heaven. The levels of the inner worlds are:

   A. Emotions and feelings
   B. Mind/intellect – concrete, analytical, philosophical reason
   C. Imagination
   D. Will
   E. Transcendence.

4. Broadening – expansion

   Consciousness can be enlarged or broadened to include increasingly larger zones of impressions and contents. This happens spherically, in all directions, not just in one direction.

5. Awakening

   The natural conscious state is that of being asleep. In this dreamlike state we see everything and everyone through a thick veil of colouring and distortions, which derive from our emotional reactions, the effect of past psychic traumas and from external influences. To awaken from this state requires courage.

6. Light – illumination

   Illumination is the passage from consciousness to intuitive awareness.

7. Fire

   The function of fire is essentially one of purification.

8. Development and evolution

   The principal symbols are:

   A. The seed
   B. Flower (lotus, rose).

9. Strengthening – intensification

   The reinforcement of all our latent, underdeveloped energies and functions. This may include transpersonal, or peak experiences.

10. Love

    Human love is an attempt to come out of oneself and to enter communion with another.

11. The way, path, pilgrimage

    The 'mystic way'. For example, Bunyan's Pilgrim's Progress, Dante's passing through inferno, purgatory, and paradise.

12. Transformation

    Transformation, or transmutation, is the theme of psychospiritual alchemy which Jung explores, related to dreams and symbols. Transformation occurs through the combined actions of elevation and descent.

13. Rebirth – regeneration

    Transformation paves the way for regeneration, which, in its most profound meaning, constitutes a 'new birth'.

14. Liberation

    Elimination of encumbrances, a process of liberation from our complexes, from our illusions and from identification with the various roles we play in life, from the masks we assume and from our idols. Freedom from fear is a goal to be won, and safeguarded every single day.

IMAGO (*See also*: Archetypes)

In biology, the sexually mature adult stage in the life cycle of insects. Used particularly by those insects that undergo metamorphosis.

The term was introduced by Jung, and later adopted by Freud, to describe the process of idealized identification with a parent, or other significant person, which is formed in childhood and persists into adulthood.

The idealized image is based on unconscious fantasies, or derived from the activities of the archetypes, and is not based on reality. A sustained image is likely to lead to confusion between the fantasy and reality.

INCEST TABOO (*See also*: Oedipus complex)

Incest is any prohibited heterosexual relations between persons of the same culturally or legally defined kinship group. It usually means between unmarried members of a nuclear family, i.e. between brothers and sisters or between parents and children.

Incest is universally condemned and usually greeted with horror. (Punishment for incest may be very severe.) It has been countenanced in exceptional circumstances, usually associated with the marriage of royal children.

Initiation ceremonies at puberty reinforce the idea that the mother and sister are forbidden to the young male as sexual partners.

Freud and Emile Durkheim, the French sociologist, both contributed to understanding the incest taboo. Freud sees the Oedipus complex - son-mother love - as a fundamental psychological conflict.

Jung interpreted incest fantasies as symbolic of wanting close emotional contact, though acknowledging the sexual feelings to be real.

To act upon the sexual urges and not acknowledge the taboo leads to abuse. To acknowledge the taboo and deny the sexual urges leads to repression with all its consequent pathology.

INDIVIDUAL PSYCHOLOGY

Alfred Adler (1870–1937)

Vienna-born physician and psychoanalyst. Wrote his first book on industrial medicine in 1898, on the health of tailors.

Adler, one of the Neo-Freudians, broke with Freud and resigned as president of the Vienna Psychoanalytic Society in 1911. He established many child-guidance centres in schools in Vienna, and is credited with being the pioneer psychiatrist of group counselling.

He disagreed with Freud over the libido theory, the sexual origin of neurosis, and the importance of infantile wishes.

Individual psychology is a broad, humanistic and holistic theory of psychology and psychotherapy. Adler believed that the main motives of human thought and behaviour lie in the individual's striving for superiority and power, partly in compensation for feelings of inferiority.

Every individual is unique, and our personality structure, including our unique goal and ways of striving for it, is our style of life, a product of our own creativity. The individual cannot be considered apart from society, for all human problems - relationships, occupation and love - are social.

The neurotically disposed person is characterized by increased inferiority feelings, underdeveloped social interest and an exaggerated, uncooperative goal of superiority. These characteristics express themselves as anxiety and aggression.

INDIVIDUAL PSYCHOLOGY EMPHASIZES:

1. Social relationships, rather than biological factors
2. Self, rather than the id and the superego
3. Striving for self-actualization, rather than the sex instinct
4. The present, rather than early experiences
5. Equality and co-operation between the sexes.

BASIC ASSUMPTIONS:

1. All behaviour has social meaning
   A. Social interest creates an attitude toward one's own place within society and relationship to others. The tasks of living are to love and to be loved; to experience friendship; to work; to develop a satisfactory self-concept, and to search for meaning.
   B. A person with high self-esteem and high social interest will move toward others in an encouraging manner.
   C. A person suffering from self-doubts or inadequacies, or

who has few concerns for the rights and needs of others, will move away from others in swamping dependency or in an independent manner which cuts other people off.

2. The human personality is a unity

   'Unity' means synthesizing our physical, emotional, intellectual, and spiritual aspects.

   Adler used the term 'style of life', a key term that describes variously:

   A. Self
   B. Personality
   C. A personal problem-solving method
   D. An attitude toward life
   E. A line of movement
   F. A pattern
   G. A technique.

   The unique life style is developed from an early age and is as characteristic as a theme in a piece of music.

3. Behaviour is subjectively determined

   Personal reality is determined through subjective experience, perceiving and learning. Every person develops a 'private logic'.

4. All behaviour is goal-directed

   By seeking to discover the payoff, or purpose of behaviour, therapists can more readily understand dysfunctional behaviour. Goals are not always conscious.

5. Motivation explains striving for significance

   Each of us moves from a feeling of relative inferiority to a feeling of superiority. This striving for success and superiority is the upward drive toward perfection.

   Neurosis and psychosis forces people to impose their (often unfounded) achievements onto others in order to boost a weakened self-esteem. This weakened self-esteem frequently leads to overcompensation which takes the form of deprecating others, a tendency that is at the root of sadism, hatred, quarrelsomeness, and intolerance.

6. Behaviour

   This may change throughout life, to meet current demands and long-term goals.

7. People are not pushed by causes

   We are determined neither by our heredity nor by our environment.

8. Self-realization is other-directed

   Self-realization, if it does not help to make the world a better place, is sterile.

9. Every person has the freedom of choice

   Some choose to remain neurotic; others choose to strive toward the goal of wholeness.

Adler's 'masculine protest' describes the drive for superiority, or completeness, arising out of a felt inferiority or incompleteness, femininity being regarded as incomplete and inferior.

THE MYTH OF MASCULINE SUPERIORITY

Society has been so structured that in the division of labour, males assume dominance and superiority over women.

In Adlerian psychology, the differences between males and females is very slight, so assumed dominance by males creates tension between the two sexes.

From a very early age, boys and girls are conditioned into an acceptance of dominance or submission. Adler insists that this masculine superiority is a myth that creates many psychological problems.

The thought of such superiority scares male children, and imposes on them an obligation they can never expect to fulfil. At the same time it compels female children to rebel against enforced inferiority.

Individual psychology emphasizes horizontal relationships, between the sexes, a position of difference but of equality, rather than vertical relationships, in which, for ever, we compare ourselves favourably or unfavourably with someone else who happens to be of a different sex. The idea is also applied to relationships in general. A hierarchy is an example of vertical relationships.

THE STAGES OF ADLERIAN THERAPY

1. The therapeutic relationship

   This encompasses the qualities of unconditional positive regard, genuineness, empathy, non-possessive warmth, self-disclosure, and concreteness.

2. Psychological investigation

   This is in four parts:

   A. The subjective situation – what is happening within the client.
   B. The objective situation – what is happening in the client's external world.
   C. Getting the answer to 'The fundamental question' – what would be different if all these problems or concerns were solved? – gives clues as to possible payoffs, or reasons why the person persists in a specific behaviour.
   D. Life-style investigation, which may involve psychometric testing, an examination of the family atmosphere, and an exploration of the client's early recollections.

3. Interpretation

   A. Is not therapist centred, it is mutual sharing of basic attitudes about life, self and others, where the emphasis is on goals and purposes, not on causes.
   B. An interpretation identifies:
   (a) Problems and feelings of deficiency
   (b) Directions taken to overcome the perceived deficiencies
   (c) The relationship between direction and other significant areas in the client's life
   (d) Specific life-task difficulties
   (e) Strategies used to avoid resolution
   (f) Feelings of superiority about avoidances
   (g) Contribution of past influences.

   Adler disapproved of the 'red pen' approach, where only weaknesses are examined. We can build only on strengths, not on weaknesses.

4. Reorientation

   Counsellor and client work together to consider what changes could be made in the client's life style. Two basic techniques are:

   (a) 'Stroking', which is synonymous with encouragement and caring.

(b) 'Spitting in the soup', which is a discouraging response, based on the idea that a bowl of soup would no longer be appetizing if spat in. When the client has insight into faulty thinking and self-defeating behaviours they become contaminated and no longer appealing.

Confronting illogical, faulty thinking is also an important part in therapy. Illogical thinking may be:

(a) Causal inference – false logic.
(b) Blowup – exaggeration.
(c) All-or-nothing – thinking in extremes.
(d) Responsibility projection – failing to own.
(e) Perfectionism – idealistic demands on self.
(f) Value-tainted – 'shoulds', 'oughts', 'bad'.
(g) Self-depreciation – punitive statements.

Faulty thinking may be corrected by:

(a) Factual description
(b) Generating alternative explanations
(c) Designing positive course of action.

ADLERIAN GENERAL COUNSELLING SKILLS

1. Active listening
2. Reflection of feelings
3. Empathic understanding
4. Challenging
5. Interpretation
6. Encouragement.

SPECIFIC THERAPEUTIC SKILLS

1. Paradoxical intention

(Adler originally called this 'prescribing the symptom'.) The client is encouraged to emphasize the symptoms or develop them even more. When people discover that they cannot intentionally do what they feared would happen, they are often able to laugh at the situation.

Frankl (*see* Logotherapy) said that such an intervention takes the wind out of the sails of fear.

2. Acting 'as if'

To 'If only I could . . .', the counsellor replies, 'Pretend, act as if you could do it that way.' Acting 'as if' is like wearing a different suit. Feeling different is important.

3. Catching oneself

When clients become aware of engaging in behaviour they want to change, they are encouraged to say, 'There I go again.'

4. Creating movement

The element of surprise may encourage the client to change behaviour. Agreeing with the faulty logic and 'going over the top', provided it is not an attack, nor sarcastic, may jolt the client into action.

5. Goal setting and commitment

Homework, assignments, and change cards related to some change in behaviour. An example of a 'change card':
'This week I will . . .' (something specific)
'I know I could sabotage my task by . . .'
'I will evaluate my achievement on . . .'

LIFE STYLE MISTAKES

1. Tendency to overgeneralize
2. False or impossible goals of security
3. Misperceptions
4. Minimization or denial of one's worth
5. Faulty values.

Adler's social relations, interpersonal behaviour, ego development, self-direction and group work have influenced many other approaches to therapy.

INDIVIDUATION (*See also*: Shadow, Persona, Personal unconscious)

A term used by Jung to describe the lifetime process by which the person becomes who she or he was meant to become, whole, indivisible and distinct from other people. It means that each one of us comes to realize that we are truly individually unique, yet we are no more than a common man or woman.

Individuation does not mean an unhealthy, narcissistic preoccupation with one's own inner world; it does mean a looking inward so that one may look outward, to the world, with clearer eyes.

Individuation is not integration, which is social adaptation and ego-bound; it is bound to self, self-experience and self-realization and emotional maturity and involves:

1. Facing the dark side of one's personality, the shadow.
2. Progressing away from the constraints of the persona.
3. Understanding and separation from the controlling influences of the collective unconscious.

Individuation leads to more fulfilling relationships, not to isolation of self. It does not shut other people out, it gathers them in.

Individuation is uniquely individual and cannot be forced on the client by the therapist.

INFERIORITY COMPLEX (*See also*: Individual psychology, Superiority complex)

A term used in individual (Adlerian) psychology to describe exaggerated feelings of inadequacy or insecurity resulting in defensive and neurotic behaviour. Inferiority complexes are usually abnormal.

As a result of its initial helplessness, an infant feels inferior, and strives to overcome this feeling of incompletion by developing to a higher level. The feeling of inferiority, and compensating for that feeling, becomes the prime motivator in moving the person from one level of development to another. Adler refers to this as the 'great upward drive' toward perfection.

Constant incapability, discouragement from others, faulty self-evaluation about one's own self-worth, enhanced by being put down and ridiculed all sow the seeds of inferiority.

People who view themselves against others on a vertical plane (a typical hierarchy), are bound to put themselves either higher or lower (better or worse) than someone else.

People who view relationships on a horizontal plane are more likely to adopt a view of equality, each recognizing her/his own unique attributes and contributions.

INSIGHT

Insight is mental discernment, direct

understanding of the meaning or implication of something. It is the illumination or comprehension of one's mental condition that had previously escaped awareness. It is where immediate and clear learning or understanding takes place without apparent trial-and-error testing behaviour.

The term derives from the work on animal behaviour by gestalt psychologist, Wolfgang Kohler.

In psychopathology it is the awareness of one's own mental condition and is considered an essential in most forms of psychotherapy. A person achieves insight when he or she understands what is causing a conflict. Insight is often accompanied by catharis.

Insight in counselling refers to the extent to which clients are aware of their problems, origins, and influences. It may be sudden – like the flash of inspiration; the 'eureka experience'. More usually it develops stage-by-stage as the client develops psychological strength to deal with what is revealed.

Insight cannot be given by one person to another. We all must arrive at it by ourselves. A function of the counselling relationship is to help the client see how to put the new-found insight into practice.

INSTINCTS (*See also*: Eros, Thanatos)

Instincts are innate, inherited, unlearned, and biologically useful behaviours. The presence of instincts does not indicate the absence of intelligence or learning.

For Freud, instincts bridged the mental and organic spheres. Instinct theory plays a prominent role in psychoanalysis, though it has been modified where now the emphasis is on instinctual, rather than on the instincts themselves as fixed motivators of behaviour.

PSYCHOANALYTIC CLASSIFICATION OF INSTINCTS

1. *Ego instincts* are non-sexual, self-preserving and associated with repression.
2. *Libido* is the sexual instinct that has both mental and physiological manifestations. Libido shows itself in ways other than sexual union. Freud considered psychiatric symptoms to be the result of misdirection or inadequate discharge of libido. Jung used the term to encompass all life processes in all species.
3. *Aggression*. Freud, unable to reconcile some of the self-destructive elements he observed in his patients, formulated the aggression instinct.
4. *Life and death instincts*. With the modification of the instinct theory, Freud, in later writings, concentrated only on the life and death instincts.

   A. *Life instinct* (Eros). Eros refers to the tendency of particles to reunite, or for parts to bind to one another, to form greater unities. Sexual reproduction is an example.
   B. *Death instinct* (Thanatos). Thanatos is defined as the tendency to return to an inanimate state. Because all organisms return to the inanimate state, Freud considered thanatos to be the dominant force.

Human instincts is a fiercely contested topic.

INSTITUTIONALIZATION

1. Institutionalization removes people from their familiar environment.
2. It means placing people in a totally alien environment, with people and circumstances they have not chosen.

INSTITUTIONALIZATION PRODUCES PEOPLE WHO:

1. Are anxious, but may have difficulty talking about their fears.
2. Are isolated.
3. Are dependent (they have returned to a previous stage of development).
4. Experience loss of self-esteem
5. Feel trapped. They may want to complain, but feel they do not have the right to.

INSTITUTIONALIZED PEOPLE HAVE THE CHOICE:

1. To fight the system and so retain self-esteem and some independence.
2. To submit to the system and totally regress.

EXCEPTIONS ARE PEOPLE WHO:

1. Use the institution as a place of comfort, to receive love and support.
2. Are emotionally integrated and able to resist the insidious effects of the institution.
3. Unconscious, and therefore not aware of what is happening.

Most people swing between dependence and independence.

INTELLECTUALIZATION (Defence mechanism) (*See also*: Working through)

Where the ego deals with threats by using the mind rather than dealing with feelings. The person excessively analyses problems in remote, intellectual terms, while emotions and feelings are ignored or discounted. The process is closely allied to rationalization.

Concentration is on the inanimate at the expense of dealing with people. Detail is concentrated on to avoid looking at the whole.

Intellectualization can act as a severe block in therapy, preventing feeling work and working through. It can be used constructively, however, to temporarily bypass affect, in order to deal with a crisis.

INTERACTION PROCESS ANALYSIS (IPA)

A system of analysing group behaviour, developed by Bales, which identifies two basic types of group behaviour: Task and Maintenance (which may be positive, or negative). Not only is the model useful for analysis roles within a group, it allows a group more control over what they do.

Twelve categories of verbal and non-verbal behaviour are identified. During group interaction, a tally is made for each member's verbal and non-verbal acts. A 'message' may be composed of a number of acts.

Tally sheets help group members:

1. To identify their level of participation
2. The roles they adopt
3. Leadership and subgroupings.

THE CATEGORIES

Task (Offering)

1. Gives: suggestions/directions (implying autonomy for others).
2. Gives: opinions, evaluation, analysis.
   Expresses: feelings, wishes.
3. Gives: orientation, information.
   Repeats: clarifies, confirms.

Task (Receiving)

4. Requests: orientation, information, repetition.
5. Requests: opinions, evaluation, analysis, expression of feeling.
6. Requests: suggestions, directions, possible ways of acting.

Maintenance (Positive)

7. Shows solidarity; raises others' status; gives help; gives rewards.
8. Shows tension release; jokes, laughs; shows satisfaction.
9. Gives: orientation, information; repeats; clarifies; confirms.

Maintenance (Negative)

10. Disagrees: shows passive rejection, formality; withholds help.
11. Shows tension: asks for help; withdraws out of group.
12. Shows: antagonism; deflates others' status; defends aggressively.

Tension often exists between task and maintaining group atmosphere.

LEADERSHIP STYLES

An autocratic leader tends to:

1. Give more verbal directions and commands
2. Give answers and opinions
3. Express concern for results
4. Appears non-verbally dominant.

A democratic leader tends to:

1. Lead the group toward its own conclusions
2. Ask questions
3. Encourage suggestions
4. Encourage participation
5. Be non-verbally animated, attentive and friendly.

A *laissez-faire* leader tends to:

1. Extend the group's knowledge by giving information.
2. Non-verbally exhibits attentive and friendly behaviour.

SUBGROUPS MAY BE IDENTIFIED BY:

1. The degree of verbal and non-verbal reciprocacy between members.
2. The degree of support or opposition to the leader and to one another.

Interaction changes during the group life:

1. TASK CATEGORIES

   Phase 1 – Orientation
   Struggle and ambiguity. Categories 3 and 4.
   Phase 2 – Evaluation
   Co-operation. Categories 2 and 5.
   Phase 3 – Control
   Determining leadership. Categories 1 and 6.

2. MAINTENANCE CATEGORIES

   Decision-making
   Agreement/Disagreement.
   Categories 9 and 10.
   Integration – Solidarity/antagonism.
   Categories 7 and 12.
   Categories 8 and 11 operate all the way through, as the group

moves from Orientation to Control. Positive and negative reactions increase as members become more involved and come closer to their goal. For a group task to be completed there needs to be a balance between task and maintenance.

This equilibrium can exist only if the positive acts occur more frequently than negative acts. Solidarity and cohesiveness are the result of a predominance of positive acts. Dysfunctional strain and discord are the result of a predominance of negative acts.

SOME GENERALIZATIONS

1. Questions seem to be followed by answers. Agreement or disagreement then follows.
2. More answers and opinions are offered than questions asked.
3. Positive acts occur twice as frequently as negative ones.
4. As group size increases, so does:

   A. Release of tension
   B. Giving suggestions and information
   C. Showing solidarity.

5. As group size decreases, so does:

   A. Tension
   B. Agreement
   C. Asking for opinions
   D. Giving opinions.

6. Groups with even numbers tend to show:

   A. Frequent disagreements
   B. Antagonism
   C. Infrequent requests for suggestions.

7. As the life of group proceeds

   A. Status, role discrimination, control and strain all increase.
   B. Solidarity increases between members who give and receive from one another.
   C. Solidarity increases between members of unequal status.
   D. The struggle to maintain status and achieve control interfere with achieving goals.

INTERNALIZATION (*See also*: Introjection, Identification)

A social psychology term that describes the process whereby one incorporates, for example, norms, morals, and values into one's inner world.

As children develop they become able to give themselves the instructions that were previously given by significant others. Full internalization is achieved when the behaviour takes place, not in response to reward or fear of punishment, but because it is perceived to be correct or appropriate.

Internalization is similar to introjection, or identification, though not used as a defence mechanism. The concept is stressed in the writings of Melanie Klein as the principal means whereby the child builds up its internal world.

INTERPERSONAL TECHNIQUES

THERAPEUTIC

1. Acceptance
2. Challenging
3. Encouraging action
4. Encouraging comparison
5. Encouraging descriptions and perceptions
6. Exploring
7. Focusing
8. Giving broad openings

9. Offering non-specific leads
10. Offering observations
11. Placing the event in time or sequence
12. Reflecting
13. Restating
14. Seeking clarification
15. Silences
16. Suggesting collaboration
17. Summarizing
18. Translating into feelings
19. Verbalizing what is implied.

NON-THERAPEUTIC

1. Apportioning responsibility/blame
2. Closed advice
3. Defending
4. Directing, leading, taking control
5. Disagreeing
6. Feigned attention, interest, involvement
7. Giving literal responses
8. Inappropriate explaining/lecturing
9. Inappropriate interpreting
10. Inappropriate self-talk
11. Inappropriate use of humour
12. Insensitive probing
13. Interrogating, threatening
14. Introducing irrelevances
15. Labelling and diagnosing
16. Making aggressive statements
17. Making judgmental statements
18. Moralizing, preaching, patronizing
19. Prying
20. Rejection
21. Using denial
22. Using stereotyped language
23. Verbal reassurances.

INTERPERSONAL THEORY (*See also*: Hierarchy of human needs, Meyer, Adolf)

Formulated by Harry Stack Sullivan (1892–1949), an American neo-Freudian who studied psychiatry as the breakdown in interpersonal relationships.

Sullivan's contribution to the psychotherapy of schizophrenia is substantial. He asserted that such people are not damaged beyond hope.

His theory draws from psychoanalysis and Meyers psychobiology.

Anxiety, for Sullivan, is the principal disruptive force in interpersonal relationships and in living. We are the product of our real or fantasized interactions with others, not of our drives and conflicts.

The child needs others in order to develop psychologically and socially.

Personality is dynamic and not static. Throughout life it is constantly subject to change and modification.

IMPORTANT CONCEPTS

1. Personality development is influenced by one's efforts to fulfil the:

   A. *Biological needs*, which are food, shelter, the physical presence of others, and sexual expression.
   B. *Security needs*, which are financial, personal recognition, self-esteem, and the sense of power. Self-esteem, or self-respect, according to Sullivan, is a sense of power in dealing with others.

2. Tension responses:
   Response A. Infant tension shows as crying. This is likely to produce tension in the mother who responds with tenderness. The result is mutual reduction of tension.

   Security thus results from the infant's ability to involve another in the fulfilling of its needs, which leads to interpersonal competence.

Response B. Infant tension shows as crying. This is likely to produce tension in the mother who responds with anxiety. The anxiety is transmitted to the infant. The result is a mutual increase in tension. Anxiety both creates and reduces self-esteem. Example: If I were adequate, the baby wouldn't cry.

3. Anxiety is transmitted via an empathic linkage from mother to baby and is disproportionate to the actual need the baby is expressing. Anxiety is experienced as something unpleasant and uncomfortable, and is therefore capable of being revived subsequently when a similar need is felt.
4. Interactions (dynamism) may be:

   A. *Conjunctive* – for example, intimacy, which lead to tension reduction.
   B. *Disjunctive* – for example, aggression, which lead to increased tension.
   Self-dynamism or self-system is a pattern by which a person avoids anxiety, and by which self-esteem and the sense of security are met. Self-dynamism is enhancing oneself through the positive appraisal of others.

5. Security operations that function within self-dynamism are:

   A. *Apathy,* which redcuces the awareness of the need.
   B. *Somnolent detachment,* which reduces the tension effect of anxiety.
   C. *Sublimation* – (*see* main entry)
   D. *Selective inattention,* which is the most frequently used security operation. It deals only with approval-enhancing stimuli. Selective inattention may be useful and healthy. It may become pathological when it excludes from awareness stimuli that are essential for integration.
   E. *Dissociating processes,* which isolate large and important parts of living from the self-system and create dynamisms of difficulty, which are:

   (a) Obsessionalism (substitution and avoidance tendencies)
   (b) Crude emotions (anger, pride, envy, jealousy)
   (c) Paranoid dynamism (transfer of blame and projection).

6. Modes of experiencing:

   A. Protaxic are immature and exist, before language.
   B. Parataxic are immature and private.
   C. Syntaxic are mature and shared.

The syntaxic mode of thinking is:

(a) Logical.
(b) Sequential.
(c) Internally consistent.
(d) Modifiable.
(e) Verifiable.
(f) Valid by consensus.

All three modes of experiencing are important in developing learning skills. Arrest of A or B may result in pathology.

7. Developmental eras

A. The infant
(a) When needs are fulfilled, with relative freedom from anxiety, the infant internalizes the 'good mother' and 'good me'.
(b) Moderate degrees of anxiety lead to internalization of 'bad mother' and 'bad me'.
(c) Disruptive levels of anxiety may lead to internalization of 'not me', with dissociation and a defect in selective inattention and isolation of feelings and impulses.

B. The child
(a) Fusion into one person of 'good mother' or 'bad mother'.
(b) Adults, when they interfere with gratification, may appear as the child's enemies. This produces anxiety when the need for tenderness is paramount.

C. The juvenile
(a) Characterized by co-operation and compromise, though not at the expense of self-respect.
(b) Extreme anxiety is likely to interfere with workable compromise.

D. The preadolescent
Marked by the need for interpersonal intimacy, with acceptance of the need to enhance each other's self-esteem.

E. The adolescent
The needs of this period:
(a) Continuing, personal security which means freedom from anxiety.
(b) Intimacy, which means collaboration.
(c) Satisfaction of genital interest (felt as lust) in orgasm.
(d) Successful transition is marked by more ability to resolve conflicts, more skill in relationships, more awareness of social responsibility, standards and values, and working toward a career.

8. Therapy. The therapist is both observer and participant in therapy, and as such, influences and is influenced.

THE STAGES OF THERAPY

A. *Inception*. The contract is established, roles and expectations clarified.
B. *Reconnaissance*. Problem patterns are identified.
C. *Detailed enquiry*. The lengthy uncovering process.
D. *Termination*. Reaching toward established goals through strengthening and broadening of the self-system.

INTERPRETATION (*See also*: Insight, Transference)

Interpretation is the act of making clear in one language what has been expressed in another; the process of clarifying and elaborating something that is obscure.

The aim of therapeutic interpretation, to bring repressed material, by way of dream-work and free association, from the unconscious into the conscious and so facilitate insight.

Psychological interpretation, which is influenced by the therapist's model or method, involves verbal communication, dreams, visions, fantasy and metaphors, and involves the therapist in:

1. Understanding the material.
2. Communicating the understanding of the material in such a way that the client not only understands it but takes it on board.
3. Interpretations are taken on board when the client accepts their relevance and begins to see how to apply them.
4. Delivering the interpretation sensitively so as not to attack defence mechanisms brutally or prematurely.

Psychoanalytic therapists place great emphasis on the interpretation of transference. Freud maintained that interpretation of dream symbols is a model for all interpretation. Other models are less rigid.

In Jung's opinion, interpretations, particularly of dreams, should bring something new to consciousness, should not moralize, and should take account of the personal context of the client. The dream belongs exclusively to the dreamer. Interpretations relate only to the personal unconscious.

INTIMACY

The state of being closely familiar with another person, not necessarily of the opposite sex and not necessarily sexual.

Intimacy with at least one other person is generally regarded as an essential ingredient of a healthy and satisfying life.

The absence of an intimate relationship, the inability to share emotions, trust others, or make a commitment to a stable, lasting relationship, is often a significant cause of mental and/or physical distress and an indication of an intimacy disorder.

The capacity for intimacy fosters self-worth and a feeling of belonging.

Women seem more able than men to converse with more warmth and openness about intimate matters. Men, generally, define intimacy in terms of shared activities, such as sports. Men are also more selective in whom they confide on intimate topics. It is even suggested that many men are incapable of making intimate statements, even when it is desirable to do so.

Generally speaking, people, regardless of sex, feel more relaxed speaking openly to women rather than to men. This is due, possibly, to the socializing process within the family.

INTROJECTION (Defence mechanism) (*See also*: Ferenczi, Internalization, Identification, Projection)

Introjection is a major influence in the development of both ego and superego.

The term was introduced by Ferenczi to describe the way in which aspects of the outside world are internalized into the ego as fantasies or mental representations.

Introjection is similar to internalization and identification, and the opposite of projection.

Jung viewed introjection as a defence against separation or threatened separation.

Feelings may also be introjected – blame, for example.

Introjection helps to keep the person in touch with 'good' objects when separated from them, and so prevents, or minimizes anxiety. Introjection of 'bad' objects permits control over them.

INTROVERSION (*See also*: Extraversion, Myers–Briggs type indicator)

In Jung's typology, the opposite of extraversion, though the majority of people lie somewhere on the extraversion/introversion dimension, rather than either/or.

People more introverted than extraverted tend to make decisions somewhat independently of constraints and prodding from the situation, people or things around them. They are quiet, diligent at working alone, and socially reserved. They may dislike being interrupted while working and may tend to forget names and faces.

They are generally independent, are diligent, reflective, and prefer to work with ideas. They are careful of generalizations and think carefully before acting. They prefer quiet working conditions.

They are in danger of misunderstanding the external and are often misunderstood by others. They tend to avoid others and to be secretive. Because they take time to act, they often lose opportunities.

INTUITION (*See also*: Myers–Briggs type indicator)

An awareness that arises from within or beneath consciousness, rather than arising from teaching, reason, or logic. Self-deception is possible on account of the subjectivity of intuition.

Intuition is often associated with the feminine principle, the Yin of oriental psychology. Creativity, lateral thinking, core construct, gut reaction are synonymous with intuition. Intuition indicates where something came from and where it is going.

ISOLATION (Defence mechanism)

Isolation protects an individual from anxiety-provoking feelings and impulses. When isolation occurs, the associated feeling and impulse are pushed out of consciousness.

When isolation is total, the feeling and impulse will be totally repressed. The person is then able to view the idea (memory or fantasy) without the feelings attached to it.

If isolation is incomplete, partial awareness of impulses may break through in the form of disturbing compulsions to perform some violent action. Sufferers may be puzzled and disturbed at their compulsions.

Isolated people may be obsessed with images and thoughts of violence or destruction. In psychodynamic terms, isolation is viewed as a conflict between impulses and controlling defensive forces.

The personality of people who use isolation tends to be orderly and obsessively compulsive. They keep their feelings very controlled and remember events in fine detail. They often respond well to rational explanations.

The urgent need in therapy is to get such clients to tap into their feelings.

J

JACKSON, DONALD, DE AVILA (1920–1968) (*See also*: Double bind, Family therapy)

American physician, family and marital therapist, and major contributor to the development of communication theory.

Jackson studied the cyclical nature of schizophrenia, the relationship of patients to their relatives and the interaction between them, and believed that schizophrenia results from faulty communication.

The concepts most associated with Jackson are Systemic therapies and Homeostasis.

JANET, PIERRE (1859–1947)

French psychologist and neurologist who was influential in uniting psychology and the treatment of mental illness.

Janet studied hypnosis under Charcot and stressed the psychological factors in hypnosis. He also contributed to the understanding of neurosis, the classification of mental and emotional disorders, particularly anxiety, phobias, and abnormal behaviour.

His best-known work is the study of hysteria, from which arose the theory of the division of the mind into conscious and unconscious parts. His 'discovery' led to dispute with Freud; both claiming, as it were, the copyright.

In his work on hysteria he attempted to classify such diverse phenomena as paralysis, sleepwalking, and amnesia, on which he was an established author.

JASPERS, KARL THEODOR (1883–1969)

German philosopher and existentialist who originally studied law, then medicine and psychiatry. He was unorthodox in his approach to learning, and studied psychiatry at his own pace and in his own way.

He published the profound book, *General Psychopathology*, and later *Philosophy*.

He clashed with the Nazis (his wife was Jewish), and he lost his post as professor at Heidelberg.

After the Second World War he devoted his energies to rebuilding the university and helping to bring about a moral and political rebirth of the German people.

He felt that an acknowledgement of national guilt was a necessary condition for the moral and political rebirth of Germany.

He ended his academic days in Basle, Switzerland. At the time of his death he had published 30 books, and left behind him 30 000 handwritten pages.

JOHARI WINDOW (*See also*: Insight, Feedback, Self-disclosure)

A name coined from the names of the psychologists, Joseph Luft and Harry Ingham.

A model of four 'windows' to represent personality. Used to gain insight through feedback and self-disclosure.

The four windows

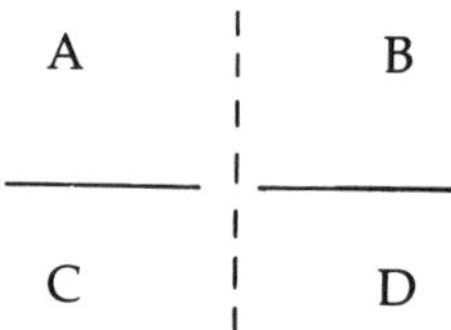

A – ARENA. KNOWN TO SELF AND OTHERS

1. Free and open exchange of information
2. Behaviour is public and freely available
3. The arena increases in size as trust grows.

B – BLIND SPOT. PERCEIVED BY OTHERS, HIDDEN FROM SELF

1. Self-awareness is lacking
2. Motives, feelings and behaviours perceived by others.
3. Communicated by what is said, and how
4. Communicated non-verbally.

C – FACADE. HIDDEN TO OTHERS, KNOWN TO SELF

1. Private and secret
2. Rarely disclosed
3. Fear of hurt, rejection, judgment.

D – UNKNOWN. HIDDEN FROM SELF AND FROM OTHERS

The realm of the unconscious and subconscious. Unconscious material is often hinted at through non-verbal language. The unconscious is made up of early childhood memories and feelings, latent potentialities, and unrecognized conflicts and complexes. It is possible to look – delicately – at subconscious material. Exploring truly conscious material is rarely appropriate except in specialized settings.

The internal boundaries of the windows are movable; up, down, or across. The extent to which the Blind spot and Facade are reduced, and the Arena enlarged, is entirely dependent upon the willingness to give and ask for feedback and to disclose. The size and shape of the Arena is determined by the balance between giving and soliciting feedback.

A LARGE ARENA SUGGESTS:

1. Behaviour that is open, above board, and not liable to be misinterpreted.
2. Other people do not have to make guesses.
3. Large Arenas are not necessary nor appropriate for every situation. Too large an Arena

may threaten casual relationships.

4. A fairly even balance between giving and soliciting feedback.

A LARGE BLIND SPOT SUGGESTS:

1. Someone who gives feedback and solicits very little.
2. A 'telling' style of communication.
3. May be highly critical, 'I speak my mind.'
4. Usually insensitive to feedback.
5. Rarely an effective listener.
6. Disclosures are out of touch, evasive or distorted.
7. Gives more feedback than solicits it.

A LARGE FACADE SUGGESTS:

1. Someone who asks questions, asks for opinions, gives little information or feedback.
2. Uses intellectualization as a defence.
3. Withholds feelings.
4. Solicits feedback but gives little.

A LARGE UNKNOWN SUGGESTS:

1. Someone who knows little about the deeper personal life.
2. May be the silent member of a group, the 'observer', the 'mystery man'.
3. A person surrounded by a shell.
4. One who says 'I learn more by listening'.
5. Not actively involved in a group.
6. Give little feedback and solicit little.
7. A small Arena is maintained at the expense of self-exploration and personal growth.

As data are moved from the Blind Spot and the Facade, the Arena is enlarged, so new material becomes available from the Unknown and the person experiences insight.

JUDGMENT (*See also*: Myers–Briggs type indicator)

The capacity to appraise, discriminate, and compare, and so arrive at a sound evaluation; to make reasonable decisions, with discernment, good sense and wisdom.

In counselling, discernment and discretion are valued, while moral judgment is considered to obstruct the client's ability to work toward insight and self-awareness.

Person-centred therapy embraces the principle of non-judgment, or non-evaluation, working toward the position where one's own values are suspended. There is the view that suspended values do influence the relationship even though they may not be voiced as verbal judgment.

K

KLEIN, MELANIE (1881–1960)

Born in Vienna, she lived most of her life in England and is linked with the Objects Relations School. Her interest in psychoanalysis arose from her time as a patient of Ferenczi, though she never trained in psychiatry.

Encouraged by Abraham, she developed her own system of child analysis and it is her contribution in child psychiatry for which she is mostly remembered. Play, she believed, is the child's symbolic way of controlling anxiety. She used free play with toys to gain insight into the fantasies, anxieties, and defences associated with the early years of life.

Klein's personality theory agrees with Freud's about the life and death instincts, and that inborn aggression is an extension of the death instinct. Oral sadism is where the death instinct is directed outward, giving rise to fantasies of the bad, devouring breast. These unconscious fantasies, from birth onward, become the origins of love and hate.

Other powerful, negative emotions, include:

1. Envy, which is derived from the fantasy of the wilfully withholding breast, finds expression in:

   A. Greed
   B. Penis envy
   C. Envy of the creativity of others
   D. Guilt over one's own creativity.

2. Jealousy develops from the Oedipus triangle. A third person is hated because that person takes the love and libidinal energy from the desired object. In Oedipal terms, the son directs hate at the father for stealing the mother's love, love that is rightfully his.

The 'good breast' is responsible for all positive, gratifying feelings associated with the life instinct, feelings that reinforce trust, and balance the life and death instincts.

Gratitude, the predominant emotion, allows the expression of trust and decreases greed. It is the origin of authentic generosity.

The term part object refers to parts of the person which are perceived by the infant, and related to as the 'whole'.

SOME MAJOR KLEINIAN CONCEPTS

1. *Anxiety*, the ego's expression of the death instinct, becomes fear of persecutory objects which, in turn, leads to fear of internalized persecutors.

   The major fears are Oral, the fear of being devoured, Anal, the fear of being controlled and poisoned, and Oedipal, the fear of castration.
2. *Introjection* and *Projection*. Both contribute to the growth of the ego through trust; and to ego defence through paranoid feelings. Which one is dominant depends on whether what is introjected or projected is perceived as good or bad.
3. *Splitting*. Characterizes the very young. It is the active separation, into good or bad, of experiences, perceptions and emotions linked to objects. Splitting interferes with the accurate perception of reality and nurtures denial. The opposite of splitting is synthesis. This takes place when the infant is able to distinguish part from whole objects.
4. *Internalization* of the good object is a prerequisite for the development of a healthy ego, firmly rooted in reality. A predominance of aggressive feelings works against a healthy ego. An ego that is based on unhealthy internalization leads to excessive idealization and to excessive splitting.
5. *Paranoid–schizoid position* – the first six months of life are characterized by:

   A. Splitting
   B. Idealization
   C. Denial
   D. Projective identification
   E. Part object relationships
   F. Persecutory fears about self-preservation.
6. *Depressive position* – the second six months of life are characterized by idealization of the good object to prevent destroying the object.

   Depressive idealization creates an overdependence on others in later stages of development.
7. *Superego*. Klein believed that the superego starts to develop within the second six months of life. A return to the paranoid–schizoid position may occur when excessive pressure from the superego prevents working through the depressive position.

   Split-off, and projected, bad objects are later introjected and form the basis of the superego. Sadism, once projected, is then reintrojected, resulting in guilt.

   The internalization of mainly bad objects is normally outweighed by internalization of good objects, though there is always some contamination by the bad objects.

   A perfectionist superego imposes the harsh demands of infantile virtues. A balanced superego responds realistically to demands for improvement on the one hand, and sublimation, on the other.
8. *The Oedipus complex*. In Kleinian theory the early stages of the complex develop from the first year of life. The desire in both sexes for the good breast becomes a desire

for the father's penis. Likewise the bad breast is displaced onto the bad penis.

When a boy perceives his father's penis to be bad, it makes a healthy father/son relationship difficult.

When the Oedipal relationship is not resolved, the boy is likely to develop sexual inhibitions and a fear of women. Castration fears arise from an oral-sadistic desire to destroy the penis.

For a girl, the good breast prepares the way for expecting a good penis. Intense oral aggression prepares the way for rejecting a positive Oedipal relationship with the mother. An Oedipus complex in a girl develops when the mother is perceived as possessing the father's penis. Penis envy arises from oral sadism, not from an envy of the male genitals. Envy of the opposite sex occurs in both sexes.

9. *Working-through* (*see also* main entry) of the depressive position consists of:

   A. Reparation (the origin of sublimation) is the mechanism of trying to repair damage done to a good object by expressing love and gratitude, and by so doing, preserving it.
   B. Reality testing increases as splitting decreases. Love from the mother accelerates reality testing.
   C. Ambivalence is the infant's awareness and acceptance of both love and hate toward the same object, with the eventual triumph of love over hate.
   D. Mourning in adult life reactivates the depressive position and guilt of infancy. In the latter, however, the mother is present to help the infant to work through toward wholeness.

10. *Fixation at the paranoid–schizoid position* may result in either A or B:

   A. Paranoid personality which combines:

   (a) Denial of reality
   (b) Excessive projective identification
   (c) Pathological splitting
   (d) Confusional states
   (e) Development of paranoia (fear of external persecutors)
   (f) Hypochondriasis.

   B. Schizoid personality which combines:

   (a) Shallow emotions
   (b) Limited capacity to tolerate guilt feelings
   (c) Tendency to experience objects as hostile
   (d) Withdrawal from object relations
   (e) Artificiality and superficiality in social adaptation.

11. *Fixation at the depressive position* may result in pathological mourning or the development of manic defences.

   A. Pathological mourning may lead to the development of a sadistic superego, which evokes extreme guilt and feelings that the whole world is empty of love.

   Pathological mourning is characterized by:

   (a) Cruelty
   (b) Demands for perfection

(c) Hatred of anything instinctual
(d) Despair
(e) Self-reproach
(f) Suicide may be an attempt to protect the good object by destroying the bad self
(g) Hypochondriacal delusions
(h) Fantasies of world destruction.

B. Manic defences include:

(a) Omnipotence, based on identification with an idealized good object, accompanied by a denial of reality
(b) Identification with the sadistic superego
(c) Introjection. Object hunger that can never be satisfied
(d) An exalted state of power
(e) Manic idealization; the merging of one's exalted self with idealized objects.

12. *Therapy*
Klein believed that analysis of children could protect them from serious guilt-producing impulses.
Klein favoured:

(a) Direct, immediate interpretations of the child's unconscious motivations.
(b) The analysis of the child's feelings, displaced from the parents, and transferred to the analyst.
(c) The analyst, from the very commencement, interprets the unconscious paranoid–schizoid and depressive fantasies within the transference.
(d) In interpreting play as symbolic expression of conflicts and anxieties, the analyst does not offer the child reassurance but works exclusively with the transference, in language the child can understand.

KRIS, ERNST (1900–1957) (*See also*: Ego)

Viennese artist who lived in London and America, and specialized in psychoanalysis and art.

One of the chief exponents of ego psychology, who believed that the ego thinks, perceives, and tests reality, all totally independently of the id. With Hartmann and Anna Freud he founded the publication, *Psychoanalytic Study of the Child*.

L

LABELLING

In its broad sense, to describe, classify, categorize and designate objects, and help us make sense and order of the world around. The term is also used to describe the process by which people are designated by some behaviour that society has called 'deviant'.

Labelling is a two-way process: the person so labelled has one set of responses; the person labelling has another set. Clusters of behaviours are attached to specific labels, or stereotypes; the role and its behaviours have to be learned and internalized.

People and society may derive gains from the labels and roles people are given and have accepted, i.e. the 'sick one'. Society may feel freed from a burden. Removing the label may itself be therapeutic, but new behaviours also have to be learned, as well as changing attitudes of others.

LACAN, JACQUES (1901–1981)

French, avant-garde, unconventional psychoanalyst and leader of the French Society of Psychoanalysis. He closely allied himself with Freud's teachings, writing, and practice.

Lacan became something of a cult figure in France, holding regular afternoon meetings in Paris, open to the general public.

LAING, R.D. (1927–1989) (*See also*: Alienation, Existential therapy)

Scottish existential psychiatrist of the radical school of therapy.

According to Laing:

1. We become alienated from our life experiences.
2. We have come to understand ourselves by relying on external criteria and appearances.
3. We are alienated from ourselves.

Laing questions our concept of sanity. The majority of us, by virtue of our alienation from self, are taken to be sane because we act like everyone else. This 'collective madness' is what we call sanity.

Radical (Laingian) therapy emphasizes the recovering of the wholeness of being human through the relationship between them.

LATENCY PERIOD

In psychoanalytic literature, a period of sexual development between the age of 4 or 5 years, and the beginning of adolescence, separating infantile from normal sexuality. During this waiting time memories and wishes remaining from the earlier infantile period are repressed. The latency period is marked by an absence of any great sexual development.

Some psychoanalysts, Erikson for example, who focus less on sexual development, point to the great social and cognitive developments of this period.

The development of social skills within the education system may provoke the development of new inferiorities.

LATENT AND MANIFEST CONTENT

Latent content refers to repressed ideas and wishes that are expressed indirectly in a dream. The latent content is revealed through decoding and interpreting the symbols and their significance to the dreamer. It is as if the latent content is the original draft of a document, which does not pass the censor, and has to be redrafted.

The redrafting of the latent content is the 'dreamwork', and what emerges is the 'manifest' content, which is acceptable, remembered, and reported. Dream interpretation is the reverse of dreamwork, because it uncovers the true meanings of the latent content. The latent content is a wish, unacceptable to the waking ego, that is fulfilled in the dream. Because it is unacceptable it has to be disguised.

LEARNED HELPLESSNESS

A term introduced by Seligman, derived from the response of dogs to inescapable stress, and related to depression in humans.

After prolonged stress, the dogs became inactive and submissive, lost appetite and failed to escape from electric shocks, from which they had previously known how to escape.

The learned helplessness model of depression maintains that when people are faced with situations, often in childhood, the outcome of which they have no control over, they learn the futility of trying to respond.

The inference is that such people become victims of circumstance, and as such cannot be held responsible for what happens to them.

They learn to exploit their weaknesses and complaints, in order to force others to do something for them.

This behaviour drives them deeper into the darkness of depression and isolates them still further from others.

Every manipulation that results in increased isolation reinforces the negative view they hold of themselves.

LEARNING STYLES (*See also*: Discovery learning)

Not everyone learns in the same way. A knowledge of different learning styles will give counsellors an increased awareness of how to facilitate interaction.

Honey and Mumford identified four learning styles:

1. Activist
2. Reflector
3. Theorist
4. Pragmatist

LEARNING HAS TAKEN PLACE WHEN PEOPLE:

1. Know something they did not know earlier, and can show it, or
2. Are able to do something they were not able to do before.

CHARACTERISTICS OF THE STYLES:

1. Activist
   A. Flexible and open-minded
   B. Happy to have a go
   C. Happy to be exposed to new situations
   D. Optimistic about anything new and, therefore, unlikely to resist change.
2. Reflector
   A. Thorough and methodical
   B. Thoughtful
   C. Good at listening and assimilating information
   D. Rarely jumps to conclusions.
3. Theorist
   A. Logical 'vertical' thinkers
   B. Rational and objective
   C. Good at asking probing questions
   D. Disciplined approach.
4. Pragmatist
   A. Keen to test things out in practice
   B. Practical, down to earth, realistic
   C. Business-like; gets to the point
   D. Technique-oriented.

Activists like to try what is novel, new or different. They are generally flexible and open-minded, with a tendency to the immediately obvious action without thinking.

Reflectors require time to review the experience. They are careful, thorough and methodical, with a tendency to hold back from direct participation.

Theorists need a sound theoretical base. They are logical vertical thinkers, with a low tolerance for uncertainty, disorder, and ambiguity.

Pragmatists work out when and how to apply what has been learned. They are practical and keen to test things out, with little interest in theory or basic principles.

No one person is all of one and none of the others. Most people have a preference for working with one particular learning style.

LEFT AND RIGHT BRAIN

The left and right hemispheres of the brain specialize in different activities.

THE 'LEFT, LOGICAL, SYSTEMATIC BRAIN':

1. Controls movements on the right side of the body.
2. Is more concerned with 'active doing'.

'Left-brain' cognitive style is predominantly concerned with:

1. Analysis and deduction
2. Convergent thinking
3. Facts, data, figures
4. The end product
5. Structure
6. Logical, sequential, linear thought
7. The mathematics mode
8. Order
9. Processing
10. Rationality
11. Reducing problems to workable segments

12. Science and technology
13. A step-by-step precision
14. Using a highly sequential approach
15. Verbal, literal, concrete language
16. Working to well-defined plans.

'Left-brain' language patterns

1. 'Why don't we look at the facts.'
2. 'These data show us that . . .'
3. 'We must work to specific objectives.'
4. 'Here is what I think – A, B, C, . . .'
5. 'You haven't explained yourself.'
6. 'Explain the logic in that.'
7. 'This is what you do – 1, 2, 3 . . .'
8. 'I'll have to work it out carefully.'

'Left-brain' non-verbal patterns

1. Creates endless lists
2. Puts everything down in strict time order
3. Spends much time on detail
4. Must get one point clear before moving on.

Some typical 'left-brain' occupations

1. Accountant
2. Administrator
3. Computer programmer
4. Engineer
5. Personnel specialist
6. Production manager
7. Purchasing agent
8. Systems analyst.

THE 'RIGHT, INTUITIVE BRAIN':

1. Controls movements on the left side of the body.
2. Is more concerned with the whole, not parts.

'Right-brain' cognitive style is predominantly concerned with:

1. Abstract topics
2. Artistic expression
3. Body image
4. Concentrating on ideas and feelings
5. Constructive tasks
6. Crafts
7. Creativity
8. Divergent, global thinking
9. Emotions
10. Focusing on the process, not the outcome
11. Using experience
12. Non-verbal knowledge through images
13. Perception
14. Prayer, meditation, mysticism
15. Problem-solving
16. Perceiving
17. Remembering faces
18. Spontaneity
19. What is visual
20. Workings symbols and fantasy, dreams
21. Working with metaphors and imagery
22. Working with opposites
23. Working with the unknown.

'Right-brain' language patterns

1. 'My gut feeling is . . .'
2. 'I sense that . . .'
3. 'Can't we look at the whole picture?'
4. 'Let's look at things on global terms.'
5. 'The solution is really quite simple.'
6. 'Common sense tells me . . .'
7. 'I know the answer, but how?'

'Right-brain' non-verbal patterns

1. Uses a lot of visual aids
2. Becomes agitated over data

3. Often appears to be disorganized
4. 'Thinks' with the eyes
5. Displays the problem graphically.

Some typical 'right-brain' occupations

1. Advertising agent
2. Counsellor/therapist
3. Graphic artist
4. Marketing manager.

Left-handed (right brain) activities are also associated with the feminine principle (Jung).

For the Mojave Indians, the left hand is the passive, maternal side of the person; the right, the active father.

IN JUNGIAN TYPOLOGY

The left brain is more associated with extraversion, sensing, thinking and judgment. The right brain is more associated with introversion, intuition, feelings and perception. For left-handed people the specialization is not so consistent. Even in right-handed people it is not an 'either or'.

Damage to the left hemisphere often interferes with language ability. Damage to the right hemisphere is likely to cause disturbance to spatial awareness of one's own body. Damage to the left brain may prove disastrous to an author, scientist, mathematician, but may not prove so damaging to a musician, craftsman or artist.

The hemispheres have a partnership function. A poet, using deep feelings, imagery and metaphor, draws on the right brain, and the left for the words to express what the right side creates.

The hemispheres may also be antagonistic, when, for example, the left hemisphere becomes too aggressive, trying to solve everything with logic and analysis, intuition and feelings are subdued.

LEWIN, KURT (1890–1947) (*See also*: Group training, Force field analysis)

German social psychologist of the Gestalt school who later resided in the USA. He attempted to apply mathematics to psychological and sociological phenomena under the name of Field theory which has had an influence on group work.

He was professor of child psychology at the University of Iowa until 1945, and director of the group dynamics research centre at the Massachusetts Institute of Technology, Cambridge until his death.

LIBIDO (*See also*: Eros, Instincts, Thanatos)

A psychoanalytic concept originally applied to sexual desires. Later it became associated with 'vital impulse' or 'vital (mental) energy'. Freud regarded the ego as a reservoir that supplies objects with libido and reabsorbs it from them, though its source is the id.

For Jung, libido is 'psychic energy', the intensity, or value of a psychic process. It has no moral, aesthetic or intellectual value. Energy can never disappear; it is dynamic, it always produces something.

Psychological conflict can be thought of as a disturbance in the flow of physical energy, a natural process if one thinks of conflict in relation to nature. In nature there is a continuous cycle of death and rebirth.

When the life and death instincts are thought of in this way, the conflict becomes more understandable.

LIFE TASKS

An individual (Adlerian) psychology term, meaning the basic challenges of life, which are:

1. Living in society
2. Working
3. Sex
4. Spiritual growth
5. Self-identity.

LIFESPAN PSYCHOLOGY (*See also*: Erikson, Erik)

Lifespan psychology is the study of people throughout life. Erikson, building on the work of earlier theorists, is the one name most associated with lifespan psychology.

Psychological development does not necessarily parallel physical maturity. Physical maturation is predictable within reasonable time limits, within specific societies and cultures.

Erikson's stages, or 'nuclear-crises', of the psychosocial development model:

Stage	Approximate age
Basic trust versus mistrust	Infancy
Autonomy versus shame and doubt	Toddler
Initiative versus guilt	Preschool
Industry versus inferiority	School age
Identity versus role confusion	Adolescence and young adulthood
Intimacy versus isolation	Young adulthood
Productivity versus stagnation	Middle adulthood
Ego integrity versus despair	Later adulthood

Some broad boundaries of life (in British culture) are:

1. Child labour
2. Juvenile marriage
3. Occurrence of the menopause
4. Pensionable age.

Bernice Neugarten's work extends Erikson's model and contributes to the understanding of the changes in middle age. Lifespan psychology now has child development studies at one end and gerontology at the other.

Lifespan psychology has seen major contributions in:

1. Relationships between generations
2. Cognitive development
3. Age and the social system
4. Social policy
5. Occupational choice.

LISTENING (*See also*: Interpersonal skills)

Sensitive, active listening is an important way to bring about personality changes in attitudes and the way we behave toward ourselves and others. When we listen, people tend to become:

1. More emotionally mature
2. More open to experiences
3. Less defensive
4. More democratic
5. Less authoritarian.

When we are listened to we listen to ourselves with more care and are able to express thoughts and feelings more clearly.

Self-esteem is enhanced through active listening because the threat of having one's ideas and feelings criticized is greatly reduced. Because we do not have to defend, we are able to see ourselves for what we truly are, and are then in a better position to change.

Listening, and responding to what we hear, is influenced by our own frame of reference. Therapeutic listening is also influenced by one's theoretical model.

POOR LISTENING HABITS IDENTIFIED

1. Not paying attention
2. Pretend-listening
3. Listening but not hearing the meaning
4. Rehearsing what to say
5. Interrupting the speaker in mid-sentence
6. Hearing what is expected
7. Feeling defensive, expecting an attack
8. Listening for something to disagree with.

THINGS TO AVOID

1. When we try to get people to see themselves as we see them, or would like to see them, this is control and direction, and is more for our needs than for theirs. The less we need to evaluate, influence, control, and direct, the more we enable ourselves to listen with understanding.
2. When we respond to the demand for decisions, actions, judgments and evaluations, or agreeing with someone against someone else we are in danger of losing our objectivity. The surface question usually is the vehicle that has a deeper need than its passenger.
3. When we shoulder responsibility for other people, we remove from them the right to be active participants in the problem-solving process. Active involvement releases energy, it does not drain it from the other person. Active participation is a process of thinking with people instead of thinking for or about them.
4. Passing judgments – critical or favourable. Judgments are generally patronizing.
5. Platitudes and clichés demonstrate either disinterest or a verbal poverty.
6. Verbal reassurances are insulting, for they demean the problem.

THINGS TO DO

1. Get into the person's frame of reference.
2. Listen for total meaning, which is content and feelings. Both require hearing and responding to. In some instances the content is far less important than the feeling for which the words are but vehicles. We must try to remain sensitive to the total meaning the message has to the speaker:

   What is she/he trying to tell me?
   What does this mean to this person?
   How does this person see this situation?

3. Note all cues:
   Not all communication is verbal. Truly sensitive listening notes:

   (a) Body posture
   (b) Breathing changes
   (c) Eye movements
   (d) Facial expression
   (e) Hand movements
   (f) Hesitancies
   (g) Inflections
   (h) Mumbled words
   (i) Stressed words.

WHAT WE COMMUNICATE BY LISTENING

We communicate interest in the importance of the speaker, respect for the speaker's thoughts, not necessarily agreement, non-evaluation and we validate the person's worth.

Listening demonstrates, it does not tell. Listening catches on. Just as anger is normally met with anger, so listening encourages others to listen. Listening is a constructive behaviour and the person who consistently listens with understanding is the person most likely to be listened to.

RESPONDING AS A PART OF LISTENING:

Passive listening, without responding, is deadening and is demeaning.

We should never assume that we have really understood until we can communicate that understanding to the full satisfaction of the other person. Effective listening hinges on constant clarification to establish true understanding.

EFFECTIVE LISTENERS:

1. Put the talker at ease
2. Limit their own talking
3. Are attentive
4. Remove distractions
5. Get inside the talker's frame of reference
6. Are patient, and don't interrupt
7. Watch for feeling words
8. Are aware of their own biases
9. Listen to the paralinguistics
10. Are aware of body language.

LISTENING WITH THE 'THIRD EAR'

The phrase 'listening with the third ear' was coined by Theodor Reik to point up the quality of psychotherapy, where active listening goes beyond the five senses. The 'third ear' hears what is said between sentences and without words, what is expressed soundlessly, what the speaker feels and thinks.

PRINCIPLES FOR THIRD-EAR LISTENING

1. Have a reason or purpose for listening
2. Suspend judgment
3. Resist distractions
4. Wait before responding
5. Repeat verbatim
6. Rephrase the message accurately
7. Identify important themes
8. Reflect content and search for meaning
9. Be ready to respond.

WE CONVEY NON-ACCEPTANCE BY:

1. Advising, giving solutions: 'Why don't you . . .'
2. Evaluating, blaming: 'You are definitely wrong . . .'
3. Interpreting, analysing: 'What you need is . . .'
4. Lecturing, informing: 'Here are the facts . . .'
5. Name-calling, shaming: 'You are stupid . . .'
6. Ordering, directing: 'You have to . . .'
7. Praising, agreeing: 'You are definitely right . . .'
8. Preaching, moralizing: 'You ought to . . .'
9. Questioning, probing: 'Why did you . . .'
10. Sympathizing, supporting: 'You'll be OK . . .'
11. Warning, threatening: 'You had better not . . .'
12. Withdrawing, avoiding 'Let's forget it . . .'

LOCUS OF CONTROL

A general term in social psychology, first introduced by Phares and developed by Julian Rotter, a social learning theorist.

Locus of control describes the ways in which we attribute responsibility for events that occur in our lives to:

1. Factors within ourselves and within our control, which include abilities, efforts, achievements, self-direction.
2. Factors outside ourselves and outside our control, which include fate, luck, chance, the influence of powerful people.

Externals are people who believe they have little or no control or influence over what happens to them.

Internals are people who believe that they do have an influence over the direction their lives take.

SOME AREAS OF DIFFERENCE

People with high external scores:

A. Often have unrealistic ambitions
B. May not always cope well with the demands of reality
C. Job satisfaction tends to be low
D. Do not always take care of equipment for which they are responsible
E. Often rely on coercive power and threats to get things done
F. Do not always handle delegation well.

People with high internal scores:

A. Are usually co-operative, self-reliant, and knowledgeable about their work.
B. Have a high sense of self-direction for their private lives and careers
C. Adapt well to change and new practices
D. Tend to pick people with superior or equal ability as partners
E. Believe in delegation.

When we fail to exercise control over our environment, we do not experience the psychological success that enables us to feel satisfied with ourselves.

HOW LOCUS OF CONTROL IS DEVELOPED

1. Child-rearing
   A. Externals, punishment, withdrawal of affection, denial of privileges, and overprotection
   B. Internals, predictable standards, fair discipline, democratic atmosphere, independence and appropriate responsibility, with a belief in self.
2. Social discrimination
   Minimal power either through class, race, or colour is more likely to lead to external orientation.
3. Prolonged incapacitation
   Long-term physical disability, may lead to external orientation.

INDIVIDUAL CHARACTERISTICS

Internals

A. Achievement oriented
B. Low anxiety levels
C. Not usually dogmatic
D. Generally trusting, not suspicious of others
E. Generally self-confident and insightful
F. Liable to resort to self-blaming behaviour
G. Generally perceive authority figures as encouraging, constructive, and supportive and operating within realistic standards

H. Extreme internals may be self-punishing.

Externals

Their characteristics are, to some degree, the opposites of the internals.

A. Not so ready to accept responsibility or blame for outcomes over which they feel they have no control.
B. Extreme externals tend to be passive in the face of difficulties.

CHANGING THE LOCUS

Any learned behaviour can be unlearned.

Change is facilitated through individual or group training programmes which concentrate on developing self-awareness and working toward new behaviours. Attitude change is never easy or quick. Sometimes it is painful and difficult. Where change is desired, and when it is entered upon willingly, and achieved with sensitivity, it can be dramatic and very rewarding.

LOGOTHERAPY

Viktor Frankl (1905–) a Viennese neurologist and psychologist and founder of the school of Logotherapy or existential analysis. He was imprisoned in German concentration camps between 1942 and 1945. He saw the meaning of his life as helping others to see a meaning in their lives.

Frankl's method of psychotherapy, sometimes referred to as the 'third Viennese school' (Freud and Adler being the first two) focuses on the meaning of human existence as well as one's search for such a meaning.

THE CONCEPTS:

1. *Freedom of the will.* In spite of physical and psychological restraints, we are free to stand against whatever circumstances confront us. We all have the potential to rise above even the most adverse conditions.
2. *The will to meaning.* To find and to fulfil meaning and purpose is fact, and we are all required to find and respond to this fact. To discover the meaning in itself produces a sense of fulfilment.
3. *The meaning of life.* Each of us has to find our own unique meaning of life.

   Therapy involves helping clients face the fact that while some circumstances may be changed, others may never be. Finding and responding to the meaning of life will then require an acceptance of whatever is involved in accepting change and also accepting what cannot be changed.

Every client should be approached 'holistically', mentally, physically, emotionally, socially, and spiritually. To gain fulfilment means to go beyond self-actualization, to become 'other-directed' and accountable.

Existential frustration refers to the individual's sense of meaninglessness. Existential vacuum refers to the emptiness that results from existential frustration. People can be helped to move out of their existential vacuum by finding meaning through love, work, suffering and death.

While Logotherapy, as an intervention, has characteristics of both psychoanalysis and spiritual counselling, it is neither. Therapy concentrates on examining the person in terms of responsibility. It does not deal directly with symptoms but with the person's attitude toward them. Logotherapy does not encourage homeostasis, it encourages tension, struggle and striving for some goal that is worthy of the person.

LONELINESS (*See also*: Existential therapy, Intimacy)

Loneliness is a personal, subjective experience of discomfort, distress, and pain resulting from the lack of intimate relationships. We are likely to feel lonely where there is an unacceptable gap between our expectation and the reality of our interaction.

Behaviourists consider loneliness to be a deficiency of quantity and type of social reinforcement.

Loneliness is associated with many psychological, physical, and social conditions. Many people feel ashamed to admit to being lonely.

Loneliness is characterized by:

1. Apathy
2. Distress
3. Emptiness as 'vast as a frozen wilderness'
4. Feeling of drifting, without rudder or line
5. Futility
6. Helplessness
7. Lack of concentration
8. Lack of motivation
9. Oversensitivity
10. Restlessness
11. Suspicion
12. Withdrawal
13. Worn-out feeling.

LONELINESS IS OFTEN PRECIPITATED BY:

1. Age
2. Disability
3. Extreme introversion
4. Infirmity
5. Isolation through environment
6. Isolation through loss of partner
7. Low self-esteem
8. Overdependence
9. Poor social skills
10. Rigidity of personality
11. Self-deprecating trait
12. Shyness
13. Single parent.

Loneliness may be coped with through denial. Social contact may be devalued, and a refuge sought in work, social activities, or addiction.

The aim of psychotherapy is to help the client live with the deep loneliness which lies at the heart of existence. Counselling should not propel the client into establishing relationships which may simply be perpetuating the denial.

M

MANDALA (*See also*: Individuation)

Hindu term for 'circle', instrument, ritual, or emblem, found all over the Orient. Mandalas are in the form of geometric diagrams, and are used to aid contemplation and concentration.

A mandala may be produced in sand in coloured threads or dust, painted on paper, or created in three dimensions.

A mandala is a mental image built up in the imagination. No one mandala is the same as another, because each is a projected image, the inner world of the creator.

The basic components of a mandala are geometric figures, counterbalanced and concentric, formed around the 'centre', which is suggested but never visually depicted.

Everyday examples of mandalas are a snow flake, or the human eye, with the pupil surrounded by the iris.

OTHER EXAMPLES OF MANDALAS:

1. Wheel of the universe
2. Mexican 'Great calendar stone'
3. Lotus flower
4. Mythical flower of gold
5. The rose
6. Labyrinth
7. Temples and cathedrals
8. Mosaic floors.

Jung believed that the spontaneous production of a mandala in dreamwork is a significant step in the person's journey toward individuation, the integration of hitherto unconscious (personal and archetypal) material by the conscious self. Mandalas are useful to induce relaxation and to get in touch with the right brain functions.

MARATHON GROUPS (*See also*: Encounter groups)

A part of the human potential movement: an intensive kind of encounter group. Such a group normally takes place over a period of time between 24 and 48 hours.

The major goal of a marathon group is confrontation and feedback; deliberately to strip away from people their ordinary defensive behaviour so that they are able to look at themselves more genuinely than they might ordinarily, in order that they might:

1. Relate to one another with integrity, authenticity, openness, and non-manipulatively and to 'level' with one another.
2. Be enabled to take the experience of open and levelling communicating with them into their significant relationships.

The emphasis is on the 'here and now plus'. The 'plus' is that during the life of the marathon, people learn to explore their past as a result of some interaction in the now.

A common arrangement is for 12–18 people to participate, usually with two co-therapists. The marathon may be recorded on video, to be replayed in the follow-up sessions, usually two months afterward.

MARTYR ATTITUDE

The martyr attitude is based on the belief that sorrows and troubles are evil machinations heaped upon the defenceless heads of suffering saints. Martyrs will invariably use the concepts of religious duty and spiritual living as flights from reality.

Behaviourally they shoulder other people's burdens and then complain to make sure that everyone around commiserates with them. The burdens of others weigh them down, and they experience little joy or peace.

Martyrs are subservient and humble and create an impression of everlasting goodness, sweetness, and light. Were the Inquisition to return, they would be the first to be burned at the stake. They often need to enjoy poor health; in a curious way it makes them feel 'good'.

Counselling, even of the most intense sort, is difficult. What martyrs gain from being ill is more than they would gain from being well. So identifying the gains and losses is a positive step along the road.

MASLOW, ABRAHAM (1908–1970)

(*See also*: Hierarchy of human needs, Humanistic psychology)

American-born Jew who became an influential figure in humanistic psychology and humanistic psychotherapy.

Maslow is probably most known for his hierarchy of human needs related to motivation and problem-solving work on self-actualization and peak experiences.

He was active in the development of the human potential movement and the founding of the Esalen Institute in California.

McGREGOR, DOUGLAS

McGregor, an industrial psychologist, used a behavioural science approach to try to improve productivity in organizations. He suggested that a manager's effectiveness, or ineffectiveness, lay in the very subtle and frequently unconscious effects of basic assumptions about people. A manager's assumptions have a direct effect on his or her managerial behaviour.

A manager with a strong tendency toward Theory-X will be geared toward direction, planning, organizing, close supervision and control of the work to be done. This person will monitor employee behaviour closely.

A manager with a strong tendency toward Theory-Y will be geared toward exploiting potential, getting staff involved in the planning process, in problem-solving and in the control of the work. This person will be more of a coach and facilitator.

Theory-X manager believes that people, generally:

1. Do not like to exert themselves, and try to work as little as possible
2. Avoid responsibility
3. Are not interested in achievement
4. Are incapable of directing their own behaviour
5. Are indifferent to organizational needs
6. Prefer to be directed by others
7. Avoid making decisions whenever possible
8. Cannot be trusted or depended upon
9. Need to be closely supervised and controlled
10. Are motivated at work by money and gains
11. Rarely change as they mature.

Theory-Y manager believes that people, generally:

1. Work hard toward objectives to which they are committed
2. Assume responsibility within these commitments
3. Have a strong desire to achieve
4. Are capable of directing their own behaviour
5. Want their organization to succeed
6. Are not passive and submissive and prefer to make decisions about their own work
7. Will make decisions within their commitments
8. If trusted and depended on, keep their end of the bargain
9. Need general support and help at work
10. Are able to change and develop.

Some managers are polarized, but most have a mixture of Theory-X and Theory-Y attitudes. Theory-Y is not a 'soft option'. It places responsibility fair and square on the individual.

METAPHOR (*See also*: Imagery, Left and Right brain)

A figure of speech, an indirect method of communication, by which two distinctly separate elements are brought together in comparison to form a new meaning. Where an abstract concept is expressed by means of analogy.

Metaphors abound in everyday conversation: the arms of a chair; the legs of a table; a sparkling personality; rivers of blood. The ability to use metaphors is a right brain activity.

The therapist needs to be able to decode the client's metaphors and so assist the development of insight. In the same way, the client needs help to understand the metaphors used by the therapist.

The difference between a symbol and a metaphor is, the symbol represents something else, while a metaphor is something else.

Interpretation of metaphors is central to psychoanalysis. It is possible to work within the metaphor, rather than tackle it directly. The use of a metaphor is useful when working with resistance, because it is indirect.

Metaphors, along with myths, parables, and symbols are used in the process of transformation, of metamorphosis, for example:

1. See/ovum – womb state;
2. Larva – separation, ego development;
3. Chrysalis – intermediate stage of growth;
4. Imago – fully unfolded being that is able to move in other dimensions.

The unconscious speaks from the collective unconscious to the conscious in symbols and analogies.

TEN CLASSICAL METAPHORS

1. From dream-sleep to awakening
2. From illusion to realization
3. From darkness to enlightenment
4. From imprisonment to liberation
5. From fragmentation to wholeness
6. From separation to oneness
7. From being on a journey to arriving at the destination
8. From being in exile to coming home
9. From seed to flowering tree
10. From death to rebirth.

MNEMONICS

The general name applied to memory aids. The principle is to enable recall of material by attaching what is to be learned to something familiar. The most effective mnemonics are simple.

Rhymed verse is an example – for remembering the number of days in the months. A well-known house – a topical mnemonic – may be used and, using imagery, to attach something new to various parts of the house, rooms, and furniture. Key words and peg words are two other systems.

Whatever system is used, learning requires effort, and frequent recall is necessary to 'fix ' the new to the established.

MOURNING (*See also*: Dying – stages of, Grief)

The period of time that follows a bereavement, which allows the expression of grief through accepted rituals. Mourning follows bereavement, is accompanied by grief and may or may not be followed by attachment to a new object.

Mourning is distinguished from grief in that it involves physiological and psychological processes. Mourning is more to do with the customs and traditions of a particular culture or society.

Grief and mourning do not necessarily occur at the same time, but for some, a period of ritualized mourning aids the grieving process. The mourning for a spouse is the loss most frequently ritualized in most societies. Mourning rituals are frequently linked with religious observance and practice.

'Operational mourning' and 'forced mourning' are two techniques used to help people convert morbid or arrested grief into a more normal mourning process.

MOURNING AND BURIAL CUSTOMS

Mourning customs are influenced by beliefs about life and death that are passed down through the generations. Religion is concerned with questions about mortality and immortality. All the major religions have a belief system that influences the way the rituals of burial and subsequent mourning are carried out.

Central to the Christian belief is the hope of resurrection. At the same time there must be an acknowledgement of the reality of the grief of parting.

The funeral will usually take place at a church or chapel, followed by a short committal at the grave-side or the crematorium.

The choice of flowers, procession and headstone is a matter of family choice, in contrast with several generations ago when the ritual was more predictable. Mourning clothes are also a matter of choice.

Normally there is some sort of social gathering as farewell. The role of the funeral director has become more prominent in recent years.

The basic belief of the Hindu religion is that the cremated body returns to its elements of fire, water, air and earth, and is thus reunited with God. The eldest son lights the funeral pyre, while mantras and sacred texts are recited by the priest.

Then follows a period of ritual where gifts of food are left for the soul of the departed. When this period is over, the bones of the deceased may be buried.

Hindus believe in reincarnation (transmigration), which is the rebirth of the soul in one or more successive existences, which may be human, animal, or in some instances vegetable.

The basis of Judaism is the first five books of the Old Testament. Death and mourning is highly ritualized. The funeral will take place within three days of death, but not on the Sabbath or on a festival day.

The body is dressed in a simple white garment and is never left unattended. Burial is the norm but some non-orthodox Jews living in other countries will permit cremation.

A seven-day period of formal mourning (Shivah) is observed after the death of a close relative.

Prayers are said, candles are lit, family and friends will visit and bring gifts of food. Though normal life will be resumed after Shivah, certain social activities are not resumed until 30 days have passed.

The followers of Islam believe that the one God was revealed through the prophet Muhammad. When a Muslim dies the body is turned to face Mecca. Death for the Muslim is but a parting for a short space of time, so prolonged grief is not encouraged.

The body is washed and wrapped in clean white sheets and buried shortly after death. Prayers are said before the burial.

Sikhs believe in one God and the equality of humankind. They also believe in reincarnation. The body is dressed in white by the family, prayers are said, then cremation takes place. Prayers and the reading of sacred scriptures continue for a further 10 days. The death of an elderly person is not a time of sadness and is usually followed by feasting and rejoicing.

Buddha is seen not so much as a god, but as a model for life. For the Buddhist, belief is demonstrated by good behaviour. Buddhists believe that the qualities of the deceased are reincarnated to become the 'germ of unconsciousness' in the womb of a mother. A monk leads the cremation service.

People of other world religions, living in an alien society, may observe compromised rituals instead of orthodox observances.

Rituals help the grieving person to make some sense of the experience, within a socially accepted framework;

it allows for a sharing of the experience and for eventual reintegration. All of this may not be so easily achieved where traditions have been eroded as in many Western societies.

MULTI-CULTURAL ISSUES

Cross-cultural counselling is similar in many ways to cross-gender counselling. Counselling and psychotherapy have their roots in white cultures, and it is possible that this way of relating is not readily accepted by people from different cultures.

However well-versed and aware we are, our counselling could benefit from a study of three important factors.

Firstly, we could learn from our clients how the history of their own culture influences them now. We also need to have explored our own cultural influences and recognized how our attitudes, beliefs, prejudices, stereotypes, and judgments influence our interactions.

Secondly, we must be prepared to take on board what our clients say of their experiences of discrimination, exploitation, stereotyping, and that indefinable but palpable phenomenon, 'awkwardness', and 'joking', and how these affect them.

Discrimination applies not only to people of different colours; many other groups of people are also subjected to as much prejudice and discrimination as people from Africa.

Thirdly, however self-aware, it is only as we become involved in cross-cultural counselling, that we will truly be able to explore our own values and attitudes toward people from different cultures.

The major influences that make for cross-cultural difficulties in counselling are language, education, religion, gender, values, beliefs, and attitudes.

Language unites people on the one hand and separates them on the other, in a way more powerful than even skin colour does.

Language conveys thoughts. Thinking is any cognitive or mental manipulation of ideas, images, symbols, words, propositions, memories, concepts, precepts, beliefs, or intentions.

Concepts are structured in hierarchies, with increasing complexity the more the original idea is broken down into properties. Conceptual thought often creates difficulty in cross-cultural counselling.

People for whom English is not their first language often have to translate what they have heard into their own language and then retranslate into English before replying. They understand the meanings of broad concepts but not every property in the hierarchy.

This difficulty is similar to two people listening to a piece of music. The one may hear only the melody; the other hears all the notes of both melody and harmony.

The way people from other cultures respond in counselling is moderated by the length of time they have spent in the new culture. Skin colour, or indeed accent (though accent is more open to moderation) are not reliable guides to how a person will respond. Many people with different skin colours are in fact second, third and fourth-generation residents of this country. In every respect they would respond as anyone else.

Methods of education vary from culture to culture. People who have come through an education system where discussion is the norm, are generally more able to deal with sophisticated concepts.

A person (no matter of what culture) who has learned mainly by rote, usually experiences difficulty handling sophisticated concepts. So it is necessary for the counsellor to be sensitively alert to the cues given out that something has not been understood.

'Talk and chalk' and rote learning are the methods of an authoritarian, obedience-dominated, system of education. An outcome of the authoritarian approach is that experiential learning is difficult.

People who have been educated under a heavily authoritarian system expect to be told what to do and what to learn. Many such people cannot see the relevance of experiential work; they have little by which to measure their learning. When they can leave a session with pages of notes or dictation, they feel satisfied that the session has been productive.

This has implications in counselling. Apart from the restriction of conceptual thinking, a relationship of equality in which the client works toward finding solutions is an alien concept to many, unproductive and time-wasting. At the same time, the fundamentals of accepted counselling practice conflict with the client's value system.

Religion has a profound bearing on values and beliefs of both client and counsellor, on the style of education and relationships with the opposite gender.

Many people have been saddled with a double authority: an authoritarian style of teaching within a religious system of education. This atmosphere of traditionalism supports the belief that women are inferior to men. Males and females from such a culture develop a deep and unhealthy fear for and of authority which shows itself in compliance and submission. It also perpetuates the male/female dominance and submission.

The male counsellor may then be related to with the same awe and reverence as the priest, as possessing the same god-like function and qualities. Clients from such a background would find a relationship of equality difficult to accept.

As most religions are male centred, clients with a religious-based culture may find it difficult to accept the credibility of female counsellors.

On the one hand, the client (of whichever gender) may not be able to enter into a relationship of active equality and will expect the counsellor to be directive and prescriptive. On the other hand, the female counsellor could be rejected because a woman in a position of perceived authority creates too much ambiguity in the client's belief system.

For centuries white nations conquered then dominated other races, and considered them ignorant and of lower intelligence. These beliefs still lurk in our cultural unconscious.

For an example of how insidious the process of cultural superiority is, one only has to look at picture books, adverts, and comics to pick out how discrimination is still being thrust at the readers or viewers. Cross-cultural counselling, then, may be as fraught with difficulty as cross-gender counselling.

Here are some specifics that might aid cross-cultural counselling:

1. We should always aim for clarity of expression in the language we use.

2. We should be aware of our use of jargon and unfamiliar figures of speech.
3. Constant checking for understanding, essential in any counselling, is crucial in cross-cultural counselling. To be aware that something said is being agreed with and not fully understood demonstrates empathy.
4. If possible, allotting extra time may be an advantage, in order to facilitate exploration.
5. We should be alert to how our personal experiences can colour our judgment. We should also be careful to separate our experiences from other people's prejudices and from myths and legends.
6. We should be aware that such moral concepts as truth, honesty, loyalty, politeness and respect may not mean the same in the client's culture, or to the client as they do in ours, or to us.
7. In some cultures, showing feelings to a comparative stranger is taboo.
8. The client's verbal and non-verbal language should not be filtered through the screen of our own standards. What we might consider 'rude' may be perfectly acceptable in the client's culture. The more we are able to suspend judgment, the more we shall be able to stay on the client's wavelength.

MULTI-MODAL THERAPY (MMT)

An eclectic, behavioural approach to therapy developed by Arnold Lazarus. The basic belief is that clients are troubled by many problems which respond to different techniques. The approach centres around the acronym BASIC I.D.

1. Behaviour
2. Affect
3. Sensation
4. Imagery
5. Cognition
6. Interpersonal relationships
7. Drugs/biology.

Multi-modal therapists seek the answer to the questions: What works, for whom, and under what conditions? The therapy is tailor-made to the individual's needs. Just as all approaches do not suit all therapists, not all approaches suit every client.

TWO PRINCIPAL PROCEDURES:

1. Bridging, where the therapist deliberately tunes into the client's dominant style before branching off into one of the other six styles. Failure to tune into the client's dominant style may lead to a failure to develop empathy, as if counsellor and client were speaking different languages.
2. Tracking is a careful assessment of the 'firing order' of the seven styles. For example:
   - C. The person first of all thinks negatively;
   - I. Then imagines an unpleasant encounter;
   - B. Then acts aggressively, result an argument.
   - S. Then experiences palpitations and sweats.

Firing orders are not fixed, though many people report a reasonably stable preference. Tracking the firing order enables clients to gain insight into what led to a particular disturbance and aids the selection of the most appropriate style.

STRUCTURAL PROFILES

Clients are asked the following questions on a six point scale. 6 most like; 0 most unlike:

Behaviour:

1. How active are you?
2. How much of a 'doer' are you?
3. Do you like to keep busy?

Affect:

1. How emotional are you?
2. How deeply do you feel things?
3. Are you inclined to strong inner reactions?

Sensation:

1. How much do you focus on the pleasure and pains derived from your senses?
2. How 'tuned in' are you to your bodily sensations – to sex, food, music, art?

Imagery:

1. Do you have a vivid imagination?
2. Do you engage in fantasy/day-dreaming?
3. Do you 'think' in pictures?

Cognition:

1. How much of a 'thinker' are you?
2. Do you like to analyse things, make plans, reason things through?

Interpersonal

1. How much of a 'social being' are you?
2. How important are other people to you?
3. Are you drawn to people?
4. Do you desire intimacy with others?

Drugs/biology

1. Are you healthy and health conscious?
2. Do you take good care of your body and physical health?
3. Do you avoid:
   A. Overeating, taking unnecessary drugs?
   B. Excessive amounts of alcohol?
   C. Exposure to other substances that may be harmful?

EXAMPLES OF A STRUCTURAL PROFILE

```
    B   A   S   I   C   I.  D.
6       X
5       |       X
4       |       |   X
3   X   |       |   |   X
2   |   |   X   |   |   |
1   |   |   |   |   |   |   X
```

THE PRINCIPLES OF THERAPY

MMT overlaps cognitive behaviour therapy and rational emotive therapy. The major points all three have in common are:

1. Most problems arise from deficient or faulty social learning.
2. The client is related more to as a trainee than as a sick person.
3. Transfer of learning to the client's everyday life is deliberately fostered through homework and other assignments.
4. Labels, diagnoses, traits and generalized descriptions are avoided.

Clients are given a multi-modal life history questionnaire, that asks crucial questions about events leading up to coming for therapy. By about the third session, the therapist has gleaned sufficient information from the questionnaire to construct a preliminary modality profile, which therapist and client discuss in detail.

A course of MMT is approximately 50 hours, and is suitable for crisis and family therapy.

SOME USEFUL TECHNIQUES

1. *Behaviour*:
   - A. Extinction: e.g. flooding
   - B. Counterconditioning: e.g. desensitization
   - C. Reinforcement: e.g. token economies, praise, time out
2. *Affect*:
   - A. Abreaction: e.g. reliving experiences
   - B. Owing and accepting feelings.
3. *Sensation*:
   - A. Tension release: e.g. biofeedback, relaxation
   - B. Sensory pleasuring: becoming aware of tactile sensations.
4. *Imagery*:
   - A. Changes in self-image: e.g. when success is maintained
   - B. Coping images: e.g. when able to create images when it was not possible to evoke such images previously.
5. *Cognition*:
   - A. Cognitive restructuring: e.g. changes in faulty reasoning, self-defeats, excessive desires for approval
   - B. Awareness: e.g. of 'firing orders'.
6. *Interpersonal*:
   - A. Modelling: using the therapist as role-model, through role-plays
   - B. Dispersing unhealthy collusions: e.g. with relatives
   - C. Non-judgmental acceptance: e.g. when clients realize they are offered something not normally available in the average relationship.
7. *Drugs/biology*:
   - A. Advising thorough medical examination where appropriate
   - B. Exercise schedule
   - C. Diet
   - D. Giving up/reducing noxious substances.

Multimodal therapy provides a framework that avoids trying to fit clients into moulds.

MUSTURBATION (*See also*: Rational emotive therapy)

A term coined by Ellis to characterize the behaviour of people whose thinking is inflexible and who always think in absolute terms.

The vocabulary of such people is peppered with such words as: 'must', 'should', 'ought', 'must not', 'should not'.

MYERS–BRIGGS TYPE INDICATOR (MBTI) (*See also*: Extraversion, Introversion, Intuition, Judgment)

The MBTI is a widely used psychometric test, based on the work of Carl Jung, and developed by Isabel Myers and her mother Katherine

Briggs. It measures eight personality preferences along four dimensions:

Extraversion	Introversion
Sensing	Intuition
Thinking	Feeling
Judgment	Perception

GENERALIZATIONS

1. People who have similar strengths in the dimensions will seem to 'click', to arrive at decisions more quickly, to be on the same wavelength. Their decisions, however, may suffer because of their similar blind spots.
2. People with dissimilar strengths in the dimensions will not be on the same wavelength and may have difficulty accepting views, opinions and actions of the other person. Decisions, when arrived at from their interaction, will generally be more sound and therefore more acceptable.
3. The parts of our dimensions we don't use much – the 'shadow' side – we are more sensitive about and more prone to react negatively when criticized. As a result conflict may occur when we must work with our shadow sides or when our deficiencies are pointed out by others.
4. We are generally attracted to people who display similar preferences. On the other hand we are often drawn to others because of the strengths we observe in them. The flip-side of our own preferences.
5. Our values, beliefs, decisions, and actions are all influenced by the four stronger dimensions of our typology.
6. Though our preferences are fixed, we can work with our shadow sides and strengthen them in order to overcome problems that result from the weaknesses.

Extraversion/introversion is the way we relate to the world around us.

EXTRAVERSION

People who are more extraverted than introverted:

1. Are generally sociable and outgoing
2. Relate to people and things around them
3. Endeavour to make their decisions in agreement with the demands and expectations of others
4. Are interested in variety and in working with people
5. May become impatient with long, slow tasks
6. Do not mind being interrupted by people.

INTROVERSION

People who are more introverted than extraverted:

1. Prefer making decisions independently of other people
2. Tend to be quiet, diligent at working alone
3. Tend to be socially reserved
4. Dislike being interrupted while working
5. Are liable to forget names and faces.

Sensing/intuition is the way we perceive the world.

SENSING

People who are more sensing than intuitive:

1. Prefer what is concrete, real, factual, structured, tangible, here-and-now
2. Tend to mistrust their intuition
3. Think in careful, detail-by-detail accuracy
4. Remember real facts
5. Make few errors of fact
6. May possibly miss a grasp of the overall.

INTUITION

People who have more intuition than sensing:

1. Prefer possibilities, theories, patterns, the overall, inventions, and the new
2. Become bored with the nitty-gritty details, the concrete and actual
3. Facts must relate to concepts
4. Think and discuss in spontaneous leaps of intuition
5. May leave out or neglect details
6. Problem-solving comes easily
7. May show a tendency to make errors of fact.

Thinking/feeling is the way we make judgments.

THINKING

People with more thinking than feeling (head types):

1. Make judgments about life, people, occurrences, and things based on logic, analysis, and hard evidence.
2. Avoid irrationality and decisions based on feelings and values.
3. Are interested in logic, analysis, and verifiable conclusions.
4. Are less comfortable with empathy, values, and personal warmth.
5. May step on others' feelings and needs without realizing it.
6. Often neglect to take into consideration the values of others.

FEELING

People with more feeling than thinking (heart types):

1. Make judgments about life, people, occurrences, and things based on empathy, warmth and personal values.
2. Are more interested in people and feelings than in impersonal logic, analysis, and things.
3. Conciliation and harmony are more important than in being on top or achieving impersonal goals.
4. Get along with people in general.

Judgment/perception is the way we make decisions.

JUDGMENT

People with more judgment than perception:

1. Are decisive, firm and sure.
2. Like setting goals and sticking to them.
3. Want to make decisions, and get on to the next project.
4. Will leave an unfinished project behind and go onto new tasks and not look back, if that is what has to be done.
5. Give priority to work over play.
6. Are good at meeting deadlines.
7. Tend to be judgmental of themselves and other people.

PERCEPTION

People who have more perception than judgment:

1. Always want to know more before making decisions and judgments.

2. Are open, flexible, adaptive, non-judgmental.
3. Are able to appreciate all sides of an issue.
4. Always welcome new perspectives and new information about issues.
5. Are difficult to pin down.
6. Hate working to deadlines.
7. Are often so indecisive and non-committal that they frustrate themselves and other people.
8. Often involved in many tasks.
9. Give priority to play rather than work.

A person's type is made up of the four dominant functions. There are sixteen types.

ISTJ – *the trustee*
ISTP – *the artisan*
ISFJ – *the conservator*
ISFP – *the artist*
INFJ – *the author*
INFP – *the searcher*
INTJ – *the scientist*
INTP – *the architect*
ESTJ – *the administrator*
ESTP – *the promoter*
ESFJ – *the seller*
ESFP – *the entertainer*
ENFJ – *the teacher*
ENFP – *the journalist*
ENTJ – *the commander*
ENTP – *the inventor*

MYTHS

A collective term for a particular kind of communication that uses symbols. Myths are basic to human nature and occur in the history of all traditions and communities. Myths help make sense out of some overwhelming aspects of human existence. They convey serious but not literal truth by means of a story. Myths influence behaviours within a culture.

The absolute authority in myths is implied rather than stated. The reality represented by a myth relates to some basic aspect of human experience. Myths usually begin with 'In the beginning'.

Myths are similar to:

1. Tales of the origins of things
2. Fairy tales and folk tales
3. Fables
4. Sages and epics
5. Legends.

CLASSIFICATION OF MYTHS:

1. The beginning

   Myths about the origin of the world are so powerful and universal that they influence all myths.

2. The ending

   The origin of (personal) death and the (catastrophic) end of the world.

3. The culture hero

   Someone who created culture (not the Creator), brought health, and made the world fit to live in.

4. The Messiah

   The cultural hero is expected to return and triumph over the forces of evil.

5. Time and eternity

   Eternity, or infinite time, is emphasized by the unchangeable order of the sun, moon and stars. The number 4, for example, is associated with earth, space, and of natural limits: air, fire, water and earth.

6. Providence and destiny (fate)

   In some myths, divine supremacy is marked by a gods mastery over fate.

7. Rebirth and renewal (reincarnation)

   The cyclical pattern of nature, with its seasons, supports the idea, not for all cultures, that life does not end with death.

8. Remembering and forgetting

   Myths of memory can take the form of collective reminiscences.

   A crucial part of the celebration of the Christian Communion is remembering.

9. High beings and celestial gods

   The sky is considered sacred everywhere, and is related to, or identical with, the highest god.

10. Kings and saints

    Myths about kings are only found in traditions that know a form of sacred kingship. Kings were believed to have union with goddesses – the 'sacred marriage'. Many legends have formed around kings and saints.

11. Transformation

    These would include initiation rites and 'rites of passage' (birth, attainment of maturity, marriage, death), as well as cosmic transformation. Baptism is a transformation rite of passage.

12. Other myths include:

    A. Eden
    B. The flood
    C. Guardian angels
    D. The serpent
    E. Tree of knowledge
    F. The rainbow
    G. The valkyries.

MYTHS AND COUNSELLING

Myths provide a means of accessing the archetypes of the collective unconscious. Psychoanalysis makes use of, for example, the myths of the Oedipus complex, the Electra complex, and narcissism.

Myths help the client to try to bridge the gap between the distorted self and reality. Understanding, interpreting and integrating the client's myths is an important therapeutic process.

N

NARCISSISM

In Greek mythology, Narcissus was the son of the river god, Cephissus, and the nymph Leiriope. Narcissus was beautiful and his mother was told that he would have a long life provided he never looked upon his own features.

He fell in love with his own reflection in the waters of a spring and pined away and died. The narcissus flower sprang up where he died.

The myth possibly arose from the Greek superstition that it was unlucky to see one's own reflection.

Freud used the myth to describe a morbid condition in which sexual energy, that naturally focuses firstly on self and then upon the parent and then onto others, remains focused on self. The person can rarely achieve satisfactory sexual relationships, due to mistrust of other people.

A narcissistic personality disorder is characterized by:

1. An exaggerated sense of self-importance
2. A tendency to overvalue one's actual accomplishments
3. A need for attention and admiration which is exhibitionistic in character
4. A preoccupation with fantasies of success, wealth, power, esteem, or ideal love
5. Inappropriate emotional reactions to the criticisms of others.

The narcissistic adult person is cut off from others, self-absorbed, vain, and somewhat superior in manner.

Counselling a person who is strongly narcissistic is a long-term process involving a relationship in which the client's self-involvement is slowly changed to involvement with others.

NEUROLINGUISTIC PROGRAMMING (NLP)

NLP, developed by Bandler and Grinder, describes how the brain works with language, and how language relates to other brain functions, and how this knowledge may enable people to achieve more satisfaction in their behaviour.

NLP builds on the work, and uses some of the techniques of other communications theorists. Techniques specific to NLP are:

1. Anchoring. Similar to the behavioural technique of conditioning.
2. Eye movements. A very precise technique, using the clients' eye movements to gain access to their inner states.
   Eye movements indicate whether we are:

   A. Making pictures
   B. Listening to internal tapes
   C. Concentrating on feelings.

Following a person's eye movements give lots of information about that person's mental processes at the moment, but not the content. When reference is made to 'right', 'left', 'down', it means the other person's, not yours.

Visual:	eyes up and right eyes up and left eyes straight ahead and out of focus.
Auditory:	eyes level right eyes level left eyes down left.
Kinesthetic:	eyes down right.

Information that comes through the kinesthetic channel is genuine and not usually open to being disguised. Each of the three 'representational systems' finds some words easier to understand than others.

Visual people work with pictures and may be recognized by:

1. Conversation which contains many visual words; 'I see what you mean'. 'I get the picture'.
2. They have a tendency to breathe high up in the chest.
3. Their voice tempo is faster than the auditory or kinesthetic modes.
4. They have a tendency to tighten the neck and shoulder muscles in order to make the pictures more clear, this is likely to lead to neck tension.
5. They are more able to recount colours and shapes, and they may be deeply affected by room colour.
6. They seldom get lost, and are able to remember directions.
   Some typical visual words:

   A. Clear
   B. Graphic
   C. Perspective
   D. Picture
   E. Shortsighted
   F. Spectacle.

Auditory people work with sounds and may be recognized by:

1. Conversations that contain a predominance of auditory words: 'That rings a bell'. 'I hear you'.
2. They have a tendency to breathe in the middle of the chest.
3. They trust sounds.
4. They do not generally trust feelings.
5. They often use internal dialogue, and in consequence may have difficulty making decisions, because thoughts go round and round.
   Some typical auditory words:

   A. Alarm
   B. Harmonize
   C. Hear
   D. Ring
   E. Static
   F. Tune.

Kinesthetic people work with feelings and may be recognized by:

1. Conversations that contain a predominance of feeling words:

'I get a feel for the problem.' 'Can you remove the stumbling block?' 'Help me untangle this knot.'

2. They have a tendency to breathe low down.
3. Their voices are deeper than the other two modes.
4. They like to have space to check out their feelings.
5. They like or hate, feel warm or cold about lots of issues. Some typical kinesthetic words:

   A. Flat
   B. Impact
   C. Impress
   D. Move
   E. Tangle
   F. Touch.

Most people favour one mode. Sometimes we use two, not often do we use all three. Sensory awareness is enhanced by opening all doors.

People who are 'thinkers' tend to filter out the communication, thus making detection of eye movement difficult. An open-ended question such as, 'Tell me about your best experience with this', may evoke a sequence of eye movements, and words to go with them, and give insight into the obscured mode.

NON-DIRECTIVE THERAPY (*See also*: Person-centred therapy)

Where the therapist attempts to engage the client in an equal participative relationship, rather than in organized and structured therapy.

The term was first used by Carl Rogers to describe his work. He later replaced it by 'client-centred' and it is now 'person-centred'.

The term is often used to distinguish a process which is different from the directive therapies, particularly behaviour therapy.

Rogers' move toward 'person-centred counselling' acknowledged the difficulties of being totally 'non-directive'. It is probably no more possible to be totally non-directive than it is to be totally objective. The very fact that time, venue, and length of session are all set, removes some of the credibility of being non-directive.

What seems to be important is the intention of the therapist and the underlying philosophy.

To be 'non-directive' means relinquishing some or most of the control to the client. The influence of the therapist, and the wish to help the client to change, some would argue, must in some way be directive.

NON-VERBAL COMMUNICATION (BODY LANGUAGE)

Verbal language is mainly conscious; body language, the language of signals, is mainly unconscious. Approximately 50% of information on the character, impact and credibility of the person is conveyed by body language. Any interpretation, therefore, of body language must be offered with the same tentativeness as one would interpret any unconscious exploration.

WORDS DISGUISE; BODY LANGUAGE REVEALS

Thoughts are easier to change than posture, expression and gesture. The study of body language is complex; Japanese mime theatre, for example, uses more than 40 positions of the eyebrow to convey different emotions. Physical factors influence much of our body language; interpretations have to be tentative.

Some examples of body language sayings:

1. Your eyes speak volumes
2. That person's a pain in the neck
3. Hang the head in shame
4. Head over heels in love
5. If looks could kill
6. Cold feet.

SOME POSSIBLE INTERPRETATIONS

Eyes

1. *Wide-open*, expressing joy, fright, surprise, amazement.
2. *Veiled*, expressing boredom, disinterest (almost arrogance), sluggishness, lack of drive, resignation.
3. *Slit*, expressing mental concentration. If exaggerated – narrow-minded, over critical, petty, jealous.
4. *Closed*, expressing protection, isolation, contemplation, inner reflection, inner enjoyment.
5. *Winking*, expressing unreliability, mistrust. Trying to create a link by expressing agreement.
6. *Screwed up*, expressing a response to fear, reluctance, displeasure. Unwilling to face facts 'eye to eye'.
7. *Blinking*, expressing embarrassment, insecurity, tension.

Looking

1. People who look away when speaking may not be sure of their opinion.
2. People who look at others feel they can support the validity of what they say. They appear more competent and confident.
3. People who look at the floor are probably overcautious and try to avoid new ideas, experiences or risks.
4. The more popular a person is within a group, the higher the level of eye contact.
5. An open look comes from an open personality.
6. *Direct*, is spontaneous, giving undivided attention, is sympathetic.
7. *Vacant*, talking round people in monologues. May also express deep thought.
8. *Seeing through*, devalues other people and creates feelings of insecurity.
9. *From below*, expressing servility, subordination. When it is coupled with leaning back this expresses humility.
10. *From above*, expressing superiority. With the head drawn back – critical distance, pride, arrogance, 'talking down the nose'.
11. *Sidelong*, expressing distrust, scepticism. With half-shut eyes – a veiled threat.
12. *Upward*, expressing adoration, request.

Using spectacles

1. Suddenly removing spectacles indicates that the person is under pressure or wants to reveal feelings.
2. Putting the spectacles on again indicates that the person wants to start again, wants to reconsider, or wants to hide feelings.
3. An earpiece in the mouth prevents a spontaneous response.
4. Moving spectacles to the front of the nose is a secret rebuke; disapproval.
5. Removing spectacles with both hands and holding on to them

shows an interest in the conversation or not yet ready to make a decision.

When we clean our spectacles during a conversation, we are showing complete lack of interest and when we fold our spectacles up and put them in their case, the conversation is ended.

NOSE MESSAGES

Wrinkled nose

'I don't like the smell of that'. A passive defence; something of a martyr. Reluctance, displeasure, aversion, disgust.

MOUTH MESSAGES

1. *Pouting lips* may be weighing pros and cons or it may be perceptive and sensitive. It may be expressing sulkiness, dislike, a wanting to get rid of something or get away from present company.
2. *Pressed lips* may be expressing non-acceptance, disagreement, criticism, disapproval. When the lips are pressed to extreme they are likely to be expressing violence. When the chin is raised, aggression is being expressed. We generally greet an enemy with pressed lips with lowered forehead.
3. *Pursed lips* are expressing rigidity, disapproval, arrogance, superficiality, and self-importance.
4. *Lip biting* is expressing embarrassment, lack of confidence, thinking what to say, or trying to prevent words bursting forth. 'Keep lips between teeth.'
5. *Turned-down mouth*; these are the 'sadness muscles'. It is also expressing something negative, or dissatisfaction. When it is accompanied by a shake of the head, strong disagreement is being expressed.

LAUGHTER AND SMILING

Laughter can make us happy, or betray our inner feelings.

Some laughter adjectives

Artificial, bitter, bleating, boasting, chilling, chortling, disdainful, embarrassed, free and easy, fresh, funny, gloating, grumbling, happy, jolly, liberated, loud, measured, mischievous, mocking, natural, noisy, pious, provocative, roaring, secretive, simple, spiteful, tormented, tremulous, weird.

Types of laughter

1. *'Ha-ha'* Free, open, hearty.
2. *'He-he'* is laughing at somebody, gloating, condescending, mocking, challenging. Keeps people at a distance.
3. *'Hee-hee'* is a secret giggle, a little snigger, ironic and spiteful.
4. *'Ho-ho'* is surprise, disbelief, usually loud, showing off, critical astonishment, protest.
5. *The smirk* – laughter with lips pressed together – is holding back, not willing to give unconditional affection, mischief, self-satisfaction, amusement known only to self.

HANDS

1. *Left/right*. The left is the emotional hand; the right hand is regarded as the 'proper' hand. In Jungian terms, left represents the feminine and right the masculine.
2. *Open hands*. Discussion accompanied by an open palm is a

trusting signal, showing interest, offers opinions, invites views.

3. *Covered hands.* With backs of hands showing, indicates concealment, insecurity, waits to be approached, keeps distance, defended.
4. *Clinging hands.* Confusion, insecurity, need support from objects, e.g. chair's arms.
5. *Don't choke me.* A hand suddenly moved across the throat may indicate fear of emotional choking.

FINGERS

1. *Clenched fists* are expressing something powerful, negative, 'keep your distance', a verbal fight.
2. *Upward thumb* is expressing authority or encouragement.
3. *Upward index finger* is self-opinionated, strictness, a 'know-all'.
4. *Finger-tapping* is expressing dominance and emphasis.
5. *Pointing index finger* is saying 'Attention!', and is expressing severe tension, blame, aggression, and argument.
6. *Index finger on lips* is asking help from the other senses, is expressing concealment, insecurity or helplessness.
7. *Index finger across mouth* is saying 'I will keep my mouth shut at all costs.'
8. *Index finger rubbing lips.* A very big lie is being suppressed. Children hide lies behind the whole hand. Adults try to avoid giving the game away by using the one finger.
9. *Index finger in mouth.* This is the Child in adult conveying simplicity, ignorance, stupidity. It often accompanies a relaxed body. May convey a perceived threat or a confused or passive person.
10. *The arrow* is where the index fingertips and thumbs meet to form an arrow. Pointed forward it is expressing self-confidence with a tendency to arrogance.
11. *Fingertips pressed together* indicates a striving for balance. Extreme concentration is when thumbs and index fingers are pressed together, and other fingers are spread.
12. *Rubbing fingertips.* A fear of confrontation or hesitancy is being expressed when all fingertips are being rubbed.
13. *Clasped hands* is indicating defence, a barricade, aggression.

STANDING

Self-confidence is indicated by the legs slightly spread, when they are wide apart, the person is eager to impress. When legs are very close together fear/tension is indicated.

When the feet are parallel the person is attentive. When they are turned inward the person is feeling insecure. When feet are turned outward the person is feeling self-confident. When the body is balanced on the inside of soles tension is indicated, and when balanced on the outside of soles nervousness is indicated.

Habitual positions reflect inner attitudes. Characteristics of a person with a balanced attitude are:

1. Firm on both feet
2. Weight distributed on the heels
3. Distance between heels about 8 inches
4. Looks balanced and relaxed
5. Upright torso
6. Arms relaxed at sides of body.

A balanced stance indicates level-headedness, self-confidence, inner freedom. A stiff, under tension stance indicates resolution, lack of flexibility/adaptability, exaggerated desire to prove oneself.

The person who pivots the body on one leg is indicating a firm and positive attitude; relaxed, liveliness, reactive, adaptability, reliability.

Shifting from foot to foot is indicating impatience, nervousness, insecurity. With the legs apart the person is expressing over-confidence, arrogance, self-importance, but may also be expressing concealed inferiority and defence. Crossed legs are indicating defensiveness yet readiness for contact. This position is often seen in newcomers to a group.

Walking. Big steps indicate decisiveness, ambition, ability to take action, initiative, broad-minded and informal. A relaxed and elastic walk, with tips of feet pointing forward, straight torso – facing the world, dynamic, drive.

The hesitant walk is characterized by little steps, tense neck and shoulders and indicates a cautious, over-adaptable person. Their inner dialogue could be something like, 'Keep on the safe side, don't take risks.' Generally they are not confident and need to express everything with meticulous and well-rehearsed care.

The mincing walk is affected, with small, quick steps with lack of rhythm and is expressing agitation, anxiety, fear. Such a person tends to make others nervous.

The relaxed walk, bordering on slouching, indicates possible immaturity, laziness, and a fear of commitment.

The swinging walk where the shoulders are carried over the hips is an indication of a forceful character who is self-opinionated and selfish.

Where the swing is from the hips and does not extend to the shoulders, self-confidence, certainty and drive are being expressed.

The dragging walk – being 'dragged along', with a round back, hollow chest, as if carrying a load, indicates a dependent, sluggish and inactive person.

The stiff walk, where there is very little rhythm, is jerky and puppet-like, indicates a person who has difficulty relating to people, is controlled by time, who avoids taking risks, is restrained in speech, longs for support, and is governed by strict, self-imposed, inflexible rules.

SITTING

1. People who sit on half the chair during discussion with the right leg forward, with torso and head forward, hands open and palms visible, are open, committed, lively and active. This is a positive attitude that encourages open discussion.
2. People who sit on the whole chair with one leg forward, with bent torso, forearms resting on open thighs and hands relaxed (backs facing outward), are expressing neutrality, open-mindedness, tranquillity, and understanding.
3. People who sprawl on the whole chair with the torso leaning backwards, hands gripped behind the neck, and legs wide apart, are expressing inflated self-confidence, lack of self-discipline, a certain recklessness, lack of decorum, undue familiarity, and lack of sensitivity.

4. Crossed legs express a natural self-confidence, equality, openness, not ready for action. Crossed legs with arms folded across chest express a 'contra' mood which is sceptical and disapproving.
5. Legs wrapped round chair indicate inflexibility, strong inner tension, and the person feels uncomfortable and helpless in others' presence.

PERSONAL SPACE

An intrusion into our personal space is threatening and disturbing and is likely to meet with a defensive reception. Invasion of space can be both physical and psychological. For example, we may react as if a character on the TV screen had invaded our personal space.

1. The intimate distance zone. Up to 2 feet maximum. (Strongly influenced by culture.) The more our intimate space is violated, the more we will use the defence tactics of crossed arms and legs, nervous shifting in chair, playing with fingers, avoiding eye contact, shrugging of shoulder, lowering of the chin.
2. The personal distance zone. Fifteen inches to 5 feet. The space reserved for family members and people we like. The most common defence tactic is to ignore, characterized by no eye contact, stiff body, preferably no talking. The more space available, the more we seem to need.
3. The social distance zone. Five to 12 feet. This is the zone for daily contacts, superficial acquaintances, colleagues, the 'boss'. This is usually the most comfortable distance for counselling.
4. Public distance zone. Twelve to 24 feet. This is the distance preferred by speakers, teachers, and actors.

CHANGING BEHAVIOUR

1. Smiling for a half minute when we don't feel like it works on negative feelings and helps clear the thoughts.
2. Positive gestures:

   A. Arms raised to chest, with palms open.
   B. Let every gesture precede the spoken word.
   C. Gesture (naturally) with alternate arms.
   D. Look relaxed.

3. Avoiding negative gestures:

   A. Do not hide your hands behind you.
   B. Do not hold on to the jacket lapels – it gives the impression of authority.
   C. Do not lower your head when reading.
   D. Do not let your shoulders slump.
   E. Do not look at the ceiling or floor.
   F. Do not fiddle with keys or money in pocket.
   G. Do not keep hands constantly below the belt line.
   H. Do not fold your arms.

Counselling uses all the senses; if all we listen to are the words, we shall have heard only half of the message. Having a heightened ability to notice changes in body language helps the counsellor to recognize how the client is responding to the interaction.

Accurate perception aids rapport and empathy.

NURTURING PARENT (*See also*: Transactional analysis)

The term describes the Parent ego state characterized by:

1. Warmth
2. Support
3. Care.

The basic need of the nurturing parent is caring.

Some typical words

Don't worry, good, darling, beautiful, I'll take care of you, let me help you, smart, there-there.

Some typical gestures and postures

Consoling touch, head nodding – 'Yes', pat on the back.

Some typical voice tones

Encouraging, supportive, sympathetic.

Some typical facial expressions

Encouraging nod, loving, sympathetic eyes.

Life position	Behaviour
1. I'm not OK You're not OK	Overindulgent
2. I'm OK You're not OK	Rescuing
3. I'm OK You're OK	Supportive
4. I'm not OK You're OK	Ingratiating

O

OBJECT (*See also*: Object relations)

A real or fantasized person or aspect of a person which is felt to satisfy or frustrate a person's need. The term is used in contrast to 'subject'. The object is that toward which action or desire is directed, so that the subject achieves instinctual satisfaction.

An object is regarded variously as the recipient of an instinctual drive, usually a part object, such as part of the body, penis or breast. It may also be regarded as a focus of ego attraction, usually a whole object or person.

The concept is central to Melanie Klein's theoretical framework of part objects of early infancy or of whole objects of later infancy.

Both part and whole objects are conceived of as either 'good' and reassuring, (satisfying), or 'bad' and persecutory (frustrating). These early experiences become models for all other experiences in later life. Various defence mechanisms provide the means whereby internal and external objects are experienced.

When the object is removed, the infant experiences great anxiety. As the capacity of the ego develops, the infant is more able to hold on to objects symbolically, even when they are absent.

OBJECT RELATIONS

A psychoanalytical term that describes the relationship of the 'subject' to the 'object'. This is not an 'interpersonal relationship'. The word 'object' indicates a commitment to a theory of instinct.

The 'subject' directs its action or desire toward gaining some instinctual gratification from an 'object'. An object is usually a person, a personal attribute, or a symbolic representation of a person, that attracts attention and/or satisfies a need. Objects are not 'things'.

Objects are not passive; they have the power to reassure or persecute; they have the attributes of goodness and badness, and to reduce tension although all this is not at a conscious level.

We learn to relate with 'objects', not merely to seek gratification, and to work toward interpersonal maturity.

The term 'object relations' is not employed in analytical psychology, though to some degree it is implied but not parallelled.

The names most associated with object relations are: Balint, Fairbairn, Guntrip, Klein, Winnicott.

OBSERVING COUNSELLING

(*See also*: Feedback)

Sometimes it is possible to observe a counsellor at work. More often, observing is associated with counselling training, where students observe each other.

Observing means listening to:

1. What is said
2. How it is said
3. What is not said
4. Watching the unconscious communication of body language.

Some guidelines:

1. Did the counsellor seem certain/uncertain in the counselling role?
2. How was the client put at ease?
3. What evidence was there of rapport?
4. What evidence was there of empathy?
5. What evidence was there of acceptance of the client by the counsellor?
6. What evidence was there of genuine concern?
7. Did the counsellor concentrate on facts at the expense of feelings?
8. How would you rate the counsellor's listening with the 'third ear', and responding skills?
9. Was there any evidence of argument?
10. How did you feel as the observer?
11. How would you describe the pace of the interview?
12. The particular comments by the counsellor that seemed most helpful were ...
13. What evidence was there of the counsellor 'reading between the lines'?
14. What body language was there?

    A. Eye contact
    B. Personal spacing and distance
    C. Gestures
    D. Body posture
    E. Facial expressions
    F. Tone of voice
    G. Timing of speech
    H. Evidence of being relaxed/tense.

The above questions are a useful self-appraisal.

OCCUPATIONAL CHOICE AND DEVELOPMENT THEORY (*See also*: Personality type – Occupational)

Also referred to as 'vocational theory' or 'career theory'.

PRINCIPAL OCCUPATIONAL CHOICE THEORIES:

1. Developmental
2. Social learning
3. Interaction
4. Social structure
5. Leisure.

1. DEVELOPMENTAL THEORY

The goal: vocational maturity through achieving a fit between changing desires/circumstances and work. Occupational life comprises:

A. Occupational choice and career development:

(a) Occupational adjustment
(b) Choice and development of leisure activities.

B. Occupational choice is a lifelong process, so long as people make decisions about work and career.
C. Factors that influence choice:

(a) Changing family circumstances
(b) Pressures from various sources
(c) Satisfactions
(d) What has to be given up?

D. Reversal of choices, which may be difficult, are influenced by:

(a) Time invested in the choice
(b) The psychological barrier of a mistake/failure
(c) Change in value system.

E. Choices involve:

(a) Capacities
(b) Educational requirements
(c) Interests
(d) Values.

F. Constraints that influence choice:

(a) Low income
(b) Limitations of parental values, school systems that entrap people in low-income occupations, and ineffective guidance.

G. A person's vocational development is influenced by:

(a) Personal development
(b) Roles
(c) Home, community, school, workplace
(d) Career
(e) Life style.

H. Satisfactory vocational development leads to vocational maturity.
I. Vocational maturity means how we cope with the process of development.

DIMENSIONS OF VOCATIONAL MATURITY

A. Autonomy:

(a) Balances dependence/independence
(b) Takes appropriate decisions
(c) Is appropriately in control
(d) Accepts responsibility.

B. Planning ability:

(a) Recognizes what has to be done
(b) Takes account of planning needs
(c) Works out how to implement plans
(d) Works out alternatives.

C. Exploration:
Uses people, materials and activities to explore all available opportunities.
D. Career decision-making:

(a) Applies decision-making principles
(b) Considers alternatives
(c) Seeks information
(d) Has a fair idea of objectives.

E. Knowledge:

(a) Knows about various occupations
(b) Knows about various work practices
(c) Knows what different occupations require

(d) Knows how to make an informed choice.

F. Realism:

(a) Recognizes limitations in knowledge and experience
(b) Does something to remedy deficiencies
(c) Has stable but flexible goals
(d) Is consistent in efforts to attain goals
(e) Identifies new objectives.

2. SOCIAL LEARNING THEORY

The goal is to learn effective career decision-making skills and to unlearn faulty anxiety-provoking reactions that affect occupational choice.

A. Genetic endowment and special abilities

(a) Gender
(b) Race
(c) Physical characteristics
(d) Physical disabilities
(e) Predispositions such as: intelligence, musical ability, artistic ability, muscular co-ordination.

B. Environmental conditions and events

(a) Job opportunities
(b) Training opportunities
(c) Policies for selection
(d) Remuneration scales for different jobs
(e) Labour laws and Union rules
(f) Physical events, such as earthquakes, droughts, floods, hurricanes
(g) Availability of and demand for natural resources
(h) Technology
(i) Changes in social organization
(j) Experience and resources within the family
(k) Education system
(l) Influence of neighbourhood or community.

C. Learning experiences

(a) Positive instrumental
Positive reinforcement through praise, recognition, appreciation
(b) Negative instrumental
Punishment and/or not receiving positive reinforcement
(c) Positive association is observing a valued model and receiving positive reinforcmeent or exposure to positive words and images associated with a course, occupation, or field of work.
(d) Negative association is exposure to negative words and images associated with a course, occupation, or field of work.

D. Task skills

(a) Problem-related skills
(b) Ability to perform to standards and values
(c) Work habits
(d) Perception and thinking processes
(e) Mental sets
(f) Emotional responses.

3. INTERACTION THEORY (*See also*: Personality types – Occupational)

The goal is to achieve a fit between personality type and job, by working with:

A. Aptitudes
B. Interests
C Personality
D. Psychometric testing.

Basic assumptions

A. Personality types:
(a) Artistic
(b) Conventional
(c) Enterprising
(d) Investigative
(e) Realistic
(f) Social.

B. People search for environments compatible with their personality type.
C. Behaviour is influenced by personality type and environment. People who achieve a fit between personality and environment, for the most part, engage in activities that do not damage their self-esteem. Where the mismatch is too great, people will try to lessen the incongruity or they will change jobs.

4. SOCIAL STRUCTURE THEORY

The goal is to achieve career policies that will:

A. Change social structure and help people overcome the negative effects of socialization.
B. Help people to take advantage of new opportunities.

Social structure theory is a sociological viewpoint that emphasizes the influences of social structure in selection and choice. Social structure influences personality development and provides a socio-economic framework for selection of occupation. A fundamental question is: Does opportunity rather than choice determine occupation?

Factors that influence choice:

A. Stratified societies
B. Education system
C. Class
D. Family expectations
E. Local availability and opportunity.

The socialization process and career desires are influenced by:

A. The selection process
B. Attitudes of teachers
C. Peer group influence
D. The home environment
E. Informal channels such as friends and relatives, social groups, the media.

The effect of socialization is that people learn their place in the occupational hierarchy. This makes career choice more socially determined than free.

People often need assistance with:

A. How to deal with unemployment
B. Precise information about job opportunities
C. How to assess various jobs
D. Adjusting/readjusting, to working life.

5. LEISURE

The goal is to help people develop a self-enhancing approach to leisure.

The dimensions of leisure:

A. Time. That which remains after basic needs have been met.
B. Freedom. To occupy one's time as one wishes.
C. Function:

(a) Self-realization which may include personal fulfilment,

personal meaning, and be therapeutic.

(b) Diversion which may be avoidance, compensation, recreational and also refreshment.

A healthy leisure approach is influenced by a self-concept that allows for leisure. The aim of counselling for leisure is to help clients create a bridge between the two concepts of self and leisure.

OEDIPUS COMPLEX

A psychoanalytic concept derived from the Greek myth, where Oedipus unknowingly falls in love with his mother and kills the rival for his love, his father.

The Oedipal triangle – father, mother, and child – applies equally to male and female children during the 'phallic' stage of development, about three to five years.

It is during this stage of development, in psychoanalytic theory, that the loving desire for the parent of the opposite sex reaches a climax. Feelings of intense rivalry are generated toward the parent of the same sex, who is the real love partner.

The rivalry resurfaces during adolescence, to be finally resolved when the young person chooses a love partner, not the parent.

The 'Electra complex' is the female equivalent, although the resolution of the conflict is different for male and female children. The male child perceives the threat of castration by his father, so he gives up his incestuous desires toward his mother. The conflict for the female child culminates in her recognition that she has no penis – castration has already taken place. The resolution of the Oedipal conflict leads to the formation of the superego and the internalization of the prohibitions and taboos of society.

Repressed Oedipal wishes are fertile ground for irrational guilt in later life. If relationships between child and parents are loving and basically non-traumatic, and if parental attitudes are neither excessively prohibitive nor excessively sexually stimulating, the Oedipal stage is passed through without difficulty.

Children subjected to trauma are likely candidates for 'infantile neurosis', an important forerunner of similar reactions in adult life.

Melanie Klein believed that Freud interpreted the myth too literally. For her, the complex started during the first year of life, and unresolved Oedipal conflict did not necessarily set the scene for all future neuroses.

It is possible that the Oedipus complex is never totally destroyed or overwhelmed, as Freud suggested, but that it persists in varying degrees throughout life.

Freud also applied the myth to the whole of society and in all cultures. Every social and psychological phenomena Freud related to the Oedipus complex. However much the concept may be open to criticism, the central place of the triangle of mother, father and child is an important understanding in any psychotherapy.

OPEN MINDEDNESS (*See also*: Authoritarian personality)

Refers to how flexible and responsive one is to examine new evidence about one's belief systems. It is partially related to one's ability to receive, evaluate, and act on information from the outside on its own merits. It also relates to how one is able to free oneself from internal pressures that would obscure or interfere with incoming information.

The open mind is relatively unencumbered by irrelevant facts within the situation which may arise from the person or from outside.

Examples of irrelevant internal pressures would be unrelated habits, beliefs and perceptual cues, irrational ego motives, power needs and the need of self-praise, and the need to allay anxiety.

Examples of external pressures would be relying on reward or punishment from external authority such as parents, peers, and other authority figures, reference groups, social and institutional norms, and cultural norms.

Open-minded people are more capable of discriminating between a message and its source and are less influenced by high status.

OPEN QUESTIONS

Wrongly used, questions can create an expectation that we will provide solutions to other people's problems. The emphasis in counselling is on using questions as aids to problem-solving. We may find it expedient to ask questions to fill certain gaps in our understanding. Should we find ourselves asking two consecutive questions without getting a response, then in all probability we have asked inappropriately and should return to responding accurately.

OPEN QUESTIONS SHOULD:

1. Seek clarification
2. Encourage exploration
3. Establish client understanding
4. Gauge feelings
5. Establish counsellor understanding.

Make effective use of 5Wh:

Who? What? Why? Where? How? Rudyard Kipling's 'Six honest serving men'

Avoid closed questions unless you want to elicit information or establish facts.

Avoid leading questions where the desired answer is implied in the question.

Avoid curiosity questions about areas not yet touched on.

Avoid closed questions that can be answered with a few words and which usually begin with the words, 'is', 'are', 'do', 'did'.

Avoid too many questions that give the impression of an interrogation.

Avoid leading questions that put the answer into the client's mouth.

Avoid probing questions which the other client is not yet ready to answer.

Avoid poorly timed questions that interrupt and hinder the helping process.

Think of responding to what the client has said, rather than asking questions.

Responding is like building a wall, brick by brick. In this way, the counsellor does not rush ahead of the client and cause anxiety by pushing indelicately into sensitive areas not yet ready to be explored.

HELPFUL WAYS OF USING QUESTIONS

1. Elaboration questions that give the client the opportunity to expand on what has already been talked about.

   'Would you care to elaborate?'

'Is there anything more?'
'Could you expand what you've just said?'

2. Specification questions that aim to elicit detail about a problem.

   'When you say he upsets you, what precisely happens?'
   'When?' 'How many times?'

3. Focusing on feelings questions that aim to elicit the feelings generated by a problem area.

   'How do you feel about that?'
   'How would you describe your feelings?'
   'Is it possible that you're feeling . . .?'

4. Personal responsibility questions which imply not only that the other has a responsibility for owning the problem, but also for making the choices that contribute to solving it.

   'How do you see your part in the break up of the relationship?'
   'Are there any skills you need to develop to help solve the problem?
   'Are there any ways you could improve the situation?'

5. Open questions are an open invitation to continue talking, particularly about feelings.

   'Could you tell me what you'd like to talk about today?' ('Could' questions tend to be the most open and help clients generate their own unique answers.)
   'What happened then?' ('What' questions tend to bring out the specific facts of a problem.)
   'How did you feel about the situation?' ('How' questions often lead toward discussion. When the word 'feel' is included, the client is usually more ready to talk about feelings.)
   'Why do you think it happened?' ('Why' questions tend to lead clients to talk about their past or present reasoning around an event or situation.)

OPERANT CONDITIONING (*See also*: Associative learning, Classical conditioning)

Operant conditioning deals with situations where the response produces something from the environment. Learning thus takes place and is not dependent on an unconditioned stimulus.

When a person, or an animal, is taught something new, classical conditioning cannot be used. To train a dog to sit up and beg, rewards have to be used. In this sense the dog has operated on the environment; it has been given a reward.

Operant conditioning has its origins in the trial-and-error observations of E.L. Thorndyke (1889). The classical observation is that a rat in a maze starts off by running randomly, seeking the food (reward).

Gradually the number of error runs is reduced until it achieves its goal. Thereafter it can very quickly and surely, operate the maze.

Trial-and-error learning involves the use of reinforcing rewards and depends on the ability to organize sensory stimuli into a pattern, though much of it depends on chance.

B.F. Skinner extended the work of Thorndyke by using a rat or a pigeon in what is known as a 'Skinner box'. Food (reinforcer) is deposited in the box whenever the animal presses a lever. When food is no longer forthcoming, the animal will stop pressing the lever. The response has undergone extinction. Operant strength is measured by how frequently the lever is pressed in a given time.

Operant conditioning has applications in human psychology. For example, a child constantly seeking attention by having tantrums at night: If attention is given (reward) the behaviour will continue. If it is ignored the tantrums will in time cease (extinction).

Both the voluntary and the autonomic nervous system can be conditioned by operant conditioning. Humans have been trained by operant methods to control their heart rate, blood pressure, and the secretion of stomach acids that may produce ulcers. Operant conditioning is the basis for biofeedback, used in Body therapies, Multi-modal therapy, and stress management.

Premack's principle about reinforcement states that any activity can reinforce any other less-frequently performed activity. Teachers use this principle when they allow children to play (more desirable activity, performed frequently) after having completed a school activity, such as writing an essay (less desirable, and less frequently performed activity).

Punishment can have dramatic effects on behaviour. Punishment is used to decrease the likelihood of a response. The results from punishment are not as predictable as result from rewards, possibly because there is no alternative to being told 'Stop!' Punishment often leads to dislike or fear of whoever does the punishing. Extreme or painful punishment may elicit undesirable, aggressive behaviour. An important difference is where the punishment is perceived to be informative and so provide an occasion for learning.

ORAL STAGE

In psychoanalytic psychology, the earliest phase of both libidinal and ego development which extends from birth to approximately 18 months.

The mouth is the main source of pleasure and centre of experience and the libido is satisfied through oral contact with a variety of objects, biting and sucking.

Though the oral stage clearly begins at birth, it is not clear if it ends with weaning.

According to pschoanalytic theory people who have an oral fixation retain their mouth as the primary eroto-genic zone, have a mother-fixation, are prone to mood swings and tend to identify with others, rather than relate to them. Fixation is the process by which a person becomes or remains ambivalently attached to an object.

Fixation, then, is failure to progress through the appropriate stages of development and is characterized by:

1. Infantile and outmoded behaviour patterns, particularly when under stress.
2. A compulsive tendency to chose objects that resemble the one on whom she/he is fixated.
3. Feeling drained of energy, because the energy is being invested in a past object.

ORGAN INFERIORITY (*See also*: Compensation, Individual psychology, Inferiority complex)

The term describes the perceived or actual congenital defects in organs of the body or their functions.

Adler referred to children who suffered from organ inferiorities as 'stepchildren of nature'. They are engaged at an early age in a bitter struggle for existence where social feelings become strangled.

A consequence of this is that there is morbid preoccupation with self and in trying to make an impression on others.

Adler also believed that a child's educational potential may be shattered by an exaggerated, intensified, and unresolved feeling of inferiority, and a goal that demands security and peace fuelled by a striving to express dominance over others.

Such children, Adler says, are easily recognized. They are 'problem children' who interpret every experience as a defeat and consider themselves to be always neglected and discriminated against, both by nature and by people.

Adults who demand of the child more that the child can do, reinforce the child's helplessness and pave the way for the realization that there are but two things over which the child has power: the pleasure or displeasure of adults.

Adler also believed that organ inferiority resulted in compensation, a striving to overcome the weakness.

P

PARABLE

Parables, fables and allegories are forms of imaginative literature or the spoken word, so constructed that the reader or listener is encouraged to look for meanings hidden beneath the literal surface of the fiction.

A poet may describe the ascent of a hill in such a way that each physical step corresponds to a new stage in the soul's progress toward a higher level of existence.

An allegory is usually a long narrative full of symbols conveying a moral message.

Well-known allegories include: *Pilgrim's Progress; Gulliver's Travels; The Divine Comedy; Paradise Lost; The Picture of Dorian Gray.*

Fables and parables are short, simple forms of allegory, usually about animals, or inanimate objects, who behave as though they are human.

Fables tend toward detailed, sharply observed realism, sometimes satirical, and use impossible events to teach their lesson. Aesop's (6th century BC) 200 or so fables is probably the most well-known collection, although other writers have achieved acclaim: John Gay and Edward Moore (England) and La Fontaine (France) are three examples.

Parables also tell a simple story, with a moral message about humans, and depend heavily on analogy. The Good Samaritan in the New Testament, is an example. Only the elite can decipher the inner core of truth of the parable. Christ's disciples had 'ears to hear'.

Parables possess a certain mystery that makes them useful for teaching spiritual values.

The therapist can use stories (fictional or true, taken from literature or the Bible, or from clinical experience) to draw analogies between the story and some aspect of the client's life, and to show how another client successfully solved a similar problem. Such a technique must be used with care, lest it put undue pressure on the client. The essential ingredient is the symbolic connection between the story told and the client's problem.

PARADOXICAL INTENTION

(*See also*: Logotherapy)

A paradox is an apparently self-contradictory statement; the underlying meaning is revealed only by careful scrutiny. Paradoxical intention is a psychotherapeutic technique used within Viktor Frankl's Logotherapy.

The therapist encourages clients (with appropriate humour, something Frankl strongly emphasizes) to do exactly and deliberately what they believe they do involuntarily, and over which they believe they have no control.

The technique is used primarily to overcome obsessions. An example would be a client who is terrified to leave the house in case she faints. The therapist might say (with relevant humour) 'Go on, faint. Faint twice. In fact, why not have a heart attack into the bargain.' When the client realizes that her intention does not produce the feared symptom, she begins to appreciate the uselessness of her behaviour. By reversing the habitual avoidance of the feared event or object the anxiety cycle is broken.

PARAPHRASING

Reflecting the content means mirroring the literal meaning of someone's words. Sometimes paraphrasing is necessary; at others, reflecting feelings is more appropriate.

Feelings are carried by words, so effective communication is hearing and responding to words and feelings. When listening, we focus initially upon the content, and are helped to do so by using Kipling's 'Six honest serving men' – 5Wh: What? When? Where? Why? What? How? If we can answer these questions, we can be sure that we have the basic ingredients of the client's experience. If we cannot answer them, we should continue to listen and seek further clarification. As experiences are shared, the missing information will be supplied.

The 5Wh help us to organize details and to know if the client is leaving things out. Our response need not be a repetition of the details. Rather, we paraphrase the client's content by summarizing and using our own words. Paraphrasing is not parroting.

A paraphrased response will capture the main points communicated by the client in a brief statement, thus ensuring that the client clearly understands our summary.

A useful format for responding to content is:

'You're saying ———————— '
Or
'In other words ———————— '
Or
'It sounds as if ———————— '

Such formulated responses can sound stilted unless freshness is retained.

PARAPRAXIS (Slips of the tongue)

General term that includes momentary amnesias, slips of the tongue and pen, errors in action, and forgetting. In psychoanalytic thought, parapraxis is caused by the intrusion of unconscious processes on the conscious, causing the 'mistake', the 'Freudian slip' that somehow betrays the truth.

Examples of parapraxes

1. 'I'm glad you're better' was the intention, which turned into, 'I'm sad you're better.'
2. 'My husband can eat what he wants' was the intention, which turned into, 'My husband can eat what I want.'
3. Man entering a restaurant with a woman.

'Do you have a table?' was the intention, which turned into, 'Do you have a bedroom?'
4. King Henry VIII greeting Anne Boleyn, 'Good morning beloved' was the intention, which turned into 'Good morning, beheaded.'

PARENTAL CHILD (*See also*: Family therapy)

A term used in structural family therapy to describe the role adopted by one of the children in the relationship with one parent.

In single-parent families the alliance may perform a function for the whole family. In a two-parent family, the alliance may lead to the exclusion of other children and will prove to be detrimental to the family structure.

PARENTING SKILLS TRAINING

Programmes specially developed to improve the way parents care for and bring up their children.

Essential elements within the parental role:

1. Communication
2. Managing stress
3. Shaping behaviour
4. Developing consistent and reliable attitudes and behaviour and the knowledge to practice them
5. An environment that is conducive to effective parenting
6. Leadership
7. Power and authority which is not oppressive
8. Co-operation with autonomy and appropriate responsibility
9. Problem-solving skills.

Teaching parenting skills:

1. Functional
   - A. (*See*: Problem-solving interventions)
   - B. (*See*: Behaviour modification)
   - C. Social skills. Socially skilled people possess a repertoire of verbal and non-verbal behaviours that enable them to behave in an appropriate manner. The main social skills are relating, communicating, being appropriately assertive, self-awareness.
2. The main therapeutic skills used are counselling and befriending (*See also*: Supportive psychotherapy).
3. Educational skills concentrate on preparing older children for parenthood, and further education classes.

PASSIVE AGGRESSION (*See also*: Aggression)

Where anger is turned against the self – masochism. The hostility is never entirely concealed. Caregivers on the receiving end of such behaviour as wrist-cutting, often feel they have been attacked by sadistic behaviour.

Understanding the feelings coupled with a matter-of-fact approach to the act is often more productive than treating the behaviour as perverse. 'Time out' may be one way of breaking the pattern of the client who persists in self-defeating behaviour.

PEAK EXPERIENCES (*See also*: Humanistic psychology, Maslow, A)

A term coined by Maslow to describe life-events that are ecstatic, overwhelmingly intense, positively valued by those who experience them, and have long-term effects.

For Maslow such an experience is where the person feels in harmony with all things, is clear, spontaneous, independent and alert, and often with little awareness of time or space.

Maslow argues that when our basic needs for security, love, and attention are not completely met, we live our lives in a constant state of deficit. When our needs are being met (perhaps never totally) we develop a sort of 'permeability', an openness, to what is. We pay total attention to an object or person regardless of use or purpose.

PEAK EXPERIENCES ARE CHARACTERIZED BY:

1. Total attention
2. Self is forgotten
3. Time and space dissolve
4. Ordinary language is inadequate
5. Feelings of humility and gratitude
6. Creativity is released
7. Sense of purpose is renewed
8. Life-style invariably is altered to pursue beauty, truth, justice and the good of others.

The experience can be neither earned nor manufactured.

Maslow also identified the Jonah complex, where we are ambivalent about such experiences of joy and we try to evade them. The Jonah complex is characterized by fears of:

1. Being overwhelmed by the experience
2. Becoming self-indulgent
3. Surrendering to fate
4. Being out of control
5. Not being able to discriminate
6. Being irresponsible.

Maslow used art, music, dance, and sex, in the search for the paths to peak experiences.

PERSONA (*See also*: Psyche)

The Latin word for person. In classical Roman theatre it was a 'mask' worn by actors to express the role being played. In Jungian psychology it is the mask or public face we put on to meet the world and which develops from the pressures of society.

It is the part of self that mediates between the unconscious and world of external reality, in much the same way as the Anima or Animus mediates between the ego and the internal world.

The difference is that the persona is concerned with the conscious and collective adaptation, the Anima and Animus are concerned with adaptation that is personal, internal, and individual.

EXAMPLES OF PERSONA:

1. Gender identity
2. A specific stage of development
3. Social status
4. Job or profession.

For Jung, the persona is the social archetype, something that involves compromises in order to live in a community.

People who identify too closely with their persona are not sufficiently self-aware, and therefore run the risk of pathology.

PERSONAL CONSTRUCT THEORY (*See also*: Constructs, Frames of reference, Repertory grid)

A model developed by George A. Kelly, based on the belief that our understanding of others and interactions with them are dependent upon getting inside their psychological world. Our thoughts, feelings and behaviours are bound up with our system of constructs.

In Kelly's view, people are 'scientists', constantly developing theories about events, creating hypotheses, then experimenting with their behaviour to test the theories.

People whose predictions or anticipations are proved correct, have a fair amount of control over their personal world. If we don't like what we experience from our behavioural experiments, we may change constructs and subsequent behaviour.

Constructive alternativism is Kelly's term to describe the idea that constructs can be abandoned or modified depending on whether or not the theory is validated.

A construct is the way we make sense of things that are alike or different from each other. While 'construct' is often used as a synonym for concept, Kelly maintained that construct had wider meaning. A construct is a cluster of characteristics shared by one event that distinguishes and makes it different from another event.

Each construct is bipolar in nature - happy and sad being the two poles of one construct. Constructs are working hypotheses, predictions, appraisals, which form psychic templates and predetermine our behaviour.

Core constructs are so central to the person's identity that, if shaken, the individual is likely to experience great anxiety.

Peripheral constructs are less crucial and can be altered more readily.

A superordinate construct is one that includes other subordinate constructs within its makeup.

A fundamental theme in personal construct theory is that there are alternative ways of looking at any event. 'Truth' does exist, but access is denied to us. We can only interpret truth and that interpretation is limited.

We are always constructing new theories and looking for new and alternative answers. When, for example, we distinguish a person as 'hostile', we predict certain responses and not others, and act accordingly.

A child develops constructs as it learns the difference between, for example, 'floor' and 'pavement'; 'pavement' and road'.

Generally we experience anxiety whenever we are aware of our constructs undergoing change. The person who could no longer determine that night would follow day would be in a state of acute anxiety.

Kelly developed the 'repertory grid' and 'self-characterization' (as if sketching a character in a play) as techniques to gain insight into a person's personal world.

Construct development does not depend upon words; the young child starts developing preverbal constructs before it can attach words to them. Effective communication depends on the extent to which one person understands the constructs of another person. Understanding personal constructs is the basis of empathy.

An application of self-characterization is fixed role therapy, where the therapist constructs a role for the client. The client is then encouraged to live this new role for a fixed period.

KELLY'S FUNDAMENTAL POSTULATE

A person's processes are psychologically channelized by the ways in which that person anticipates events.

1. Processes indicates that the person is a behaving organism
2. Channelized refers to a network of flexible but structured pathways
3. Anticipated – prediction and motivation; the 'push and pull' of personal constructs.

KELLY'S ELEVEN COROLLARIES:

1. *Construction*. Events are anticipated by interpreting similarities and differences.
2. *Individuality*. Individuals differ from one another in the way events are interpreted.
3. *Organization*. We all develop our own construction system; how we interpret events and relationships between constructs.
4. *Dichotomy*. Our construction system is composed of a limited number of bipolar constructs.
5. *Choice*. A choice is made between one part of a construct or the other that will extend, not limit, the total construction system.
6. *Range*. Constructs are limited and apply only to specific events.
7. *Experience*. The construction is modified in the light of experience.
8. *Modulation*. Constructs may be modified according to the permeability of the construct to allow new elements in. A construct is permeable if it admits newly perceived elements to its context. It is impermeable if it rejects elements on the basis of their newness. Some constructs are impermeable, rigid, and frozen. Elements are the things or events a person uses to compare the construct with.
9. *Fragmentation*. Generally we successfully handle different, and sometimes opposing construction subsystems.
10. *Commonality*. The constructs of different people may be similar, depending on the similarity of their psychological processes.
11. *Sociality*. The extent to which people can play a part in the social process of others depends on how accurately they interpret constructs.

Personal construct theory is a highly systematized, rational, intellectual, precise, and 'scientific' method of psychotherapy and counselling. On taking this into account, it may not appeal to some people who prefer to work more with feelings.

PERSONAL UNCONSCIOUS (*See also*: Collective unconscious)

A term in Analytic (Jungian) psychology to describe the surface layer of the unconscious, resting on the collective unconscious. It consists mainly of subliminal perceptions and repressed experiences which are influenced by the collective unconscious.

PERSONALITY DISORDER

This is an umbrella term that provides cover for a number of psychological disorders not easily grouped in any other way. It was originally used for any mental disorder that showed some sort of maladjustment in motivation and maladaptive behaviour.

The term, which generally excludes neuroses and psychoses, means pathological developments in one's overall personality in which anxiety or distress do not feature prominently.

Personality disorders are deeply ingrained patterns of thought and behaviour that are generally recognized during adolescence or earlier, and usually continue throughout adult life. Someone suffering from personality disorder may also suffer from a mental illness.

1. The paranoid type shows excessive sensitiveness to setbacks, humiliation or rebuffs.

   There is also a tendency to misconstrue the friendly actions of others as hostile or contemptuous and a strong tendency to respond aggressively when personal rights appear to be attacked.
2. The cyclothymic type shows pronounced mood that may be persistently depressed or persistently elated, or swinging between the two.
3. The explosive shows instability of mood, with liability to unrestrained outbursts of anger, hate, violence, or affection.
4. The obsessional. This is similar to obsessional neuroses, differing only in the severity, with feelings of personal insecurity, doubt and incompleteness and excessive conscientiousness. The person is plagued by insistent and unwelcome thoughts or/and impulses. Rigidity of thought and excessive doubt are also characteristic.
5. Hysterical personalities are characterized by shallow, unstable emotions, dependency on others, and craving for appreciations and attention. They are suggestible, theatrical, and sometimes sexually immature.
6. Dependent personalities are passively compliant with the wishes of people in authority. They have difficulty coping with the demands of daily living.
7. The sociopathic type have a disregard for social obligations. They show lack of feeling for others, are impetuous. They may have a tendency to violence with an unconcern for their actions. They tend to be emotionally cold and lack remorse.

   They are often abnormally aggressive, irresponsible, with a low tolerance level. They are frequently plausible and tend to blame others for what they themselves do.

PERSONALITY TYPE (OCCUPATIONAL) (*See also*: Occupational choice and development theory)

PERSONALITY CHARACTERISTICS

1. ARTISTIC TYPE

   A. Complicated
   B. Emotional
   C. Feminine
   D. Imaginative
   E. Impulsive
   F. Independent
   G. Introspective
   H. Intuitive
   I. Non-conforming
   J. Original.

Possible occupations

   A. Actor
   B. Architect
   C. Artist
   D. Drama teacher
   E. Writer.

2. Conventional type

   A. Conforming
   B. Conscientious
   C. Inflexible
   D. Inhibited
   E. Obedient

F. Orderly
G. Persistent
H. Practical
I. Self-controlled
J. Unimaginative.

Possible occupations

A. Bookkeeper
B. Key punch operator
C. Mail clerk
D. Teller
E. Typist.

3. ENTERPRISING TYPE

A. Acquisitive
B. Adventurous
C. Ambitious
D. Domineering
E. Energetic
F. Exhibitionistic
G. Impulsive
H. Optimistic
I. Self-confident
J. Sociable.

Possible occupations

A. Administrator
B. Banker
C. Car dealer
D. Manager

4. INVESTIGATIVE TYPE

A. Analytical
B. Critical
C. Curious
D. Independent
E. Intellectual
F. Introverted
G. Methodical
H. Rational.

Possible occupations

A. Astronomer
B. Anthropologist
C. Biologist
D. Mathematician.
E. Research analyst.

5. Realistic type

A. Asocial
B. Conforming
C. Frank
D. Genuine
E. Masculine
F. Materialistic
G. Persistent
H. Practical
I. Stable
J. Uninsightful.

Possible occupations

A. Aircraft mechanic
B. Civil engineer
C. Electrician
D. Filling station attendant.

6. SOCIAL TYPE

A. Co-operative
B. Responsible
C. Friendly
D. Helpful
E. Idealistic
F. Insightful
G. Kind
H. Persuasive.

Possible occupations

A. Clergyman
B. College professor
C. Counsellor
D. Personnel director
E. Social worker.

PERSON-CENTRED THERAPY
(Carl R. Rogers (1902–1987)) (*See also*: Core conditions, Frames of reference, Non-directive therapy)

Rogers, an American, whose study of theology convinced him that he was not suited to pulpit ministry, turned to psychology and psychoanalysis.

His study of children led him to question the validity of some of the fundamental tenets of psychoanalysis.

Rogers developed the non-directive approach to counselling, based on his unshakeable belief that clients needed to have much more control over the therapeutic process than they were given in traditional therapy.

The person-centred approach (as it is now called) emphasizes the capacity and strengths of clients to direct the course and direction of their own therapy. The concept of self-actualization is at the centre of person-centred therapy, in common with other humanistic therapies, philosophies, and approaches.

Fundamental to the method is the relationship established between therapist and client, based on the core conditions of:

1. *Empathy*, the ability to appreciate a client's personal meanings, and to accompany that client as he or she progresses through therapy.
2. *Non-possessive warmth*. A warmth that is given genuinely for the needs of the client, not for the needs of the therapist. It enables, it does not stifle.
3. *Unconditional positive regard*. A genuine regard without strings attached. It is a demonstration of sincere trust, that allows the client to verbalize that which is so often unallowable.
4. *Genuineness or congruence*. The degree to which we are freely and deeply ourselves, and are able to relate to people in a sincere and undefensive manner. Genuineness is being real.

Person-centred therapists are strongly anti-technical, anti-skill and anti-techniques. They prefer to talk about attitudes and behaviours, and creating growth-promoting climates.

Their view of their clients is that they are intrinsically good, capable of directing their own destinies and capable of self-actualization.

The focus is on entering the client's frame of reference and understanding and tracking the client's personal meanings. This does not mean that the therapist is passive. Being able to enter the client's frame of reference means active listening and a continual struggle to lay aside preconceptions that would hinder the process. The person-centred therapist also believes in the importance of rejecting the pursuit of authority or control over others. Power is there to be shared.

The answers to two basic questions are sought in therapy, 'Who am I?' 'How can I become myself?'

The person-centred approach, in common with many other therapies, is less successful with severely disturbed psychotic clients. Person-centred principles have been applied in the classroom, in colleges, in organizations and in groups. Critics of the approach argue that it is naive and does not help the client face reality.

The fundamental theory is in the form of an 'if-then' hypothesis. If the core conditions are present, then growth and change will take place.

PERSON-CENTRED CONSTRUCTS

1. The *Actualizing tendency* is an inherent tendency to develop in ways that serve to maintain or enhance the individual. The term includes the concepts of need-reduction and drive-reduction, which have three tendencies: to seek tensions that cause pleasure, to be creative, and to learn to walk.

2. *Experience*. This includes all that is potentially available to awareness, both conscious and unconscious: the psychological aspects of physiological functions; the stimulations received through the senses; the influences of memory.
3. *Feeling* is an emotional experience plus its personal, cognitive meaning.
4. *Awareness*, which may vary between 'dim' or 'sharp', represents some part of experience. Experiences become available to awareness when they are not denied or defended. As the symbols of awareness do not always match reality, it is necessary to separate out the real from the unreal.
5. *Self* refers to the organized, consistent perceptions of the 'I', and the relationship of 'I' to others. The ideal self is the self-concept the person would most like to possess. Self experiences are the crude material from which the self-concept is formed.

   Confusion and tension result in a state of vulnerability when there is incongruity between the self-concept and actual experience, Unawareness of incongruity between self and experience makes us vulnerable to anxiety and disorganization.
6. *Anxiety and threat*. Anxiety is a state of unease or tension the cause of which is unknown. Threat exists when an actual or anticipated experience is incongruent with the self-concept and the total experience. A threat to the maintenance of self-concept results in a behavioural defence.
7. *Psychological maladjustment* is where certain significant experiences are denied or distorted so as not to admit them to awareness. This results in incongruity between self and experience.
8. *Intensional/Extensional*. When we react or perceive in an intensional manner, we tend toward rigidity and to:

   A. See experiences in absolute and unconditional terms
   B. Overgeneralize
   C. Be ruled by concept or belief
   D. Fail to relate facts to time and space
   E. Confuse fact and evaluation
   F. Rely on abstract reasoning rather than on reality testing.

   When we react or perceive in an extensional manner, we tend toward flexibility and to:

   A. Differentiate between experiences
   B. Relate facts to time and space
   C. Be ruled by facts, not by concepts or beliefs
   D. Use a variety of ways to evaluate experiences
   E. Be aware of different levels of abstraction
   F. Test inferences and abstractions against reality.

9. *Congruence of self and experience*. Therapy enables people to reorganize their self-concept, in order to accommodate unacceptable characteristics, hitherto inconsistent with the self-concept. To the (striving toward) truly open person, awareness and experience are totally congruent. The best possible psychological adjustment is synonymous with complete congruence or openness.

10. *Maturity*. We exhibit mature behaviour when we:
    - A. Perceive realistically
    - B. Perceive in an extensional manner
    - C. Are not defensive
    - D. Accept individual uniqueness
    - E. Are responsible for our behaviour
    - F. Evaluate experiences on the evidence of our own senses
    - G. Are prepared to change our evaluations on the evidence of new experiences
    - H. Prize ourselves and others.
11. *Conditions of worth*. Worth is often conditional on the approval of significant others, and on taking over their values. Conditional worth disturbs our self-valuing process and interferes with full functioning.

    When we have an internal locus of evaluation we assume responsibility for valuing ourselves according to our own perceptions. When we have an external locus of evaluation we judge others by our own values and standards.
12. *Frame of reference* (*see* entry).

STAGES IN THERAPY

Stage 1

- A. Client communicates about externals.
- B. Feelings are not owned.
- C. Constructs are rigid.
- D. The client is reluctant to engage in close relationships.

Stage 2

- A. Feelings are sometimes described but not owned.
- B. Keeps subjective experience at a distance.
- C. Problems are perceived as external to self.

Stage 3

- A. Feelings and personal meanings in the past are described, usually as unacceptable or bad.
- B. Expressions of self are in objective terms.
- C. Self tends to be seen as a part of others.
- D. Personal constructs are rigid.
- E. Some recognition that problems are personal and not external.

Stage 4

- A. Free and full description of feelings and personal meanings.
- B. Intense feelings are not described in the present.
- C. The possibility of feelings breaking through causes alarm.
- D. Unwilling to experience feelings.
- E. Personal constructs become more free.
- F. What was absolute now becomes possibility.
- G. Some recognition of self-responsibility.

Stage 5

- A. Easier to express feelings in the present.
- B. Owning of feelings.
- C. Immediacy of feelings is less fearful.
- D. More able to tolerate contradictions and ambiguities.
- E. Personal constructs and meanings are open to question.
- F. More acceptance of self-responsibility.

Stage 6

A. Acceptance, and immediate expression, of previously denied feelings.
B. Feelings expressed bring liberation through catharsis.
C. Acceptance of the validity of working in the present.
D. Self is real, not an object.
E. Flexible constructs replace inflexible ones.

Stage 7

A. The client feels comfortable with living in present experiencing.
B. The immediacy of feelings are experienced with enhanced richness.
C. Able to risk expressing feelings.

The therapist's task is to facilitate clients' awareness of, and trust in, self-actualization. The therapeutic process is centred in the client and it is the client's inner experiencing that controls the pace and the direction of the relationship.

When clients are accepted, and when the core conditions are present, they feel safe enough to explore their problems and gradually come to experience the parts of themselves they normally keep hidden from themselves and from others.

PHALLIC STAGE (*See also*: Electra complex, Oedipus complex)

A psychoanalytic term to describe the third stage of psychosexual development in which there is interest in the sexual organs. Sexual gratification occurs through direct experience with the genitals. The phallic stage occurs between the age of three and seven years, when we unconsciously desire to possess the parent of the opposite sex.

PHENOMENOLOGY (*See also*: Existentialism, Jaspers, Karl T.)

Phenomenology is a school of philosophy that arose in the early years of the present century. It is the study of all human experience as free as possible from presupposition or bias. Phenomenology is the basic method of existentialism.

Phenomenologists limit their study to conscious experiences without trying to elicit underlying hypothetical causes. The data they produce are formulated from the subject's point of view.

Phenomenologists as a rule reject the idea of the unconscious. They believe we can learn more about human nature by studying how people view themselves and their world than we can by observing their actions.

In that phenomenologists are more concerned with internal mental processes and the inner life and experiences of individuals – self-concept, feelings of self-esteem and self-awareness – than with behaviour, they have certain similarity to cognitivists.

Phenomenologists believe that we are free agents, that we are not acted upon by forces beyond our control, but that we have a great degree of control over our own destiny. The issue of free will versus determinism.

Most humanistic therapies, with their emphasis on self-actualization, are grounded in phenomenology.

Counsellors who use a phenomenological approach concentrate on what is happening now. Most personality theories look at the person from the outside; phenomenology attempts to enter the person's own psychological experience, to try to understand what something means to that person. A phrase often used by Carl Rogers, 'from the internal frame of reference of the individual', sums up the phenomenological experience.

PLEASURE PRINCIPLE (*See also*: Reality principle)

A term in Psychoanalytic psychology to describe the basic human tendency of the person to maintain a pleasant, tolerable energy level through the relief of inner tension and in so doing to avoid pain and to seek pleasure.

The terms 'pleasure' and 'pain' may be misleading; 'gratification' and 'unpleasure' may be more accurate.

The pleasure principle is conspicuous in the first years of life and is moderated by the development of the reality principle. It is not so much that pleasure is actively sought, but that discomfort is actively avoided in order to keep instinctual tension in the best possible balance.

Rather than regard the pleasure and the reality principles in opposition to each other, it might be advantageous to think of them as two integral parts that each operate in a different way to keep the organism balanced, in much the same way as do the parts in a thermostat.

POST-TRAUMATIC STRESS DISORDER (PTSD) (*See also*: Critical incidents, Crisis intervention)

The term first appeared in the third edition of the *Diagnostic and Statistical Manual of Mental Disorders* (DSM-111), grouped under anxiety disorders. After the Second World War, the condition became known as 'concentration-camp syndrome'. PTSD is a feature of many catastrophic events, and is particularly linked to war conditions.

The essential feature is the development of characteristic symptoms following a psychologically traumatic event that is generally outside the range of human experience and where the symptoms persist for at least one month. The event would be distressing to almost anyone and would involve, for example:

1. Serious threat to life or physical integrity.
2. Serious threat or harm to one's children, spouse, or other close relatives and friends.
3. Sudden destruction of home or community.
4. Seeing another person who has recently been, or is being, seriously injured or killed as the result of accident or violence.

The traumatic event is persistently re-experienced in at least one of:

1. Recurrent and intrusive distressing recollections of the event. Children often engage in repetitive play in which themes or parts of the trauma are expressed.
2. Recurrent, distressing dreams of the event.
3. Sudden acting or feeling as if the traumatic event was recurring. This may include reliving the experience, illusions, hallucinations, and dissociative episodes (flashbacks), that may occur at any time.
4. Intense psychological distress at exposure to events that symbolize or resemble an aspect of the traumatic event, including anniversaries.

Avoidance of the topic, or numbing of responses, may show as:

1. Strenuous efforts to avoid thoughts or feelings associated with the trauma or to avoid activities or situations that arouse recollections of the event.
2. Inability to recall an important aspect of the trauma.
3. Marked lack of interest in significant activities. In young children there may be loss of recently acquired skills.
4. Feelings of detachment or estrangement.
5. Restricted range of emotions.
6. Pessimism about the future.

Symptoms may persist and may show as:

1. Difficulty falling or staying asleep
2. Irritability or outbursts of anger
3. Difficulty in concentrating
4. Ever on the alert
5. Easily startled
6. Anxiety when exposed to situations that resemble the traumatic event.

Stressors in PTSD would include:

1. Rape or assault
2. Military combat
3. Natural and manufactured catastrophes
4. Physical or sexual abuse.

CRITICAL INCIDENT STRESS DEBRIEFING

Debriefing, ideally, should take place on day 2, 3 or 4 following the incident. Day one is too soon. After day four, perceptions, feelings and reactions begin to harden and the debriefing begins to have less healing value.

The debriefing should be conducted by an experienced group facilitator who has experience of stress management. Only people with direct experience of the event should be present with the facilitator.

Debriefing is not an evaluation of behaviour, but a time for sharing feelings and experiences, not relating those of other people. It is necessary to warn participants that they may feel worse at first talking about these things, but it will help to prevent more serious problems developing.

Staff who provide support to traumatized and bereaved people need recognition, support, stress relief, adequate supervision, and the chance to record their experience, and to properly round off their participation when the time is right. Individual counselling may also be required, to help people work through their grief reactions.

PRECONSCIOUS (*See also*: Censor, Defence mechanisms, Working through)

In psychoanalysis, the area of the mind between the conscious and the unconscious. The 'antechamber' to consciousness. It is also referred to as the descriptive unconscious or the foreconscious.

The contents of the preconscious – knowledge, emotions, images – although not immediately in the conscious, are accessible to it because the censorship is absent.

Material can be described as temporarily forgotten; suppressed, and not repressed.

The preconscious is important in the process of working through, a process necessary to consolidate the insight gained through interpretation.

PREJUDICE (*See aso*: Authoritarian personality, Open-mindedness)

The literal meaning refers to forming an attitude without just grounds, or without sufficient evidence. It is also an adverse or hostile attitude toward a group or its individual members.

A prejudice may be either positive or negative and may be about a particular thing, event, person or idea. Prejudice is characterized by irrational, stereotyped beliefs and views and their accompanying emotions and values.

Prejudice tells more about the bearer of the attitude than about the persons who are the objects of the prejudice. Prejudiced behaviour is discrimination.

An essential characteristic of prejudice is the need to separate into acceptable and non-acceptable, which act as 'filters' or evaluators. The self-image we have is closely tied in with the image of the group as a whole.

PRESENTING PROBLEM

What clients complain of; the client's 'admission ticket' to therapy. The presenting problem may be in the nature of a 'trial balloon'; not of primary importance, but of sufficient import to generate some anxiety. The presenting problem can be thought of, in musical terms, as an 'overture'. An audience does not judge the performance by the overture; they wait to hear the full work.

In psychoanalytic and humanistic therapies, the presenting problem is regarded as symbolic of the client's underlying difficulties.

In therapies that concentrate on behaviour, the presenting problem is regarded as significant, and treated accordingly. The professional discipline and theoretical orientation of the therapist will influence how the presenting problem is handled.

PRIMAL THERAPY

A psychologically violent, defence-shattering method developed by Arthur Janov. The aim of primal therapy is, through catharsis, to unblock repressed, painful feelings about one's unmet needs as an unborn child.

Janov refers to 'primal pain', arising from the 'major primal scene' – the infantile experience or fantasy about parental intercourse; for clients to recognize and then express their deepest feelings about their parents and their primal traumas.

Primal trauma refers to some painful experience: the experience of birth, and especially severe punishment, the death of a parent, witnessing parental coitus (the primal scene), or the knowledge of not being loved.

The theory behind primal therapy derives from Otto Rank, Winnicott, Balint and Laing. The French obstetrician Leboyer has stressed the importance of the first few minutes outside of the womb in establishing the mother–child bond.

The theory is that the pain of the trauma experienced before, during, and in the early months after birth, is kept from conscious awareness, but at the cost of neurotic symptoms and psychological disorders later in life.

Primal therapy uses various techniques and methods to deal with the traumas of conception, implantation (the struggle of the fertilized ovum to implant itself on the wall of the womb), birth and infancy. It consists in helping the client relive primal scenes until the 'primal pool' has been systematically emptied; dismantling the defences to leave only a 'real self'.

The point is stressed; that 'recall' and 'remember' are activities of the mind; to 'relive' is absolute. Blocking the pain creates neuroses; feeling the pain undoes it.

Clients are encouraged to confront memories whenever they surface, on the principle that every time catharsis occurs, a little more of the primal pool is drained away, and with it, neurotic symptoms. Having gone through the dark underworld of reliving the pain, post-primal clients have satisfied or completed their childhood needs, and are able to disengage from their (often unrealistic) longings for what their parents might have given them.

As therapy is directive, confrontative, and traumatic, therapists are 'on-call' day or night for several weeks following therapy.

PROBLEM-SOLVING INTERVENTIONS (*See also*: Action plans, Goals and goal-setting)

These are goal-directed techniques aimed at improving the abilities of an individual or a family. Symptoms such as anxiety and depression may be due to the client's inadequate attempts at resolving certain situations. When new problem-solving skills are learned, the symptoms may fade.

Effective problem-solving can only take place when well-defined phases are pursued:

1. Define the problem
2. Decide a method of attack for the problem
3. Generate alternatives
4. Test alternatives for reality
5. Choose an alternative
6. Plan for action
7. Implement the plan
8. Evaluation
9. Next steps.

Often, when confronted with a problem, we are deluded into a false sense of security by counterproductive steps:

1. Denying the problem exists
2. Ignoring it, hoping it will go away
3. Blame something or someone for it
4. Blame oneself.

Before one can start on the problem-solving process it is necessary to acknowledge that one exists and that we intend to do something.

Step 1 – Define the problem

This diagnostic stage helps to identify if there is conflict and if so, where.

1. Whose problem is it?
2. Who is doing what, to whom?
3. Are the perceptions accurate?
4. Is communication distorted?
5. What is at stake?
6. What decisions have to be made?

Defining the problem provides clarity, understanding, and purpose.

Step 2 – Decide a method of attack

1. Is there anyone else who can help?
2. Do you need any more information?
3. Do you know anyone else who has successfully solved this problem?
4. What sources can you tap?

Step 3 – Generate alternatives

1. Brainstorm, if possible with someone else.
2. Think through each alternative,

looking at positive and negative aspects.

Step 4 – Test alternatives for reality

1. Don't eliminate possibilities too quickly.
2. Try operating the 'detailed response' before rejecting something. This means that before a suggestion is rejected, you must have generated at least three positive statements about it.
3. Work out a 'for' and 'against' for each possibility.
4. When all possibilities have been filtered through the detailed response, arrange them in a hierarchy of feasibility.

Step 5 – Choose an alternative

1. Use Force field analysis (*see* entry).
2. The chosen alternative must be within one's capability and within available resources.

Step 6 – Plan for action

It is necessary to choose a planning process that is appropriate to the potential solution. There is a danger of becoming so engrossed in the planning that the original problem, or the alternatives, are lost sight of.

Step 7 – Implement the plan

Use Rudyard Kipling's 'Six honest serving men' 5Wh: Who? What? Why? When? Where? How?

Step 8 – Evaluation is at two levels

1. An evaluation of the action plan itself; how far did the plan meet the set goals and objectives. It may be necessary to go back to step 6.
2. The second level evaluates how effective the overall problem-solving was. Just how far did the plan contribute to the outcome.

Step 9 – Next steps

Follow-up is essential. If the original problem still exists, use 5Wh. It may be necessary to go back to step 1 and work through the process once more. Follow-up may also be helpful to consolidate the learning experience.

Problem-solving is aided by:

1. Having a healthy self-respect, which also means accepting the consequences of one's own personal worth and contributions.
2. A healthy other-respect. This may mean giving credit to those who think differently. It also means being able to listen to what others say.
3. A healthy optimism that problems can be solved if everyone is willing to work at them to find an acceptable solution.
4. A respect for, but not fear of, conflict as being potentially creative.
5. A willingness to invest energy and to take risks.

SKILLS ESSENTIAL IN PROBLEM-SOLVING

1. Active listening, clarifying, paraphrasing, self-disclosure
2. Diagnostic skills (steps 1–2)
3. Decision-making skills (steps 2–5)
4. Data-collecting skills (steps 5–6)
5. Design and planning skills (steps 5–8)
6. Organizing/administrative skills (step 7)
7. Analysis skills (step 8).

Counsellors can help clients to develop their problem-solving skills and so reduce the helplessness they feel at being confronted with a problem that seems unsurmountable.

PROJECTION (Defence mechanism)

'It's happening to you, not to me.'

In psychoanalysis, the process by which one's own traits, emotions, dispositions, ideas, wishes, and failings are attributed to other, which are then perceived as an external threat.

Projection of aspects of oneself is preceded by a denial that one feels such an emotion, has such a desire or wish, but that someone else does possess these feelings and tendencies. In the process some conflict is repressed.

The Kleinian approach views projection as a normal aspect of psychological development, and not indicative of neurosis.

In psychoses, projection takes the form of delusions of persecution.

CHARACTERISTICS OF PEOPLE WHO USE PROJECTION:

1. Excessive fault-finding
2. Very sensitive to criticism
3. Prejudice
4. Collect injustices.

An example would be where a student cheats in an exam, then justifies his action by claiming that all students cheat.

Openness and concern for the client's rights and maintaining a professional formality are helpful. Confrontation is likely to lead to the relationship being terminated. Being able to work within the client's frame of reference is essential, without necessarily giving agreement to what is often an underlying paranoid feeling.

PROJECTIVE IDENTIFICATION (Defence mechanism) (*See also*: Empathy, Scapegoating)

Where unacceptable parts of self are put on to another person, identification with the object of the projection then takes place.

It serves to protect the ego against the anxieties of being persecuted by others and being separated from them. Thus it leads to a divorce from reality. The object is discerned as threatening, and therefore must be controlled.

Projective identification allows one to distance oneself from others, while at the same time to make oneself understood by applying pressure on others to experience feelings similar to one's own.

Projective identification has a non-pathological function; it is an early form of empathy, and of symbol formation, both of which are essential in therapy. It is also a feature in the process of scapegoating.

PROVOCATIVE THERAPY (*See also*: Rational emotive therapy Paradoxical intention)

Provocative therapy grew out of dissatisfaction with Person-centred therapy. The aim is to elicit behaviours and feelings that are more appropriate and of which the client approves, than at present are being expressed.

TECHNIQUES USED:

1. Confrontation
2. Feedback
3. Paradox
4. Humour
5. Action techniques
6. Negative modelling to mirror the client's behaviour in exaggerated form
7. Therapeutic double-bind.

The therapist often acts as 'devil's advocate', to goad the client into altering some aspect of behaviour. Provocative therapy does not subscribe to most of the cautions embraced by other approaches. It provides an abrasive, stimulating experience, mainly through a manipulation of the client–therapist relationship.

While the method (like all others) is open to criticism, the authors claim success, particularly with long-term hospitalized psychotic patients.

PSYCHE

The oldest and most general meaning of 'psyche' is by the early Greeks, who regarded it as 'soul', or the very essence of life. In classical mythology, the heroine in the story of Cupid and Psyche.

A certain Greek king had three daughters, of whom Psyche, the youngest, was so beautiful that people worshipped her and neglected Venus. Venus (Aphrodite) was so jealous she sent her son Cupid (Eros) with instructions to make her fall in love with some ugly old man.

Cupid instead fell in love with Psyche himself. He told her that she must never see him, but one night, while looking at him by the light of a lamp, he awoke and fled.

Psyche was desolate and searched far and wide for him. She finally submitted herself to Venus who set her four impossible tasks: to sort a huge pile of different seeds into their respective piles; to acquire some golden fleece from the terrible rams of the sun; to fill a crystal container from an inaccessible stream; to descend into the underworld and fill a small box with beauty ointment. This last task was made all the more difficult because Psyche would have to harden her heart to compassion.

Psyche completed all her tasks, the first three with assistance from ants, a green reed and an eagle. The final task she accomplished by saying 'No'. Cupid persuaded Zeus, the Father of the God to let him marry Psyche, he agreed and Psyche was made immortal.

In Greek folklore the soul was pictured as a butterfly – another meaning of both 'psyche' and 'soul'. The soul or spirit, distinguished from the body.

The mind functioning as the centre of thought, feeling, and behaviour, and consciously or unconsciously adjusting and relating the body to its social and physical environment.

In Analytical psychology the psyche is the sum total of all the conscious and unconscious psychic processes. The soul is regarded as the sum total of personality, comprising the persona, the outward face or attitude, the mask, the anima (in men) and the animus (in women), the inward attitude or face.

The four main functions of the psyche are Intuition, Sensing, Thinking, and Feeling. Each approaches reality from a different point of view and with a different question. Each grasps a different part of reality.

PSYCHIC PAIN (*See also*: Primal therapy)

Psychic pain is pain of the heart, mind and spirit. It is as real and powerful as any physical pain. Suppression of psychic pain very often leads to physical disorders.

Psychic pain is often the pain of the deepest sadness, where the person feels 'like a dried out husk', and where tears – normally therapeutic

– dry up in the eyes before they can be shed.

Many people are taught that it is a worthy thing to endure physical pain. In the same way there is the myth that to admit to psychic pain is a sign of weakness. Suppression of psychic pain drives it deeper into the mind and into the body, and healing is therefore made much more difficult. Locked in pain wastes valuable creative energy and leads to exhaustion.

Many people are now experimenting with new therapies to relieve physical pain. People who can be encouraged to express their psychic pain through counselling are likely to discover a generally improved state of physical health. Pain and anger are close companions. The ability to express anger is one way of expressing the underlying pain.

Psychic pain begins to be experienced at the moment of birth; it is the price we pay for separation. It is also the price we have to pay for forming relationships, for within every relationship lies the seeds of separation. Psychic pain may be caused by such experiences as:

1. Bereavement
2. Divorce
3. Enforced isolation
4. Helplessness
5. Loneliness
6. Poverty
7. Loss of purpose
8. Loss of self-esteem.

PSYCHOANALYSIS (Sigmund Freud (1856–1939)) (*See also*: Ego, Id, Superego)

Freud was born in Moravia, settled and worked in Vienna, and died in London. His psychology and psychotherapeutic method is described as 'depth psychology'.

When working with patients under hypnosis (with Josef Breuer), Freud observed that often there was improvement in the condition when the sources of the patients' ideas and impulses were brought into the conscious.

Also observing that patients talked freely while under hypnosis, he evolved his technique of free association. Noting that sometimes patients had difficulty in making free associations, he concluded that painful experiences were being repressed and held back from conscious awareness. Freud deduced that what was being repressed were disturbing sexual experiences – real or fantasy.

Repressed sexual energy and its consequent anxiety find an outlet in various symptoms that serve as ego defences. The concept of anxiety now includes feelings of guilt, fear, shame, aggression, hostility, and fear of loneliness at the separation from someone on whom the sufferer is dependent.

Psychoanalysis, behaviourism, and humanistic psychology is the trilogy of the main orientations to psychotherapy.

Psychoanalysis includes investigating mental processes not easily accessed by other means. It is a method of investigating and treating neurotic disorders, and the scientific collection of psychological information. The main purpose of psychoanalysis is to make unconscious material conscious.

PSYCHOSEXUAL (LIBIDINAL) DEVELOPMENT

1. The oral phase which centres around feeding and the associated organs – mouth, lips, and tongue.

2. The anal phase which is the main source of pleasure and libidinal gratification comes from the activities surrounding the retaining and passing of faeces.
3. The phallic phase in which the genital organs become the principal object of interest, with exhibitionist and voyeuristic wishes.
4. The latency period is a relatively quiescent period following the resolution of the Oedipus complex and the consolidation of the superego; the lull before the stormy puberty and adolescence.
5. The genital phase is the final stage of psychosexual development, usually around late adolescence.

THE MAIN TECHNIQUES OF PSYCHOANALYSIS:

1. Free association (*see* entry)
2. Interpretation of dreams, resistance, and parapraxes
3. Analysing the transference.

PSYCHOANALYTIC ASSUMPTIONS

1. The concepts are applicable to normal and abnormal behaviour.
2. The existence of a tripartite mental apparatus – id, ego, and superego.
3. The idea of psychological adaptation – where the mental apparatus attempts to reduce conflict as much as possible.
4. The idea of psychic determinism – that all aspects of the mental life are determined, that nothing in the mental life is due to chance, any more than in the physical world.
5. That there is both a conscious and an unconscious world.

BASIC CONCEPTS

1. The pleasure principle – the tendency of all natural impulses or 'wishes' to seek their own satisfaction, independent of all other considerations.
2. Instincts. Throughout life, three basic instincts may either work together or oppose each other.

   A. Eros – self-preservation, libido.
   B. Thanatos – death, destruction. Operates to lead what is living back to an inorganic state.
   C. The aggressive instinct is derived from and is the main representation of the death instinct.

3. The conscious and the unconscious

   A. Consciousness has the function of a sense organ for the perception of physical qualities. Material becomes conscious from both the external world and from within.
   B. The unconscious has two levels, the unconscious proper, which contains repressed material, admissible to the conscious only through analysis, and the preconscious, which refers to material, though unconscious, that is available and accessible.

4. The mental apparatus

   A. The id is the oldest of these systems. It contains everything that is inherited and fixed in the constitution. It is filled with energy from the instincts and strives to operate the pleasure principle. It is a chaos, a cauldron of seething emotions. It knows no judgment, values, good or evil, and knows no morality. It is not governed by logic.

B. The ego (or 'I') is derived from bodily sensations and mediates between the id and the outside world. It represents reason and common sense and operates the reality principle to control the destructive potential of the id's pleasure principle. It solves problems and perceives. Freud described the id as a horse and the ego as its rider.

C. The superego is the sum of the influences of parents and family (modified by other people), culture and race. It is moralistic and it may be benign or punitive, harsh, and restricting.

The superego operates the ego-ideal, based on the admiration the child feels for its ideal parent. The ego-ideal consists of precepts ('You ought to be like this') and prohibitions ('You ought not to be like that'). Both precepts and prohibitions result from the struggle to resolve the Oedipus complex and also represent conscience.

5. Anxiety is a reaction to actual danger or a signal involving the perception of impending danger which may be Realistic (from the environment); Moral (conflict with the superego), or Neurotic (conflict with the id's impulses).
6. Psychical energy, cathexis and anti-athexis. The id, ego, and superego are charged with psychical energy, similar to an electric charge. Cathexis is a neologism invented by Freud, analogous to the flow of an electrical charge. Anti-cathexis is a blocking of the discharge of energy.
7. Bisexuality. Freud believed that all human beings are constitutionally psychosexually bisexual. As evidence of this he points to the biological fact that male and female have vestiges of the organs of the other sex, and that libido is asexual. Both the woman and the man develop out of the child with a bisexual disposition.

NORMAL DEVELOPMENT

This may be viewed as:

1. A passage through successive stages of sexual maturation without major fixations and regressions.
2. Developing an ego that copes reasonably effectively with the external world.
3. Developing a superego based on constructive identifications.
4. Not developing punitively, moralistic, and evolving defence mechanisms.

Psychoanalytical belief is that neuroses are acquired only during early childhood. The neurotic person is unable to heal the disordered ego and the misery is perpetuated.

The ego pays the price of its defences by being denied access to repressed material by which neurotic conflict would be resolved and is weakened by its repression.

Personality functioning is impaired when psychical energy is used in harmful, defensive anti-cathexes.

Neurotic symptoms will continue so long as the repressions continue.

PSYCHOANALYTIC THERAPY

1. A neurotic person is someone who is incapable of enjoyment and efficiency.
2. To be capable of enjoyment, and to live efficiently, the neurotic person needs to place the libido in real objects instead of transforming it into symptoms.
   To live efficiently, the ego needs to have the energy of the libido at its disposal, rather than wasting it in repressions. The superego needs to be allowed libidinal expression and the efficient use of the ego.
3. The objectives of psychoanalysis are to free impulses, strengthen reality-based ego-functioning, and to so alter the contents of the superego that it operates less punitively.

THE STAGES OF PSYCHOTHERAPY

1. The opening phase
2. The development of transference
3. Working through
4. Resolution of the transference.

THE PROCESS OF PSYCHOTHERAPY

1. Free association
2. Working with resistance
3. Interpretation. The means whereby repressed, unconscious material is made conscious
4. Interpretation of dreams.

'SCHOOLS' OF PSYCHOTHERAPY USING VARIATIONS OF PSYCHOANALYSIS:

1. *Freudian psychoanalysis*. Followers of Sigmund and Anna Freud
2. *Analytical psychology*. Followers of Jung
3. *Individual psychology*. Followers of Adler
4. *Interpersonal*. Followers of Sullivan and Horney
5. *Object relations or 'British School'*. Followers of Balint, Fairbairn, Guntrip, Winnicott.

Each of the main schools has developed its own methods of training and accreditation. Knowledge derived from psychoanalysis has led to insights into:

1. Art
2. Religion
3. Social organization
4. Child development
5. Education.

MAJOR CRITICISMS OF PSYCHOANALYSIS:

1. Self-fulfilling
2. Overemphasizes sexuality
3. Untestable and unscientific
4. Deterministic and pessimistic
5. Politically repressive
6. Antifeminist
7. Ignores social and interpersonal dynamics
8. Elitist, costly, and time-consuming.

PSYCHOBIOGRAM (*See also*: Psychobiology)

Adolf Meyer emphasized the relationship between biology, psychology, and sociology in understanding human behaviour in his Life chart, which is a chronological record of the condition and performance of eight 'vulnerable systems'.

A psychobiogram is a record of the role each of the systems plays in shaping the biography or life of the client. It is also a record of, and the interplay between, the various experiences, memories, and feelings associated with the chronological data.

THE EIGHT 'VULNERABLE SYSTEMS':

1. Cerebrum
2. Digestive
3. Heart and circulation
4. Kidneys
5. Respiratory organs
6. Sexual
7. Thymus
8. Thyroid.

The psychobiogram is useful to show the complex lateral and vertical relationships between significant life events.

PSYCHOBIOLOGY (*See also*: Interpersonal theory, Psychobiogram)

Adolf Meyer (1866–1950), Swiss–American psychiatrist who developed a therapy based on the view that a person's personality is developed from biological, social, and psychological influences.

Meyer believed that a biographical study of personality provides both a guide for extracting essential data and for analysing the relationship between that data and the client's symptoms.

Meyer concentrated on developing a client's Life chart – a record of the conditions and the performance of the functions of eight vulnerable systems of the body, and the role each of these plays in shaping the client's personality.

Meyer called this study of the interrelationship of all the factors in a person's life, distributive analysis. Helping the client understand, and therefore to cope better, he called distributive synthesis. Therapy starts with distributive analysis, and ends with distributive synthesis.

The life chart is important in evaluating strengths, weaknesses and resources, with concentration on the healthy parts of the personality. Early concentration is on sleep, nutrition, and regulation of daily routine.

Meyer believed that it was important to use words and ideas familiar to the client.

Focus is on the present, conscious reactions to life, only relating to the past where there is a direct influence on the present and on attaining long-term goals. Therapy is an active process, where the therapist feels comfortable advising, suggesting, and re-educating. All of this may be called 'habit training' of current life situations.

PSYCHODRAMA

Psychodrama is a range of psychotherapeutic techniques in which people dramatize their personal problems within a group setting. The technique was introduced in the 1920s by the Viennese psychiatrist J.L. Moreno.

Although the situations in psychodrama are simulated, they can generate insight and release emotions through catharsis. A stage setting is generally used, the therapist acting as the 'director', with group members playing various roles. Some of the techniques are:

1. *Soliloquy*: the person verbalizes his or her psychological reactions to various remembered or imagined situations.

2. *Self-presentation*: the person plays the part of various significant others.
3. *Self-realization*: the person enacts his or her past and future life plan.
4. *Role reversal*: the person takes the part of someone else with whom interaction is difficult.
5. *Mirroring*: a member of the audience attempts to copy the behaviour of the person, to enable that person to see self through someone else's eyes.
6. *Sculpting* is, for example, where one person is asked to describe his/her place within a group (often a family), by using space/position, not words.

PSYCHODYNAMIC (*See also*: Psychoanalysis)

The word dynamic, as applied to psychology, implies movement and change, particularly in relation to such concepts as process, instincts, insight and development. It is more than the identification and enumerating attributes of the mind.

Psychodynamic means every psychological theory which uses the concept of inner drives; the interaction of mental forces within the psyche can be described as psychodynamic. Thoughts, feelings, and behaviours are viewed as manifestations of inner drives.

PSYCHOSYNTHESIS (Roberto Assagioli (1888–1974))

Psychosynthesis was developed by Assagioli, an Italian psychiatrist who broke away from Freudian orthodoxy early this century and developed an integrated approach to psychiatry.

Psychosynthesis is a synonym for human growth, the ongoing process of integrating all the parts, aspects, and energies of the individual into a harmonious, powerful whole. Assagioli drew upon psychoanalysis, Jungian and existential psychology, Buddhism, Yoga, and Christian traditions and philosophies.

THE FUNDAMENTALS OF PSYCHOSYNTHESIS:

1. Psychological pain, imbalance, and meaninglessness are caused where the various elements of the psyche are unconnected or clash with one another.
2. When these elements merge, we experience a release of energy, a sense of well-being and a deeper meaning of life.
3. Assagioli's map of the psyche (In diagrammatic form, egg shaped.)

   A. The lower unconscious contains one's personal psychological past in the form of repressed complexes, long-forgotten memories and dreams and imaginations.
   B. The middle unconscious, wherein reside the skills and states of mind.
   C. The higher unconscious or superconscious, from where we receive our higher intuitions and inspirations. The higher unconscious is also the source of higher feelings and spiritual energies.

4. The field of consciousness lies within the middle unconscious. It is the part of which we are directly aware and contains sensations, images, thoughts, feelings, desires, and impulses. It also

includes power to observe, analyse, and make judgments.

5. The conscious self or 'I' lies in the centre of the field of consciousness.

   One's task is to gain experience of the essence of self, or 'I'. Awareness of the conscious self is essential for psychological health. The personal self is a reflection of the transpersonal self, in much the same way as the moon reflects the light from the sun.
6. The higher or transpersonal self is the true self, the permanent centre, situated beyond or above the conscious self. Identification with the transpersonal self is a rare occurrence.
7. The collective unconscious. The psyche is bathed in the sea of the collective unconscious of dreams, myths, legends, and archetypes.

The lines that delimit the various parts of the diagram are analogous to permeable membranes, permitting a constant process of 'psychological osmosis'.

ASSAGIOLI'S MAP OF THE PSYCHOLOGICAL FUNCTIONS

(In diagrammatic form, star-shaped.)

1. Sensation
2. Emotion-feeling
3. Impulse-desire
4. Imagination
5. Thought
6. Intuition
7. Will
8. Personal self, or 'I'.

ASSAGIOLI'S PERSONALITY TYPOLOGY

1. The will type, whose characteristics are prompt and decisive action, courage, the power to conquer, role and dominate both physical surroundings and other people.

   There is a strong tendency to suppress all emotions and as a consequence cares little for their own or other people's feelings. This suppression of feelings often leads this person into committing heroic acts of courage.

   Mentally this person is alert with clear vision, unencumbered by emotions. Although not trusting of intuition, in the realm of abstract thinking this person excels, having a quick and sure grasp of principles, general laws, and universal connections.
2. The love type is often attached to material possessions, money or property, and the good things of life. The love may be expressed through the mind and emotions. Many love people are underdeveloped sexually with a distinct possibility of egotistical love. The love type can be self-indulgent and a lover of comfort, with a tendency to laziness and to follow the crowd.

   Intuition is highly developed in the love type, who have an interest in psychology and a communion with inner worlds of others.

   Generally the love type is kind and receptive, sociable, and often afraid of solitude. They are sometimes too readily influenced by others.
3. The active–practical type, whose characteristics are based on intelligent activity and the practical use of tools, is coupled with a highly developed manual dexterity. They are comfortable in the 'real' world of things. Material objects, particularly money, interest them, so

they often pursue activities for gain. Money is power.

This type wants immediate and lively reactions; to go slowly is a punishment. Feelings, and all that require psychic sensitivity, are foreign to this type, as is the feminine principle of the psyche; the practical mind sees no relevance or meaning. This type of person struggles to understand the psychology of women.

Mentally this type deals well with concrete and practical problems, but the more abstract ones leave them, cold.

4. The creative–artistic type is characterized by the search for harmony, peace, union, and beauty. They have an excellent sense of colour and exhibit good taste. They are often beset by unsatisfied ambitions, internal and external conflict.

   They are prone to mood swings, between optimism and pessimism; between uncontrolled happiness and despair. They are easily disturbed by violence, vulgarity, and ugliness.

   They are sensitive to psychic phenomena, and they rely on their intuition which is well-developed. They are always searching for the meaning hidden behind everything they perceive. They are imaginative, dreamy, and impracticable and may live in fantasy world. Men of this type feel at home with feminine psychological characteristics.

5. The scientific type is characterized by an interest in the appearance of things, as perceived through the five senses. There is no real interest in moral, aesthetic, or any other type of values.

   The emotions of this type are totally directed toward impersonal objects. They are passionately attached to ideas and theories and their energies are directed toward intellectual ends.

   Their minds are constantly on the alert, investigating, posing questions, solving problems, searching, probing, experimenting, proving, and discovering.

6. The devotional–idealistic type is attracted to an ideal, which is often an ideal personality.

   The ideal may be religious, political, social, or philosophical. Sometimes their severely ascetic attitude turns to hatred of the body as a hindrance toward their spiritual ambition.

   They often love or hate with a passion that makes them narrow-minded, intolerant, critical, and uncompromising. They generally lack a sense of proportion and humour and have a tendency to impose their views on others. At the same time they are sincere and not egotistical. The Inquisitors are quoted as such a type, torturing and killing in an effort to save the soul of their victim.

   The high level of intuition which some develop is identified with the feminine principle. The active subtype do not develop the same degree of intuition and identify more with the masculine principle, with combativeness and aggression; the person who is always prepared to do battle for a just cause.

7. The organizational type express themselves in action and are thoroughly objective. They demonstrate will and purpose, a clear mind, constructive activity

and practical ability and are methodical and persistent 'doers'. They organize the co-operation and work of other people to achieve the desired end.

This type like to formalize laws with meticulous care, and they tend toward rigidity, which often manifests itself as bigotry. They are strong disciplinarians, both external and internal, and use discipline in order to eliminate loss and waste of time, energy, and materials, to avoid friction and establish, in the end, more productive co-operation.

The organizational type relies heavily on tradition, habit, and custom, and when these fail, or break down, the person is thrown into confusion; as if their anchor has gone.

THE TASK OF PSYCHOSYNTHESIS

No person is exclusively one type; we are mixtures. Most of us could identify one, or two types that are more of us than the others. When we have identified the type(s), our task is how to utilize the knowledge we have acquired to effect self-potential.

EXPRESSION, CONTROL AND HARMONIZATION

Each person faces this three-point task.

Expression:

1. Accepting the characteristics
2. Recognizing the potentialities
3. What our type can teach us
4. The opportunities and dangers
5. The kind of service to the world.

Control

1. Controlling and correcting excesses.
2. Working on the opposites.

Harmonization

1. Cultivating undeveloped faculties
2. Develop the will to change
3. Seek the company of people who demonstrate the desired attributes.

PSYCHOSYNTHETIC TASKS

The will type

1. To develop love, understanding, empathy, and compassion in such a way that they become capable of expressing goodwill.
2. To develop sensitivity, intuition, and the ability to co-operate with, rather than to solely dominate, compete with, and direct others.
3. To feel comfortable without solitude and to learn to live with others.
4. To transform egotistical will into service to others.

The love type

1. To attain non-attachment and to eliminate from real love the elements of greed and possessiveness, and allow for liberty of the other person.
2. To separate love from the egocentric elements.
3. To develop a stronger will to help them control their love.

The active–practical type

1. To cultivate the qualities of the love and the creative types.
2. To recognize the intangible world, intuition, psychological qualities, beauty.
3. To learn how to relax and be silent.

The creative–artistic type

1. To learn to seek a mid-path between polarities and extremes.

2. To work with reality and the practical.
3. To respect the limitations of others.
4. To develop more self-discipline, though not at the expense of inspiration.
5. To develop a more responsible attitude toward money.

The scientific type

1. To control the thirst for knowledge and apply it to specific areas.
2. To approach relationships with warmth, compassion and goodwill.
3. To cultivate the appreciation of subjective qualities, of internal experiences and intuition, love, and beauty.

The devotional–idealistic type

1. To distinguish true from idealistic love and to transform devotion to an ideal into true love.
2. To learn to suspend judgment and to accept that there are other 'ways'.
3. To learn to be more impersonal and objective.
4. To develop tolerance and intellectual humility.

The organizational type

1. To avoid becoming too identified with the formal and the predictable, and to beware of the organization becoming an end in itself.
2. To work toward modifying the tendency to rely on the practical and the objective, the concrete and the visible, by developing loving service and the true good of all, free from officiousness and rigidity.
3. To apply the developed principles of co-ordination and synthesis to personal or transpersonal development.

ASSAGIOLI'S CONCEPT OF SUBPERSONALITIES

Subpersonalities are distinct, miniature personalities, living together within the personality, each with its own cluster of feelings, words, habits, beliefs, and behaviour. They are often in conflict with one another and engaged in a constant jockeying for position.

They are remnants of helpful and unhelpful influences left over from a time when they were needed for survival to meet lower-level needs. For example, a policeman subpersonality is helpful in keeping one on the right side of the law, but becomes tyrannical when it always pushes one into punishing other people for minor breeches of one's self-imposed standards.

Examples of subpersonalities:

Boffin	Policeman
Executioner	Professor
Gaoler	Rebel
Granite	Saboteur
Monk/Nun	Seducer
Nurse	Spider
Playboy	Tiger

THE GOALS OF PSYCHOSYNTHESIS

1. To free ourselves from the infirmity of illusions and fantasies, unrecognized complexes, of being tossed hither and thither by external influences and deceiving appearances.
2. To achieve a harmonious inner integration, true self-realization,

and a right relationship with others.

3. To recognize when we have identified with one or another subpersonality and disidentify from its control.

These goals are achieved through knowledge of one's personality, control of the various elements of the personality, and working with the subpersonalities, to free oneself from their tyranny. Psychosynthesis speaks of 'guiding', not therapy.

PRINCIPAL METHODS AND TECHNIQUES:

1. Catharsis
2. Creativity
3. Critical analysis
4. Dialogue
5. Dreamwork
6. Evocative words and affirmation
7. Free drawing
8. Gestalt
9. Guided imagery
10. Homework
11. Journal keeping
12. Meditation
13. Movement
14. Subpersonality work.

BROAD CLASSIFICATION OF TECHNIQUES:

1. *Analytical*. To help identify blocks and enable the exploration of the unconscious.
2. *Mastery*. (*See* Assagioli's map of the psychological functions, above.) The eight psychological functions need to be gradually retrained to produce permanent positive change.
3. *Transformation*. Creating a soil in which the seeds of change can blossom. The goal is the refashioning of the personality around a new centre.
4. *Meditative*. To awaken and integrate intuition, imagination, creativity and higher feelings.
5. *Grounding*. The learning and growth of a session is brought into the concrete terms of daily life. Grounding makes use of:

   A. Carrying out the choices made in the session, actively using imagination.
   B. Standing or moving in ways that express new qualities or attitudes.
   C. Mental images to evoke positive emotional states.
   D. Repeating key phrases or affirmations throughout the day.
   E. Practising chosen behaviours.

6. *Relational*. To deal with the common obstacles within relationships and communication, and to cultivate qualities such as love, openness, empathy.

Psychosynthesis is an evolutionary psychology, to help us to become increasingly aware of our vast potentials, and to bring them into service in the world. It can help us to balance all aspects of the human personality; intellect, emotion, body, intuition, and imagination.

Psychosynthesis can facilitate courage and patience, wisdom and compassion. It refers to the ongoing synthesis of the psyche, a process that transcends specific models and methods.

R

RACKET FEELINGS (*See also*: Transactional analysis)

A transactional analysis term to describe the habitual ways of feeling bad about oneself, learned from parents and other significant people. They are the feelings of our parents, they do not rightly belong to us, but we act as if they do.

An example would be that when our parents were under pressure they may have become anxious, depressed, confused, or nervous. If they did not take appropriate adult action to eliminate the tension or pressure, the likelihood is that we learned a racket by responding in the same way. Rackets originate from the Not OK Child of our parents; our Child then repeats these to avoid taking constructive action.

RANKIAN DIALECTIC (Otto Rank (1884–1939)) (*See also*: Birth trauma)

Viennese, non-medical psychoanalyst who developed his own theory of personality which forced a break from Freud. Rank extended his theory to the study of myth, legend, and art; he believed that every person has a need to express creativity.

For him the basis of neurosis lies in the birth trauma. Every crisis of development has its origins in separation, wishing to return to the womb's safety.

The fundamentals of the process are to assist the client away from union or likeness, which affirms one's worth, and toward separation or difference, which forces self-identity.

Moving from separation toward union is only possible when one is certain of one's own identity. Union causes guilt for needing someone and also has the fear of smothering, of engulfment, and of dying.

Union implies surrender of one's will to another, in order to enjoy brief happiness. It does not allow full recognition of uniqueness.

Moving from union to separation is asserting one's own uniqueness that causes guilt for abandoning someone. Every new experience of union and separation is a rebirth, with its fear of the unknown outcome. This is growth.

Every person needs to experience a love relationship, to know self-worth and to experience a release from the fear of difference. The process is completed when assertion of uniqueness and separation takes place within the love relationship.

The will is the principal mover, or change agent. Neuroses are where people do not recognize the responsibility for their own will.

THERAPEUTIC PROCESS

The process of therapy is to help clients replay all the past struggles with relationships, especially intimacy, and the fear of death. Resistance is seen as the client's assertion of will.

Dependency on the therapist gives way to separateness as the client's self-worth is affirmed. Therapy focuses on the present struggle with the therapist who helps the client free his or her will.

RAPPORT (*See also*: Bonding, Core conditions, Empathy)

Generally, a comfortable, relaxed, unconstrained, mutually accepting interaction between people. The basic accord, harmony, or quality, the foundation for any therapeutic relationship, without which healing and growth cannot take place. The term was originally used to describe the relationship between hypnotists and their subjects.

Rapport develops in the presence of:

1. Active listening
2. Accurate, sensitive responding
3. Reflecting feelings
4. The presence of empathy
5. A sincere desire to understand
6. An ability to be fully present with the client, wherever that might be.

RAPPORT HAS THREE ESSENTIAL INGREDIENTS:

1. Harmony, something for which we strive, sometimes achieve, and so easily lose. It is an elusive shadow which, somehow, we must turn into substance.
2. Compatibility, which is influenced by such factors as:
   - A. Personality
   - B. Appearance
   - C. Intelligence
   - D. Emotional stability
   - E. Understanding
   - F. Kindness/tenderness
   - G. Common interest.
3. Affinity, which is the quality of the relationship. Counselling forms a significant bond between counsellor and client, who have become bonded together for a specific purpose. When that purpose has been fulfilled, the relationship, the bond of affinity, will be severed. The more one invests in a relationship, the stronger the bond grows; and the breaking of it may bring pain.

Rapport is not something a person gains, like a certificate of competence. It is a transient state, more easily lost than achieved. It is always under threat from misinterpreting, lack of awareness of the interaction with the client, and ineffective listening.

RATIONAL EMOTIVE THERAPY (RET)

A comprehensive method of psychotherapy developed by Albert Ellis. RET considers dysfunctional behaviour to be the result of faulty beliefs and irrational and illogical thinking. The method has elements in common with both cognitive and behavioural therapy.

The method uses an A–B–C–D sequence.

A = Activating event
B = Beliefs which influence C
C = Consequences
D = Dispute

Highly charged emotional consequences are invariably created by our belief systems. Undesirable emotional consequences can usually be traced to irrational beliefs. When irrational beliefs are disputed (D), disturbed consequences disappear.

BASIC RET PROPOSITIONS:

1. We are born with the potential to be rational as well as irrational.
2. Our tendency to irrational thinking, self-damaging habits, wishful thinking, and intolerance is influenced by culture, community and family group.
3. We tend to think, feel, and behave at the same time.
4. RET therapists believe that a highly cognitive, active-directive, homework-assigning, hard-headed, and discipline-oriented system is likely to be more effective than other systems.
5. A warm relationship is neither necessary, nor a sufficient condition for effective personality change.
6. RET makes use of a variety of techniques to achieve a deep-seated cognitive change, rather than a removal of symptoms.
7. All serious, emotional problems can be attributed to magical and faulty thinking. Logical, observable and experimental thinking will eliminate these problems.
8. Insight is cold comfort if all it does is to let us see we have problems.

We must accept that the real difficulty is in ourselves, not in other people nor in what happens to us.

THREE BASIC PRINCIPLES:

1. While present behaviour is related to the past, it is beliefs about the events and not the events themselves that cause problems in the present.
2. Although we may have been emotionally disturbed in the past, our faulty beliefs continue the process. We actively reinforce them by the way we think and act.
3. Only repeated rethinking of our irrational beliefs and repeated actions designed to undo those beliefs, and the crooked thinking that goes with them, are enough to create lasting change.

PHYSIOLOGICAL BASIS OF PERSONALITY

1. We are born with a strong tendency to want, and to insist upon, the best in life.
2. We condemn ourselves and others when we do not get what we want.
3. We tend to think childishly all our lives and only with great difficulty achieve and maintain realistic and mature behaviour.
4. Self-actualizing capacities are frequently defeated by our inborn and acquired self-sabotaging strategies.

SOCIAL ASPECTS OF PERSONALITY

1. When others approve of us and accept us, when we love and are loved, we tend to approve of ourselves as 'good' and 'worthwhile'.

2. Emotional disturbances are often caused when we care too much about what others think. This leads us to believe that we can only accept ourselves when others accept us.
3. A corollary of this is that we have an exaggerated compulsion to do anything to be liked.

PSYCHOLOGICAL ASPECTS OF PERSONALITY

We become psychologically disturbed when we feel upset at C, after experiencing a disturbing event at A.

Beliefs at B could run something like:

'I can't stand this.'
'It's awful.'
'I'd just as soon be dead.'
'I'm worthless.'
'It's all your fault.'

The illogicality of this is that:

We may not like what has happened, but we can stand it.
Why can't we?
What is awful?

It would be more precise to say:

'It may be very inconvenient', or
'It may be unhelpful'.

Being precise aids logical thinking. To think we can control the world is magical, irrational thinking. When we upset ourselves we then start to condemn ourselves for being upset.

To help people change, concentrate on B.

A is past. The feelings of C, though real, are strongly influenced by B. Concentrating attention on B, diverts attention from both A and C.

THE THERAPEUTIC PROCESS

1. No matter what feelings the client brings out, the therapist tries to get back to the irrational ideas that lie beneath the feelings.
2. The therapist does not hesitate to contradict, and may use personal experience or experience from other people.
3. The therapist never misses a chance to draw attention to, and attack 'shoulds', 'oughts', 'musts'.
4. The therapist will use the strongest philosophic approach possible, saying something like, 'If the worst thing possible happened, would you still be worthless?'
5. The therapist does not dwell on feelings, but uses them to point to irrational beliefs and ideas.
6. While showing acceptance, unconditional regard, and confidence in the client's abilities, the therapist, when necessary, is stern and insists that the client is capable of doing better.
7. The therapist at all times tries to get the client to see the irrational ideas, without telling, or explaining.
8. The therapist may use strong, confrontative language to give the client an emotional shock.
9. The therapist is empathic but not sympathetic.
10. The therapist constantly checks the client's understanding of what is being taught, and does this by getting the client to repeat and clarify what has just been said.
11. Unlike some therapies, the RET therapist does a lot of the talking, and takes the lead.

In all of this, the client is understood and although deep feelings are there, the client is given little chance to become immersed in them or to abreact strongly to them.

THE CLIENT EXPERIENCES:

1. Full acceptance
2. Renewed confidence
3. Self-responsibility
4. Hope of recovery
5. Reduction in defences

RET is used in numerous settings with individuals and groups.

TECHNIQUES COMMONLY USED

1. Repeating forceful, rational, coping statements.
2. Rational emotive imagery to change inappropriate feelings to appropriate ones.
3. Unconditional acceptance, even when the client's behaviour is stupid or blameworthy.
4. Role-play of difficult situations, during which the therapist will interrupt to draw attention to faulty thinking.
5. Clients learn to conduct forceful dialogue with themselves; to express irrational beliefs and then to dispute them.

   These dialogues may be tape-recorded and played back for the therapist to hear.
6. When clients feel strongly ashamed for doing what they want to do, for fear of disapproval, they are encouraged to accept a 'shame-attacking exercise', like doing something ridiculous in public. They work on themselves until they no longer feel ashamed or embarrassed.
7. RET uses humour to attack people's oversensitiveness, and dogmatic 'musts'. RET discourages dependence by teaching clients to help themselves; to monitor their thoughts, feelings and behaviours; not to blame events or people; to restructure their perceptions and evaluations, and to stand on their own feet.

MAJOR IRRATIONAL BELIEFS

1. I must do well and must win approval for all my performances, or else I rate as a rotten person.
2. You must act kindly and considerate toward me, or else you are a thoroughly bad person.
3. I must live under good and easy conditions, so that I get practically everything I want without too much effort and discomfort. If I don't, the world is doomed, and life hardly seems worth living.

MAJOR IRRATIONAL IDEAS

1. I must have sincere love and approval almost all the time from all the significant people in my life.
2. In every circumstance, and at all times, I must be:

   A. Cheerful
   B. Comfortable
   C. Compassionate
   D. Competent
   E. Confident
   F. Consistent
   G. Controlled

   } The seven great Cs.
3. Life proves awful, terrible, horrible, or catastrophic when things do not go the way I would like them to go.
4. When I feel miserable it comes from outside pressures and I have little ability to control my

feelings or rid myself of depression and hostility.

5. It is easier to avoid facing life's difficulties and self-responsibilities than to undertake some rewarding forms of self-discipline.
6. My past remains all-important, and because something once strongly influenced my life, it has to keep deciding my feelings and behaviour in the present.
7. People and things should turn out better than they do. If I don't quickly find good solutions to life's hassles it's awful and horrible.
8. I achieve happiness by doing nothing, or by passively and without commitment, 'enjoying myself'.
9. I must always have a high degree of order or certainty to feel comfortable.

   I need some supernatural power on which to rely.
10. If something seems dangerous or fearsome, I must become terribly occupied with and upset about it.
11. My general worth and self-acceptance depend on the goodness of my performances, and on other people's approval.
12. People who harm me, or commit misdeeds, are bad, wicked, or villainous individuals. I should severely blame, damn, and punish them for their sins.

RET teaches clients to change these self-statements into 'wanting', 'wishing', 'preferring', instead of 'needing' and 'demanding'.

RATIONALIZATION (Defence mechanism)

'I would be different if . . .'

In general, it means the process one uses to make clear something that is confused, irrational, and unclear.

In psychoanalytic terms it means, in addition, giving an intellectual, rational explanation in an attempt to conceal or justify attitudes, beliefs, or behaviour that might otherwise be unacceptable.

An example would be where the person who fails a driving test blames the failure on a 'migraine'. To that person the rationalized reason is more acceptable than the truth.

REACTION FORMATION (Defence mechanism)

'I've never wanted to hit anyone in my life.'

In psychoanalytic terms a mechanism that is used to defend the ego against the anxiety of expressing a repressed wish, whereby we believe as though the opposite were true.

It is where one's anxieties about an unacceptable impulse are kept at bay by developing behaviour patterns that are directly opposed, as a means of controlling the impulses.

To the observer these reactions seem highly exaggerated and/or inappropriate. Reaction formation is closely associated with obsessive–compulsive disorder. An example would be the heavy drinker who gives up alcohol and becomes an ardent 'ban the drink' campaigner.

REALITY PRINCIPLE (*See also*: Pleasure principle)

In psychoanalytic psychology, mental activity is governed by the pleasure and the reality principles.

The gratification of pleasure (or the avoidance of discomfort) (the reduction of tension) is balanced by the ability of the reality principle (the leading principle in the ego) to accommodate the facts of, and the objects existing in, the outside world.

The reality principle allows postponement of gratification to accommodate other immediate needs, or to secure greater pleasure at a later time.

Normal development is seen as acquiring and strengthening the reality principle so that it acts as a brake on the more primitive pleasure principle.

REALITY THERAPY

A therapeutic system developed by William Glasser, based on the idea that individuals are responsible for what they do.

Responsible behaviour is defined as that which satisfies one's needs, while at the same time not denying others from satisfying theirs.

Reality therapy focuses on the present and upon getting people to understand that all choices are made in order to meet needs.

When needs are not met we suffer, and often we cause others to suffer also. Reality is based on the concept that our brain works as a control system, like a thermostat.

People are like a building supported by the five pillars or needs of *survival*, to *belong*, to *exercise power*, to *have fun*, and *experience freedom*. When any one pillar weakens, the whole structure becomes unstable.

People with failed identities are those who have not learned the behaviours necessary for them to meet their psychological needs. They may, therefore, need to learn the behaviours and skills that will help them out of their self-involvement, out of their fantasy world in which they feel more comfortable.

The task of the Reality therapist is to educate clients to become more responsible and realistic, and more successful at attaining their goals.

GLASSER IDENTIFIES TWO BASIC NEEDS:

1. To love and be loved. This means involvement.
2. To feel self-worth and to feel the worth of others. This means performing tasks of worth.

GLASSER BELIEVES:

1. The concept of mental illness to be a scientific fantasy
2. That symptoms are chosen because the individual is lonely and failing now
3. That no symptom is chosen without reason
4. A symptom serves to reduce the pain of loneliness
5. That successful involvement means facing loneliness, pain, and failure
6. We choose symptoms
7. Symptoms disappear when needs are successfully fulfilled by means of responsible behaviour.

Reality therapy differs from orthodox psychotherapy in that it:

1. Rejects the concept of mental illness and all the conventional diagnostic labels.
2. Concentrates on the present as the razor's edge upon which we live our lives. Our memory of the past is capricious; to remember accurately would be too painful.
3. Rejects the phenomenon of transference as a misleading and false idea.

4. Pays little attention to the unconscious and the dreams that go with it. Reality therapy deals only with what the client is presently aware of.
5. Concentrates on clients' perceptions of their behaviour, and judges if that behaviour is conducive to meeting their declared goals.
6. Attempts to teach clients better ways to deal with the world, thus helping them to choose more effective behaviours.

THE CLIENT HAS TWO CHOICES:

1. To deny reality, with its irresponsible behaviour, loneliness, pain, and lack of involvement; the failed identity.
2. To face reality, with its responsible behaviour, love, worth, and involvement; the success identity.

SOURCES OF A SUCCESS IDENTITY

1. People we love and admire and who love and admire us
2. The causes and concerns on which we spend our time
3. Our behaviour in crises
4. Feedback from others
5. Beliefs, values, and philosophy of life
6. Status and position in life
7. Physical appearance and structure.

A success identity or a failure identity starts to form around the age of four years, as we develop (or fail to develop) social and verbal skills, intellect and thinking ability.

Children who identify themselves as 'successful' or 'unsuccessful' quickly associate themselves with similar people.

REALITY THERAPY AND EDUCATION

Many educational systems confirm an embryonic failure identity in children. Many children fail at school because teachers deny children their primary needs for humanity and love.

Schools could help to develop a success identity by:

1. Focusing on thinking and problem-solving skills, not on rote learning.
2. Making learning relevant to the child's world.
3. Giving prime importance to reading, writing, and speaking skills.
4. Having mixed-sex classes and all ages.
5. Doing away with grading systems.
6. Having classroom meetings and non-judgmental discussions.

STEPS IN REALITY THERAPY

1. Establish rapport and empathy and ask the clients what they most want.
2. Asking, 'What are you doing now?' focuses on goals and those behaviours most open to changes to achieve the goals.
3. Would their choice get what they want?
4. Creating an effective plan hinges on the previous three steps.
5. Strong commitment to the plan means strong follow-through.
6. Reality therapists are not interested in excuses when plans are not followed through, particularly when clients rake up the past as their excuse.
7. The therapist does not resort to punishment, but will use (where appropriate) temporary restric-

tion of freedom, temporary removal of privileges.

8. It may take a long time for some people to realize that they can take some control of their world.

The determined therapist will gradually become part of the client's inner world.

The overall goal for therapy, and for living, is a success identity. Attaining a success identity has the following ingredients:

1. Neither denying nor ignoring the reality of the world in which we live.
2. Behaving responsibly, including formulating and carrying out plans.
3. Loving and being involved with and committed to others, as well as being loved in return.
4. Engaging in activities that are worthwhile to ourselves and to others.
5. Living up to a reasonable standard of ethical behaviour.

Reality therapy is an attempt to help people choose effective and responsible behaviours that will fulfil the needs that drive them.

Clients learn that they can exercise control, however weak that control may seem, and that they need not be controlled by the world. They learn that responsibility and consequences go hand in hand.

REASSURANCE (*See also*: Core conditions, Frames of reference, Hope)

Verbal attempts by the therapist to relieve anxiety by trying to prove to the client that things are not as bad as the client thinks.

Unwarranted, false reassurances are a violation of respect, for they are an attempt to diminish the problem in the eyes of the client.

Verbal reassurances, given inappropriately, may make the client 'dry up'. Sometimes it is essential for clients to experience the depths of their feelings in order to work through them toward understanding and insight.

Unwarranted reassurances are very often attempts to minimize the feelings or the problem. They may reflect therapists' inability to handle their own anxiety and frustration.

Reassurances may be a refusal to acknowledge the reality of the client's perceptions. If the client perceives something as a mountain, then a mountain it is. Unwarranted reassurances can frighten the client off. If the therapist (the expert) can't handle feelings, what hope has the client?

Positive reassurance is conveyed indirectly through the skills of active listening and responding, within a relationship in which the core conditions are demonstrated. The more closely we enter another person's frame of reference, the less likely we shall be to offer empty, unwarranted, and false reassurances.

REBIRTHING (*See also*: Birth trauma, Primal therapy)

A therapy that enables people to re-experience their own birth, in order to free themselves from the constraining beliefs and experiences associated with birthing. The thesis is that all the trauma associated with birth forms the basis for all following anxiety.

How, as adults, we cope with stressful events, depends on:

1. How easy or how difficult or prolonged the labour was.

2. How we were handled, rudely removed, or not separated from our mother after birth and allowed to start the bonding process.
3. The advocates of natural childbirth believe in the importance of making the extrauterine experience as compatible, so far as possible, with the intrauterine existence.

Rebirthing uses two basic techniques: special breathing and positive affirmations.

REDUNDANCY COUNSELLING

(*See also*: Dying – stages of (Kubler–Ross))

The effects of redundancy can be devastating to the person, the immediate family, and also to society. It may be the most psychologically mutilating event the individual has ever experienced.

Redundancy affects the person concerned, and the one having to give the news. The whole organization is subjected to the trauma. Whatever the reasons, when the axe falls, the innocent often feel they have a hand in the execution.

A disturbing fact is that people, particularly managers who have been once made redundant, are more at risk of a second or third redundancy.

THE STAGES OF REDUNDANCY:

1. Planning in secret; often accompanied by rumours and suspicion
2. Announcement of redundancy and selection of personnel to go
3. Individuals leave the organization and enter a period of unemployment
4. Search for new jobs.

THE PSYCHOLOGICAL PHASES OF REDUNDANCY

1. Shock and denial
2. Anger
3. Bargaining
4. Depression
5. Acceptance

All models have their limitations, and it does not mean that every person will follow the model through as presented. Neither does it mean that there is a logical progression through the stages. It is more likely that the person will fluctuate between the various stages and maybe experience all of them within a short space of time, and return to a previous stage many times before 'acceptance'. In many cases of redundancy, acceptance only comes with being re-employed.

Stress following redundancy is to be expected for the following reasons:

1. Expectations have been cut short.
2. Being unemployed is not the norm.
3. They may not find the answer to the question, 'Why me?' It is possible that the individual does have a part to play in what has happened, for example, he/she may not have kept abreast of personal development, something expected by many organizations. This expectation may be justified, particularly where the organization provides opportunity for self-development. At the same time, effective management may have detected the lack before and been able to take constructive action, not redundancy.

Redundancy counselling, which covers dismissal or other severance, is concerned mainly with helping people change in order to improve their chances of new employment.

The new employment may have to be different from the previous one, but it should feel psychologically good, according to the following criteria:

1. Provides one with an opportunity to use one's special abilities.
2. Permits one to be creative and original.
3. Enables one to look forward to a stable and secure future.
4. Provides one with a chance to earn a reasonable income.
5. Gives one an opportunity to be of service to others.

Some people want only practical advice; others need an opportunity to explore their feelings before they can make a decision, having explored various options.

THE STAGES OF REDUNDANCY COUNSELLING

1. Dealing with the crisis
2. Careers advice
3. Coaching (interviewing skills, preparing CVs, and presentation)
4. Where to look, whom to approach, coping with rejections, and follow-up after re-employment.

Counselling should be an integral part of the organization's redundancy package. Some people have the necessary coping skills, and have an already established network of support and contacts, but may need some help with the practicalities.

Some, because of their stress levels (which may, of course, involve the family) may need more personal counselling before they are able to think clearly enough to take action.

Some are so devastated that they experience a full-blown grief reaction and will need a lot of personal counselling.

REDUNDANCY COUNSELLING BENEFITS THE ORGANIZATION BY:

1. Taking the problem off the organization's shoulders
2. Showing concern, thereby keeping up morale
3. Enabling difficult decisions to be made
4. Helping to keep confidence in the organization.

SERVICES USUALLY OFFERED BY COMPANIES SPECIALIZING IN REDUNDANCY COUNSELLING:

1. Negotiating the 'golden handshake'
2. Financial, pensions, and investments advice
3. Legal advice
4. Health check-up
5. Crisis/personal counselling
6. Vocational/career guidance
7. Analysis of interests and skills, strengths and weaknesses, aptitude and psychometric tests, and advice from clinical psychologists
8. Self-marketing skills: interviewing, presentation, preparing CVs and letters
9. Exploring new opportunities: working abroad, self-employment, retraining
10. Getting lists of vacancies and contacting recruiting agencies
11. Providing office facilities, including secretarial assistance
12. Advice on handling offers of work.

An important step forward is when the person can say, 'My job is redundant; I am not.'

RE-EVALUATION COUNSELLING

(*See also*: Six-category intervention)

Also known as 'co-counselling'. Developed in the USA by Harvey Jackins for lay people to help each other, without the cost involved in professional intervention.

It is a self-directed, peer approach, where two people work together and help each other deal with tensions and emotional pain.

The assumption behind the approach is that illness is often related to failure to recognize the existence of feelings such as anger, loneliness, and inadequacy, locked away in the subconscious.

Each person in turn, for an agreed length of time - usually one hour - acts as the counsellor to the other. The counsellor helps the client to express pent-up, painful, suppressed feelings.

THE FOUR STAGES

1. Catharsis
2. Insight of re-evaluation of traumatic events
3. Celebration
4. Goal-setting and redirection.

The client takes responsibility for what takes place in the session.

The task of the counsellor is to:

1. Give total attention
2. Give total support
3. Offer security for the client's self-disclosure.

The counsellor does not:

1. Interpret
2. Advise
3. Analyse
4. Categorize.

The counsellor may:

1. Ask open-ended questions
2. Offer suggestions, to free the client from being stuck.

CLIENTS AND COUNSELLORS ARE TAUGHT TO:

1. Make self-affirming statements to each other
2. Talk descriptively, not analytically
3. Use repetition to uncover emotions
4. Verbalize random thoughts and associations.

Co-counselling, because it is reciprocal, hinges on both people having enough psychological strength and awareness to take on the counselling role. Co-counselling philosophy is that there are three basic personal energies or capacities:

1. To love and be loved
2. To understand the world and to be understood
3. To take charge of life, to be self-directing, to be the agent of free choice, and to be part of a larger whole.

The purpose of personal energy is to celebrate these capacities and their relationship to one another so as to enhance the person who proclaims them.

The objectives of co-counselling are to train the clients to:

1. Take charge of their feelings
2. Provide them with skills for releasing distressed feelings of:
   - A. Anger, through loud sounds and vigorous, harmlessly directed storming movements
   - B. Fear, through trembling
   - C. Grief, through sobbing
   - D. Embarrassment, through laughter.

THE EFFECTS OF CATHARSIS:

1. The break up of rigid, compulsive and non-effective behaviours
2. The release of previously bound-up energies
3. A more satisfying and rewarding relationship with the world.

TRANSFERENCE IS WORKED THROUGH BY:

1. Getting the client to identify and verbalize just how the counsellor is like someone else to whom feelings are directed.
   This is repeated until no more likenesses remain.
2. Getting the client to identify and verbalize just how the counsellor is not like the other person, so that the counsellor is perceived for whom he or she really is.

It is the client who, at all times, decides to work at a certain level. Deeper penetration is never forced by the counsellor.

REFERENCE GROUP

A social psychology term to describe any group with which a person feels some identification or emotional affiliation, in order to evaluate and to regulate our opinions and actions.

When we aspire to a different group, and use it as our frame of reference, we may become dissatisfied with our own, and, as a consequence, experience deprivation.

On the other hand, aspiring to a higher group may act as a motivator to achievement, particularly if we internalize the other group's views and general perspective of the world so that they become ours.

Examples of the reference group at work would be a young aspiring athlete who may use gold-winning athletes as a reference group. Another example is that of young people who often experience competition between the family group and the reference group of peers.

The process of attitude change from one reference group to another, although it is doubtful if the change is ever total, is often fraught with conflict. Attitudes and their accompanying behaviours are acquired through identification; changing those attitudes often means jettisoning previously held attitudes and beliefs.

REFERRAL

Where one counsellor refers a client to another more qualified counsellor or agency.

It is important to know to whom one should refer clients for the most appropriate help, so it is essential to build up an extensive referral file.

A referral should never be taken lightly, neither should it be delayed longer than necessary to ensure the best possible outcome.

REFERRAL IS LIKELY TO BE DELAYED BECAUSE OF:

1. The counsellor's hurt pride at not being able to continue with the client until completion.
2. Not creating an awareness in the mind of the client from the start that referral is a possibility.
3. Not admitting limitations.
4. Not working through and helping the client understand why referral is indicated.
5. Not being able to separate from the client.

Sometimes there is a tendency to

refer too quickly. Perhaps the counsellor may see the need for referral, and this is totally rejected by the client. The limitations should then be brought into the open and discussed. The counsellor then may need to seek expert help if work with the client is to be productive.

REFLECTING (*See also*: Paraphrasing)

Reflecting concentrates on the feelings within a statement. Paraphrasing and reflecting are invariably linked and it may be artificial to try to separate them.

Reflecting feelings accurately depends on empathic understanding.

Pity = feeling *for*
Sympathy = feeling *like*
Empathy = feeling *with*

Neither pity nor sympathy is constructive.

Reflecting involves both listening and understanding then communicating that understanding. If understanding remains locked up within us, we contribute little to the helping process.

Being able to reflect feelings involves viewing the world from the clients' frames of reference; what their thoughts, feelings, and behaviours mean to them.

Effective responding shows that we accept people.

It does not act as a 'stopper' on their flow of talk and their emotions. They do not feel inadequate, inferior, or defensive talking to us, or as though they are being talked down to.

TO RESPOND EFFECTIVELY:

1. Observe facial and bodily movements.
2. Listen to words and their meanings.
3. Tune into your own emotional reactions to what the client is communicating.
4. Sense the meaning of the communication.
5. Take into account the degree of client self-awareness.
6. Respond appropriately.
7. Use expressive, not stereotyped, language.
8. Use vocal and bodily language that agree with each other.
9. Check the accuracy of your understanding.

REFRAMING (*See also*: Family therapy, Neurolinguistic programming)

A technique of challenging the client's perceptions of the problem then changing those perceptions so that the problem, or parts of it, become more manageable.

The facts may remain unchanged, and indeed may not be changeable, but how we perceive something influences our behaviour. Helping the client separate concrete facts from their perception of the facts is therapeutic.

Reframing lifts the problem out of the symptoms into a new frame that does not carry the implications of the old. Reframing is an important technique used in Family therapy and in Neurolinguistic programming.

REGRESSION (Defence mechanism)

'I hate you, hate you' (with foot stamping).

This is a return to an earlier (fixated) level of functioning, with the feelings and behaviours attached to it.

Regression is prompted by an unconscious desire to avoid anxiety, tensions, and conflicts evoked at the present level of development.

The psychoanalytic theory of regression is that remnants of the stages of development remain and are activated when under threat, so that we repeat the behaviour appropriate to that stage of development. This return, however, does not remove anxiety. The current anxiety is replaced by a re-experiencing of the anxiety encountered at the regressed stage.

In cognitive therapy, regression is referred to as a temporary falling back upon an earlier form of thinking, in learning to deal with something new.

An example of regression would be the young husband who, following the first quarrel with his new wife, 'runs back to mother'.

REICH, WILHELM (1897–1957) (*See also*: Body-centred therapy)

One of Freud's most controversial followers who believed that neurosis results not from a damning up of sexual energy, but from a blockage of normal orgasm.

Neurotic symptoms do not fully discharge sexual energy and the tension which is produced results in bodily symptoms. Sexual energy may be converted into anxiety, and undischarged energy may result in sadism or aggression.

For Reich, ejaculation does not mean true organismic potency which is measured by the total involvement of one person with another during orgasm. In societies with strong barriers against sexual expression, full orgasmic potency is uncommon. Potency is being positively attached to one's partner within a relationship that involves self-regulation of sexual desires.

Reich developed what he called 'Orgone' or 'Life energy' theory, which was incorporated by Alexander Lowen in Bioenergetics.

SOME IMPORTANT REICHIAN CONCEPTS

1. Hysterical character armour trait
   - A. An unstable defence against genital impulses that are easily aroused accidentally.
   - B. This trait interferes with a person's motivation toward intellectual achievement, because too much time and energy is spent avoiding potentially dangerous situations and people.
   - C. The trait is characterized by:
     - a. Sexual or seductive behaviour
     - b. Soft and rolling body movements
     - c. Superficiality
     - d. Excitability
     - e. Flightiness
     - f. Fearfulness
     - g. Temperamental behaviour
     - h. Suggestibility
     - i. Easy disappointment.
2. Compulsive character armour trait
   - A. A rigid defence against loss of control over aggressive and sadistic impulses.
   - B. An attempt to avoid uncertainty.
   - C. Even minor breaks in routine can cause overwhelming concern.
   - D. This trait makes the person fear punishment and the

associated guilt of accidental arousal of unwanted impulses.

E. The trait is characterized by:

a. Fear of losing control
b. Over-concern for orderliness
c. Circumstantial thinking
d. Ruminations
e. Indecision
f. Blockage between thoughts and feelings
g. Stiff body movements.

3. Phallic–narcissistic character armour trait

   A. Is created by an over-identification with the phallus (or with the fantasy, in women).
   B. Phallic–narcissistic men have a basic hostility toward women.
   C. The trait is characterized by:

   a. Outward coldness
   b. Reserve
   c. Living on a 'short-fuse'
   d. Outspoken
   e. Provocative
   f. Power-seeking.

4. Masochistic character armour trait

   A. Contrary to the usual view on masochism (that the person experiences pain as pleasure), Reich's view is that this trait prevents the individual experiencing pleasure in any form.
   B. A beating would be less painful than experiencing someone's love.
   C. While there is an intensive craving for love, the masochist cannot accept it.
   D. Masochists convince others that they are unlovable, so they avoid love and loving.
   E. They are hurt the most by love; the very love they most crave.
   F. The trait is characterized by a sense of lifelong suffering, endless complaining, and self-damaging words and actions that have the effect of punishing and provoking others into not loving.

Orgone therapy identifies and analyses underlying character traits before progress is possible. Interpersonal issues between client and therapist must also be resolved before constructive work can be done.

Attention is paid to what the client says, but more importantly, to how it is said.

A Reichian therapist will work with the character armour as it manifests itself, particularly in muscular tensions.

RELATIONSHIP PRINCIPLES

EFFECTIVE PEOPLE:

1. Build on other people's ideas
2. Express warmth and affection
3. Handle personal anger constructively
4. Influence others
5. Listen with understanding
6. Receive warmth and affection
7. Tolerate conflict and antagonism
8. Tolerate conflicting views of others
9. Tolerate other people's behaviour
10. Have aspirations for self
11. Are aware of their own feelings
12. Are aware of other people's feelings
13. Are willing to continue self-awareness
14. Have close personal relationships

15. Value independence
16. Value innovativeness
17. Are open-minded
18. Show peace of mind
19. Have physical energy
20. Have high self-esteem/self-worth
21. Are self-expressive
22. Tolerate differences in others
23. Trust people
24. Are versatile
25. Are willing to discuss their own feelings.

RELATIONSHIP PRINCIPLES OF COUNSELLING

1. INDIVIDUALIZATION

A. Individualization means recognizing and respecting the other person's uniqueness.
B. It recognizes not just *a* human being but *this* human being – just as she/he is.
C. Every person has the need and the right to be related to as unique.
D. Clients need our undivided attention and privacy to be able to discuss their unique problem.
E. People whose uniqueness is not respected react by only giving information and not disclosing feelings.
F. When people are related to with uniqueness, when they feel understood, they will enter more willingly into the helping relationship.
G. Relating to others in this way may not come easily.
H. Training is essential to:

a. Recognize and deal with our biases and prejudices
b. Acquire knowledge of human behaviour
c. Develop listening and responding skills
d. Learn to move at the client's pace
e. Learn to respond with empathy
f. Develop perspective
g. Develop a flexible approach.

I. We can enhance individualization by:

a. Thoughtfulness and care
b. Privacy
c. Preparation
d. Engaging the client
e. Flexibility.

2. EXPRESSING FEELINGS

A. Every client has the right to be permitted, and indeed encouraged, to express both positive and negative feelings within an atmosphere of understanding and acceptance, and without feeling judged.
B. We should neither discourage nor condemn feelings. It is often therapeutic to encourage the expression of feelings.
C. Any problem, however practical its focus, has an emotional component.
D. The expression of feelings is encouraged:

a. To relieve pressures and tensions and free the client for positive, constructive action.
b. To understand more clearly the client and the problem.
c. To help us assess the client's strengths and weaknesses.
d. To provide psychological support. Feelings shared bring closeness.

e. When feelings are brought into the open there is more chance that something constructive can be done with them.
f. Feelings shared help to deepen the counselling relationship.
g. To create a safe environment.

E. Feelings are facts.
F. Feelings have a voice. They will speak for themselves. We must ensure that we listen to them.
G. We can enhance the expression of feelings by:

a. Being relaxed
b. Adequate personal preparation
c. Active and purposeful listening
d. Not trying to rush the process.

Some cautions

A. Psychological awareness is essential to deal constructively with other people's feelings, and the feelings generated within us.
B. The relationship must encourage true expression of feelings.
C. Give free time and space to the client.
D. Keep your foot on the emotional brake. Feelings expressed too soon, too much, may be destructive.
E. Clients' feelings should not become our burden.
F. Do not fall into the trap of offering premature or empty verbal reassurances.

3. INVOLVEMENT MUST BE CONTROLLED

No emotional involvement means separation.

Controlled emotional involvement means effective contact.

Over-involvement means engulfment.

Over-involvement/over-identification is caused by a deficiency of self-awareness.

The components of controlled involvement are:

A. *Sensitivity*. Listening to feelings, verbal cues, non-verbal cues, paralinguistic cues.
B. *Understanding* what these feelings mean to this person means getting inside the client's frame of reference, seeing through the client's eyes, hearing through the client's ears, feeling through the client's experience.
C. *Responding*. Responses convey understanding. A response may be Internal, founded on attitudes, feelings, and understanding; External, verbal or non-verbal.

Avoid empty phrases such as:

'I know how you feel.'
'This must be hard on you.'

We can never know how another person feels. We only know how we feel, how we felt. We trust that our level of understanding is helping us get somewhere near the client's feelings.

4. SELF-DETERMINATION (SELF-DIRECTION)

A. Self-determination is our basic right of freedom to choose our own direction, even though that decision may clash with the values, beliefs, and desires of other people.

B. We all have the responsibility to live our own life, and achieve life's goals, as we perceive them.

C. One of the functions of counselling is to help clients mobilize their inner resources so that they are more able to make balanced decisions.

D. Many people feel helpless to make decisions because the alternatives are unclear. Helping them tease out what is involved often enables them to make a decision and to take responsibility for what they decide to do.

E. We may face a dilemma. If, in our view, a proposed course of action is destructive, could we still be objective and positive toward the client? If our values clashed, could we continue counselling without trying to persuade, manipulate, take responsibility, or try to control the client?

F. Clients need help to:

a. See their problem with a new perspective.
b. Explore alternatives and the possible consequences.
c. Express their thoughts and feelings about choices.
d. Explore their thoughts, feelings and behaviours within a relationship in which they feel safe.

The counsellor, as it were, helps clients clear some of the mist away from the window, thus allowing them to look out and see a little more clearly.

G. Self-determination is not licence. It is influenced by:

a. The rights of others.
b. The client's capacity to make informed decisions.
c. Civil and criminal law, and the client's own moral law,
d. In work, the Contract of Employment.

Clients who violate their own moral law do spiritual harm to themselves. If a decision would be so contrary to the client's own moral law as to be destructive, it is questionable if we are really helping to solve a problem if we do not challenge that decision.

For every individual right of choice there are accompanying duties and responsibilities in our relationship with others. When we practice self-determination it does not mean that we are indifferent to what clients do; neither does it mean that we have to approve. We accept their basic right.

5. CONFIDENTIALITY (*See also*: Ethics)

A. Confidentiality means not revealing secret details about another person disclosed during counselling.

B. Everything said in a counselling interview is confidential; not everything is secret.

C. A belief that absolutely everything the client says must never be shared with anyone else can lead to problems.

D. If it becomes imperative that some information must be passed on, full discussion with the client is essential.

E. Some people who use counselling at work, as distinct from independent counsellors, must consider the rules of professional conduct of their organization.

F. Wherever possible agreement to disclose should be received, to avoid feelings of betrayal.
G. It is helpful to ask: Is this information concerned mainly with the client as a person or with the organization?
H. Purely personal material, unless it impinges on the client's working life and influences performance, is of no concern to anyone else.
I. The dividing line between 'personal' and 'organizational' is finely drawn.
J. Only after a weighing up of all the pros and cons will we realize why the balance is tipped the way it is, and so make our decision to keep something or pass it on.
K. What are secrets?

a. The private secret is that which, if we reveal, would libel, injure, or cause great sadness to the person concerned.
b. The pledged secret is when one person shares something with another, and is assured that it will remain in confidence.
c. The entrusted secret is the explicit or implicit understanding that the confidant will not divulge the information.

Feelings as well as facts should not be shared indiscriminately. Confidentiality is limited by:

a. Whose needs predominate
b. Who would be harmed
c. The organizational needs
d. The needs of the wider society.

6. ACCEPTANCE (*See also*: main entry)

A. Acceptance is:

a. A warm regard for people as persons of unconditional self-worth.
b. Valuing people no matter what their condition, thoughts, behaviours, or feelings.
c. Respect and liking for people as separate, unique persons.
d. Willingness to allow people to possess their own feelings.
e. Regard for the attitudes of the moment, no matter how negative or positive; no matter how much such attitudes may contradict other attitudes the person held in the past.

B. Inherent in the idea of acceptance is that the counsellor does not judge the client by some set of rules or standards.
C. Counsellors must be able to suspend their own judgments, and not let them intrude on the interaction.
D. Acceptance is a special kind of loving that moves out toward people:

a. As they are – warts and all
b. Maintaining their dignity and personal worth, with their:
c. Strengths and weaknesses
d. Qualities, likeable, unlikeable
e. Positive and negative attitudes
f. Constructive and destructive wishes
g. Thoughts/feelings/behaviours, but without:

h. Wish/pressure to make the person be someone else
i. Wish to control, criticize, or condemn
j. Attaching 'if' clauses; e.g. 'I will love you if . . .' Clients will test our unconditional acceptance

E. When we accept clients just as they are, they accept us – just as we are and it helps them to accept other people as they are.
F. Acceptance is dependent on self-awareness. The more psychologically aware we are, the more able we shall be to help others mobilize their feelings and energies and to direct them toward change, growth, and fulfilment.
G. Obstacles to acceptance

a. Lack of knowledge of human behaviour.
b. Blockages within self.
c. Attributing one's own feelings to the client.
d. Biases and prejudices.
e. Unfounded reassurances.
f. Confusion between acceptance and approval.
g. Loss of respect for the client.
h. Over-identification with the client.

7. NON-JUDGMENT

A. People who are troubled need help, not judgment.
B. An attitude of judgment, based on the firmly held belief that assigning guilt or innocence or the degree to which the client is responsible or not for causing the problem has no place in the therapeutic relationship.
C. Judgment without the appropriate authority is a violation of basic human rights.
D. Clients who are nurtured within a relationship of non-judgment learn not to pass judgment upon themselves.
E. People find the courage and the strength to change when in such a relationship.
F. When we pass judgment upon others, if we examine ourselves we will find the very thing on which we pass judgment also present within.
G. 'Non-judgment' does not mean being valueless or without standards. It does mean not trying to mould others to fit into our value systems. Our values may be right for us, but totally wrong for other people. Counsellors, however, are not human chameleons. They must remain true to their own values and standards.
H. Guilt or innocence, blame, condemnation, and punishment are all part of judgment.
I. People feel attacked when judgment is passed on them but less attacked when their observed behaviour is questioned.
J. We communicate the unspoken judgment lurking within. When we feel non-judgment, that feeling is communicated.
K. We may not like all clients, but it is our duty to strive toward freedom from prejudices which will lead us into passing judgment.
L. We can work toward non-judgment by:

a. Recognizing, and carefully scrutinizing, our own values and standards, some of which we may need to jettison

b. Trying to see the world from the client's frame of reference
c. Not jumping to conclusions
d. Not saying, 'I know how you feel'
e. Not comparing the client to someone else
f. Not becoming over-involved
g. Not responding to the client's inappropriate feelings toward us, which may indicate transference.

REPERTORY GRID (*See also*: Personal construct theory)

A technique developed by George Kelly to rank or rate a person's elements against bipolar constructs on a matrix.

Elements for the grid are supplied either by the counsellor or elicited from the client.

AN EXAMPLE OF A GRID

A rating of 7 (most like) to 1 (least like).

Mother (MO) Father (FA) Partner (PA) Sister (SI) Brother (BR) Friend (FR) Self (SE)

One client's assessment of his brother:

7	MO	FA	PA	SI	BR	FR	SE	1
Kind	—	—	—	—	3	—	—	Cruel
Pleasant	—	—	—	—	5	—	—	Unpleasant
Handsome	—	—	—	—	6	—	—	Ugly
Masculine	—	—	—	—	6	—	—	Feminine
Strong	—	—	—	—	7	—	—	Weak
Large	—	—	—	—	7	—	—	Small
Valuable	—	—	—	—	3	—	—	Worthless
Open	—	—	—	—	2	—	—	Closed
Active	—	—	—	—	5	—	—	Passive
Warm	—	—	—	—	2	—	—	Cold
Sexual	—	—	—	—	7	—	—	Not sexual
Gentle	—	—	—	—	1	—	—	Tough
Clean	—	—	—	—	5	—	—	Dirty

SOME BIPOLAR CONSTRUCTS

1. Clear–unclear
2. Clever–stupid
3. Friendly–aggressive
4. Happy–sad
5. Hard working–lazy
6. Interesting–boring
7. Like–dislike
8. Loving–selfish
9. Naughty–good
10. Sensible–silly
11. Beautiful–ugly.

REPRESSION (Defence mechanism)

'It never happened.'

The basic meaning of the word to repress means to put down, suppress, control, censor, exclude. In all depth psychology it is where an idea or feeling is banished or not allowed to enter consciousness. It is the cornerstone concept of psychoanalytic theory.

Primal repression is where primitive, forbidden id impulses are blocked and prevented from ever reaching consciousness.

Primary repression is where anxiety-producing mental content is forcefully removed from consciousness and prevented from re-emerging, and where ideas and feelings are acted upon before they can become conscious.

Secondary repression is where ideas and feelings once conscious are now excluded from consciousness. Repressed material makes its presence known through symbolic behaviour, dreams, neuroses, and parapraxes.

Repression prevents ideas, wishes, anxieties, impulses, and images from becoming conscious, and rejects to the unconscious mind ideas, wishes, anxieties, impulses, and images that have become conscious. If they did come into the conscious, the person would produce anxiety, apprehension, or guilt.

The effects of repression can be seen in someone who has performed a shameful act, and then develops total amnesia for the act and all the surrounding circumstances.

RESISTANCE (Defence mechanism) (*See also*: Counter-transference, Transference)

In psychoanalysis, the client's unconscious efforts to thwart the aims and process of therapy. The client does this by blocking unconscious, repressed material from breaking through into the conscious.

Because of the client's resistance, access to the unconscious can be gained only by indirect means, the chief being free association. Resistance must be overcome if the client is to integrate unconscious material into the conscious and move forward toward the loss of symptoms.

Resistance is not a 'once-and-for-all' phenomenon; it is continually being experienced. By analysing the resistances, the client gains freedom from them. The analyst uses positive transference to overcome resistance.

The paradox is that many people who engage in therapy experience resistance to it. Most people would experience resistance if they felt, for example, censured and judged.

Anticipated change may also create resistance. Clients are more likely to undertake change with less resistance when in a supportive relationship, than when they feel undesired change is being forced upon them.

TYPES OF RESISTANCE:

1. *Intentional resistance* protects the ego by not adhering to the fundamental rule of free association.
2. *Transference resistance* (*see* Transference).
   Transference love is ambivalent, a mixture of affection with a reverse side of hostility, exclusiveness, and jealousy. Transference invariably becomes negative, turning into resistance.
3. *Resistance from the symptoms*. The client would stand to lose something if the neurosis is cured.
4. *Id resistance*. The id resists because it is being forced into a change of direction.
5. *Superego resistance* results from the unconscious sense of guilt or need for punishment and will strenuously resist analysis.

OVERCOMING RESISTANCE CANNOT BE HURRIED, IT CAN BE HELPED BY:

A. The client's need for recovery.
B. The client's intellectual interest.
C. Positive transference.
D. Making the expression of resistance as safe as possible.
E. Honour the resistance by careful listening, without discounting what is revealed.
F. Acknowledge the resistance not by agreeing with it, but by recognizing the difficulty the client is experiencing.
G. Reinforce that there must be valid reasons for resisting at this time.

EXPLORING THE RESISTANCE

A. Distinguish between valid and invalid resistance. Valid resistance is directed at the specific topic; invalid resistance is a smokescreen of feelings to divert the counsellor's attention. Invalid resistance is often linked to generalities and bringing up the past.

B. Any probing of the resistance must be carried out with extreme caution. The probing is carried out with the express consent of the client.

C. The aim is to reduce needless resistance that interferes with the clients healthy functioning.

INDICATORS OF RESISTANCE INCLUDE:

1. A tendency to argue
2. Avoidance of new learning
3. Refusal to co-operate in suggested programmes
4. Refusal to look at new possibilities
5. Always wanting to generalize, and not deal with specifics
6. Intellectualizing, and refusing to work with feelings
7. Rudeness, antagonism, anger, or any other strongly negative feeling.

Resistance may be created by the therapist, either from what is said or done, or not said or done. The therapist whose empathy has lapsed, and is no longer relating to the client from the internal frame of reference is in danger of creating the conditions in which resistance will flourish.

RETROFLECTION

A term in Gestalt therapy to describe a split within the self; a resisting of aspects of the self by the self. It means that we do to ourselves what we originally did or wanted to do to others. When we use retroflection we have difficulty with the boundaries between self and the environment.

To illustrate retroflection: Whenever there is conflict I say to myself, 'It's all my fault. I've done it again. It's always the same with me.' This 'owning' of everything is different from owning one's responsibility. This is taking the total blame. While some of it may be correct, is it all correct? Can we hold ourselves responsible for what is patently outside of our control?

When carried to extreme, retroflection leads to isolation, as we increasingly take responsibility for other people's actions and feelings. With this is an associated guilt of having left undone something we could have done, either to prevent it happening, or to lessen the burden when it has.

S

SCAPEGOATING

The Old Testament Day of Atonement ritual uses two he-goats. One is chosen by lot as a sacrifice to God, the other is symbolically burdened with the sins of the Israelites and driven off into the wilderness. (Leviticus Chapter 16, verses 7–10 and 20–22.)

By extension, a scapegoat has come to mean any individual or group that innocently bears the blame of others. The Christian teaching of Christ's death and atonement, reflects the notion of the innocent suffering for the guilty.

In groups, scapegoating describes the way in which one person can be isolated and excluded, in order to relieve group tension and stress. The scapegoated person usually possesses one or more characteristics that influence the process, such as:

1. Mental or physical handicap or illness
2. Racial, sexual, colour, or language difference
3. Vulnerability – difference in rank or status, or in families, rank order.

Scapegoating can be seen within societies, where minority groups are blamed for everything that goes wrong in the community, which relieves the others from having to take any responsibility. Scapegoating uses the defence mechanisms of displacement, projection and projective identification.

SCRIPTS (*See also*: Transactional analysis)

A script is one's preconscious life-plan decided by the age of 6 or 7 years. It is based on injunctions (don't do . . .) and counterinjunctions (usually in the form of slogans).

A counterscript is a preconscious life-plan decided by the child's parent. The aim of therapy is to free people from following their scripts and counterscripts.

The script positions:

1. I'm OK; You're OK, the healthy position.
2. I'm OK; You're not OK, this is a distrustful position, and is taken

up by a child who is suspicious of people.
3. I'm not OK; You're OK, is the position of the child who usually feels low or depressed.
4. I'm not OK; You're not OK, is the position of a child who feels that life just isn't any good, and that there is no escape from it.

SELF-ACTUALIZATION
(*See also*: Humanistic psychology, Maslow. A.)

The capacity of human beings to grow and develop toward emotional and psychological maturity and self-fulfilment.

The term is used by most humanistic therapies to describe the dominating, motivating life force that drives the individual toward ever-developing, ever-perfecting his/her capacities to the highest heights and deepest depths. Therapies that emphasize minimal therapist direction, or person-centred philosophy, also embrace the principle of self-actualization.

Self-actualization is the road; to be self-actualized is the goal, striven for but never absolutely attained.

Self-actualization involves the successful mastery of conflicts that always involve anxiety. It is closely linked with 'peak experiences', though not synonymous with them. Our drive for self-actualization may conflict with our rights and duties and responsibilities to other people who are involved.

THE CHARACTERISTICS OF SELF-ACTUALIZATION

1. Psychological growth and maturation
2. The awakening and manifestation of latent potentialities
3. Ethical, aesthetic, and spiritual experiences and activities.

1. For Maslow, self-actualization is:

   A. A liberating of the person from factors that stunt personal growth.
   B. Freeing of the person from the neurotic problems of life – infantile, fantasy, or otherwise 'unreal'.
   C. Enabling the person to face, endure, and grapple with the real problems of life; a moving from unreal toward real issues.

2. Self-actualization is not:

   A. A state of no conflict
   B. A state of once-and-forever full unity
   C. An absence of problems.

SELF-ACTUALIZING THERAPY

A humanistic therapy that helps people to recognize and engage their core conflicts and so use the released energy to live more creatively. Actualizing therapy derives from:

1. Maslow's theory of self-actualization
2. Carl Rogers' person-centred philosophy
3. Rollo May's humanistic/existentialism
4. Alexander Lowen's bioenergetics therapy
5. Viktor Frankl's logotherapy.

The fundamental belief is that all human beings possess an innate drive toward self-actualization. This approach may be used in groups or in individual therapy.

CLIENTS ARE HELPED TOWARD FULL POTENTIAL BY:

1. Overcoming their core conflicts
2. Becoming aware of, and being able to express, feelings
3. Accepting their weaknesses and limitations
4. Discovering their own unique meaning of life
5. Working toward growth and development of personality.

THE TECHNIQUES:

1. Reflecting experiences and feelings
2. Self-disclosure for both client and counsellor
3. Exercises to get in touch with feelings through body work
4. Values clarification
5. Role play
6. Role reversal
7. Breathing exercises to release emotions
8. The use of touch to replace aggressive feelings with feelings of love.

Actualizing therapy is not usually appropriate for people who are very disturbed, being more suited to people who are motivated to develop different parts of their self-awareness.

SELF-AWARENESS (*See also*: Johari window)

To be aware of one's own personality, qualities and continuing identity. Self-awareness is one's physical, mental, emotional, moral, spiritual, and social qualities being integrated, powerfully organized and working toward our fullest potential.

It is the capacity to understand and use one's qualities, to focus attention, and process information in accord with the self-concept.

SELF-AWARENESS CAN BE THOUGHT OF AS:

1. Known to self and others
2. Perceived by others, hidden from self
3. Hidden to others, known to self
4. Hidden from self and from others.

Consciousness of self, open or hidden, varies according to:

1. Routine or ritual situations – e.g. work – generally call for a low level of self-awareness.
2. Special situations, important relationships, learning new skills, personal development, and interpersonal training all require a heightened self-awareness.

SELF-AWARENESS MAY BE ENHANCED BY:

1. Art work
2. Body work
3. Dance
4. Feedback
5. Group work
6. Hypnosis
7. Imagery
8. Left/right brain work
9. Meditation
10. Personal therapy
11. Self-analysis.

SELF-CONCEPT

The self is central for integration and in how we relate to people.

ALLPORT'S VARIOUS PARTS OF SELF:

1. Bodily self
2. Self-identity
3. Self-esteem
4. Self-extension
5. Self-image

6. Self as rational agent
7. Self-striving.

In social psychology terms, self is a combination of the opinions and attitudes absorbed from significant others.

IN JUNGIAN PSYCHOLOGY, SELF:

1. Is made up of conscious and unconscious contents and dwarfs the ego in every way.
2. Is the whole range of human experience.
3. Expresses the unity of the personality. Adler describes the 'creative self'. Assagioli talks of the 'transpersonal self', with many subpersonalities.

Awareness of self is not:

1. An intellectual concept
2. A byproduct of the superego
3. The result of suggestion
4. A parapsychological phenomenon
5. A state of lowered awareness.

THE SELF IS A TWO-PERSON:

1. The personal, or conscious self; that which separates us from other people.
2. The inner, or transpersonal self; that which unites us with other people.

THE SELF-CONCEPT

1. The most important single factor affecting the way we communicate is our self-concept – how we see ourselves and the situations in which we find ourselves.
2. The self-concept is:

   A. The centre of our personal universe
   B. Our frame of reference
   C. Our personal reality
   D. A screen through which we see, hear, evaluate, and understand.

People with weak self-concepts distort the way they think others perceive them. They fear that disagreeing with others may give the impression of not liking them. People with weak self-concepts may have difficulty in:

1. Communicating with others
2. Admitting that they are wrong
3. Expressing feelings – positive or negative
4. Accepting criticism
5. Voicing ideas that are different from those held by other people.

The self-concept is formed by our relationship with significant others who convey their approval or disapproval, acceptance or rejection. To develop a positive self-concept we need love, respect, and acceptance from significant others.

SELF-DISCLOSURE

The process by which we let ourselves be known to others.

DISCLOSURES MAY BE:

1. Intentional (mainly conscious)
2. Unintentional (mainly unconscious)
3. Verbal (mainly conscious)
4. Non-verbal (mainly unconscious)
5. Thoughts, feelings, and behaviours.

Clear verbal and non-verbal disclosures increase the chance of accurate reception without the need for complicated decoding.

Appropriate disclosure is critical in relationships, for it enhances them, keeps them alive and helps to avoid alienation. One person's low disclosure is likely to block another person's willingness to disclose.

People who are genuine - in touch with their own inner empathy - are also in touch with what they are experiencing and send authentic messages to others.

Disclosure involves both negative and positive aspects of self. Not everyone finds it easy to disclose positive aspects of themselves, possibly due to low self-esteem.

DISCLOSING MEANS THAT WE HAVE TO ANTICIPATE:

1. Our own feelings
2. The other person's reactions
3. The possible effect on the relationship.

We may interfere with people's genuine self-disclosure by:

1. Being secretive; this leads to a high degree of information control
2. Colluding with them; in which case, fantasy and reality become confused
3. Faking disclosures; which prevents the other person from making genuine disclosures.

QUESTIONS OF APPROPRIATENESS OF DISCLOSURE:

How much?
What area?
How many areas?
How intimate?
To whom?
In what context?
Why am I doing it?

ENCOURAGING SELF-DISCLOSURE

1. *Assertion*. Learning to express, where appropriate, positive and negative feelings.
2. *Challenging*. To give feedback non-aggressively.
3. *Development of relationships*. Breadth and depth of disclosures tend to increase naturally as relationships develop.
4. *Expressiveness*. To be able to express feelings appropriately (or not express them, but recognize and acknowledge them), not just talk about them.
5. *Feedback options:*

   A. To agree
   B. To restate initial disclosure
   C. Reflect the other person's message
   D. Send an 'I' message
   E. Remain silent.

6. *Immediacy*. To be able to respond immediately and say what otherwise would remain unsaid.
7. *Positive/negative disclosure*. Genuine intimacy is characterized by a willingness to let ourselves be known genuinely.
8. *Questions*. Questions often avoid having to disclose. Questions should be used with discrimination.
9. *Reciprocity*. Relationships can be prevented from becoming shallow, by matching levels of disclosure.
10. *'I' messages*. Recognizing, owning and expressing one's own feelings, not someone else's.
11. *Specificity*. Generalizations are too vague for people to relate to.
12. *Verbal and non-verbal disclosures*. People can be taught to disclose by such means as:

A. Modelling/teaching
B. Rehearsal/practising
C. Homework
D. Audiovisual aids.

SELF-DISCLOSURE (CLIENT)

Where the client makes a conscious decision to disclose feelings, thoughts, attitudes, behaviours – past or present – to the therapist. Client disclosure is an essential element in most types of psychotherapy.

Where this is not happening, therapy is seriously impeded. The degree of disclosure is related to the degree of trust within the relationship. Therapist trustworthiness, a non-judgmental attitude, and acceptance all facilitate disclosure.

Exploring how disclosure could facilitate or hinder counselling may help those clients who have difficulty disclosing. Clients may be helped toward disclosure by considering the potential gains and risks.

POSSIBLE GAINS:

1. Lessened loneliness and alienation
2. Greater intimacy
3. More friendships
4. Self-responsibility
5. More assertive
6. Makes it easier for others to disclose
7. Discovering others
8. Self-acceptance
9. More control of own life.

POSSIBLE RISKS:

1. Rejection
2. Not liking self
3. Feelings of shame
4. Being misunderstood
5. Wary of confidentiality
6. Feeling tense/vulnerable
7. Too much intimacy too soon
8. Too many close relationships
9. Too much self-knowledge
10. Equilibrium of relationship disturbed
11. Breaking taboos about disclosures.

Reluctance to disclose may also be related to ethnic or religious influences.

SELF-DISCLOSURE (THERAPIST)

Where therapists are open and use disclosure apropriately, clients are more likely to be equally disclosing. Counsellor disclosure involves appropriate sharing of:

1. Attitudes
2. Experiences
3. Feelings
4. Reactions to the client
5. Views.

Counsellor disclosure may be more appropriate in well-established relationships. Disclosures should reflect the needs of the client, not the needs of the counsellor.

Self-disclosure is embraced in humanistic therapies, but seldom in psychoanalytic therapies, where to self-disclose would get in the way of working through the transference.

Inappropriate or mistimed disclosures may increase rather than decrease the client's anxiety. The focus may be removed from the client if the disclosure is lengthy or inappropriate.

DISCLOSURE IS APPROPRIATE IF:

1. It keeps the client on target and does not distract.
2. It does not add to the client's burden.

3. It is not too often.

The greatest block to self-disclosure is fear of not being accepted, of thinking oneself to be different, odd, unworthy, fit only to be judged. Cautious, ritualized communication inhibits self-disclosure.

TO BUILD SELF-DISCLOSURE SKILLS

1. Be direct
2. Be sensitive
3. Be relevant
4. Be non-possessive
5. Be brief
6. Be selective.

EXAMPLE

Peter was talking to Roy about his father's recent death. He was having difficulty expressing himself until Roy said,

'My father died four years after mother. When he died I felt I'd been orphaned. Is that something like how you feel?'

Peter sat for several minutes in deep silence before saying,

'You've put into words exactly how I feel. May I talk about my childhood and how Dad and I got on?'

SELF-ESTEEM

The positive and negative evaluations we make of, and apply to, ourselves. Self-esteem indicates the extent to which we believe ourselves to be significant, capable, and worthy.

Self-esteem is generally applied to feelings of worthiness. We may have a good, average, or bad opinion of ourselves.

A surprising point about self-esteem is the enormous range of variation between individuals. Some people think the whole world is theirs for the taking; others almost feel they have no right to exist.

Generally we see our value mirrored in the eyes of society, a process that starts in childhood, and to some extent our self-esteem is derived from a comparison between ourselves and other people.

Comparison with the peer group, for example, is important, and is based on popularity, power over others, task competence, and honour/virtue.

Some people attempt to bolster their self-esteem at the expense of others' self-esteem, but this in the long-term is not fruitful.

Freud believed that the male child who has been the mother's favourite will forever keep the feeling that he is a conqueror. Yet other children, even within the same family, grow up with the feeling that their very existence is a terrible mistake. There is no 'self-esteem blueprint' for parents to work on.

We all possess an actual self and an ideal self. The ideal self, what we know we could be, should be, or would like to be, derives from:

1. Parental expectations
2. Instructions received on how to behave
3. The values of parents
4. The values of heroic figures from real life, biography, and fiction.

At the highest level, self-esteem depends on making sense of our relationship to the rest of the universe. Low self-esteem operates in the gap between the actual self and the ideal self.

In some cultures self-esteem is based largely on membership of family, social groups, tribe, or nation.

Initiation rites are designed to break down individual self-esteem and replace it with self-esteem based on group membership.

Low self-esteem is often associated with:

1. Abuse
2. Anxiety states
3. Delinquency
4. Depressive illness
5. Disability, disfigurement
6. Prejudice
7. Psychosomatic disorders

Self-esteem rating scales correlate strongly with scales measuring anxiety, depression, and neuroticism, and in many cases there is overlap of items.

Low self-esteem is an enormous public health problem. People who report low self-esteem usually say that it has been present since early childhood or at least adolescence.

Observers have commented that females generally suffer more from low self-esteem than do males. Depression, often associated with low self-esteem, is also thought to be closely linked to gender issues.

SELF-FULFILLING PROPHECY

A concept developed by the sociologist, R.K. Merton. A self-fulfilling prophecy is so designed that the findings cannot help but prove the truth of the theory. The school teacher who predicts that a certain student will fail, tends to react to that student in ways that increase the likelihood of failure.

The term is also used in a psychological sense, usually in a negative way, where clients put themselves down. Another example would be where parents who fear a child will turn against them, bring it about by constantly predicting to the child what will happen.

The principle of 'expectancy' is used positively in therapy; the client expects to be helped. 'Paradoxical self-fulfilling prophecy' can also be used, where the therapist predicts the opposite of the desired behaviour, to provoke the client in achieving the desired behaviour.

SEXUALIZATION (Defence mechanism)

Where an object or function is invested with a sexual significance not inherently possessed. The defence is used to ward off anxieties associated with prohibited impulses or desires.

An example would be where a person can only become sexually aroused by the wearing of a certain garment.

SHADOW

A Jungian term that describes:

1. The thing a person has no wish to be
2. The negative, dark, primitive side of the self
3. What is inferior, worthless, uncontrollable and unacceptable.

The shadow cast by the ego is what makes us fully human. It is kept in check by the ego and the persona. The more we attempt to live in the persona, the more potent will be the shadow's strength. Analytical therapy aims to bring more of the shadow in to the light.

The shadow involves the personal unconscious, instincts, the collective unconscious, and archetypes.

The shadow is itself an archetype and as such it is impossible to eradicate. The contents of the shadow are powerful, and capable of overwhelming the most well-ordered ego.

EVIDENCESOF THE SHADOW APPEARS IN:

1. Projections, both negative or positive, which are powerful and potentially destructive, and may be directed against individuals, groups, or whole societies.
2. Dreams, as a 'shady' character, a 'tempter', in the same sex as the dreamer, but with characteristics that the dreamer would consciously not embrace.

IN ANALYTICAL THERAPY, THE CLIENT IS HELPED TO:

1. Own, accept, come to terms with, and integrate the shadow as something personal and not attributable to other people.
2. Develop an awareness of the images and situations most likely to produce shadow projections.
3. Analyse the shadow and so break its compulsive hold.

SILENCE

Silence is referred to in psychotherapeutic literature as:

1. An indicator of resistance
2. A necessary and productive part of the therapeutic process
3. An intervention by the therapist
4. An integrating process.

Silences enable the client to make associations and connections and engage in problem-solving. Breaking the silence may interfere with the client's internal processes.

The positive value of silences is stressed in the person-centred and humanistic approaches, as a means of adding depth to the relationship.

Silence enables clients to hear what they and the counsellor have said, and releases attention to observe non-verbal behaviour.

Counsellors who are never silent deprive themselves and their clients of the opportunity to listen to the deeper meanings that lie beyond words.

Silence happens between people, rather than within one of them, and is an essential characteristic of the relationship.

Silences may arise from resentment, through not having been listened to, being argued with, put down, or been given incorrect, mistimed, or unacceptable interpretations.

In family therapy, 'dysfunctional silence' is used by one member of the family, in order to sabotage change.

Silence on the other hand is essential in techniques such as meditation, relaxation, and imagery.

When silence is thought to be resistance or blocking, the therapist may use a prompt, by repeating something said previously, or by drawing attention to the nature of the silence.

Therapists may have to work hard on their ability to tolerate silence. What could be a constructive silence is easily ruined by too quick an intervention.

SINGLE-SESSION THERAPY (*See also*: Brief therapy)

Single sessions may be planned, where it is known by both therapist and client to be one session, though longer than the accepted 'therapeutic hour'.

SUGGESTED PRINCIPLES:

1. Identify one salient issue.

2. View the client's difficulties as a stepping stone to development.
3. Engage the client fully.
4. Keep interpretations to the minimum.
5. Understand with empathy.
6. Start the client on the road toward problem-solving.
7. Limit the number of issues to be explored.
8. Make provision for follow-up at the client's request.

Unplanned single sessions are also known as 'therapeutic drop out', where the client terminates after one session. Studies show that a significant percentage of those who do drop out found what they were seeking, and had no real desire to enter into ongoing therapy.

SIX-CATEGORY INTERVENTION (*See also*: Re-evaluation counselling)

A method developed by John Heron. It is client-directed, with counsellor interventions directed toward catharsis and support.

THE SIX INTERVENTIONS:

1. PRESCRIPTIVE

Interventions that aim to influence and direct the client's behaviour in such a way that:

A. The client is free to accept or reject them
B. They do not interfere with the client's freedom of choice.

Prescriptive interventions take the form of:

A. Advice, in a specific area of expertise
B. Suggestions or commendations
C. Requests
D. Demands or commands
E. Modelling behaviour
F. Giving a lead
G. Verbally and non-verbally directing the client's behaviour
H. Attitudes and beliefs about behaviour
I. Particular goals to be achieved.

2. INFORMATIVE

Interventions that aim to impart new knowledge:

A. Which the client sees as relevant
B. That do not increase dependence
C. Encourage the client to be an active partner in the learning process.

Informative interventions give:

A. General knowledge
B. Information specific to the client's situation
C. Information about the client's behaviour.

3. CONFRONTING

Interventions that:

A. Challenge attitudes, beliefs and behaviours
B. Support the client while highlighting the defences being used
C. Enable the client to achieve insight.

Confronting interventions include:

A. Direct, descriptive, non-judgmental, personal-view feedback

B. Interrupting the pattern of negative thinking or acting, by:

a. Distraction
b. Introducing a new topic
c. Contradicting
d. Proposing a total change of activity.

C. Mirroring in a supportive way the client's negative verbal or non-verbal behaviour
D. Using direct questions to get at what is being defended
E. Challenging restrictions; the use of 'shoulds' and 'oughts', and generalizations, for example
F. Unmasking, which uses information not given by the client
G. Interpretation of the clients defences
H. Discharge feedback is demonstration by the counsellor, in sound and movement, of pent-up anger and frustration.

Confronting interventions that are punishments or attacks cause the client to counterattack. They only succeed when clients feel that the counsellor is attacking their defences, not them.

4. CATHARTIC

Interventions that aim to help the client release repressed emotions:

A. Anger, through storming
B. Grief, through tears and sobbing
C. Fear, through trembling
D. Tension, through yawning
E. Embarrassment, through laughter.

Cathartic, interventions include:

A. *Literal description* where, in the first person and in the present tense, the client describes a traumatic event in detail. Detail would include sounds, sights, smells, what people said and did.
B. *Repetition* where the client repeats emotionally charged words or phrases. Non-verbal cues indicate emotionally charged content such as faltering tone, sudden emphasis, puckering of mouth, or eyes, twitching of fingers or limbs, sudden change of posture, change in breathing pattern.
C. *Association* when the client is encouraged to verbalize a sudden, unbidden thought, or to repeat a slip of the tongue. Unbidden thoughts may be detected mainly by the eyes looking anywhere but at the counsellor, and by hand movements, indicating discomfort.
D. *Acting into* means encouraging the client to deliberately act out the sounds and movements of the emotions, to tap into a genuine discharge of emotion.
E. *Self-role play* is a basic cathartic intervention. Clients become themselves in a past traumatic scene, with its words and wishes and feelings. The counsellor becomes the recipient of the client's emotionally charged message.
F. *Monodrama* (*see also*: Gestalt therapy) is where the client has a different chair for each role in the conflict. The client

switches from chair to chair and creates a dialogue between the characters in each chair.

G. *Primary contact*. The counsellor gazes into the client's eyes and, at the same time, holds the client's hands and gives total attention.

H. *Touch*. When the client is on the verge of tears and sobbing, touch is supportive and may allow the floodgates to open.

I. *Bodywork*, after the style of bioenergetics, with breathing and exaggerated movements.

J. *Contradiction* encourages the client to use phrases that:

a. Contradict the negative self-image, accompanied voice tone and body language that agree with the verbal message.

b. Express negative views with voice and body language that contradict the feelings.

c. Use a double-negative to exaggerate tone of voice, facial expression, and body language.

K. *Fantasy* may be used in a number of ways to bypass intellect.

L. *Relaxation* and reverie to work on associations.

M. *Transpersonal work*, e.g. meditation.

Balance of attention. Old, painful emotions cannot be discharged unless the client has sufficient attention outside the traumatic experience.

The counsellor may help generate attention by directing the client's attention to something in the immediate environment, to the counsellor, getting the client to describe a recent, pleasant experience, to relax or do controlled breathing.

5. CATALYTIC

These interventions are those that:

A. Enable the client to work toward self-determination and self-recovery.

B. Convey to the client that the counsellor is paying attention, is supportive, and is trying to understand.

Catalytic interventions include:

a. *Free attention*, not being distracted, either by the external or by internal thoughts and feelings, using gaze, posture, facial expressions and touch, being totally supportive, waiting and expecting with hope, being non-anxious, being tuned into the client.

b. *Active listening skills* include:

Reflecting the last words after a pause, selective reflecting, where attention is focused on significant words or phrases;

Paraphrasing, putting into one's own words the gist of what the client has said;

Empathy building, making every effort to work within the client's frame of reference.

c. Checking for understanding is a summary that reinforces understanding, aids empathy building, and encourges further elaboration.

d. Discreet self-disclosure by the counsellor encourages trust and acceptance.

e. Open questions by the counsellor encourage further exploration.

f. Problem-solving structured exercises that work logically from identifying symptoms toward an agreed action plan.
g. Self-discovery, through reality games and growth games.
h. Theoretical structure, where the counsellor offers relevant theories and conceptual models.
i. Analysis of variables, as they relate to how the counsellor perceives the possible reasons.
j. Examination of options, how the counsellor perceives the various alternatives to the client's decision.

6. SUPPORTIVE

Supportive interventions are those that:

A. Affirm the person's worth and value
B. Are given unconditionally
C. Are caring and authentic
D. Do not collude with the client's defences, and negative self-opinions.

Supportive interventions include:

A. Free attention
B. Touch
C. Expressing positive feelings
D. Expressing care and concern
E. Validation and positive affirmation
F. Sharing what is happening in the relationship
G. Self-disclosure.

A negative self-image makes it difficult for some clients to accept supportive interventions. Productive interventions fall into one or other of the six categories. No one intervention is superior to another. To be productive, any intervention has to be caringly supportive. All interventions must have a catalytic element.

SOCIAL THERAPY

This is provided by the therapeutic communities and community psychiatry where services are offered outside the hospital setting.

The focus of intervention is the patients' relationship with their physical environment and with other people. The aim is to alter existing conditions, by influencing both the social system and the person within the system.

Altering the system may be through political action, welfare rights, and acting as patient advocate. Social therapy within an institution focuses on group relationships, staff–patient relationships, and the way in which decisions are made and how power is allocated.

PIONEERS IN SOCIAL THERAPY:

1. T.F. Main (The Cassel Hospital)
2. Maxwell Jones (The Henderson Hospital)
3. R.D. Laing and associates (Kingsley Hall)
4. The Richmond Fellowship
5. The Tavistock Institute.

Practitioners of social therapy minimize traditional professional status, relying instead on creating a therapeutic network of resources.

SOCIOGRAM

A sociometric diagram or chart designed by Jacob L. Moreno to plot the structure of personal relations within a group.

Such a chart would indicate each individual's:

1. Acceptance or rejection
2. Relative popularity
3. Leadership capacities
4. Prejudices
5. Perceived intelligence.

Members who are isolated can be identified as well as those at the centres of negative or positive attention.

SOMATIZATION (Defence mechanism)

Where psychic disturbances are converted into physical symptoms that preoccupy the individual. The physical symptoms are not in keeping with any actual physical disturbance.

Somatization is a way of dealing with emotional conflicts or internal or external stressors.

In desomatization, infantile somatic responses are replaced by thoughts and feelings.

In resomatization, there is regression to earlier somatic forms when the person cannot face unresolved conflicts.

SPLITTING (Defence mechanism)

A psychoanalytic term to describe a division within the psyche. The term is used in three different ways:

1. Horizontal splitting

   Division one – conscious, preconscious, unconscious
   Division two – the three agencies of the psyche: id, ego and superego.

2. Vertical splitting

   Division one – acceptance of reality
   Division two – denial of reality.

3. Paranoid–schizoid position
   Division one – compartmentalizing people as good or bad
   Division two – dealing with contradictions.

Splitting is commonly seen in clients with behavioural and antisocial problems.

CHARACTERISTICS OF PEOPLE WHO USE SPLITTING:

1. Others are seen in black or white terms.
2. They think in 'all or nothing' terms.
3. They categorize people into all good or all bad.
4. They idealize or disparage.
5. They draw wrath upon themselves by turning people against them.

A permissive therapeutic atmosphere is essential.

STATUS (*See also*: Individual psychology)

The relative position of a person or thing, with rights, responsibilities and duties, especially social or professional that are inherent in it.

Status assumes vertical relationships, based on a hierarchy, prestige, and honour. Status is what a person is; role is what that person does. One person usually occupies a number of different statuses, each corresponding to membership in some group or social category.

STATUS MAY BE:

1. *Ascribed* status is often based on gender, age, family relationships, and birth, not on merit.

2. *Achieved* status is acquired through achievement, education, occupation,, marriage, special abilities.

Status is closely allied to authority, power, conformity, norms, leadership, and compliance.

Groups of people of unequal status generally find interaction difficult. Status and rank are marked by clearly distinguishable symbols that serve to guide behaviour. Symbols come to be admired and prized as evidence of success.

STEKEL, WILHELM (1868–1940)

Rumanian born, German-speaking Jew, an early student and colleague of Freud. He was one of the founder members of the Vienna Psychoanalytic Circle. He was a close friend of Alfred Adler and they influenced each other's work.

Unorthodox and creative, he used his own personality in therapy more than was acceptable at that time.

His alliance with Freud ended in 1912 when he went on to develop his own brief and more direct approach, which he called Active analysis.

STRESS MANAGEMENT (*See also*: 'A'-type personality, Fight/flight response, Post-traumatic stress syndrome)

Stress is any change that a person must adjust to. It is an effect and not a cause; the effect is felt only within the individual and is essentially the rate of wear and tear in the body. The subjective sensations of stress are feeling tired, jittery, or ill.

Hans Selye says that stress produces 'adaptive reactions' as a defence. He refers to this as the 'General adaptive syndrome' (GAS).

THE GAS HAS THREE STAGES:

1. Alarm reaction
2. Resistance
3. Exhaustion.

When we interpret something as threatening, the body prepares us to fight or run away:

1. Blood flow to brain increases.
2. Blood is redirected from the extremities to the trunk and head.
3. Hands and feet become sweaty.
4. Hearing becomes more acute.
5. Heart and respiratory rates increase.
6. Muscles tense.
7. Thought processes speed up.
8. Vision becomes clearer.

Chronic stress is the result of the body not being given relief from the biochemical changes that occur during the 'fight or flight' response.

What produces stress in one person may have no effect whatsoever in someone else. One person cannot make assumptions about what is not 'distressing' for another person.

Only when something is perceived as hostile does it have the power to act as a stressor, although stress events are not necessarily negative or unpleasant.

Stress has been found to be related to many physical ailments, and every organ of the body may become the focus for felt stress.

SOURCES OF STRESS

1. Environmental
2. Physiological
3. Emotional
4. Mental

5. Behavioural
6. Transpersonal.

Social readjustment rating scale (SSRS) (Holmes and Rahe) identifies ten significant areas related to life events and stress:

1. Economics
2. Education
3. Family
4. Group and peer relationships
5. Health
6. Marriage
7. Occupation
8. Recreation
9. Religion
10. Residence.

Holmes and Rahe developed a scale of 43 'Life change units' (LCUs). People who accrue 200 or more points at any one time, over a period of about a year, are prone to physical disease or psychiatric disorder.

THE TOP TEN LCUs

1.	Death of spouse (partner)	100
2.	Divorce	73
3.	Marital (partner) separation	65
4.	Death of close family member	63
5.	Detention in prison or other institution	63
6.	Significant personal injury or illness	53
7.	Marriage	50
8.	Being dismissed from work	47
9.	Reconciliation with partner	45
10.	Retirement from work	45

MEASURES TO REDUCE LIFE EVENTS STRESS

1. Become familiar with life events and their degree of change.
2. Display one's Life change chart in a prominent place and review it frequently.
3. Practice recognizing significant life events.
4. Identify feelings about significant events.
5. Learn to control events, not vice versa.
6. Do not make decisions in a hurry.
7. Plan significant events well in advance.
8. Practice keeping calm.

HELPING PEOPLE TO RECOGNIZE AND DEAL WITH STRESS

How many of the following phrases do you regularly use?

A. I'm just as tired when I wake up.
B. I can't face another day.
C. I'll take another day off sick.
D. Oh God! another dreary day.
E. I couldn't care less.
F. If I sit down, I'll never get started again.
G. I'm bad tempered lately, it's not like me.
H. Life's one long, boring slog.
I. Life's maddening, nothing's ever right.
J. I need a drink.

Mind indicators of stress

A. Frequent headaches
B. Lapses in memory
C. Ringing/buzzing in the ears
D. A particular thought won't go away
E. Can't settle down to get on with things
F. Constantly put tasks off
G. Great difficulty concentrating
H. Head feels full of cotton wool
I. As if thinking through a fog.

Social indicators of stress

A. People are more difficult than usual.

B. People make too many demands.
C. Too much change is happening.
D. No one to confide in.
E. Life is nothing but work and sleep.
F. Family problems.
G. Don't really know anyone really well.

Body indicators of stress

A. Legs twitch in bed.
B. Frequently have cramp in bed.
C. Aches and pains in the back of the neck.
D. Shoulders, neck and back ache a lot.
E. Hands often tremble.
F. Sigh often.
G. Can't get enough breath in the lungs.
H. Suffer from diarrhoea.
I. Rings on fingers get very tight.
J. Tummy feels knotted.
K. Tummy gets very gassy.
L. Bladder needs to be emptied a lot.
M. Sleep is difficult.
N. Wake in the early hours.
O. Difficulty getting back to sleep.
P. Get very hot at night.
Q. Heart-beat seems loud and fast at night.
R. Heart seems to skip a beat.

Emotional indicators of stress

A. Often very near to tears
B. Rarely laugh these days
C. Can't react with the same feeling
D. Life is flat
E. Upset by the least little thing
F. Feel as taut as violin string
G. Don't feel or care about anything/anybody.

'A'-TYPE PERSONALITY AND STRESS (*See also*: 'A'-type personality)

1. Undertakes more than one job at any one time, which results in poorly done work.
2. Tries to cram too much work into a given time, results in a race against the clock.
3. Competitive about almost everything, sometimes with hostility and aggression.
4. An intense, sustained drive to achieve self-selected but usually poorly defined goals, coupled with extraordinary mental alertness.

Categories of occupational stress:

1. Work load
2. Occupational frustration
3. Occupational change.

The stress levels of people caught on the occupational treadmill of long hours, intensive study, promotion, and relocation (usually with increased financial commitments) will, inevitably, increase. The spirit of work of the '90s is geared toward the 'A'-type personality.

ASSERTIVENESS AND STRESS (*See also*: Assertiveness)

Assertive behaviour is a middle way between passive or aggressive behaviour. People who behave passively feel humiliated, put down, worthless, not appreciated, and stressed because they have allowed someone to walk all over them. People who behave aggressively feel stressed because of the angry feelings generated within themselves and in other people.

When people feel good after communicating with others, it is usually because:

1. They have said what they want to say.
2. They have listened and been listened to.
3. They have maintained their self-esteem.

Making decisions often causes stress and conflict because of the way difficult events are perceived and interpreted. Fears about making a faulty decision add to the stress.

SYMPTOMS OF DECISIONAL STRESS:

Feelings of imminent loss if a wrong decision is made. Losses may be material, social, reputation, self-esteem.

Effects of stress on decision-making

1. One's ability to handle information is undermined.
2. Crisis management becomes the norm.
3. There is a tendency to make irrational/hasty decisions.
4. Sometimes the inability to make a decision is total.

Helping people reduce decisional stress

1. Explore and evaluate alternative choices.
2. Explore and evaluate risks.
3. Encourage action, however small.
4. Don't overload with information.
5. Don't encourage making 'any old decision'.
6. Teach relaxation and positive imagery.
7. Use a 'for and against' approach.

HELPING PEOPLE MANAGE TIME

Time is a conveyor belt of small and large decisions, all of which shape our lives. Some decisions produce frustration, lowered self-esteem and stress. Inappropriate decisions give rise to the symptoms of ineffective time management.

1. Rush and hurry
2. Chronic hesitation between alternatives
3. Fatigue or apathy alternate with non-productivity
4. Deadlines are often missed
5. Few periods of rest or companionship
6. The sense of being overwhelmed by demands and details
7. For most of the time having to do what they don't want to do
8. They may not have any clear idea of what they would prefer to be doing.

People can be helped toward effective time management by:

1. Establishing goals
2. Establishing goal priorities
3. Creating time by constructing a realistic and practical programme to take care of essential tasks
4. Taking time to learn how to make decisions.

Encourage them to take time to reflect on:

1. How their day has gone.
2. Were intervals between work genuine times of recreation?
3. Was their eating healthy?
4. Did they eat/drink more than they could handle?
5. What mood are they in at bedtime?

6. Are they on the emotional treadmill of anxiety about some aspect of work?
7. Are they having a relationship problem?

HELP PEOPLE SET GOALS (*See also*: Goals and Goal-setting)

One step toward a goal is one step behind. Focus on the goal, not on the route. Help them to think how not to spend 80% effort to get 20% reward.

SOME GOLDEN DO'S TO HELP PEOPLE AVOID STRESS

1. Learn to say 'No' – assertively. The consequences of saying 'No' have to be weighed against the consequences of saying 'Yes', when it is really 'No' you want to say.
2. Tackle high-priority tasks first. Low-priority tasks may go away.
3. Don't become so schedule-conscious that interruptions create more stress.
4. Create personal time and space every day. Everyone around benefits.
5. Make one decision every day. Start with something small, but significant.
6. Practice deep relaxation daily.

STRESSFUL THINKING (*See also*: Cognitive therapy)

Many people are caught in the trap of negative thinking. A sense of inferiority or inadequacy puts a stumbling block in the pathway of achievement. Negative thinking is destructive and wasteful of precious energy. Negative thoughts interfere with relaxation and increase stress. Self-confidence leads to self-realization and successful achievement.

Aids to thought control

1. Explore and list negative thoughts.
2. Use imagination positively.
3. Use 'thought stop'.
4. Substitute a positive thought to replace the invasive negative thought.
5. Make positive thinking an ally.

IRRATIONAL IDEAS AND STRESS (*See also*: Locus of control, Rational emotive therapy)

1. Negative thinking uses irrational ideas.
2. Negative thinking creates stress.
3. Negative self-talk leads to negative feelings.
4. Many irrational ideas are based on impossible standards, generally imposed on us by other people and taken on board, lock, stock, and barrel.
5. Rationality enhances goal attainment.
6. Irrationality hinders goal attainment.

MAIN STRESS-MANAGEMENT TECHNIQUES

1. Assertiveness training (*see* entry)
2. Autogenic training (*see* entry)
3. Body awareness (*see* Bioenergetics)
4. Biofeedback
5. Breathing (as practised in yoga)
6. Coping skills training
7. Exercise
8. Imagination (*see* entry)
9. Meditation
10. Nutrition
11. Relaxation. This can be learned in one week, practising two 15-minute sessions a day. (*See also*: Autogenic training)

12. Rational emotive therapy (*see* entry)
13. Self-hypnosis
14. Thought stopping (*see* Cognitive therapy)
15. Time management.

STROKES (Transactional analysis)

Strokes describe the recognition we receive from others. Strokes can be verbal, non-verbal, or both. A wave of the hand. 'Hello, how are you today?' A slap.

1. *Positive* strokes are warm and enhance self-esteem, and evoke the feeling of 'I'm OK, You're OK.' Expressing love, caring, respect, and responding to an expressed need are all positive strokes.
2. *Negative* strokes are cold and knock self-esteem and evoke the feeling of 'I'm not OK.' Expressing hating is a negative stroke.'I can't stand you' is a negative stroke.
3. *Conditional* strokes are given to get something in return. 'I will love you if . . . ' (*See also*: Unconditional positive regard)
4. *Unconditional* strokes are given without any attached strings; with no hidden motives.

We need positive strokes to maintain physical and mental well-being. Institutionalized infants have been known to die when deprived of stroking. As we grow, words are often substitutes for physical stroking we received as children.

So often strokes are given when we have done something. We also need strokes just for being who we are. We also need to learn to ask for strokes when we need them. 'I'd really appreciate a big hug right now.' 'Give me a kiss, darling.'

A positive self-esteem makes it in order to stroke oneself. 'I did a really good job and I'm pleased with myself.'

SUBLIMATION (Defence mechanism)

'I'm dedicating my life to prayer, instead of sex.'

In psychoanalysis, the channelling of what would be instinctual gratification into new, learned behaviour; something that is more conforming to social values and behaviours.

It is usually referred to in a sexual context and classical psychoanalytic theory regarded creative and artistic tendencies as manifestations of sublimation. In the same way, intellectual curiosity is said to be a sublimation of scophilia (the desire to look; voyeurism, Peeping Tom).

Anna Freud maintained that sublimation indicated a healthy progression, in that it produces an acceptable solution to infantile conflicts which otherwise might lead to neurosis.

In a more general sense sublimation is the redirection of energy from social unacceptable behaviour into something more acceptable.

An example would be the person who finds an outlet for aggression through competitive sports.

SUICIDE

Any deliberate act of self-damage which the person cannot be certain to survive and, to some degree, had the intention of death.

Durkheim's classification of suicide is:

1. *Egoistic*. Suicide resulting from a deep sense of personal failure coupled with a lack of concern for the community with which the subject was inadequately involved.

2. *Altruistic*. Suicide based on sacrificing oneself for the good of others, coupled with a sense of community feeling.
3. *Anomic* (*See also*: Anomie, Alienation).
   Suicide based on the belief that life no longer has meaning, resulting from a sense of anomie, loneliness, isolation, and loss of contact with the norms of society. Society has failed to control and regulate the behaviour of individuals.

Parasuicide is where there is little or no intention that death should result.

Attempted suicide is where an act that would have led to death has been prevented.

Almost all people in the 'pre-suicidal' state experience ambivalent feelings. They want to die and also to be saved. They want to escape from an intolerable situation, and they also wish that the intolerable situation could be so transformed that they could continue living.

Prevention may be possible in the pre-suicidal state, because of the ambivalence, but people of immature personality, may not experience ambivalence.

Depression is the chief cause of suicide. People who are suffering from situational depression (sometimes called 'reactive') very often respond positively to psychotherapy.

Clinical (also called 'endogenous') depression is difficult to handle with psychotherapy but usually responds to medical intervention.

Loneliness often leads to situational depression. Relationship difficulties may also lead to depression and are a common cause of suicide and parasuicide.

Chad Varah of the Samaritans says that befriending often swings the ambivalent person in favour of living and toward finding an alternative to death.

SUMMARIZING

SUMMARIZING IS USED TO:

1. Focus scattered facts, thoughts, feelings and meanings
2. Prompt the client to further explore a particular theme
3. Close a particular theme
4. Help the client to find direction
5. Help to free a client who is stuck
6. Provide a 'platform' to view the way ahead
7. Help the counsellor when feeling stuck
8. Help clients to view their frame of reference from another perspective.

A summary:

1. Outlines the relevant facts, thoughts, feelings, and meanings.
2. May include a mixture of what was said and what was implied.
3. Gives a sense of movement.
4. Requires checking with the client for accuracy.
5. Should be simple, clear, and jargon-free.

EXAMPLE OF SUMMARIZING

'Have I got this straight? You said that you are very confused with all that's happening. Your boyfriend wants you to have a baby, but you're not sure about that. You would like to carry on with your career, it means a great deal to you; at the same time you do want to have children, but not yet.

You would like to get married before you start a family but your boyfriend doesn't think like that. You're afraid that if you stick to your principle, you may lose your boyfriend. Is that about it?'

SUPEREGO (*See also*: Ego, Id)

The superego is the last of the components of the psychic apparatus to develop. It has been called 'the heir to the Oedipus complex'.

It is that part of the ego in which self-observation, self-criticism, and other reflective activities develop. It is formed gradually within the ego as a mechanism for maintaining the ego-ideal.

The ego-ideal is the standard of perfection we create for ourselves.

The ego-ideal is derived from loved or admired (rather than judging and threatening) figures and images. It is responsible for the sense of guilt and self-reproaches so typical in neuroses.

The superego behaves as a moral judge, criticizing the thoughts and acts of the ego, causing feelings of guilt and anxiety when the ego gratifies or tends to gratify the primitive impulses of the id.

The superego evolves, to a large extent, as a result of repression of the instincts, it is thus more closely related to the id than to the ego.

In the developing process, standards, restrictions, and punishments imposed by authority figures are internalized into the superego which then becomes self-governing.

The immature superego tends to be rigid and punitive. Modification over time, and with experience, permits adult sexual behaviour.

The upheaval and aggressive acting out behaviour of adolescence can be understood in terms of the instinctual release previously curbed by the superego. One of the major tasks of adolescence is to modify the development of the superego.

Freud's first use of 'superego' related to his belief that obsessional ideas were self-reproaches for some sexual act performed with pleasure in childhood.

Some people suffer from excessive conscience, characterized by excessive work, earnestness, and rituals, rarely allowing themselves pleasure.

Only when we can achieve some separateness from superego can we live satisfactorily, even though sometimes the price of disobedience is guilt.

SUPERIORITY COMPLEX (*See also*: Individual psychology, Inferiority complex)

In literal terms this means the conviction that one is better than, or superior to, others. Adler used the term to describe the mechanism of striving for recognition and superiority as a compensation for the feelings of inferiority, inadequacy and insecurity.

Inferiority is acted upon through the processes of socialization and education. The superiority complex helps to rid the developing child of feelings of inferiority.

The striving for power and dominance may become so exaggerated and intensified that it then must be called pathological. When this happens, the ordinary relationships of life will never be satisfactory.

The pathological drive to achieve power is characterized by:

1. Effort
2. Haste and impatience

3. Violent impulsiveness
4. Lack of consideration for others
5. Dominance from an early age
6. Defensiveness
7. Feeling of being against the world, and the world is against the subject
8. Achievements that do not benefit anyone but the subject
9. Trampling on others to get to the top
10. Human relationships matter little
11. Pride, vanity, and the desire to conquer
12. Constantly putting other people down in order to feel elevated
13. A marked distance between the subject and other people
14. Joy in life is rarely experienced.

SUPERVISION (*See also*: Evaluation)

Supervision, an accepted and necessary need within counselling, is sometimes referred to as the mentor relationship.

Supervision helps counsellors to increase their skills and develop understanding and sensitivity of their own and the clients' feelings.

The supervisory relationship is not primarily a therapeutic one. The task of the supervisor falls somewhere between counselling and tutoring. Supervision is developmental, helping the counsellor examine his/her relationship with particular clients and the counselling process.

The supervisory relationship forms a three-way relationship of client, counsellor and supervisor. Supervision is often resisted, because people don't use it fully. Counsellors who disregard the supervision relationship will lose out, and run the risk of their counselling becoming stale.

THE COMPONENTS OF SUPERVISION

1. Support and encouragement
2. Teaching and integrating theoretical knowledge and practice
3. Assessment in the maintenance of standards
4. Transmission of professional values and ethics.

APPROACHES TO SUPERVISION

1. Characteristics of case-centred supervision
   - A. Exploration of case material
   - B. Concentrated mainly on what took place
   - C. Little exploration of the counselling relationship
   - D. A teacher/pupil relationship
   - E. Discussion is more in the 'then-and-there', than in the 'here-and-now'.
2. Characteristics of counsellor-centred supervision
   - A. The counselling relationship and what is happening within the counsellor
   - B. Feelings are more readily acknowledged
   - C. Carried out in an uncritical atmosphere
   - D. Transference and counter-transference are more openly explored.
3. Characteristics of interactive supervision
   - A. Takes into account both the case and the counselling relationship.
   - B. The interaction between client and counsellor may in some way be reflected in the supervisory relationship. Recognizing

the interaction and working with it is likely to provide the counsellor with invaluable first-hand experience.

SUPPORTIVE PSYCHOTHERAPY

Supportive therapy is any form of therapeutic procedure in which direct help is provided. It is a form of therapy offered:

1. To people who have been so emotionally damaged that any dramatic change is unlikely
2. To people in crisis.

Some clients are likely to need support for many years.

The aim of supportive therapy is to:

1. Help the client maintain some degree of independent living
2. Restore abilities and inner resources
3. Enhance self-esteem
4. Establish realistic expectations of therapy
5. Prevent deterioration
6. Enable the client to function with minimum support
7. Involve others in the support.

TECHNIQUES OF SUPPORTIVE THERAPY

1. Assertiveness training
2. Change of environment
3. Encouragement/praise
4. Explanation
5. Give advice to network supporters
6. Guidance
7. Increase social contacts
8. Reassurance
9. Relaxation training
10. Social skills training
11. Suggestion
12. Helping to set goals and courses of action.

DANGERS OF SUPPORTIVE THERAPY

1. The therapist may become discouraged and cease to work for any change
2. The risk of dependency
3. May be relegated to therapists with least experience.

Supportive therapy works more at the cognitive behavioural levels and avoids probing the client's deeper conflicts.

SUPPRESSION (Defence mechanism) (*See also*: Repression)

In a broad sense suppression is the voluntary and conscious elimination of some behaviour such as a bad habit, or suppression of unacceptable ideas.

In psychoanalytic terms suppression refers to conscious, voluntary inhibition of activity, in contrast to repression, which is unconscious, automatic, and prompted by anxiety, not by an act of will.

Disturbing ideas, feelings, memories are banished from the conscious to the preconscious.

Suppression is less total than repression, and because it resides in the preconscious is more accessible to the conscious. While issues are deliberately cut off, they are not avoided; discomfort is present but is minimized.

SYMBOLS AND SYMBOLISM (*See also*: Analytical psychology, Imagery, Psychosynthesis)

Symbols are objectives or activities that represent, and stand as substitutes for, or are thought to typify, something else.

Material objects may be used to

represent something invisible such as ideas. The dove is a symbol of peace.

Symbols are products of feeling and intuition and erupt spontaneously from the imagination.

Symbolism is the practice of representing things by means of symbols, or of attributing symbolic meanings or significance to objects, events or relationships.

IN PSYCHOANALYTIC THEORY A SYMBOL IS:

1. An unconscious representation of something not directly connected with it
2. A representation of intrapsychic conflict
3. Usually an expression of repressed sexual material
4. The only way the unconscious may be reached.

The real meaning is not normally available to the conscious mind and only makes itself known through dreams.

Dream symbolism is important in the process of concealing unconscious wishes or conflicts, through displacement and condensation, or revealing them through interpretation.

The use of symbols and the transfer of interest from one thing to another is an important step in children's development.

The development and use of language hinges on the ability to work with symbols.

EXAMPLES OF SYMBOLIC AGENTS:

1. Codes
2. Diagrams
3. Images
4. Maps
5. Pictures
6. Words.

SYMBOLS APPEAR IN:

1. Dreams
2. Religious iconology
3. Mythology
4. Altered states
5. Hallucinations
6. Fairy tales
7. Legends
8. Folk tales
9. Novels
10. Meditation and contemplation.

IN ANALYTICAL PSYCHOLOGY SYMBOLS ARE:

1. Dreams that express themselves as images
2. Captivating pictorial statements
3. Obscure, metaphoric, and mysterious portrayals of a person's inner world
4. Individual representation of universal phenomena
5. Archetypal in quality.

Working with symbols is a way of bypassing ego-control and intellectual filtering, and of getting in touch with the urges, feelings, ideas, and impulses that would not be tolerated in the conscious.

SYNCHRONICITY

A Jungian term to describe meaningful connections between events that are plainly related, yet:

1. Do not always obey the laws of cause and effect.
2. Do not appear to obey the rules of time and space.
3. Link the psychic and the material worlds.

Jung attempted to prove the concept by examining the correspondence between astrological birth signs and choice of marriage partners. While this experiment was heavily criticized, Jung was putting across the idea that events, assumed to be linked by chance, may be connected by synchronicity.

Many of us have experienced situations which we have been tempted to call 'coincidences', but which have had profound personal meaning.

Evidence of synchronicity may be more apparent when the threshold of consciousness is lowered, when just dropping off to sleep, or when engaging in active imagination.

By keeping the possibility of synchronicity in mind, we may be protected from feeling, on the one hand, that everything is due to fate, or, on the other hand, from resorting to explaining everything on a cause and effect basis. Taking this middle way will show to the client a respect for an experience which, at the moment, we may not be ready to understand.

SYSTEMATIC DESENSITIZATION

Desensitization is the reduction or the extinction of sensitivity to something specific that causes a problem, for example allergies.

The same behavioural principle, pioneered by J. Wolpe, is applied in the treatment of anxiety and phobic behaviours by counter-conditioning.

THE TECHNIQUE:

The client is exposed, under relaxed conditions, to a series of stimuli that increasingly approximate to the anxiety-provoking one, until the stimuli no longer produce anxiety.

THE STAGES:

1. Relaxation training which the client is urged to practise twice daily.
2. The construction of a hierarchy of anxiety-provoking stimuli, ranked according to the level of anxiety they evoke, from least to greatest.
3. Presentation of scenes during relaxation, starting with the least anxiety-provoking, and working in a step-by-step progression through the hierarchy.

   Some people find it very difficult to relax, to carry out visualization, or to produce hierarchies that accurately reflect their problem.

Variations on the theme

Some therapists use a tape recorder for home desensitization. Some work in groups, while others carry out the process in real situations.

T

TAVISTOCK METHOD (Groups)
(*See also*: Bion, W.R.)

The Tavistock method originated with Bion, working with small study groups at the Centre for Applied Social Research in the London Tavistock Institute of Human Relations.

Bion's military experience in psychiatry convinced him that the individual could not be considered except as part of a group. The emphasis later gradually shifted from the roles adopted by people in groups, to the dynamics of leadership.

BASIC ASSUMPTIONS OF GROUPS

1. A group is formed from a collection of people when there is interaction between members who are aware of their shared relationship, from which a common group task emerges.
2. Various forces bring groups into being, such as external threat, collective regressive behaviour, and attempts to satisfy needs for affection, dependency, safety, and security.
3. When a collection becomes a group it behaves as a system and is greater than the sum of its parts, though the primary task may be masked.
4. The primary task of any group is to survive.
5. The fantasies and projections of its members gives the group a life of its own.
6. Group members are used in the service of the primary task.
7. A person's present behaviour is an expression of that person's individual needs and also the needs of the group.
8. Whatever the group says or does, the group is always talking about itself.
9. Knowledge of the group process increases people's insights into their own and other people's behaviour in the group.
10. Groups have manifest (overt) and latent (covert) aspects.
11. People always have hidden agendas – parts of themselves that they consciously or unconsciously do not intend to reveal.

12. The basic assumption group is composed of the combined hidden agendas of:
    - A. Unconscious wishes
    - B. Fears
    - C. Defences
    - D. Fantasies
    - E. Impulses
    - F. Projections.
13. The basic assumption group is in conflict with the task.
14. The tension between the task and the basic assumption group is usually balanced by:
    - A. Individual defence systems
    - B. Ground rules
    - C. Expectations
    - D. Group norms.
15. Survival assumptions:
    - A. Dependency
      - (a) The aim is to gain security and protection from either the designated leader or the assumed leader.
      - (b) The group behaves in such a way that it hopes it will be rescued, controlled, and directed by the leader.
      - (c) The group expresses disappointment and hostility when the leader does not rescue.
      - (d) Authoritative leaders often fall foul of the dependency assumption.
    - B. Fight/flight
      - (a) Fight is characterized by active aggression, scapegoating, and physical attack.
      - (b) Flight is characterized by withdrawal, passivity, avoidance, and ruminating on past history.
      - (c) Fight leadership is bestowed on the person who mobilizes the group's aggressive forces; but this leadership is generally short-lived.
      - (d) Flight leadership is bestowed on the person who successfully moves the group away from the 'here and now' to the 'then and there' and so reduces the importance of the task.
    - C. Pairing is characterized by warmth and affection, creating intimacy and closeness, and by mutual support that excludes others in the group.
    - D. Oneness exists where the group surrenders self to some outside cause, all-powerful force, in order to feel a sense of well-being and wholeness.

Organizations seek to satisfy one or other of the survival assumptions. Examples are:

1. Dependency, e.g. the Church
2. Fight/flight, e.g. the military and industry
3. Pairing, e.g. the political systems
4. Oneness, e.g. mysticism and cosmic consciousness.

THE FUNCTION OF THE FACILITATOR IS TO:

1. Confront the group, without intentionally offending group members.
2. Draw attention to group behaviour, but not to individual behaviour.
3. Point out how the group uses individuals to express its own emotions.
4. Show how it exploits some members so that others can excuse themselves.

5. Focus on what is happening in the group.
6. Present observations in such a way as to increase the group's awareness.

FACILITATOR INTERVENTIONS MAY BE:

1. Description of what is observed.
2. Process observation – how the group pursues its task.
3. Thematic development – interactions that threaten the performance of the task, often drawing analogies from myth, legend and fairy tale.
4. Enlightenment – remarks aimed at instant enlightenment.
5. Shock – remarks that point to absurdities, aimed at producing shock and immediate awareness.

ISSUES CONFRONTING GROUP MEMBERS

1. *Authority*
2. *Responsibility*
3. *Boundaries*. A fundamental precept of group relations is that work is not possible unless some boundaries – known to all members – are established and maintained. Boundaries must be strong yet permeable.
4. *Projection* occurs in all human relationships and is particularly observable in groups in the form of:

   A. Scapegoating
   B. Hostility often directed at the facilitator
   C. Struggles for power
   D. People who project their weaknesses onto others are also in danger of giving away their strengths.

5. *Group structure*

   A. Control – the group objectives and contract
   B. Restraints – ground rules
   C. Selected emphasis – expectations and assumptions of both facilitator and members
   D. Elaborate structures hinder the group process
   E. Minimal structures enhance the group process
   F. Visible structures build trust
   G. Invisible structures open the door to manipulation.

TELEPHONE COUNSELLING

The telephone, the central feature of many crisis intervention agencies, is seldom used for counselling over longer periods. Potential clients, those who have not yet plucked up courage to engage in a more formal counselling relationship, can use the telephone.

The telephone allows for anonymity, gives control to the client and reduces intimacy, something that many clients find frightening.

Difficulties of telephone counselling are mainly the lack of visual contact and total reliance on verbal language.

Listening, essential in any counselling, is crucial in telephone counselling. Effective listening is listening to what is said, the way it is said (paralinguistics), what is not said, and being aware of silences.

The way the person responds helps to build rapport, and is aided by the frequent (but not habitual, or unrelated) use of minimal responses such as 'H-m', 'Yes', 'Right', 'OK', 'Carry on'.

Non-verbal language is always being transmitted so we should avoid doing anything we would not normally do in face-to-face counselling. Taking notes, or doodling may create an intuitive distraction.

Telephoning advice:

1. Look welcoming
2. Imagine you are looking the speaker in the eye
3. Try to convey warmth by avoiding a clipped, crisp, business-like, hurried approach.
4. Avoid looking at the clock, aware of a pressing engagement. Be honest, tell the caller, and arrange a return call.

If the telephone is held in your left hand, you are more likely to use your right brain function for feelings and to explore.

If the telephone is held in your right hand, you are more likely to use your left brain to analyse and to be precise.

Empathy is more right- than left-brain oriented.

TERRITORIALITY (*See also*: Non-verbal communication)

The tendency to defend or protect one's space against invasion or attack by other members of the same species. The 'territory' may be real, physical, psychological, or personal.

A related concept is that of individual space. The space around us within which others are not tolerated.

People often display territorial behaviour, e.g. resenting someone else sitting in their preferred chair.

THANATOS (*See also*: Eros)

In ancient Greek religion, Thanatos, the twin brother of Hypnos (sleep), is the death principle, sometimes raised to the status of a god.

In psychoanalysis, the death instinct struggles with Eros, the life instinct, and is expressed in such behaviours as denial, rejection, and turning away from pleasure.

TOKEN ECONOMIES

A behavioural technique based on the earning and exchange of tokens. The technique derives from the theories of conditioning and learning.

A number of psychiatric units operate a token system, especially with very regressed, chronic patients, to induce socially appropriate behaviour.

Tokens (which can later be exchanged for food and privileges, such as watching television) are given for dressing properly, interacting with other patients or staff, not engaging in psychotic talk, helping with the cleaning. Such programmes have proved effective in changing both the patient's behaviour and the general ward atmosphere.

TOUCH (*See also*: Body therapy)

The touch of significant others, especially the mother, or principal care-giver, plays an important part in the development of security in the infant. Through its senses the infant learns that it is loved, and develops a confident personality.

Deprivation of touch can give rise to neurotic or psychotic behaviour in later life, such as 'touch hunger' or 'touch revulsion'.

The psychoanalytic approach operates a 'non-touch' rule, which affords no escape for the client, and frees the therapist from possible collusion and self-gratification.

Body therapists, however, use a great deal of touch. For them, touch is healing. The cardinal guideline is that the therapist is not 'touch hungry' or seductive. The touch should be for the benefit of the client, not for the counsellor.

TRANSACTIONAL ANALYSIS (TA) (*See also*: Adapted child, Adult, Child, Critical parent, Ego states, Free child, Games, Nurturing parent, Racket feelings, Scripts, Strokes, Transactions). Berne, E. (1910–1970)

TA is a system of analysis and therapy developed by Berne. The theoretical framework comprises:

1. Various 'selves' or ego states – Parent, Adult, Child – which form the personality
2. Transactions between people and between one's various selves
3. An individual existential position
4. A preconscious lifeplan or 'script'

TA is also a method of groupwork that emphasizes the person's ability to change, the role of the inner parent in the process of change, and the person's control of the ego states.

THE THEORETICAL FRAMEWORK EXPANDED:

1. Structural analysis

   A. Critical parent functions are to set limits, discipline, make rules and regulations about how life should be; the do's and don'ts. The critical parent uses such words as 'always', 'never', 'should', 'should not', 'must', 'ought to', 'have to', 'cannot', 'good', and 'bad'. The critical parent judges and criticizes.

   B. Nurturing parent functions are to give advice, guide, protect, teach how to, and keep traditions. Group work helps people become aware of the influence of parents, then to sort out what makes sense and what does not.

   C. Adult functions are to work on facts, to compute, store memories and feelings, to use facts to make decisions. The adult decides what fits, where, and what is most useful.

      The adult gathers data on the parent and the child and makes decisions based on available data, and plans the decision-making process.

   D. Natural child functions. The natural child is loving, spontaneous, carefree, fun-loving, and exciting. The natural child is adventurous, curious, trusting and joyful.

   E. Adapted child functions are being angry, rebellious, frightened, and conforming.

      The adult can turn off either or both of the other ego states. Control is not repression; it means changing the ego state. Control is about choice and decisions.

2. Transactions

These are the basic units of human communication; any exchanges between the ego states of any two people. Transactions may be verbal and non-verbal. Transactions operate at an overt social level and at a covert psychological level.

Transactions may be:

(a) Parallel, e.g. parent to parent, and parent to parent.
(b) Crossed, e.g. parent to parent, and parent to child.
(c) Ulterior, e.g. adult to adult, and child to adult.

3. *Contamination*

This is where the child takes on the values, prejudices, opinions and feelings of significant others without filtering them through the adult.

4. *Strokes*

Recognition from others may be:

A. Positive, evoking the feeling of 'I'm OK, you're OK'. Stroking is being.
B. Negative, evoking the feeling of 'I'm not OK, you're OK'.
C. Conditional strokes are given for something done. 'I will love you if . . . '
D. Unconditional strokes are given just for being.
E. Positive, unconditional stroking benefits the giver as well as the receiver.

5. Existential or basic positions (scripts):

A. *I'm OK; you're OK*. Associated words: good, healthy, success, competent, confident, challenging, and creative.
B. *I'm OK; you're not OK*. Associated words: arrogant, do-gooder, distrustful, and bossy.
C. *I'm not OK; you're OK*. Associated words: depression, resignation and suicide.
D. *I'm not OK; you're not OK*. Associated words: futile, schizoid, alienation.

People whose child feels Not OK become more used to negative strokes than to positive ones.

They may yearn for compliments, but cannot accept them, and cannot trust the person who gives them.

6. Stamps and rackets

Stamp collecting is storing bad feelings as an excuse for doing things you might not otherwise do. Stamps are not needed if the basic position is I'm OK; you're OK.

Rackets are habitual ways of feeling bad, learned from significant others. They are other people's feelings taken on board and acted upon.

7. Time structuring

We fill our time depending on which of the four basic positions our child has taken and what kind of stroking our child wants.

A. *Withdrawal*. No overt communication, e.g. in a railway carriage.
B. *Rituals* are socially prescribed forms of behaviour, e.g. the 'Hello – Goodbye' sequence.
C. *Activities* are socially significant because they offer a framework for various recognitions and satisfactions.
D. *Pastimes* are semi-ritualistic; topical conversations that last longer than rituals but are still mainly socially programmed, e.g.'let's talk about cars/babies/the weather'.
E. *Games* (over ninety have been described) are unconscious. A conscious game is manipulation. Games involve stamp collecting.

F. *Intimacy* is the most satisfying solution to the need for positive stroking. To be able to enter intimacy, a person must have awareness and enough spontaneity to be liberated from the compulsion to play games.

8. Injunctions, attributions, and discounts

Injunctions are irrational negative feeling messages expressed pre-verbally and non-verbally. They are restrictive, reflecting fears and insecurities.

Examples of injunctions:

(a) 'Don't be you, be me, or someone else.'
(b) 'Don't grow up.'
(c) 'Don't count, be unimportant.'

Examples of slogans as injunctions:

(a) 'Be a man, my son.'
(b) 'God helps those who help themselves.'

Attributions:

(a) Are being told what we are, what we must do, and how we must feel.
(b) Are generally approving of obedience and disapproving of disobedience.

Injunctions and attributions lie at the heart of a judgmental attitude. The developing child's autonomy may be sacrificed on the altar of parental control.

9. Scripts

A. A script is a preconscious set of rules by which we structure our life plan.
B. Scripts are decided before the age of 6 or 7 years.
C. Scripts are based on injunctions and attributions.
D. Scripts determine how we approach relationships and work.
E. Scripts are based on childlike illusions that automatically influence our lives.

Berne proposed that the parent of the opposite sex tells the child what to do, and the parent of the same sex demonstrates how to do it.

CONSIDERATIONS FOR THERAPY

TA helps clients to become aware of how they hurt themselves, the changes they need to make, and the inner forces that hinder change.

Therapeutic change is based on decisions and action. If we do not decide or act, no one will, or can, do it for us. When we accept a 'can't' we agree with the clients that they are helpless. Clients make a contract with themselves to work toward specific changes in behaviour.

ROLES IN THE DRAMA TRIANGLE (GAME)

1. *The persecutor* is someone who sets unnecessarily strict limits on behaviour, or is charged with enforcing the rules but does so with brutality.
2. *The rescuer* is someone who, in the guise of being helpful, keeps others dependent on him/her.
3. *The victim* is someone who (without cause) feels he/she is being unjustly treated.

All three roles are interchangeable and may all be played by the client in turn.

TRANSACTIONS (*See also*: Transactional analysis)

A Transactional analysis term to describe the basic unit of communication.

Any verbal or non-verbal exchange between the various ego states of two or more people. A conversation is a series of transactions.

Transactions may be overt – at a social level, or covert – at a psychological level, and may be:

1. *Parallel*. For example, between adult and adult. Both parties are comfortable with the transactions.
2. *Crossed*. For example, from adult to adult, but the response is from child to parent.
3. *Ulterior*. For example, on the surface it is from adult to adult, but it is so constructed as to hook into the child of the other person who then responds from the child ego state.

TRANSFERENCE (*See also*: Bonding, Counter-transference)

The situation in therapy in which the client displaces on to the therapist feelings, attitudes and attributes which derive from previous figures in the client's life.

The client then responds to those feelings, as though the therapist were a significant figure in the client's past.

A form of memory in which repetition in action replaces recollection of events.

QUALITIES THAT DISTINGUISH TRANSFERENCE

1. Inappropriateness
2. Intensity
3. Ambivalence
4. Inconsistency.

Transference may be positive, e.g. feelings of liking or love, or negative, e.g. feelings of dislike, insecurity, nervousness, anger, hostility.

The term is also used to describe the tendency to transfer onto any current relationship feelings and emotions that properly belong to a previous relationship.

Transference allows old conflicts to resurface and to be worked through. The therapist is careful to avoid responding to the displaced feelings and behaviour.

Negative transference will interfere with therapy.

Negative transference shows in direct attacks on the therapist or, by acting out negative feelings rather than exploring them, and unwillingness to work through resistances.

Intense positive transference may make excessive emotional demands on the therapist and prevent exploration of feelings.

FREUD'S POSITION

1. Transference is a resistance to true remembering.
2. Transference produces a conflict between getting better and getting the better of the therapist.
3. Negative transference feelings are more likely to occur in male clients.
4. Narcissistic people are not likely to experience transference.
5. Transference means wanting to change the therapeutic relationship into something else.

In positive transference the therapist is:

1. All important to the client
2. A constant topic of conversation

3. Idealized
4. Constantly praised
5. A significant person of dreams and fantasies.

Transference, if not recognized and worked through, may lead to a deterioration in the relationship, little progress, and a plateau in therapy.

JUNG'S POSITION

1. Almost all cases requiring lengthy treatment involve transference.
2. Transference of some degree is present in any intimate relationship.
3. Transference is natural, it cannot be demanded.
4. Accurate empathy reduces transference.

CARL ROGERS' POSITION

1. Understanding the client is easier than handling the transference.
2. Strong transference (in person-centred therapy) occurs in a relatively small number of cases, though some is present in all.
3. When the displaced feelings become realistically placed, transference attitudes disappear, because they have become meaningless.
4. The more the therapist interprets, controls, questions, directs, criticizes, questions, and evaluates, the more dependency is created, and the stronger the degree of transference.

   Transference is likely to develop where the therapist is perceived as 'the authority'.

TRANSFERENCE PATTERNS:

1. Idealizing the therapist is characterized by:

   A. Profuse complimenting
   B. Agreeing
   C. Bragging about the therapist to others
   D. Imitating the therapist's behaviour
   E. Wearing similar clothes
   F. Hungering for the therapist's presence
   G. Dreams that involve the therapist.

2. Attributing supernatural powers to the therapist is characterized by regarding the therapist as:

   A. All-knowing
   B. Divine-like
   C. The 'expert'
   D. Able to grant requests for advice
   E. Someone to be afraid of.

3. Regarding the therapist as provider is characterized by the client's:

   A. Displaying out-of-place emotion, and weeping
   B. Displaying helplessness and dependence
   C. Being indecisive
   D. Asking for advice
   E. Asking for touch, to be held
   F. Professing to have no strength without the therapist
   G. Being effusively grateful.

4. Regarding the therapist as one who thwarts is characterized by being:

   A. Self-protective
   B. Watchful
   C. Reticent
   D. Resentful
   E. Annoyed at lack of direction
   F. Hostile.

5. Regarding the therapist as unimportant is characterized by:
   A. Always changing the subject
   B. Talking and never listening
   C. Unwilling to explore
   D. Dismissive of ideas.

Working with transference means focusing directly on the expressed feelings and making them explicit.

TRANSPERSONAL PSYCHOLOGY

(*See also*: Existential therapy, Psychosynthesis)

Sometimes referred to as the 'fourth force', the successor to humanistic psychology. It seeks to expand or extend consciousness beyond the usual boundaries of the ego personality and beyond the limitations of time and/or space. It is concerned with the ultimate questions about human existence.

Transpersonal psychotherapy is concerned with traditional conce ns but includes personal awareness and growth beyond the reaches of traditionally accepted limits of health. What matters is the experience of being at one with humanity.

Transpersonal experiences are distinguished from 'religious' or 'spiritual' experiences, in that they are not required to fit into some prearranged pattern of dogma.

A transpersonal view of the world goes beyond ego boundaries and sees all parts as being equal in their contribution to the whole, and all humans as having the same needs, feelings, and potentials.

Transpersonal therapists have trained themselves to see the light within themselves and others. Transpersonal work is not about learning something new, but unlearning distorted knowledge already acquired.

MOTIVATIONS OF DIFFERENT THERAPIES

1. Psychoanalysis - sex
2. Behaviourism - reward and punishment
3. Humanism - self-actualization
4. Transpersonal - all of these plus:
   A. Freedom
   B. Wholeness
   C. Connection
   D. Play
   E. Creativity
   F. Exploration.

TOPICS OF CENTRAL INTEREST:

1. Awe
2. Being-values
3. Being
4. Bliss
5. Cosmic awareness
6. Ecstasy
7. Essence
8. Maximal interpersonal encounter
9. Maximal sensory awareness
10. Meta-needs
11. Mystical experiences
12. Oneness
13. Peak experiences
14. Spiritualizing everyday life
15. Self-actualization
16. Spirit
17. Synergy
18. Transcendence
19. Transcendental phenomena
20. Ultimate meaning
21. Ultimate values
22. Unitive consciousness
23. Wonder.

A transpersonal therapist would assist a client, not in order to come to terms with a dysfunctional society, for example, but to discover inner potentials in order to transcend the difficulty.

In addition to using techniques from all of the traditional approaches, the transpersonal therapist may use:

1. Meditation
2. Voluntary disidentification to provide a means of avoiding the effects of stress
3. Learning to enter altered states
4. Bodywork
5. Breathing exercises
6. Movement.

CORE CONCEPTS IN TRANSPERSONAL PSYCHOLOGY

1. *Self*. I am not defined by others; neither do I define myself; I am defined by the other.
2. *Motivation*. My motivation is not to satisfy need, neither to exercise choice; it is to surrender.
3. *Personal goal*. My personal goal is not adjustment, neither is it self-actualization; it is union.
4. *Social goal*. My social goal is not socialization, neither is it liberation; it is salvation.
5. *The process* I go through is not healing, ego-building or ego-enhancement; it is enlightenment and ego-reduction.
6. *Role of helper*. The role of my helper is not analyst, neither is it facilitator; it is guide.
7. *Focus*. The focus of my attention is not toward the individual, neither is it toward the group; it is toward a supportive community.

SOME TRANSPERSONAL THERAPY BELIEFS:

1. To do therapy is to receive therapy.
2. We cannot help anyone; we can only help ourselves.
3. Therapy is a day-by-day process.
4. We demonstrate what we believe.
5. What a therapist is saying is only a small part of the therapeutic effort.
6. Everyone has the potential to be someone else's therapist, client, or both.
7. Therapy focuses on internal rather than on external resources.
8. Focus is on self-energy, not allowing others to invalidate us.
9. Thoughts determine outcome.
10. We have to find our own unique pathway, then tread it.
11. We need to learn to trust our internal voices.

TRANSPERSONAL METHODS INCLUDE:

1. Altered states
2. Analytic therapy
3. Arica
4. Monasticism/Mysticism
5. Psychosynthesis
6. Sufism
7. Yoga
8. Zen.

TRUST (*See also*: Attachment, Bowlby, Erikson, Lifespan psychology)

Trust is the basis of many human experiences and relationships. For Erikson, trust develops gradually and requires consistent and concentrated effort to maintain it.

Trust is associated with creativity, personal growth, and productivity.

CHARACTERISTICS OF TRUSTING PEOPLE:

1. Acceptance of values and attitudes
2. Belief in equality
3. Concentrates on problem-solving
4. Co-operate with others
5. Decisions are arrived at easier
6. Freedom of expression

7. Spontaneity
8. Highly dependable
9. Highly genuine
10. Openness in communication
11. Recognized for competence
12. Relate with warmth and empathy
13. Respect others
14. Self-accountable
15. Supportive of others
16. Treat others with regard
17. Understanding of thoughts, feelings and behaviours
18. Willing to take risks.

CHARACTERISTICS OF MISTRUST:

1. Always wanting to 'play it safe'
2. Closed communication
3. Cold/rejecting
4. Concerned with hierarchy and status
5. Desire to control
6. Feelings of superiority
7. Focused on solutions
8. Highly competitive
9. Hostile behaviour
10. Incompetent
11. Inconsistent standards and behaviour
12. Lack of respect for others
13. Not consistently reputable
14. Suspicion
15. Unwilling to give credit
16. Unwilling to take risks.

When trust is destroyed, hurt and anger develop, as does a fear of ever trusting again. Effective counselling hinges on developing a trusting climate.

BUILDING TRUST:

1. Accepting the feelings of others
2. Being consistent
3. Being present and involved
4. Communication that is unambiguous
5. Effective eye contact
6. Empathic listening
7. Expressing feelings
8. Giving and receiving feedback
9. Initiating actions
10. Initiating communication
11. Respecting trusting behaviour in others
12. Using 'I' talk
13. Using affirming language and behaviour.

BEHAVIOURS OF TRUSTING/ OPEN PEOPLE:

1. Are personal, not hiding behind roles
2. Respond to current feelings and perceptions
3. Focus on relationships
4. Spontaneous
5. Sharing of self
6. Respond to the uniqueness of others
7. Concerned for self-growth and growth of others
8. Not afraid to follow hunches and impulses
9. Focus more on positive than negative behaviours
10. Focus on the 'here and now'
11. Focus on strengths
12. High congruence between verbal and non-verbal communication.

U

UNCONSCIOUS

This refers to mental processes of which the subject is unaware. In psychoanalysis it is a division of the psyche and the storehouse of repressed material of which the individual is not consciously aware. The discovery of the clinical importance of the unconscious became the cornerstone of psychoanalysis.

FREUD'S THREE PSYCHIC AGENCIES:

1. The unconscious
   - A. Exists at the deepest level of the psyche, beneath the conscious and the preconscious.
   - B. Only the id is entirely within the unconscious.
   - C. Unconscious material is brought into the conscious only through dreams, word associations, free associations, parapraxes, and symptoms.
   - D. Unconscious material comprises fantasies and images or representations that make their way into the conscious symbolically.
2. The preconscious
   - A. A region somewhere between the unconscious and the conscious.
   - B. Preconscious material is ready to become conscious.
3. The conscious

In Analytic psychology the unconscious is represented by:

1. The personal unconscious
   The surface layer of the unconscious. It is everything that the person acquires throughout life, everything forgotten, repressed, subliminally perceived, thought and felt, as well as complexes and imagos.
2. The collective unconscious
   The deeper part of the unconscious. Archetypal material that has never been in the personal conscious.

For Jung the unconscious is hypothetical, because it can only be inferred and is not amenable to direct observation. Working with the unconscious is central to most psychodynamic therapies. Behavioural and cognitive therapies do not work directly with the unconscious.

UNCONDITIONAL POSITIVE REGARD (UPR) (*See also*: Core conditions)

A non-possessive caring and acceptance of the client, irrespective of how offensive the client's behaviour might be. Unconditional positive regard is one of the core conditions of person-centred therapy to facilitate change.

It is where we communicate a deep and genuine caring, not filtered through our own feelings, thoughts, and behaviours.

Conditional regard implies enforced control, and compliance with behaviour dictated by someone else.

EXAMPLES OF UPR

1. She always responds to me with warmth and interest.
2. Her feelings toward me do not depend on how I feel toward her.
3. I can express whatever feelings I want, and she remains the same toward me.
4. I can be very critical of her or very appreciative, without it changing her feelings toward me.

V

VALUES

Values are what we consider good or beneficial to our well-being. Values are learned beliefs, largely culturally determined, and show in our attitudes.

Values are part of our personality and direct how we behave, think, and therefore influence how we feel. Needs, on the other hand, are innate; values are acquired through experience.

SIX BASIC VALUE SYSTEMS:

1. *Political*. The pursuit of power, characterized by:

   A. Influence
   B. Personal prestige
   C. Control
   D. Authority
   E. Strength
   F. Money as evidence of success
   G. Social status and recognition.

2. *Aesthetic*. The pursuit of beauty, symmetry, and harmony, characterized by:

   A. Artistic expression
   B. Style and charm rather than practicality
   C. The dignity of people
   D. Self-sufficiency and individuality
   E. Taste, appearance, and elegance
   F. Money as a means to an end
   G. Could be regarded as 'snobs' with expensive tastes.

3. *Social*. The pursuit of humanitarianism, characterized by:

   A. Social does not mean 'outgoing'
   B. Love of fellow beings
   C. Kind, sympathetic, warm, giving
   D. Charitable, unselfish
   E. Belief in freedom
   F. Ready to offer aid and assistance
   G. Consequences of actions are carefully considered
   H. Frightened off by cold, unsympathetic people.

4. *Theoretical*. The pursuit of truth and knowledge, characterized by:

A. Thinking, learning, probing, analysing, explaining
B. Critical, logical, empirical
C. Science, research, information, theory
D. Organizing material
E. Detached, unemotional
F. Problem-solving, develop theories, form questions
G. Knowledge is power
H. Often a low tolerance of people who do not place the same value on knowledge.

5. *Economic*. The pursuit of what is practical and useful, characterized by:

A. Knowledge is useful only if it can be applied to produce something useful immediately.
B. Efficiency and effectiveness are measured by profit and prosperity.
C. Extreme frugality gives the impression of being stingy or selfish.
D. Must conserve resources and use them wisely.
E. May judge the success of others by their wealth.

6. *Religious*. The pursuit of faith, characterized by:

A. Renouncing experience and logic
B. Mystic seeker, unity with nature
C. Life is a divine creation
D. Life is ordained and planned
E. Self-denial, prayer, meditation.

VALUES CLARIFICATION

In counselling, the following questions are useful to help clients understand full values:

1. How freely was it chosen?
2. What alternatives were there?
3. What effects would any alternatives have?
4. How has the value been acted upon?
5. Is the value acted upon repeatedly?
6. How does the value help reach potential?
7. Has the value been publicly affirmed?

A full value must have all seven criteria.

SOME WORK VALUES

The degree of worth a person attributes to particular aspects of work. Dimensions of work include the opportuities offered by the work for a person to satisfy the following needs:

1. To be creative
2. To earn money
3. To be independent
4. To enjoy prestige and status
5. To serve others
6. To do academic work
7. To have a stable and secure job
8. To enjoy one's colleagues
9. To have good working conditions.

WILL THERAPY (*See also*: Birth trauma)

Otto Rank replaced the emphasis on the Oedipus complex as the source of psychic conflict by his concept of birth trauma.

WILL THERAPY EMPHASIZES:

1. Creativity as a basic human need
2. Liberating the client from separation anxiety
3. Responsibility for one's own choices
4. Responsibility for one's own creative self-expression
5. The person's will in guiding and integrating the self.

WILL THERAPY HELPS CLIENTS TO:

1. Return to their birth trauma
2. Accept separateness
3. Discover how to take risks
4. Take charge of their life
5. To accept being different and to have their uniqueness accepted by others.

Rank's work has had a profound effect on the philosophy of humanistic therapies.

WILL TO POWER (*See also*: Individual (Adlerian) psychology)

A term used by Adler to describe the individual striving for superiority and dominance over other people in order to overcome the opposite feelings of inferiority and inadequacy. The striving for competence.

WINNICOTT, DONALD W. (1896–1971)

One of the British School of Psychoanalysts, who introduced the idea of the importance of maternal holding and mirroring of the infant's emotional states. Winnicott's theories have had a particular impact in the field of social work and child analysis.

WORD ASSOCIATION TEST (*See also*: Free association)

Also called free association test. Used

as a test of psychological reactions in which the person responds to a stimulus word with the first word that comes to mind. Conclusions are drawn about the associated words.

Jung, building upon the work of Bleuler, Galton, and Wundt, perfected the technique for tapping the personal complexes.

Freud also used free association and described various pathways as chain, thread, train, or line of association. Where Freud and Jung differed is that Freud continued to use free association, while Jung developed his work with the archetypes to overcome complexes.

Time delay is experienced when the stimulus word evokes an emotionally charged response, if the word relates to something the person felt was unpleasant.

The test is rarely used now, although its principles are useful adjuncts in counselling.

WORKING THROUGH

The process of helping the client to move from resistance to insight and permanent change. Working through acts as a kind of catalyst between analysis of transference and the overcoming of the amnesia for the crucial childhood experiences.

The client discovers piecemeal, over an extended period of time, the full implications of some interpretation or insight. Working through is the period that elapses between interpretation and its acceptance and integration.

The concept, though introduced by Freud, and central to psychoanalysis, is common to most of the psychodynamic therapies. The term is also used to describe the gradual acceptance of loss in the process of grief and mourning.

WOUNDED HEALER (*See also*: Dream therapies)

A Jungian term to describe the potential healing power of the therapist's own pain. Therapist and client are both part healer and part sufferer.

Therapists project their own experience of being wounded onto the clients in order to know the clients in an emotional sense. We cannot take clients where we ourselves have not travelled.

When the therapist's vulnerability is acknowledged, the client becomes an active partner in the process, and not just a passive recipient of help, ladled out by the perfect counsellor. The therapist is not then perceived as the healthy expert, and the client as sick and unskilled.

The 'wounded healer' suggests a cost to the therapist. Jung referred to the 'healing art', linked to compassion.

The concepts of the wounded healer finds an echo in Hephaestus (Vulcan), the mythical lame son of Zeus and Hera, Queen of the Heavens. Ridiculed in the hostile world of Olympus because of his club foot and rolling gait, he found refuge in his work. As a craftsman at the forge fire he transformed raw material into beautiful objects.

Hephaestus, the only imperfect major deity, is the archetype of the wounded healer whose creativity cannot be separated from his or her emotional wounds. The motivation to heal comes from our own sense of being wounded.

Hephaestus could never (in his eyes) be beautiful, so he created beauty. His body didn't work perfectly, but what he created was perfect.

The client who works through his or her woundedness with the help of the wounded therapist, can then become the wounded healer for someone else.

Y

YIN–YANG

The ancient Chinese believed that a life-force flows through all things. In ourselves it flows along meridians or pathways (used in acupuncture) that correspond to different organs of the body. The energy that flows between the two opposite poles of Yin and Yang is known as 'chi'. These opposite poles equate roughly with masculine/feminine, and positive/negative.

Yin and Yang are the two complementary principles that make up all aspects of life. Yin is conceived of as a dark square (depicting Earth, and earthly forces), female, passive, cool, moist, contracting, and absorbing. It is present in even numbers, in valleys and streams, and is represented by the tiger, the colour orange, and a broken line. Within our bodies, the Yin organs are those that are hollow, and involved in absorption and discharge, such as the stomach and bladder.

Yang is conceived of as Heaven, a white circle (depicting Heaven and celestial forces), male, light, hot, dry, active, expanding, and penetrating. It is present in odd numbers, in mountains, and is represented by the dragon, the colour azure, and an unbroken line. The Yang organs in the human body are the dense, blood-filled organs such as the heart and lungs.

The interaction between the Yin and the Yang is represented by the famous symbol of the circle divided into two equal sections by a sigmoid line across the diameter. The white (Yang) section has a black spot within, and the black (Yin) section has a white spot within it, to symbolize that everything living, and all that we do, must contain within it the seed of its opposite.

The sigmoid line is a symbol of the movement of communication and serves the purpose of implying the idea of rotation, of perpetual motion, metamorphosis, and continuity in situations that are characterized by contradictions; life and death is an example.

The two forces are said to proceed from the Supreme ultimate (T'ai Chi), and their interplay on one another is a description of the processes of the universe. As Yin increases, Yang decreases, and vice versa.

The concept of Yin–Yang is linked with the five elements of fire, water, metal, earth, and wood. Yin–Yang, and the five elements, support the Chinese belief in a cyclical theory of becoming and dissolution, and an interdependence between the world of nature and the events of man.

In the human body, a proper balance of Yin and Yang is seen as being necessary for complete health. If one or other predominates, mental or physical problems will arise.

Z

Z-PROCESS ATTACHMENT THERAPY

The method, developed by Zaslow, evolved out of Bowlby's attachment theory, which uses confrontation, prolonged holding, and verbal communication to convert the client's felt rage, frustration, and grief into constructive energy.

Zaslow's view of psychopathology was of disturbed bonding, requiring active methods, not psychotherapy. Therapy aims at repairing broken attachment.

The face, with eye contact, is the major focus of infant bonding. Therapy, therefore, consists of holding sessions and prolonged gaze, carried out by one therapist and other people who want to show love and are concerned for the client. One person may be used for a small child; for older children and adults, the therapist and seven other people will be used, holding different parts of the body.

Protest, resistance, and rage are evoked by holding the person helpless against all attempts to break free, and by using tactile stimulation, e.g. tickling.

During holding, the therapist asks questions related to age-appropriate behaviour, personal identity, and autonomy. True contact is made when the client looks with rage into the eyes of the therapist. With contact made, a relationship can start to be formed.

Holding sessions are followed by talking sessions to work through the issues that have been raised. This therapy is used in the treatment of autistic children and adults suffering from schizophrenia.

Bibliography

GENERAL BIBLIOGRAPHY

The following books form the core of the references, and therefore are not listed under the various subjects.

Arieti, S., (ed.) (1974) *American Handbook of Psychiatry*, vol. 2, Basic Books, New York.

Atkinson, R.L., Atkinson, R.C., Smith, E.E. and Hilgard, E.R. (1987) *Introduction to Psychology* (9th edn), Harcourt Brace Jovanovich Publishers, Florida, Orlando.

Biestek, F.P. (1975) *The Casework Relationship*, George Allen and Unwin, London.

Campbell, A.V. (ed.) (1987) *A Dictionary of Pastoral Care*, SPCK, London.

Chetwynd, T. (1984) *Dictionary for Dreamers*, Paladin, London.

— (1986) *A Dictionary of Symbols*, Paladin, London.

Corsini, R. (ed.) (1984) *Current Psychotherapies* (3rd edn), F.E. Peacock, Illinois, Itasca.

Drever, J. (1979) *A Dictionary of Psychology* (2nd edn), Penguin, Harmondsworth.

Egan, G. (1976) *Interpersonal Living*. Brooks/Cole, Monterey, Calif.

— (1986) *The Skilled Helper: A Systematic Approach to Effective Helping*, Brookes/Cole, Monterey, Calif.

— (1986) *Exercises in Helping Skills*, Brookes/Cole, Monterey, Calif.

Encyclopaedia Britannica (1976).

Great Illustrated Dictionary, Reader's Digest.

Everyman's Encyclopaedia (1989) J.M. Dent and Sons, London.

Harré, R. and Lamb, R. (1983) *The Encyclopaedic Dictionary of Psychology*, Blackwell, New York.

Kaplan, H.I. and Sadock, B.J.S. (eds) (1989) *Comprehensive Textbook of Psychiatry/V*, Williams and Wilkins, New York.

Miller, B.F. and Keane, C.B. (1978) *Encyclopaedia and Dictionary of Medicine, Nursing, and Allied Health*, W.B. Saunders, London.

Nelson-Jones, R. (1983) *The Theory and Practice of Counselling Psychology*, Holt, Rinehart and Winston, New York.

— (1983) *Practical Counselling Skills*, Holt, Rinehart and Winston, New York.

—— (1986) *Human Relationship Skills*, Holt, Rinehart and Winston, New York.

Patterson, C.H. (1986) *Theories of Counselling and Psychotherapy* (4th edn), Harper and Row, New York.

Reber, A.S. (1985) *A Dictionary of Psychology*, Penguin, Harmondsworth.

Rycroft, C. (1972) *A Critical Dictionary of Psychoanalysis*, Penguin, Harmondsworth.

Samuels, A., Shorter, B. and Plant, F. (1986) *A Critical Dictionary of Jungian Analysis*. Routledge and Kegan Paul, London.

Stewart, W. (1985) *Counselling in Rehabilitation*, Croom Helm, London.

Tschudin, V. (1991) *Counselling Skills for Nurses*, Bailliére Tindall, London.

Walrond-Skinner, S. (1986) *A Dictionary of Psychotherapy*, Routledge and Kegan Paul, London.

BIBLIOGRAPHY

'A'-TYPE PERSONALITY

Friedman, M. (1969) *Pathogenesis of Coronary Artery Disease*, McGraw Hill, New York.

Friedman, M. and Rosenman, R. (1974) *Type 'A' Behaviour and Your Heart*, Knopf, New York.

Jenkins, C.D. (1971) Psychologic and social precursors of coronary disease. *New England Journal of Medicine*, 284, 309.

ABRAHAM, KARL

Abraham K. (1953) A short study of the development of the libido, viewed in the light of mental disorders. In: *Selected papers*. Basic Books, New York.

ACCEPTANCE

Dryden, W. (1988) *Therapists' Dilemmas*. Harper and Row, London.

Jung, Carl G. (1958) *The Collected Works – Psychology and Religion* (vol. 11), Routledge & Kegan Paul, London.

Kraus, H. (1950) The role of social casework in American social work. *Social Casework*, 31 (9).

ACKERMAN, NATHAN WARD

Ackerman, N.W. (1958) *The Psychodynamics of Family Life*, Basic Books, New York.

—— (1966) *Treating the Troubled Family*, Basic Books, New York.

ACTING OUT – ACTING IN

Abt, L.E. and Weisman, S.L. (1965) *Acting out – Theoretical and Clinical Aspects*, Grune and Stratton, New York.

Bradshaw, J. (1990) *Homecoming: Reclaiming and Championing Your Inner Chlid*, Piatkus Books, London.

Deutsch, F. (1947) Analysis of postural behaviour. *Psychoanalytic Quarterly*, 16, 195–213.

Freud, S. (1914) Remembering, repeating and working through, In: *Standard Edition* (vol. 12). Hogarth Press, London.

—— (1940) An outline of psychoanalysis. In, *Standard Edition* (vol. 23), Hogarth Press, London.

Gaddini, E. (1982) Acting out in the psychoanalytic session, *International Journal of Psychoanalysis*, 63, 57–64.

Johnson, A.M. and Szurek, S.A. (1952) The genesis of anti-social

acting out in children and adolescents, *Psychoanalytic Quarterly*, 21, 323.
Mahl, G.F. (1967) Some clinical observations on non-verbal behaviour in interviews. *Journal of Nervous and Mental Diseases*, 144, 492–505.
Sandler, J. *et al.* (1970) Basic psychoanalytic concepts: Acting out. *British Journal of Psychiatry*, 117, 329.
Schwartz, L. and Schwartz, R. (1971) Therapeutic acting out. *Psychotherapy: Theory, research and practice*, 8, 205–7.

ACTION PLANS

Egan, G. (1988) *Change-Agent Skills*, University Associates, San Diego, Calif.

ADAPTATIONAL PSYCHODYNAMICS

Rado, S. (1962) *Psychoanalysis of Behaviour* (vols. 1 and 2), Grune and Stratton, New York.

ADVICE

Burnard, P. (1989) *Counselling Skills for Health Professionals*. Chapman and Hall, London.
Hollis, F. (1966) *Casework: A Psychosocial Therapy*, Random House, New York.

AGGRESSION

Pollard, J. *et al.*(1944) *Frustration and Aggression*. Kegan Paul, London.
Venables, E. (1971) *Counselling*. National Marriage Guidance Council, England.
U'Ren, R.C. (1980) *The Practice of Psychotherapy*, Grune and Stratton, New York
Yalom, I.D. (1980) *Existential Psychotherapy*, Basic Books, New York.

ALEXANDER, FRANZ G.

Alexander, F.G. (1930) *The Psychoanalysis of the Total Personality*. Nervous and Mental Disease Publishing, New York.
— (1948) *Fundamentals of Psychoanalysis*. W.W. Norton, New York.
— (1960) *Western Mind in Transition: An Eyewitness Story*. Random House, New York.
— and Healy, W. (1935) *Roots of Crime*. A.A. Knopf, London.

ALIENATION

Bebout, J. (1974) It takes one to know one: Existential concepts in encounter groups. In, Wheeler, A. and North, R.L. (eds) *Innovations in Client-Centred Therapy*, J. Wiley, Chichester.
Ivey, A.E. and Simek-Downing, L. (1980) *Counselling and Psychotherapy Skills Theory and Practice*, Prentice-Hall, Englewood Cliffs, New Jersey.
Jung, Carl G. (1958) *The Collected Works – The Structure and Dynamics of the Psyche* (vol. 8), Routledge and Kegan Paul, London.
Littlewood, R. and Lipsedge, M. (1989) *Aliens and Alienists*. Hyman, London.
Lynch, J. (1977) *The Broken Heart*, Basic Books, New York.

ALTRUISM

Badcock, C.R. (1986) *The Problem of Altruism*, Basil Blackwell, Oxford.
Latané, B. and Darley, J.M. (1970) *The Unresponsive Bystander: Why*

Doesn't He Help? Appleton-Century-Crofts, New York.

Rivers, R. (1971) The evolution of reciprocal altruism. *Quarterly Review of Biology*, 46, 35–57.

Rushton, J. (1980) *Altruism, Socialisation and Society*. Prentice Hall, New Jersey.

ANALYTICAL PSYCHOLOGY

Jung, Carl G. (1958) *The Collection Works – Psychological Types* (vol. 6), Routledge and Kegan Paul, London.

—— (1958) *The Collected Works – The Practice of Psychotherapy* (vol. 16), Routledge and Kegan Paul, London.

ANIMA AND ANIMUS

Jung, Carl G. (1958) *The Collected Works – Two Essays on Analytical Psychology* (vol. 7), Routledge and Kegan Paul, London.

Jung, Emma (1978) *Animus and Anima*. Spring Publications, New York.

Wickes, F.G. (1988) *The Inner World of Man*, Sigo Press, Boston, Mass.

ANOMIE

Littlewood, R. and Lipsedge, M. (1989) *Aliens and Alienists*, Hyman, London.

ANOREXIA NERVOSA

Boskind-Lodahl, M. (1981) Cinderella's stepsisters: A feminist perspective on anorexia nervosa and bulimia. In, Howell, E. and Bayes, M. (eds) *Women and Mental Health*. Basic Books, New York.

Crisp, A.H. (1980) *Anorexia Nervosa: Let Me Be*, Academic Press, London.

Crisp, A.H., Harding, B. and McGuinness, B. (1974) Anorexia nervosa: psychoneurotic characteristics of parents, relating to prognosis. *Journal of Psychosomatic Research*, 18, 167–73.

Fransella, F. and Button, E. (1983) The 'construing' of self and body size in relation to maintenance of weight gain in anorexia nervosa. In Darby, P.L. (ed) *Anorexia Nervosa: Recent Developments in Research*, Alan Liss, New York.

MacLeod, S. (1981) *The Art of Starvation: Anorexia Observed*. Virago, London.

Melville, J. (1983) *The ABC of Eating: Coping with Anorexia, Bulimia and Compulsive Eating*, Sheldon Press, London.

Minuchin, S., Rosman, B.L. and Baker, L. (1978) *Psychosomatic Families: Anorexia Nervosa in Context*, Harvard University Press.

Vaughan, E.(1979) Counselling anorexia. *Marriage Guidance Journal*, September.

ANXIETY

Gregory, R.L. (ed.) (1987) *The Oxford Companion of the Mind*, OUP, Oxford.

Weekes, C. (1962) *Self Help for your Nerves*, Angus and Robertson, London.

ARCHETYPES

Jung, Carl G. (1958) *The Collected Works – Psychological Types* (vol. 6). Routledge and Kegan Paul, London.

ASSERTIVENESS

Alberti, R.E. (1977) *Assertiveness: Innovations, Applications and Issues*, Impact Press, San Louis, Obispo.

— and Emmons, M. (1974) *Your Perfect Right* (rev. edn). Impact Press, San Louis, Obispo.

Bower, S.A. and Bower, G.H. (1976) *Asserting Your Self*. Addison-Wesley, Reading, Mass.

Byrum, B. (1988) The nuts and bolts of assertive training. *The 1988 Annual: Developing Human Resources*, University Associates, San Diego, Calif.

Cawood, D. (1988) *Assertiveness for Managers*, International Self-Counsel Press, Canada.

Dickson, A. (1982) *A Woman In Your Own Right*. Quartet Books, London.

Fensterheim, H. and Baer, J. (1980) *Don't Say 'Yes' When You Want To Say 'No'*. Futura, New York.

McFall, R.M. and Twentyman, C.T. (1973) Four experiences on the relative contributions of rehearsal, modelling and coaching to assertion training. *Journal of Abnormal Psychology*, 81, 199–218.

Rich, A.R. and Schroder, H.E. (1976) Research issues in assertiveness training. *Psychological Bulletin*, 81, 1081–96.

Sharpe, R. (1989) *Assert Yourself*, Cogan Page, London.

Stubbs, D.R. (1986) *Assertiveness at Work*, Pan Books, London.

ASSOCIATIVE LEARNING

Bower, G.H. (1972) Mental imagery and associative learning. In, Gregg, L.W. (ed.), *Cognition in Learning and Memory*, Wiley, New York.

Hilgard, E.R. (1981) *Theories of Learning* (5th edn). Prentice-Hall, Englewood Cliffs, New Jersey.

Pavlov, I.P. (1927) *Conditioned Reflexes*, OUP, New York.

Skinner, B.F. (1938) *The Behaviour of Organisms*, Appleton-Century-Crofts, New York.

Thorndyke, E.L. (1898) Animal intelligence: An experimental study of the associate process in animals. *Psychological Monographs*, 2(8).

ATTACHMENT

Ainsworth, M.D.S. *et al.*(1978) *Patterns of Attachment*, John Wiley, Chichester.

Bowlby, J. (1969) *Attachment and Loss*, vol. 1, *Attachment*, Penguin, Harmondsworth.

— (1973) *Attachment and Loss*, vol. 2, *Separation*, Penguin, Harmondsworth.

— (1980) *Attachment and Loss*, vol. 3, *Loss*, Penguin, Harmondsworth.

— (1975) Attachment theory, separation anxiety and mourning. In, Hamburg, D.A. and Brodie, H. (eds), *American Handbook of Psychiatry* (vol. 6). Basic Books, New York.

Fraiberg, S. (ed.) (1980) *Clinical Studies in Infant Mental Health*, Tavistock, London.

Lamb, M.E. (1982) Parental influences on early socio-emotional development. *Journal of Child Psychology and Psychiatry*, 23, 185–90.

Parkes, C.M. and Stevenson-Hinde, J. (eds) (1982) *The Place of Attachment in Human Behaviour*, Tavistock, London.

Robertson, J. and Robertson, J. (1971) Young children in brief separations, In, Eissler, R.K. *et al.* (eds), *The Psychoanalytic Study of the Child* (vol. 26), Yale University Press, New Haven, Connecticut.

ATTITUDE

Ruch, F.L. and Zimburdo, P.G. (1971) *Psychology of Life*, Scott, Foresman, Glenview, Illinois.

AUTHORITARIAN PERSONALITY

Adorno, T.W., Frenkel-Brunswick, E., Levinson, D.J. and Stanford, R.N. (eds) (1950) *The Authoritarian Personality*. Harper, New York.
Ruch, F.L. and Zimbardo, P.G. (1971) *Psychology of Life* (8th edn), Scott, Foresman, London.
Stubbins, J. (1977) Stress and disability, In, Stubbins, J. (ed.) *Social and Psychosocial Aspects of Disability*. University Press, Baltimore.

AUTOGENIC TRAINING AND RELAXATION

Inglis, B. and West, R. (1983) *The Alternative Health Guide*, Michael Joseph, London.
Jacobson, E. (1974) *Progressive Relaxation*, University of Chicago Press, Chicago.
Luthe, W. (1969) *Autogenic Training*, Grune and Stratton, New York.
Schultz, J. and Luthe, W. (1959) *Autogenic Training: A Psychophysiologic Approach to Psychotherapy*. Grune and Stratton, New York.

BEHAVIOUR THERAPY

Bandura, A. (1969) *Principles of Behaviour Modification*, Holt, New York.
Beck, A., Rush, J., Shaw, B. and Emery, G. (1979) *Cognitive Therapy of Depression*, Guildford Press, New York.
Eysenck, H.J. (1967) *The Biological Basis of Personality*, Charles C. Thomas, Springfield, Illinois.
Franks, C.M., Wilson, G.T., Kendall, P. and Brownell, K. (1982) *Annual Reviews of Behaviour Therapy: Theory and Practice* (vol. 8), Guildford Press, New York.
Goldstein, A. and Foa, E. (eds) (1980) *Handbook of Behavioural Interventions: A Clinical Guide*, Wiley, New York.
Rachman, S.J. and Wilson, G.T. (1980) *The Effects of Psychological Therapy*, Pergamon, Oxford.
Rimm, D.C. and Master, J.C. (1979) *Behaviour Therapy: Techniques and Empirical Findings*, Academic Press, London.
Skinner, B.F. (1953) *Science and Human Behaviour*, Macmillan, New York.
Wolpe, J. (1958) *Psychotherapy By Reciprocal Inhibitions*, Stanford University Press, Stanford, Calif.
Yates, A.J. (1980) *Biofeedback and the Modification of Behaviour*, Plenum, New York.

BEREAVEMENT COUNSELLING

Cooper, J. (1980) Parental reaction to stillbirth. *British Journal of Social Work*, 10, 55–69.
Glick, I. *et al*. (1974) *The First Year of Bereavement*, Wiley, New York.
Lewis, C.S. (1961) *A Grief Observed*, Faber and Faber, London.
Poss, S. (1981) *Towards Death With Dignity*, National Institute Social Services Library, No. 41, London.
Pritchard, E. *et al*. (eds) (1977) *Social Work With The Dying Patient and His Family*, Columbia, New York.
Schoenberg, B. (ed.) (1980) *Bereavement Counselling*. Greenwood Press, London.

BIBLIOTHERAPY

Howie, M. (1983) Bibliotherapy in social work, *British Journal of Social Work*, 13, 287–319.
Rubin, R. (ed.) (1976) *Bibliotherapy Source Book*, Oryn Press, Phoenix.
—— (1978) *Using Bibliotherapy: A Guide to Theory and Practice*, Oryx Press, Phoenix.

BINSWANGER

Binswanger, L. (1967) *Being-in-the-World*, Harper and Row, New York.

BION, W.R.

Bion, W.R. (1961) *Experiences in Groups*, Basic Books, New York.
—— (1970) *Attention and Interpretation: A Scientific Approach to Insight in Psychoanalysis and Groups*, Basic Books, New York.

BIRTH TRAUMA

Leboyer, F. (1975) *Birth Without Violence*, Knopf, New York.
Moxon, C. (1926) Freud's death instinct and Rank's libido theory. *Psychoanalytic Review*, 13, 294–303.
Rank, O. (1929) *The Trauma of Birth*, Harcourt Brace, New York.

BLEULER, EUGENE

Bleuler, E. (1950) *Dementia Praecox or the Group of Schizophrenias*, International University Press, New York.
—— (1950) *Textbook of Psychiatry*, George Allen and Unwin, London.

BODY AWARENESS

Lowen, A. (1973) *The Language of the Body*, Macmillan, New York.
Schutz, W.C. (1967) *Joy*, Grove Press, New York.
Stevens, J.O. (1971) *Awareness*, Real People Press, Moab, Utah.

BODY-CENTRED THERAPY

Feldenkrais, M. (1972) *Awareness Through Movement*, Harper and Row, New York.
Inglis, B. and West, R. (1983) *The Alternative Health Guide*, Michael Joseph, London.
Lowen, A. (1971) *The Language of the Body*, Macmillan, New York.
Rolf, I. (1975) *Structural Integration*, Viking/Esalen, New York.

BODY-IMAGE

Critchley, M. (1950) The body-image in neurology, *Lancet*, 1, 335–41.
Feldman, M.M. (1975) The body-image and object relations: Exploration of a method utilising repertory grid techniques. *British Journal of Medical Psychology*, 48, 317–32.
Fisher, S. and Cleveland, S.E. (1985) *Body-image and Pesonality*. Van Nostrand, New York.
McCrea, C.W., Summerfield, A.B. and Rosen, B. (1982) Body-image: A selective review of existing measurement techniques. *British Journal of Medical Psychology*, 55, 225–33.
Schilder, P. (1950) *The Image and Appearance of the Human Body*. International Universities Press, New York.

BONDING

Bowlby, J. (1969) *Attachment and Loss*, vol. 1, *Attachment*, Penguin, Harmondsworth.
Dryden, W. (1989) The therapeutic alliance, In, *Key Issues for Counseling in Action*, Sage Publications, London.
Lorenz, K.Z. (1966) *On Aggression*, Methuen, London.

BOWLBY, E. JOHN M.

Bowlby, E. John M., (with E.M. Durbin) (1938) *Personal Aggressiveness and War*, Kegan Paul, London.

—— (1946) *Forty-four Juvenile Thieves*, Bailliere Tindall and Cox, London.
—— (1951) *Maternal Care and Mental Health*, WHO Monograph Series, No. 2.
—— (1953) *Child Care and the Growth of Love*, Penguin, Harmondsworth.
—— (1969) *Attachment and Loss*, Vol. 1, *Attachment*, Penguin, Harmondsworth.
—— (1973) *Attachment and Loss*, Vol. 2, *Separation: Anxiety and Anger*, Penguin, Harmondsworth.
—— (1980) *Attachment and Loss*, Vol. 3, *Loss: Sadness and Depression*, Penguin, Harmondsworth.
—— (1979) *The Making and Breaking of Affectional Bonds*, Tavistock, London.
—— (1988) *A Secure Base*, Routledge and Kegan Paul, London.

BRAIN-STORMING

Francis, D. (1987) *50 Activities for Unblocking Organisational Communication*, Gower, Aldershot.

BRIEF THERAPY

Balint, M. *et al.* (1973) *Focal Psychotherapy*, Tavistock, London.
Barten, H.H. (1971) *Brief Therapies*, Behavioural Publications, New York.
Budman, S. (ed.) (1981) *Forms of Brief Therapy*, Guildford Press, New York.
Butcher, J.N. and Koss, M.P. (1978) Research on brief and crisis oriented therapies, In, Bergin, A.E. and Garfield, S.L. (eds) *Handbook of Psychotherapy and Behaviour Change*, Wiley, New York.
Small, L. (1971) *The Brief Psychotherapies*, Brunner/Mazel, New York.

BRITISH SCHOOL OF PSYCHOANALYSIS

Balint, M. (1952) *Primary Love and Psychoanalytic Technique*, Hogarth Press, London.
Bowlby, J. (1969) *Attachment and Loss*, vol. 1, *Attachment*, Penguin, Harmondsworth.
—— *(1973) Attachment and Loss*, vol. 2, *Separation: Anxiety and Anger*, Penguin, Harmondsworth.
—— (1980) *Attachment and Loss*, vol. 3, *Loss: Sadness and Depression*, Penguin, Harmondsworth.
Fairbairn, W.R.D. (1952) *Psychoanalytic Studies of the Personality*, Tavistock, London.
Guntrip, H. (1961) *Personality Structure and Human Interaction*, Hogarth Press, London.
Sutherland, J.D. (1980) The British object relations theorists. *Journal of American Psychoanalytic Association*, 28, 829–58.
Winnicott, D.W. (1965) *Collected Papers*, Hogarth Press, London.

BULIMIA NERVOSA

Fairburn, C.C. (1982) Eating disorders. In , Kendell, R.E. and Zealley, A.K. (eds) *Companion to Psychiatric Studies* (3rd edn), Churchill Livingstone, Edinburgh.
Melville, J. (1983) *The ABC of Eating: Coping with Anorexia, Bulimia and Compulsive Eating*, Sheldon Press, London.
Russell, G. (1979) Bulimia nervosa: An ominous variant of anorexia nervosa. *Psychological Medicine*, 9, 429–48.

BURN OUT

Cherniss, C. (1980) *Staff Burn Out: Job Stress in the Human Services*, Sage, London.
Cooper, C.L. and Payne, R. (1978) *Stress at Work*, Wiley, Chichester.

Faber, B. and Heifetz, L.J. (1982) Process and dimensions of burn out in psychotherapists, *Professional Psychology*, 13, 293–301.

Orlinsky, D.E. and Howard, K.I. (1977) The therapist's experience of psychotherapy. In, Gurman, A.S. and Razin, A.M. (eds), *Effective Psychotherapy*, Pergamon, New York.

Parry, G. and Gowler, D. (1983) Career stresses on psychological therapists. In, Pilgrim, D. (ed.) *Psychology and Psychotherapy*, Routledge and Kegan Paul, London.

Pines, A.M. and Arunsen, E. (1981) *Burn Out*, The Free Press, New York.

CASTRATION COMPLEX

Freud, S. (1908) On the sexual theories of children, *Standard Edition*, vol. 9, Hogarth Press, London.

Hare, E.H. (1962) Masturbatory insanity: the history of an idea. *Journal of Mental Science*, 108, 1–25.

CATHARSIS (and ABREACTION)

Freud, S. and Breuer, J. (1983–5) Studies on hysteria, *Standard Edition*, vol. 2, Hogarth Press, London.

CHALLENGING

Ivey, A.E. and Gluckstern, N. (1976) *Basic Influencing Skills: Leader and Participant Manuals*, Microtraining, North Amherst, Mass.

Ivey, A.E., Ivey, M.B. and Sinek-Downing, L. (1987) *Counselling and Psychotherapy: Integrating Skills, Theory and Practice* (2nd edn), Prentice Hall, Englewood Cliffs, NJ.

CO-DEPENDENCE

Beattie, M. (1987) *Co-dependent No More: How to Stop Controlling Others and Start Caring for Yourself*. Harper and Row, New York.

—— (1989) *Beyond Co-dependency and Getting Better at all Times*, Harper and Row, New York.

Pfeiffer, J.A. (1991) Co-dependence: learned dysfunctional behaviour. *The 1991 Annual: Developing Human Resources*, University Associates, San Diego, Calif.

Mellody, P., Miller, A.W. and Miller, J.K. (1989) *Facing Co-dependence: What it Is, Where it Comes From, How it Sabotages Our Lives*, Harper and Row, New York.

COGNITIVE BEHAVIOUR MODIFICATION

Agras, W.S. (1985) *Panic; Facing Fears, Phobias and Anxiety*, Freeman, New York.

Craighead, W.E., Kazdin, A.E. and Mahoney, M.J. (1981) *Behaviour Modification: Principles, Issues, and Applications*, 2nd edn, Houghton Mifflin, Boston.

Turner, S.M., Calhoun, K.S. and Adams, E. (eds) (1981) *The Handbook of Clinical Behaviour Therapy*, Wiley, New York.

COGNITIVE DISSONANCE

Brown, R. (1985) *Social Psychology*, 2nd edn, Free Press, New York.

Festinger, L. (1957) *A Theory of Cognitive Dissonance*. Stanford University Press, Stanford.

Osgood, C. and Tannenbaum, P. (1955) The principle of congruity in the prediction of attitude change. *Psychological Review*, 62, 42–55.

COGNITIVE THERAPY

Beck, A.T. (1976) *Cognitive Therapy*

and the Emotional Disorders, International Universities Press, New York.

Lazarus, A.A. (1971) *Behaviour Therapy and Beyond*, McGraw Hill, New York.

Rimm, D.C. and Masters, J.C. (1974) *Behaviour Therapy: Techniques and Empirical Findings*, Academic Press, New York.

Wolpe, J. (1969) *The Practice of Behaviour Therapy*, Pergamon, Oxford.

COLLECTIVE UNCONSCIOUS

Bennet, E.A. (1961) *C.G. Jung*, Barrie and Rockliff, London.

Jung, C.G. (1933) *Modern Man in Search of a Soul*, Routledge and Kegan Paul, London.

—— (1959) *The Archetypes and the Collective Unconscious*, Routledge and Kegan Paul, London.

Samuels, A. (1985) *Jung and the Post-Jungians*, Routledge and Kegan Paul, London.

COLLUSION

Berne, E. (1970) *Games People Play*, Penguin, Harmondsworth.

Laing, R.D. (1971) *Knots*, Tavistock, London.

COMMUNICATION

Berne, E. (1964) *Games People Play*, Grove, New York.

Combs, G.W. (1981) Defensive and supportive communication. *The 1981 Annual Handbook for Group Facilitators*. University Associates, San Diego, Calif.

Filley, A.C. (1975) *Interpersonal Conflict Resolution*, Scott, Foresman, Glenview, Illinois.

Gibb, J.R. (1961) Defensive communication. *Journal of Communication*, 11, 141–8.

Jones, J.E. (1972) Communication modes: an experiential lecture. *The 1972 Annual Handbook for Group Facilitators*, University Associates, San Diego, Calif.

Rogers, C.R. and Roethlisberger, F.J. (1952) Barriers and gateways to communication. *Harvard Business Review*, 30, 46–52.

COMPENSATION

Adler, A. (1937) *Understanding Human Nature*, George Allen and Unwin, London.

COMPLEXES

Jung, C.G.(1958) *The Collected Works – Psychological Types*, vol. 6, Routledge and Kegan Paul, London.

CONCRETE THINKING

Brainers, C.J. (1978) *Piaget's Theory of Intelligence*, Prentice-Hall, Englewood Cliffs, NJ.

CONFLICT

Deutsch, M. (1973) *The Resolution of Conflict*. Yale University Press, New Haven, Conn.

Festinger, L. (1957) *A Theory of Cognitive Dissonance*, Stanford University Press, Stanford.

Lewin, K. (1935) *A Dynamic Theory of Personality*, McGraw Hill, New York.

Main, A.P. and Roark, A.E. (1975) A consensus method to reduce conflict. *Personnel and Guidance Journal*, 53, 754–759.

CONSCIENCE

Baelz, P. (1977) *Ethics and Beliefs*, Sheldon Press, London.

Brooke, R. (1985) Jung and the phenomenology of guilt. *Journal of*

Analytical Psychology, April.

Donagan, A. (1979) *The Theory of Morality*, University of Chicago Press, Chicago.

Freud, S. (1923) The ego and the id, *Standard Edition*, vol. 19, Hogarth Press, London.

CONSCIOUS

Freud, S. (1926) Inhibitions, symptoms and anxiety, *Standard Edition*, vol. 20, Hogarth Press, London.

—— (1940) An outline of psychoanalysis, *Standard Edition*, vol. 23, Hogarth Press, London.

Gurwitsch, A. (1957) *The Field of Consciousness*, Duquesne University Press, Pittsburgh.

Jung, Carl G. (1934) *The Collected Works - The Practice of Psychotherapy*, vol. 16, Routledge and Kegan Paul, London.

Taylor, J.G. (1970) Consciousness: Theory versus non-theory. *Bulletin of the British Psychological Society*, 23, 43–46.

CONSTRUCT

Bannister, D. and Fransella, F. (1980) *Inquiring Man*, 2nd edn, Penguin, Harmondsworth.

Fransella, F. and Bannister, D. (1977) *A Manual for Repertory Grid Technique*, Academic Press, London.

Kelly, G.A. (1955) *The Psychology of Personal Constructs*, W.W. Norton, New York.

—— (1963) *A Theory of Personality*, W.W. Norton, New York.

CONTRACT

Sage, C.J. (1976) *Marriage Contracts and Couple Therapy*, Brunner/Mazel, New York.

CONVERSION

Freud, S. (1894) The neuro-psychoses of defence, *Standard Edition*, vol. 3, Hogarth Press, London.

—— (1980) Some general remarks on hysterical attacks, *Standard Edition*, vol. 9, Hogarth Press, London.

—— and Breuer, J. (1983–5) Studies on hysteria, *Standard Edition*, vol. 2, Hogarth Press, London.

COPING SKILLS INTERVENTIONS

Goldfried, M.R. (1971) Systematic desensitisation as training in self control. *Journal of Consulting and Clinical Psychology*, 37, 228–34.

—— and Davison, G.C. (1976) *Clinical Behaviour Therapy*, Holt, Rinehart and Winston, New York.

Meichenbaum, D. (1974) Self instructional methods, In Kanfu, F.K. and Goldstein, A.P. (eds) *Helping People Change*, Pergamon, New York.

—— *et al.*(1975) The nature of coping with stress, In Saracen, I. and Spielberger, C. (eds), *Stress and Anxiety*, vol. 2, Wiley, New York.

CORE CONDITIONS

Mitchell, K.M. *et al.* (1977) A reappraisal of accurate empathy, non-possessive warmth and genuineness. In Gurman, A.S. and Razin, A.M. (eds), *Effective Psychotherapy*, Pergamon, New York.

Thorne, B. (1987) Beyond the core conditions, In Dryden, W. (ed.), *Key Cases in Psychotherapy*, Croom Helm, London, pp. 48–77.

Troemel-Ploetz, S.(1980) 'I'd come to you for therapy'; Interpretation, redefinition and paradox in Rogerian Therapy, *Psychotherapy: Theory, Research and Practice*, 17, 246–57.

Truax, C.B. and Mitchell, K.M. (1971) Research on certain therapist interpersonal skills in relation to process and outcome, In Bergin, A.E. and Garfield, S.L. (eds), *Handbook of Psychotherapy and Behaviour Change*, Wiley, New York.

CORONARY-PRONE BEHAVIOUR

Jenkins, C.D. (1971) Psychological and social precursors of coronary disease. *New England Journal of Medicine*, 283, 244–55.

Paffenberger, R.S., Wolf, P.A. and Notkin, J. (1966) Chronic disease in former college students, *American Journal of Epidemiology*, 83, 314–28.

COUNTER-TRANSFERENCE

Blanck, L. and Blanck, R. (1979) *Ego Psychology II: Psychoanalytic Developmental Psychology*, Columbia University Press, New York.

Cutler, R.L. (1958) Counter-transference effects in psychotherapy, *Journal of Consulting Psychology*, 22, 349–56.

Freud, S. (1922) *Introductory Lectures on Psychoanalysis*, George Allen and Unwin, London.

Jacobs, M. (1988) *Psychodynamic Counselling in Action*, Sage, London.

Jung, C.G. (1946) *The Psychology of the Transference*, Routledge and Kegan Paul, London.

Patterson, C.H. (1985) *The Therapeutic Relationship: Foundations for an Eclectic Psychotherapy*, Brooks/Cole, Monterey, Calif.

Rogers, C.R. (1981) *Client Centred Therapy*, Constable, London.

Watkins, C.E. (1989) Counter-transference: Its impact on the counseling situation. In Dryden, W. (ed.), *Key Issues for Counselling in Action*. Sage, London. Originally in *Journal of Counselling and Development* (1985) 63, 356–9.

CREATIVITY

Golann, S.E. (1962) The creativity motive, *Journal of Personality*, 30, 588–600.

Martin, L.P. (1990) Inventory of barriers to creative thought and innovative action. *The 1990 Annual: Developing Human Resources*, University Associates, San Diego, Calif.

Morgan, J.S. (1968) *Improving Your Creativity on the Job*, AMACOM, New York.

Rogers, C.R. (1959) Toward a theory of creativity. In Anderson, H.H. (ed.) *Creativity and Its Cultivation*, Harper and Row, New York.

CREDIBILITY

Griffin, K. (1967) The contribution of studies of source credibility to a theory of interpersonal trust in the communication Process, *Psychology Bulletin*, 68, 104–21.

Johnson, D.W. (1973) *Contemporary Social Psychology*, Lippincott, Philadelphia.

—— and Matross, R. (1977) Interpersonal influence in psychotherapy: A social psychological view, In Gurman, A.S. and Razin, A.M. (eds), *Effectiveness in Psychotherapy*, Pergamon, New York.

Parloff, M.B. *et al.* (1978) Research on therapist variables, in relation to process and outcome. In Garfield, S.L. and Bergin, A. E. (eds), *Handbook of Psychotherapy and Behaviour Change*, Wiley, New York.

CRISIS THERAPY

Aquilea, D.C. and Messick, J.M. (1974)

Crisis Intervention: Theory and Methodology, V. Mosby, St Louis.

Everstine, D.S. and Everstine, L. (1983) *People in Crisis*, Brunner/Mazel, New York.

Ewing, C.P. (1978) *Crisis Intervention as Psychotherapy*, OUP, Oxford.

Golan, N. (1978) *Treatment in Crisis Situations*, Free Press, New York.

Langsley, D.G. (1981) Crisis intervention: an update. In Masserman, J.H. (ed.), *Current Psychiatric Therapies*, vol. 20, Grune and Stratton, New York.

CRITICAL INCIDENTS

Cohen, N. (1989) Lockerbie's other victims, *The Independent*, Feb. 8, p. 15.

Hodgkinson, P.E. (1988) Psychological after-effects of transportation disaster. *Medicine, Science and the Law*, 28(4), 304–9.

—— (1989) Technological disaster – survival and bereavement, *Social Science and Medicine*, 29(3), 351–6.

Morris, B. (1989) Hillsborough, *Insight*, 9, 8–9.

Wright, M.(1990) Planning a trauma counselling service. *Counselling*. British Association for Counselling, August 1990.

DEFENCE MECHANISMS

Fairbairn, W.R.D. (1952) A revised psychopathology. In *Psychoanalytic Studies of the Personality*, Tavistock, London.

Freud, Anna (1937) *The Ego and the Mechanisms of Defence*. Hogarth Press, London.

Freud, S. (1896) Further remarks on the neuro-psychoses of defence, *Standard Edition*, Hogarth Press, London.

—— (1926) Mourning and melancholia, vol. 14; Introductory lectures, vol. 16; Inhibitions, symptoms and anxiety, vol. 20 (1940) An outline of psychoanalysis, vol. 23. *Standard Edition*, Hogarth Press, London.

Hartmann, H. (1964) *Essays on Ego Psychology*, International Universities Press, New York.

Kline, P. (1981) *Fact and Fantasy in Freudian Theory*, Methuen, London.

Laughlin, H.P. (1970) *The Ego and its Defences*, Appleton-Century-Crofts, New York.

Madison, P. (1961) *Freud's Concept of Repression and Defence*, Minnesota University Press, Minneapolis.

DEFINITION

British Association for Counselling. 1 Regent Place, Rugby, Warwickshire CV21 2PJ.

Woolfe, R. (1989) *Counselling Skills: A Training Manual*, The Scottish Health Education Group, Edinburgh.

DÉJÀ VU

Reed, G. (1972) *The Psychology of Anomalous Experience: A Cognitive Approach*, Hutchinson University Library, London.

DELUSIONS

Bion, W.R. (1961) *Experience in Groups*, Tavistock, London.

DEMORALIZATION

Frank, J.D. (1971) Therapeutic factors in psychotherapy. *American Journal of Psychotherapy*, 25, 350–61.

—— (1974) Psychotherapy: the restoration of morale, *American Journal of Psychotherapy*, 31, 271–4.

DEREFLECTION

Frankl, V.E. (1955) *The Doctor and the*

Soul: from Psychotherapy to Logotherapy, Knopf, New York.
—— (1962) Basic concepts of logotherapy. Paper read before the Annual Meeting of the American Ontoanalytic Association in Chicago, 7 May 1961. Reprinted in *Journal of Existential Psychiatry*, No. 8, Spring 1962. The Institute of Psychosynthesis, London.
—— (1967) *Psychotherapy and Existentialism*, Simon and Schuster, New York.
—— (1969) *The Will to Meaning: Foundations and Applications of Logtherapy*, New American Library, New York.
—— (1978) *The Unheard Cry for Meaning*, Simon and Schuster, New York.

DIRECTION

Ivey, A. and Gluckstern, N. (1976) *Basic Influencing Skills: Leader and Participant Manuals*, Microtraining, North Amherst, Mass.

DISCOVERY LEARNING

Frost, J.L. (ed.) (1968) *Early Childhood Education Rediscovered*, Holt, Rinehart and Winston, New York.
Piaget, J. (1959) *The Language and Thought of the Child*, 3rd edn, Routledge and Kegan Paul, London.

DISSOCIATION

Fenichel, O. (1945) *The Psychoanalytic Theory of Neurosis*, Norton, New York.
Laughlin, H.P. (1967) *The Neuroses*, Appleton-Century-Crofts, New York.
—— (1970) *The Ego and its Defences*, Appleton-Century-Crofts, New York.

DISTANCING

Adler, A. (1937) *Understanding Human Nature*, George Allen and Unwin, London.

DOUBLE BIND

Bateson, G. *et al.* (1956) Toward a theory of schizophrenia, *Behavioral Science*, 1, 251–264.
Berger, M.M. (1981) *Beyond the Double Bind: Communication and Family Systems*, Brunner/Mazel, New York.
Sluzki, C.E. and Ransom, D.C. (eds) (1976) *Double Bind: The Foundation of the Communication Approach to the Family.* Grune and Stratton, New York.

DREAM THEORIES

Baken, P. (1976) The right-brain is the dreamer. *Psychology Today*, November, pp. 66–8.
Freud, S. (1900) The interpretation of dreams, *Standard Edition*, vol. 4, Hogarth Press, London.
Fromm, E. (1951) *The Forgotten Language*, Rinehart, New York.
Garfield, P.L. (1976) *Creative Dreaming*, Futura Press, London.
Jones, R.M. (1970) *The New Psychology of Dreaming*, Grune and Stratton, New York.
Jung, C.G. (1934) The practical use of dream analysis, In, *The Practice of Psychotherapy*, vols 12 & 16, *The Collected Works of C.G. Jung*, Routledge and Kegan Paul, London.
—— (1936) Individual dream symbolism in relation to alchemy. In, *Psychology and Alchemy* vols 12 and 16, *The Collected Works of C.G. Jung*, Routledge and Kegan Paul, London.
—— (1964) *Man and His Symbols*, Doubleday, Garden City.
Koestler, A. (1964) *The Act of Creation*, Macmillan, New York.
Ornstein, R.E. (1975) *The Psychology of Consciousness*, Pelican, Harmondsworth.
Shohet, R. (1985) *Dream Sharing*, Turnstone Press, Wellingborough.

Ullman, M. (1983) *Working with Dreams*, Hutchinson, London.
Wickes, F.G. (1988) *The Inner World of Childhood: A Study in Analytical Psychology*, Sigo Press, Boston.
Zdenek, M. (1983) *The Right-Brain Experience*, Corgi, London.

DYING - STAGES OF

Kubler-Ross, E. (1970) *On Death and Dying*, Tavistock, London.
Poss, S. (1981) *Towrds Death with Dignity*, George Allen and Unwin, London. (National Institute Social of Services Library No. 41.)

EGO

Cattell, B. (1965) *The Scientific Analysis of Personality*, Penguin, Harmondsworth.
Freud, S. (1938) An outline of psychoanalysis, *Standard Edition*, vol. 19, Hogarth Press, London.
—— (1923) The ego and the id, *Standard Edition*, vol. 19, Hogarth Press, London.
Hartmann, H. (1964) *Essays in Ego-psychology*. Hogarth Press, London.

EGO STAGES (LOEVINGER)

Loevinger, J. (1976) *Ego Development*, Jossey-Bass, San-Francisco, Calif.
Pinedo, V. (1978) Loevinger's ego stages as the basis of an interventional model, *The 1978 Annual Handbook for Group Facilitators*. University Associates, San Diego, Calif.

EGOCENTRISM

Cox, M.V. (1980) *Are Young Children Egocentric?* St. Martin's Press, New York.
Piaget, J. (1923) *The Language and Thought of the Child*, 3rd edn 1959, Routledge and Kegan Paul, London.

EMPATHY

Barrett-Leonard, G.T. (1981) The empathy cycle: Refinement of a nuclear concept. *Journal of Counselling Psychology*, 28, 91–100.
Bergin, A.E. and Solomon, S. (1970) Personality and performance correlates of empathic understanding in psychotherapy, In, Hart, J.T. and Tomlinson, T.M. (eds), *New Directions in Client Centred Therapy*, Houghton Mifflin, Boston.
Curtis, J. (1981) Effect of therapist self-disclosure on patients' impressions of empathy, competence and trust. *Psychological Reports*, 48, 127–36.
Katz, R.L. (1963), *Empathy* Macmillan, London.
Mitchell, K.M. *et al.* (1977) A reappraisal of accurate empathy, non-possessive warmth and genuineness, In, Gurman, A.S. and Razin, A.M. (eds), *Effective Psychotherapy*, Pergamon, New York.
Rogers, C.R. (1961) *On Becoming A Person: A Therapist's View of Psychotherapy*, Constable, London.
—— (1975) Empathic: an unappreciated way of being. *Counselling Psychologist*, 3, 2–10.
Truax, C.B. and Carkhuff, R.R. (1967) *Towards Effective Counselling and Psychotherapy*, Aldine Press, New York.

ENCOUNTER GROUPS

Burton, A. (ed.) (1969) *The Theory and Practice of Encounter Groups*, Jossey-Bass, San Francisco.
Libermann, M.A. *et al.* (1973) *Encounter Groups: First Facts*, Basic Books, New York.
Rogers, C.R. (1970) *Encounter Groups*, Harper and Row, New York.

Schultz, W.C. (1975) *Elements of Encounter*, Bantam, New York.

Stoller, F.H. (1972) Marathon groups: toward a conceptual model, In, Solomon, L.N. and Berson, B. (eds) *New Perspectives on Encounter Groups*, Jossey-Bass, San Francisco.

ENVY

Adler, A. (1937) *Understanding Human Nature*. George Allen and Unwin, London.

Klein, M. (1957) Envy and gratitude, In *The Writings of Melanie Klein*, vol. 3, Basic Books, New York.

Rosenfeld, H.A. (1965) *Psychotic States*, Hogarth Press, London.

EQUITY THEORY

Walster, E., Walster, G.W. and Bershid, W. (1978) *Equity Theory and Research*, Allyn and Bacon, Boston.

ERIKSON, ERIK H.

Erikson, Erik H. (1958) *Young Man Luther*, Faber, London.

—— (1963) *Childhood and Society*, 2nd edn, W.W. Norton, New York.

—— (1964) *Insight and Responsibility*, W.W. Norton, New York.

—— (1968) *Identity*, Faber, London.

ETHICS

Bolton, N. (ed.) (1979) *Philosophical Problems in Psychology*, Methuen, London.

Code of Ethics and Practice for Counsellors, (AGM/9/90) British Association for Counselling, Rugby.

Corey, G. *et al*. (1979) *Professional and Ethical Issues in Counselling and Psychotherapy*. Brooks-Cole Publishing, Monterey, Calif.

Mackie, J.M. (1977) *Ethics*, Penguin, Harmondsworth.

Stolz, S. *et al*. (1978) *Ethical Issues in Behaviour Modification*, Jossey-Bass, San Francisco.

Szasz, T. (1965) *The Ethics of Psychoanalysis*. Delta, New York.

EVALUATION

Cormier, W.H. and Cormier, L.S. (1979) *Interviewing Strategies for Helpers: A Guide to Assessment, Treatment, and Evaluation*, Brooks/Cole, Monterey, Calif.

Goodyear, R.K. (1981) Termination as a loss experience for the counsellor. *Personnel and Guidance Journal*, 59, 347–50.

Ivey, A. (1983) *International Interviewing and Counselling*. Brooks/Cole, Monterey, Calif.

Maholick, L.T. and Turner, D.W. (1979) Termination: that difficult farewell. *American Journal of Psychotherapy*, 33, 583–91.

Ward, D.E. (1989) Termination of individual counselling: Concepts and strategies In Dryden, W. (ed.) *Key Issues for Counselling in Action*, Sage, London.

EXISTENTIAL THERAPY

Binswanger, L. (1967) *Being-in-the-World*. Harper and Row, New York.

Boss, M. (1971) *Existential Foundations of Medicine and Psychology*, Aronson, New York.

Deurzen-Smith, E. van (1988) *Existential Counselling in Practice*, Sage, London.

Frankl, V.(1973) *Psychotherapy and Existentialism*, Penguin, Harmondsworth.

Laing, R.D. (1967) *The Divided Self*, Penguin, Harmondsworth.

—— (1967) *The Politics of Experience*, Penguin, Harmondsworth.

Macquarrie, J. (1972) *Existentialism*, Penguin, Harmondsworth.

May, R. (1977) (rev. edn) *The Meaning of Anxiety*, W.W. Norton, New York.

—— (1981) *Freedom and Destiny*, W.W. Norton, New York.

Yalom, I.D. (1981) *Existential Psychotherapy*, Basic Books, New York.

FAMILY THERAPY

Bowen, M. (1978) *Family Therapy in Clinical Practice*, Jason Aronson, New York.

Foley, D. (1974) *An Introduction to Family Therapy*, Grune and Stratton, New York.

Framo, J. (1982) *Exploration in Marital and Family Therapy: Selected Papers of James, L. Framo*, Springer, New York.

Gurman , A. and Kniskern, D. (1981) *Handbook of Family Therapy*, Brunner/Mazel, New York.

Hoffman , L. (1981) *Foundations of Family Therapy*, Basic Books, New York.

Minuchin, S. (1974) *Families and Family Therapy*, Harvard University Press, Cambridge.

Satir, V. (1972) *Peoplemaking*, Science and Behaviour Books, Palo Alto.

FEEDBACK

Blanchard, K. and Johnson, S. (1982) *One Minute Manager*, Morrow, New York.

Hanson, P.G. (1975) Giving feedback: An interpersonal skill. *The 1975 Annual Handbook for Group Facilitators*, University Associates, San Diego, Calif.

Laundgren, D.C. and Schaffaer, C. (1976) Feedback processes in sensitivity training groups. *Human Relations*, 29(8), 763–782.

Pareek, U. and Venkateswara, R. (1990) Performance coaching. *The 1990 Annual: Developing Human Resources*, University Associates, San Diego, Calif.

Rogers, C.R. (1970) *Encounter Groups*, Harper and Row, New York.

FEMININITY/MASCULINITY

Ardener, S. (ed.) (1981) *Defining Females: The Nature of Women in Society*, (Oxford University Womens Studies Committee) Croom Helm, Beckenham.

Baker-Miller, J. (1978) *Towards a New Psychology of Women*, Penguin, Harmondsworth.

Brown, L. and Liss-Levinson, N. (1981) Feminist therapy, In, R. Corsini (ed.) *Handbook of Innovative Psychotherapies*, Wiley, New York.

Chaplin, J. (1988) *Feminist Counselling in Action*, Sage, London.

Chaplin, J. (1989) Counselling and gender, In, Dryden, W., Charles-Edwards, D. and Woolfe, R. (eds), *Handbook of Counselling in Britain*, Tavistock/Routledge, London.

Dickson, A. (1982) *A Woman In Your Own Right*, Quartet Books, London.

Fisher, S. (1970) *Body Experiences in Fantasy and Behaviour*, Meridith Corporation, New York.

Jung, Emma (1978) *Animus and Anima*, Spring Publications, Dallas.

Miller, J.B. (1978) *Towards a New Psychology of Women*, Penguin, Harmondsworth.

Orbach, S. and Eichenbaum, L. (1986) *Understanding Women*, Pelican, London.

FERENCZI, S.

Ferenczi, S. (1924) (Written in collaboration with Otto Rank) *The Development of Psychoanalysis*, Nervous and

Mental Disease Publishing, New York.
—— (1924) *Thalassa: A Theory of Genitality*, Internationale Psychoanalytische Bibliothek, Leipzig.
—— (1950–1955) *Selected Papers*, Hogarth Press, London.

FLOODING

Boudewyns, P.A. and Shipley, R.H. (1982) Confusing negative practice with flooding: a cautionary note. *Behaviour Therapist*, 5, 47.
Emmelkamp, P.M. and Mersch, P.P. (1982) Cognition and exposure *in vivo* in the treatment of agoraphobia: Short term and delayed effects. *Cognitive Therapy and Research*, 6, 77–90.
Gelder, M. (1975) Flooding: results and problems from a new treatment for anxiety, In, Thompson, T. and Dockens, W. (eds), *Applications of Behaviour Modification*, Academic Press, New York.
Marks, I.M. (1972) Flooding (implosion and related treatments, In, Agras, W.S. (ed.), *Behaviour Modification: Principles and Clinical Applications*, Little Brown, Boston.
—— (1978) Exposure treatments, In, Agras, W.S. (ed.), *Behaviour Modification: Principles and Clinical Applications* (2nd edn), Little Brown, Boston.
—— (1978) Behavioural psychotherapy of adult neurosis, In, Garfield, S. and Bergin, A.E. (eds) *Handbook of Psychotherapy and Behaviour Change*, Wiley, New York.
Rachman, S. *et al*. (1973) The treatment of obsessive-compulsive neurotics by modelling and flooding *in vivo*. *Behaviour Research and Therapy*, 11, 463–71.

FORCE FIELD ANALYSIS

Egan, G. (1988) *Change-Agent Skills B: Managing Innovation and Change*, University Associates, San Diego, Calif.
Lewin, K. (1969) Quasi-stationary social equilibria and the problem of permanent change, In, Bennis, W.G., Benne, K.D. and Chin, R. (eds), *The Planning of Change*, Holt, Rinehart and Winston, New York.

FOULKES, SIGMUND, H.

Foulkes, S.H. (1948) *Introduction to Group Analytic Psychotherapy*, William Heinemann Medical Books, London.
—— (1957) (with E. Anthony) *Group Psychotherapy*, Penguin, Harmondsworth.
—— (1964) *Therapeutic Group Analysis*, Allen and Unwin, London.
—— (1975) *Group Analytic Psychotherapy*, Gordon and Breach, London.

FRAMES OF REFERENCE

Rogers, C.R. (1961) *On Becoming A Person: A Therapist's View of Psychotherapy*, Constable, London.

FREE ASSOCIATION TEST

Bellack, L. (1961) Free association: Conceptual and clinical aspects. *International Journal of Psychoanalysis*, 42, 9–20.
Freud, S. (1910) Five lectures on psychoanalysis, *Standard Edition*, vol. 11, Hogarth Press, London.
Zdenek, M. (1983) *The Right-Brain Experience*, Corgi, London.

FREUD, ANNA

Freud, Anna (1936) *The Ego and the Mechanisms of Defence*, Institute of Psychoanalysis, London.
—— (1968) *Normality and Pathology in Childhood*, Hogarth Press, London.

FREUD, SIGMUND

Freud, S. (1914) *Standard Edition*, Hogarth Press, London.

FROMM, ERICH

Fromm, E. (1941) *Escape From Freedom*, Farrar and Rinehart, New York.
—— (1947) *Man for Himself*, Routledge and Kegan Paul, London.
—— (1950) *Psychoanalysis and Religion*, Victor Gollancz, London.
—— (1955) *The Sane Society*, Routledge and Kegan Paul, London.
—— (1956) *The Art of Loving*, George Allen and Unwin, London.
—— (1960) *Zen Buddhism and Psychoanalysis*, Souvenir Press, London.
—— (1961) *Marx's Concept of Man*, Penguin, Harmondsworth.
—— (1968) *The Revolution of Hopes*, Harper and Row, New York.

GENUINENESS (CONGRUENCE)

Barrett-Leonard, G.T. (1962) Dimensions of therapist response as causal factors in therapeutic change, *Psychology Monographs*, 76, No. 43, whole No. 562.
Rogers, C.R. and Truax, C.B. (1967) The therapeutic conditions antecedent to change: A theoretical view, In, Rogers, C.R. (ed.) *The Therapeutic Relationship and its Impact*, University of Wisconsin Press, Wisconsin.
Watkins, J.G. (1978) *The Therapeutic Self*, Human Sciences Press, New York.

GESTALT THERAPY

Downing, J. and Marmorstein, R. (1973) *Dreams and Nightmares: A Book of Gestalt Therapy Sessions*, Harper and Row, New York.
Fagan, J. and Sheppard, I.L. (eds.) (1970) *Gestalt Therapy Now:Theory, Techniques, Applications*, Harper Colophon, London.
Hatcher, C. and Himelstein, P. (eds) (1976) *The Handbook of Gestalt Therapy*, Jason Aronson, New York.
Kofka, K. (1935) *Principles of Gestalt Psychology*, Harcourt, Brace and World, New York.
Kohler, W.(1930) *Gestalt Psychology*, Kegan Paul, London.
Perls, F.S. (1969) *Ego, Hunger and Aggression: The Beginnings of Gestalt Therapy*, Random House, New York.
—— (1969) *Gestalt Therapy Verbatim*, Stevens, J.O. (ed.), Bantam, New York.
—— (1969) *In and Out of the Garbage Pail*, Real People Press, Moab, Utah.
—— (1973) *The Gestalt Approach: An Eye Witness to Therapy*, Science and Behaviour Books, Palo Alto, Calif.
Polster, E. and Polster, M. (1974) *Gestalt Therapy Integrated: Contours of Theory and Practice*, Random House, New York.
Riet, V. Van De, Korb, K. and Gorrell, J.J. (1980) *Gestalt Therapy*, Oxford, Pergamon.
Steven, B. (1970) *Don't Push the River*, Real People Press, Moab, Utah.

GRIEF

Anthony, E.J. and Kopernick, A. (eds) (1973) *The Impact of Disease and Death*, Wiley, New York.
Backer, B. *et al.* (1982) *Death and Dying*, Wiley, New York.
Burton, L. (ed) (1974) *Care of the Child Facing Death*, Routledge and Kegan Paul, London.
Cronk, H.M. (1972) This business of dying, *Nursing Times*, 68, 1100.
Freud, S. (1917) Mourning and melancholia, *Standard Edition*, vol. 14, Hogarth Press, London.

Kubler-Ross, E. (1970) *On Death and Dying*. Tavistock, London.

Lindermann, E. (1944) Symptomatology and management of acute grief. *American Journal of Psychiatry*, 101, 141.

Machin, L. (1990) *Looking at Loss: Bereavement Counselling Pack*, Longman, Harlow.

Parkes, C.M. (1972) *Bereavement: Studies of Grief in Adult Life*, Tavistock, London.

Poss, S. (1981) *Towards Death with Dignity*, George Allen and Unwin, London. (National Institute Social Services Library, No. 41.)

Schoenberg, B. *et al.* (1974) *Anticipatory Grief*, Columbia University Press, New York.

Smith, C.R. (1982) *Social Work with the Dying and Bereaved*, BASW/Macmillan, London.

GROUP THERAPY

Whiteley, J.S. and Gordon, J. (1979) *Group Approaches in Psychiatry*, Routledge and Kegan Paul, London.

Yalom, I.D. (1975) *The Theory and Practice of Group Psychotherapy*, 2nd edn, Basic Books, New York.

GROUP TRAINING

Agazarian, Y. and Peters, R. (1981) *The Visible and Invisible Group*, Routledge and Kegan Paul, London.

Douglas, T. (1983) *Groups*, Tavistock, London.

Hare, A.P. (1976) *Handbook of Small Group Research*, 2nd edn, Collier Macmillan, London.

Homans, G.C. (1950) *The Small Group*, Random House, New York.

Sprott, W.J. (1958) *Human Groups*, Penguin, Harmondsworth.

GUILT AND SHAME

Coleman, V. (1982) *Guilt: Why it Happens and How to Overcome it*, Sheldon Press, London.

Freud, S. (1951) *Civilisation and Its Discontents*, Hogarth Press, London.

Lewis, H. (1971) *Shame and Guilt in Neurosis*, International Universities Press, New York.

Smith, R.W. (ed.) (1971) *Guilt, Man and Society*, Doubleday, Garden City, New York.

Stein, E.V. (1968) *Guilt: Theory and Therapy*, Westminster, Philadelphia.

Thrane, G. (1979) Shame. *Journal for the Theory of Social Behaviour*, 9, 139–66.

HARTMANN, HEINZ

Hartmann, H. (1939) *Ego Psychology and the Problem of Adaptation*, International Universities Press, New York.

—— (1964) *Essays on Ego Psychology*, Hogarth Press, London.

HIERARCHY OF HUMAN NEEDS

Maslow, A.H. (1970) *Motivation and Personality*, Harper and Row, New York.

Pfeiffer, S. (1972) The Maslow need hierarchy, *The 1972 Annual Handbook for Group Facilitators*, University Associates, San Diego, Calif.

HOPE

Christensen, B. and De Blaissie, R.R. (1980) Counselling with parents of handicapped adolescents. *Adolescence*, 15, 58.

Dembo, T. (1955) Suffering and its alleviation: A theoretical analysis. *Report for the Association for the Aid of Crippled Children*, New York.

HORNEY, KAREN

Horney, K. (1937) *The Neurotic Personality of Our Time*, W.W. Norton, New York.
—— (1939) *New Ways in Psychoanalysis* Kegan Paul, London.
—— (1950) *Neurosis and Human Growth*, W.W. Norton, New York.

HUMANISTIC PSYCHOLOGY

Assagioli, R. (1980) *Psychosynthesis*, Turnstone Books, Wellingborough.
Fadiman, J. and Frager, R. (1976) *Personality and Personal Growth*, Harper and Row, New York.
Fagan, J. and Sheppard, I.L. (eds) (1970) *Gestalt Therapy Now: Theory, Techniques, Applications*, Harper Colophon, London.
Ferrucci, P. (1982) *What We May Be*, Turnstone Press, Wellingborough.
Laing, R.D. (1967) *The Divided Self*, Penguin, Harmondsworth.
Maslow, A.H. (1969) *Motivation and Personality*, Harper and Row, New York.
Ornstein, R.E. (1975) *The Psychology of Consciousness*, Pelican, Harmondsworth.
Rogers, C.R. (1961) *On Becoming a Person: A Therapist's View of Psychotherapy*, Constable, London.
Rowan, J. (1983) *The Reality Game*, Routledge and Kegan Paul, London.

HUMOUR

Cade, B.W. (1982) Humour and creativity. *Journal of Family Therapy*, 4, 35–42.
Chapman, A.J. and Foot, H.C. (1976) *Humour and Laughter: Theory Research and Applications*, Wiley, Chichester.
—— (1977) *It's a Funny Thing, Humour*, Pergamon Press, Oxford.
Freud, S. (1905) Jokes and their relation to the unconscious, *Standard Edition*, vol. 8, Hogarth Press, London.
Fry, W.F. (1963) *Sweet Madness, A Study of Humour*, Pacific Books, Palo Alto, Calif.
Goldsten, J.H. and McGhee, P. (eds) *Psychology of Humour: Theoretical Perspectives and Empirical Issues*, Academic Press, New York.
McGhee, P.E. (1976) *Humour: Its Origins and Development*, W.H. Freeman, San Francisco.
—— and Golesten, J.H. (1983) *Handbook of Humour Research*, 2 vols, Springer-Verlag, New York.
—— and Chapman, A.J. (1980) *Children's Humour*, Wiley, Chichester.

ID

Freud, S. (1923) The ego and the id, *Standard Edition*, vol. 19, Hogarth Press, London.
Jung, C.G. (1963) *Memories, Dreams and Reflections*, Routledge and Kegan Paul, London.
Schur, M. (1963) *The Id and the Regulatory Principles of Mental Functioning*, International Universities Press, New York.

IDENTIFICATION

Bandura, A. (1969) *Principles of Behaviour Modification*, Holt, New York.
Dicks, H.V. (1967) *Marital Tensions*, Routledge and Kegan Paul, London.
Erikson, E.H. (1968) *Identity, Youth and Crisis*, Faber and Faber, London.
Freud, S. (1950) The origins of psychoanalysis, *Standard Edition*, vol. 4, Hogarth Press, London.
Jung, Carl G. (1958) *The Collected Works - Psychological Types*, Vol. 6, Routledge and Kegan Paul, London.
Klein, M. (1955) On identification, *New Directions in Psychoanalysis*, Karnac, Maresfield Reprints, London.

Pincus, L. (ed.) (1960) *Marriage: Studies in Emotional Conflict and Growth*, Methuen, London.

Schafer, R. (1976) *A New Language for Psychoanalysis*, Yale University Press, New Haven, Connecticut.

IMAGERY

Assagioli, R. (1965) *Psychosynthesis*, Turnstone Press, Wellingborough.

—— (1976) *Transpersonal Inspiration and Psychological Mountain Climbing*, PRF Issue No. 36, Institute of Psychosynthesis, London.

—— (1969) *Symbols of Transpersonal Experiences*, Institute of Psychosynthesis, London.

Crampton, M. (1974) *A Historical Survey of Mental Imagery Techniques in Psychotherapy*, Quebec Centre of Psychosynthesis, Montreal.

Desoille, R. (1966) *The Directed Daydream*, PRF Issue No. 18, Institute of Psychosynthesis, London.

Ferrucci, P. (1982) *What We May Be*, Turnstone Press, Wellingborough.

Gallegos, S.E. and Rennick, T. (1984) *Inner Journeys*, Turnstone Press, Wellingborough.

Hammer, M. (1967) The directed daydream technique. *Psychotherapy: Theory, Research and Practice*, 4, 173–81.

Jung, Carl G. (1958) *The Collected Works – Psychological Types*, vol. 6, Routledge and Kegan Paul, London.

Kelly, G.F. (1972) Guided fantasy as a counselling technique with youth. *Journal of Consulting and Clinical Psychology*, 19, 355–61.

Kosbab, F.P. (1974) Imagery techniques in psychiatry. *Archives of General Psychiatry*, 31, 283–90.

Leuner, H. (1984) *Guided Affective Imagery; Mental Imagery in Short-term Psychotherapy*, Thieme-Stratton, New York.

Lyles, J. (1982) Efficacy of relaxation training and guided imagery in reducing the awareness of cancer chemotherapy. *Journal of Consulting and Clinical Psychology*, 50, 509–24.

Ornstein, R.E. (1975) *The Psychology of Consciousness*, Pelican, Harmondsworth.

Oyle, I. (1975) *The Healing Mind*, Celestial Arts, Millbrae, Calif.

Pelletier, K.R. (1977) *Mind as Healer, Mind as Slayer*, Dell, New York.

Shorr, J.B. (1974) *Psychotherapy Through Imagery*, Intercontinental Medical Book Corporation, New York.

—— *et al.* (1980) *Imagery: Its Many Dimensions and Applications*, Plenum Press, New York.

Singer, J.L. (1974) *Imagery and Daydream Methods in Psychotherapy and Behaviour Modification*, Academic Press, New York.

Zdenek, M. (1983) *The Right-Brain Experience*, Corgi, London.

IMAGO

Jung, Carl G. (1958) *The Collected Works – Psychological Types*, Vol. 6, Routledge and Kegan Paul, London.

INCEST TABOO

Freud, S. (1913) Totem and taboo, *Standard Edition*, vol. 13, Hogarth Press, London.

Jung, C.G. (1911) *Collected Works – Symbols of Transformation*, vol. 7, Routledge and Kegan Paul, London.

INDIVIDUAL PSYCHOLOGY

Adler, A. (1924) *The Practice and Theory of Individual Psychology*, Littlefield, Adams, Totowa, New Jersey.

—— (1933) *Social Interest: A Challenge to*

Mankind, George Allen and Unwin, London.

—— (1937) *Understanding Human Nature*, George Allen and Unwin, London.

—— (1958) *What Life Should Mean To You*, Capricorn Books, New York.

Ansbacher, H.L. and Ansbacher, R.R. (1956) *The Individual Psychology of Alfred Adler*, Harper and Row, New York.

—— (1974) Alder and Virchow: New light on the name 'Individual Psychology, *Journal of Individual Psychology*, 30, 43–52.

—— (1978) *Cooperation Between the Sexes: Writings on Women, Love and Marriage, Sexuality and its Disorders*, Doubleday, New York.

Dinkmeyer, D., Pew, W. and Dinkmeyer, D. (1979) *Adlerian Counselling and Psychotherapy*, Brooks/Cole, Monterey, Calif.

Dreikurs, R. (1953) *Fundamentals of Adlerian Psychology*, Hawthorn, New York.

—— (1967) *Psychodynamics, Psychotherapy and Counselling*, Alfred Adler Institute, Chicago.

Eckstein, D. (1976) Early recollection changes after counselling: A case study. *Journal of Individual Psychology*, 32(2), 212–223.

—— (1981) An Adlerian primer. *The 1981 Annual Handbook for Group Facilitators*, University Associates, San Diego, Calif.

Kern, A. *et al*. (1978) *A Case of Adlerian Counselling*, Alfred Adler Institute, Chicago.

Leibin, V.M. (1981) Adler's concept of man, *Journal of Individual Psychology*, 37, 3–4.

Mosak, H., and Dreikurs, R. (1973) Adlerian psychotherapy, In, Corsini, R. (ed.) *Current Psychotherapies*. F.E. Peacock, Itasca, Ill.

O'Connel, W. (1971) *Action Therapy and Adlerian Theory*, Charles C. Thomas, Springfield, Ill.

Shulman, B. (1973) Confrontation techniques in Adlerian psychotherapy, In, Shulman B. (ed.) *Contributions to Individual Psychology*, Alfred Adler Institute, Chicago.

INDIVIDUATION

Jung, C.G. (1917) *Collected Works – Two Essays on Analytical Psychology*, vol. 7, Routledge and Kegan Paul, London.

INSIGHT

Kohler, W. (1925) *The Meaning of Apes*, Kegan Paul, New York.

INSTINCTS

Fletcher, R. (1968) *Instincts in Man*, Allen and Unwin, London.

McDougall, W. (1908) *An Introduction to Social Psychology*, Methuen, London.

INSTITUTIONALIZATION

Ainsworth-Smith, I. (1987) *What Institutionalisation Does to a Person*, Chaplain's Office, St George's Hospital, London.

INTELLECTUALIZATION

Freud, Anna (1937) *The Ego and the Mechanisms of Defence*, Hogarth Press, London.

INTERACTION PROCESS ANALYSIS

Bales, R.F. (1950) *Interaction Process Analysis*, Addison-Wesley, Reading Mass.

—— (1958) The equilibrium problem in small groups. In, Hare, A.P., Borgatta, E.F. and Bales, R.F. (eds), *Small Groups: Studies in Social Interaction*, A. A. Knopf, New York.

— and Slater, P.E. (1955) Role differentiation in small decision-making groups. In, Parson, T. and Bales, R.F. (eds), *The Family, Socialisation and Interaction Process*, Free Press, Glencoe, Ill.

Byrum-Gaw, B. (1980) Interaction process analysis, *The Annual Handbook for Group Facilitators*, University Associates, San Diego, Calif.

INTERNALIZATION

Hartmann, H. (1939/1958) *Ego Psychology and the Problems of Adaptation*, International Universities Press, New York.

Meissner, W.W. (1981) *Internalisation in Psychoanalysis*, International Universities Press, New York.

Schafer, R. (1976) *A New Language for Psychoanalysis*, Yale University Press, Newhaven, Conn.

INTERPERSONAL TECHNIQUES

Hayes, J.S. and Larson, K. (1968) *Interacting With Patients*, Macmillan, London.

INTERPERSONAL THEORY

Sullivan, H.S. (1953) *The Interpersonal Theory of Psychiatry*, Tavistock, London.

— (1964) *The Fusion of Psychiatry and Social Sciences*, Norton, New York.

INTERPRETATION

Cheshire, N.M. (1975) *The Nature of Psychodynamic Interpretation*, Wiley, London.

French, T. (1970) *Psychoanalytic Interpretations*, Quadrangle Books, Chicago.

Freud, S. (1900) The interpretation of dreams, *Standard Edition*, vols. 4 and 5, Hogarth Press, London.

Jung, C.G. (1954) The practical use of dream analysis, *Collected Works*, vol. 16, Routledge and Kegan Paul, London.

Leites, N. (1977) Transference interpretations only? *International Journal of Psychoanalysis*, 58, 275–87.

Strachey, J. (1934) The nature of the therapeutic action of psychoanalysis, *International Journal of Psychoanalysis*, 15, 127–59.

INTIMACY

Duck, S.W. (1983) *Friends for Life*, Harvester Press, New York.

Hinde, R.A. (1979) *Towards Understanding Relationships*, Academic Press, New York.

INTROJECTION

Ferenczi, S. (1909) Introjection and transference, In *First Contributions to Psychoanalysis*, Hogarth Press, London.

Freud, S. (1917) Mourning and melancholia, *Standard Edition*, vol. 14, Hogarth Press, London.

Klein, M. (1955) On Identification, In, *New Directions in Psychoanalysis*, Tavistock Publications, London.

Schafer, R. (1976) *A New Language for Psychoanalysis*, Yale University Press, Newhaven, Conn.

INTUITION

Capra, F. (1983) *The Turning Point*, Fontana, London.

Jung, Carl G. (1958) *The Collected Works – Psychological Types*, Vol. 6, Routledge and Kegan Paul, London.

JANET, PIERRE

Janet, P. (1907) *The Major Symptoms of Hysteria*, MacMillan, New York.

— (1924) *Principles of Psychotherapy*, George Allen and Unwin, London.

— (1925) *Psychological Healing*, George Allen and Unwin, London.

JOHARI WINDOW

Hanson, P.C. (1973) The Johari window: A model for soliciting and giving feedback, *The 1973 Annual Handbook for Group Facilitators*. University Associates, San Diego, Calif.

Luft, J. (1966) *Group Processes: An Introduction to Group Dynamics*, National Press, Palo Alto, Calif.

JUDGMENT

Rogers, C.R. (1980) *A Way of Being*, Houghton Mifflin, Boston.

KLEIN, MELANIE

Klein, M. (1932) *The Psychoanalysis of Children*, L. and V. Woolf, Institute of Psychoanalysis, London.

—— (1948) Mourning and its relation to manic-depressive states, In, Klein, M. (ed.), *Contributions to Psychoanalysis, 1921–1945*, Hogarth Press, London.

—— (1952) Notes on some schizoid mechanisms, In M. Klein, P. Heimann, S. Isaacs, J. Riviere (ed.), *Developments in Psychoanalysis*, Hogarth Press, London.

—— (1957) Envy and gratitude, In, *The Writings of Melanie Klein*, vol. 3, Basic Books, New York.

—— (1961) *Narrative of a Child Analysis*, L. and V. Woolf, Institute of Psychoanalysis, London.

KRIS, ERNST

Kris, E. (1952) *Psychoanalytic Exploration in Art*, George Allen and Unwin, London.

LABELLING

Becker, H. (1963) *Outsider: Studies in the Sociology of Deviance*, Free Press, New York.

Goffman, E. (1963) *Stigma: Notes on the Management of Spoiled Identity*, Penguin, Harmondsworth.

Horowitz, A.V. (1982) *The Social Control of Mental Illness*, Academic Press, New York.

Lemert, E. (1967) *Human Deviance, Social Problems and Social Control*, Prentice-Hall, Englewood Cliffs, New Jersey.

Scheff, R. (1966) *Being Mentally Ill*, Aldine Press, Chicago.

Szasz, T. (1973) *Ideology and Insanity*, Calder and Boyars, London.

Wing, J.K. (1978) *Reasoning About Madness*, Oxford University Press, Oxford.

LACAN, JACQUES

Lacan, J. (1978) *Four Fundamental Concepts of Psychoanalysis*, Penguin, Harmondsworth.

LAING, R.D.

Laing, R.D. (1967) *The Divided Self*, Penguin, Harmondsworth.

—— (1967) *The Politics of Experience*, Penguin, Harmondsworth.

LATENCY PERIOD

Eriksion, E.H. (1963) *Childhood and Society*, Penguin, Harmondsworth.

LEARNED HELPLESSNESS

Seligman, M.E.P. (1973) Fall into helplessness. *Psychology Today*, 7, 43–48.

—— (1975) *Helplessness*, Freeman, San Francisco.

LEARNING STYLES

Bates, M.H. and Maudsley, D. (1985) *From Learning to Teaching: A Learning Centred Approach the Development of Teaching Styles*. (Source unknown.)

Honey, P. and Mumford, A. (1986) *The Manual of Learning Styles*. Published privately, Peter Honey, Ardingly House, 10 Linden Ave., Maidenhead, Berks., UK

— (1989) *Learning Opportunities*. Published privately, Peter Honey, Ardingly House, 10 Linden Ave., Maidenhead, Berks., UK

LEFT AND RIGHT BRAIN

Buzan, T. (1983) *Use Both Sides of Your Brain*, E.P. Dutton, New York.

Edwards, B. (1982) *Drawing on the Right Side of the Brain*, Collins, London.

Ornstein, R.E. (1975) *The Psychology of Consciousness*, Pelican, Harmondsworth.

Rossi, E. (1977) The cerebral hemispheres in analytical psychology. *Journal of Analytical Psychology*, 22, 32–51.

Sperry, R.W. (1986) Hemisphere disconnection and unity in conscious awareness. *American Psychologist*, 23, 723–33.

Stevens, A. (1982) *Archetype: A Natural History of the Self*, Routledge and Kegan Paul, London.

Wonder, J. and Donvan, P. (1984) *Whole-Brain Thinking*, William Morrow, New York.

Zdenek, M. (1983) *The Right-Brain Experience*, Corgi, London.

LIBIDO

Freud, S. (1923) Three essays on sexuality, *Standard Edition*, vol. 7, Hogarth Press, London.

Jung, Carl G. (1958) *The Collected Works – Psychological Types*, vol. 6, Routledge and Kegan Paul, London.

LIFESPAN PSYCHOLOGY

Baltes, P.B. and Schale, K.W. (eds) (1973) *Life-span Developmental Psychology: Personality and Socialisation*, Academic Press, London.

Datan, N. and Ginsberg, L.H. (eds) (1975) *Life-Span Developmental Psychology: Normative Life Crises*, Academic Press, London.

— (eds) (1980) *Transition of Aging*, Academic Press, London.

Erikson, E.H. (1963) *Childhood and Society*, Penguin, Harmondsworth.

Goulet, L.R. and Baltes, O.B. (eds) (1970) *Life-span Developmental Psychology: Research and Theory*, Academic Press, London.

Neugarten, B.L. (ed.) (1968) *Middle Age and Aging*, University of Chicago Press, Chicago.

LISTENING

Reik, T. (1972) *Listening With the Third Ear*, Pyramid Publications, New York.

Rogers, C.R. and Farson, R.E. (1975) *General Motors Salaried Supervisor Seminar*, General Motors Education and Training Department, Flint, Michigan.

Wismer, J.N. (1978) Communication effectiveness: Active listening and sending feeling messages, *The 1978 Annual Handbook for Group Facilitators*, University Associates, San Diego, Calif.

LOCUS OF CONTROL

Collins, B. (1974) Four components of the Rotter internal–external scale belief in a difficult world, a just world, a predictable world and a politically responsive world. *Journal of Personality and Social Psychology*, 29, 381–91.

DuCette, J. and Wolk, S. (1972) Locus of control and levels of aspiration in black and white children. *Review of Educational Research*, 42, 493–504.

Goodstadt, B. and Hjelle, L.A. (1973) Power to the powerless: Locus of control and the use of power. *Journal of Personality and Social Psychology*, 8, 155–156.

Levenson, H. (1974) Activism and powerful others: Distinctions within the concept of internal–external control. *Journal of Personality Assessment*,38, 177–83.

Pareek, U. and Rao, T.V. (1974) *A Status of Population Research in India: Behavioural Sciences*. Tata/McGraw Hill, New Delhi, India.

Phares, E.J. (1968) Differential utilisation of information as a function of internal–external control. *Journal of Counselling Psychology*, 36, 649–662.

Rotter, J.B. (1966) Generalised expectancies for internal versus external control of reinforcement. *Psychological Monographs: General and Applied*, 80 (1), Whole No. 609.

Ryckmann, R.M. and Sherman, M.F. (1973) Locus of control and perceived ability level as determinants of partner–opponent choice. *Journal of Social Psychology*, 3, 125–130.

Tiffany, D.W., Cowan, J.R. and Tiffany, P.M. (1970) *The Unemployed*, Prentice-Hall, Englewood Cliffs, New Jersey.

Tseng, M.S. (1970) Locus of control as a determinant of job proficiency, employability and training satisfaction of vocational rehabilitation clients. *Journal of Counselling Psychology*, 17, 487–491.

Venkateswara, R. (1985) The entrepreneurial orientation inventory. *The 1985 Annual: Developing Human Resources*, University Associates, San Diego, Calif.

LOGOTHERAPY

Frankl, V.E. (1955) *The Doctor and the Soul: From Psychotherapy to Logotherapy*, Knopf, New York.

—— (1962) *Basic Concepts of Logotherapy.* Paper read before the Annual Meeting of the American Ontoanalytic Assocation in Chicago, 7 May 1961. Reprinted in *Journal of Existential Psychiatry*, No. 8, Spring 1962. The Institute of Psychosynthesis, London.

—— (1967) *Psychotherapy and Existentialism*, Simon and Schuster, New York.

—— (1969) *The Will to Meaning: Foundations and Applications of Logotherapy*, New American Library, New York.

—— (1978) *The Unheard Cry for Meaning*, Simon and Schuster, New York.

LONELINESS

Bowlby, J. (1979) *The Making and Breaking of Affectional Bonds*, Tavistock, London.

Hobson, R.F. (1974) Loneliness. *Journal of Analytical Psychology*, 19, 71–89.

Peplau, L.A. and Perlman, D. (1982) *Loneliness*, John Wiley, New York.

Thiel, H.G., Parker, D. and Bruce, T.A. (1973) Stress factors and the risk of myocardial infarction. *Journal of Psychosomatic Research*, 17, 43–57.

MANDALA

Cirlot, J.E. (1971) *A Dictionary of Symbols* (2nd edn), Routledge and Kegan Paul, London.

Jung, C.G. (1964) *Man and His Symbols*, Doubleday, Garden City.

—— (1961) *Memories, Dreams, Reflections*, Random House, New York.

—— (1963) *Mysterium Coniunctionis*, Bollingen Series 20, No 14, Princeton University Press, New Jersey.

—— (1959) *The Archetypes and the Collective Unconscious* – Part II – Aion. Bollingen Series 20, No. 9, Princeton University Press, New Jersey.

Ornstein, R.E. (1975) *The Psychology of Consciousness*, Pelican, Harmondsworth.

Zdenek, M. (1983) *The Right-Brain Experience*, Corgi, London.

MARATHON GROUPS

Bach, G.R. (1966) The marathon group: Intensive practice of intimate interaction. *Psychological Reports*, 18, 995–1002.

— and Goldberg, H. (1974) *Creative Aggression*, Avon, New York.

Mintz, E.E. (1971) *Marathon Groups: Reality and Symbol*, Appleton-Century-Crofts, New York.

MARTYR ATTITUDE

Rowe, D. (1971) Poor prognosis in a case of depression as predicted by the repertory grid. *British Journal of Psychiatry*, 118, 297–300.

Sadler, W.S. (1936) *Theory and Practice of Psychiatry*, H. Kimpton, London.

MASLOW, ABRAHAM HAROLD

Maslow, A.H. (1954) *Motivation and Personality*, Harper and Row, New York.

— (1962) *Toward a Psychology of Being*, Nosstrand, Princeton.

— (1971) *The Farther Reaches of Human Nature*, Penguin, Harmondsworth.

McGREGOR, DOUGLAS

Glaser, R. and Glaser, C. (1983) Manager's dilemma: Theory X and Theory Y, *The 1983 Annual for Facilitators, Trainers and Consultants*, University Associates, San Diego, Calif.

McGregor, D. (1961) *The Human Side of Enterprise*, McGraw-Hill, New York.

— (1967) *The Professional Manager*. Bennis, W.G., McGregor, C. (eds) McGraw–Hill, New York.

MEDITATION

LeShan, L. (1974) *How to Meditate*, Bantam, New York.

Naranjo, C. and Ornstein, R. (1971) *The Psychology of Meditation*, Viking Press, New York.

Saraswati, Swami J. (1975) *Yoga, Tantra, and Meditation*, Balantine, New York.

Tart, C. (ed) (1972) *Altered States of Consciousness*, Doubleday Anchor, New York.

METAPHOR

Andolf, M. *et al*. (1983) *Behind the Family Mask*, Brunner/Mazel, New York.

Black, M. (1962) *Models and Metaphors*, Cornell University Press, Ithaca, New York.

Cade, B. (1982) Some uses of metaphor. *Australian Journal of Family Therapy*, 3, 135–40.

Edinger, E. (1972) *Ego and Archetype*, Putnam, New York.

Gordon, D. (1978) *Therapeutic Metaphors*, Meta Publications, Calif.

Grof, S. (1976) *Realms of the Human Unconscious*, Dutton, New York.

Metzner, R. (1980) Ten classical metaphors of self-transformation. *Journal of Transpersonal Psychology*, 12 (1), 47–62.

MOURNING

Averill, J.R. (1975) Grief: its nature and significance. In, Carr, A.C. *et al*. (eds) *Grief: Selected Readings*, Health Sciences Publishing, New York.

Gorer, G. (1965) *Death, Grief and Mourning in Contemporary Britain*, Cresset, London.

Liebermann, S. (1978) Nineteen cases of morbid grief. *British Journal of Psychiatry*, 132, 159–73.

Machin, L. (1990) *Looking at Loss: Bereavement Counselling Pack*, Longman, Harlow.

Paul, H. and Grosser, G. (1965) Operational mourning and its role in conjoint family therapy. *Community Mental Health Journal*, 1, 339.

Rosenblatt, P., Walsh, R. and Jackson, D. (1976) *Grief and Mourning in Cultural Perspective*, HRAF Press, New Haven, Conn.

MULTICULTURAL ISSUES

Dummett, A. (1980) Nationality and citizenship, In, *Conference Report of Further Education in Ethnic Minorities*, National Association for Teachers in Higher Education.

Hall, E.T. (1976) *Beyond Culture*, Doubleday, New York.

Jones, E.E. (1985) Psychotherapy and counselling with black clients. In, Pederon, P. (ed.) *Handbook of Cross-cultural Counselling and Therapy*, Praeger, London.

Katz, J.H. (1978) *White Awareness: Handbook for Anti-racism Training*, University of Oklahoma Press, Norman.

Lago, C. and Thompson, J. (1989) Counselling and race. In Dryden, W., Charles-Edwards, D. and Woolfe, R. (eds), *Handbook of Counselling in Britain*, Tavistock/Routledge, London.

Sue, D.W. (1981) *Counselling the Culturally Different*, Wiley, New York.

MULTI-MODAL THERAPY (MMT)

Brunell, L.F. and Young, W.T. (eds) (1981) *Multi Modal Handbook for a Mental Hospital*, Springer, New York.

Fay, A. and Lazarus, A.A. (1981) Multi modal therapy and the problem of depression, In, Clarkin, J.F. and Glazer (eds) *Depression: Behavioural and Directive Treatment Strategies*, Garland Press, New York.

Kwee, M.G.T. (1981) Towards the clinical art and science of multi modal psychotherapy. *Current Psychological Review*, 1, 55–68.

Lazarus, A.A. (1973) Multi Modal Behaviour Therapy: Treating the BASIC I.D. *Journal of Nervous and Mental Disease*, 156, 404–411.

—— (ed.) (1976) *Multi Modal Behaviour Therapy*, Springer, New York.

—— (1981) *The Practice of Multi Modal Therapy*, McGraw-Hill, New York.

MYERS–BRIGGS TYPE INDICATOR (MBTI)

Briggs-Myers, I. (1980) *Gifts Differing*, Consulting Psychologists Press, Palo Alto, Calif.

—— (1980) *Introduction to Type*, Consulting Psychologists Press, Palo Alto, Calif.

—— and McCaulley, M.H. (1985) *Manual: A Guide to the Development and Use of the Myers-Briggs Type Indicator*, Consulting Psychologists Press, Palo Alto, Calif.

Kiersey, D. and Bates, M. (1984) *Please Understand Me*, Prometheus Nemesis Book Company, Del Mar.

Wickes, F.G. (1950) *The Inner World of Man*, Methuen, London.

MYTHS

Bayley, H. (1912) (reprinted 1974) *The Lost Language of Symbolism: An Inquiry into the Origin of Certain Letters, Words, Names, Fairy Tales, Folklore, and Mythologies*, Ernest Benn, London and Tonbridge.

Cassirer, E. (1946) *Language and Myth*, Harper and Row, New York.

Ehrenwald, J. (1966) *Psychotherapy: Myth and Method*, Grune and Stratton, New York.

May, R. (1973) The function of myth in sickness and health, In, Wittenberg, E.G. (ed.) *Interpersonal Explorations in Psychoanalysis*, Basic Books, New York.

NARCISSISM

Freud, S. (1913) On narcissism, *Standard Edition*, vol. 13, Hogarth Press, London.

Jacoby, M. (1981) Reflections on H. Kohut's concept of narcissism. *Journal of Analytical Psychology*, 26 (1), 19–32.

Kohut, H. (1977) *The Analysis of the Self*, International Universities Press, New York.

—— (1977) *The Restoration of the Self*, International Universities Press, New York.

Ledermann, R. (1979) The infantile roots of narcissistic personality disorder. *Journal of Analytical Psychology* 26(4), 107–26.

NEUROLINGUISTIC PROGRAMMING

Bandler, R. and Grinder, J. (1976) *Structure of Magic*, vols. 1 and 2. Science and Behaviour Books, Palo Alto, Calif.

—— (1979) *Frogs into Princes*, Real People Press, Moab, Utah.

—— (1982) *Reframing*, Real People Press, Moab, Utah.

Grinder, J. *et al.* (1973) *Guide to Transformational Grammar*, Holt, Rinehart and Winston, New York.

Laborde, G.Z. (1987) *Influencing with Integrity*, Syntony Publishing, Palo Alto, Calif.

NON-DIRECTIVE THERAPY

Frank, J.D. (1973) *Persuasion and Healing*, 2nd edn, Johns Hopkins Press, Baltimore.

Pope, B. (1977) Research of therapeutic style, In, Gurman, A.S. and Razin, A.M., *Effective Psychotherapy*, Pergamon, New York.

NON-VERBAL COMMUNICATION (BODY LANGUAGE)

Argyle, M. (1969) *Social Interaction*, Methuen, London.

—— (1975) *Bodily Communication*, Methuen, London.

—— (1978) *The Psychology of Interpersonal Behaviour*, 3rd edn, Penguin, Harmondsworth.

Hall, E.T. (1973) *The Silent Language*, Doubleday, Garden City.

Morris, D. (1977) *Manwatching*, Jonathan Cape, London.

—— Collett, P., Marsh, P. and O'Shaughnessy, M. (1979) *Gestures; Their Origins and Distribution*, Jonathan Cape, London.

Pease, A. (1981) *Body Language*, Sheldon Press, London.

The Secrets of Body Language (1990) Reader's Digest Association, London.

OBJECT

Freud, S. (1915) Instincts and their vicissitudes, *Standard Edition*, vol. 14, Hogarth Press, London.

Klein, M. (1952) Some theoretical conclusions regarding the emotional life of the infant, In, Rivére, J. (ed.), *Developments in Psychoanalysis*, Hogarth Press, London.

OBJECT RELATIONS

Dicks, H.V. (1967) *Marital Tensions*, Routledge and Kegan Paul, London.

Fairbairn, W.R.D. (1952) *Psychoanalytic Studies of the Personality*, Tavistock, London.

—— (1963) Synopsis of the object relations theory of the personality, *International Journal of Psycho-analysis*, 44, 224–225.

Guntrip, H. (1968) *Schizoid Phenomena, Objects Relations and the Self*, Hogarth Press, London.

Kernberg, O. (1976) *Object Relations Theory and Clinical Psychoanalysis*, Jason Aronson, New York.

Scharff, D.E. (1982) *The Sexual Relationship: An Object Relations View of Sex and the Family*, Routledge and Kegan Paul, London.

Shapiro, R. (1979) Family dynamics and object relations theory, In, Feinstein, S. and Giovacchini, P. (eds), *Adolescent Psychiatry*, vol. 7, University of Chicago Press, Chicago.

Sutherland, J.D. (1963) Object relations theory and the conceptual model of psychoanalysis, *British Journal of Medical Psychology*, 36, 109–24.

—— (1980) The British object relations theorists: Balint, Winnicott, Fairbairn, Guntrip. *Journal of the American Psychoanalytic Association*, 28, 829–59.

OCCUPATIONAL CHOICE AND DEVELOPMENT THEORY

Blau, P.M. *et al.* (1956) Occupational choice: a conceptual framework. *Industrial and Labour Relations Review*, 9, 531–43.

Ginzberg, E. (1972) Toward a theory of occupational choice: A restatement. *Vocational Guidance Quarterly*, March, 169–76.

Holland, J.L. (1973) *Making Vocational Choices: A Theory of Careers*, Prentice-Hall, Englewood Cliffs, NJ.

Krumboltz, J.D., Mitchell, A.M. and Jones, G.B. (1976) A social learning theory of career selection. *The Counselling Psychologist*, 6(1), 71–81.

Super, D.E. (1980) A life-span, life-space approach to career development, *Journal of Occupational Behaviour*, 16, 282–98.

—— and Bohn, M.J. (1970) *Occupational Psychology*, Tavistock, London.

OEDIPUS COMPLEX

Freud, S. (1913) Totem and taboo, *Standard Edition*, vol. 13, Hogarth Press, London.

—— (1924) The dissolution of the Oedipus complex, *Standard Edition*, vol. 19, Hogarth Press, London.

Gabriel, Y. (1983) *Freud and Society*, Routledge and Kegan Paul, London.

Hamilton, V. (1982) *Narcissus and Oedipus*. Routledge and Kegan Paul, London.

Klein, M. (1945) The Oedipus complex in the light of early anxieties, In, *Contributions to Psychoanalysis*, Hogarth Press, London.

Leowald, H.W. (1979) The waning of the Oedipus complex. *Journal of the American Psychoanalytic Association*, 27, 751–75.

OPENMINDEDNESS

Rokeach, M. (1960) *The Open and Closed Mind*, Basic Books, New York.

OPERANT CONDITIONING

Honig, W. and Staddon, J.E.R. (eds) (1977) *Handbook of Operant Behaviour*, Prentice-Hall, Englewood Cliffs, NJ.

PARABLE

Cade, B.W. (1982) Some uses of metaphor. *Australian Journal of Family Therapy*, 3, 135–40.

Felner, C. (1976) The use of teaching stories in conjoint family therapy. *Family Process*, 15, 427–33.

TeSelle, S. (1975) *Speaking in Parables: A Study in Metaphor and Theology*, SCM Press, London.

PARADOXICAL INTENTION

Frankl, V.E. (1969) *The Will to Meaning*, New American Library, New York.

PARAPRAXIS

Freud, S. (1901) The psychopathology of everyday life, *Standard Edition*, vol. 6, Hogarth Press, London.

PARENTAL CHILD

Minuchin, S. (1974) *Families and Family Therapy*, Tavistock, London.

PARENTING SKILLS TRAINING

Abin, R.R. (1976) *Parenting Skills – Workbook and Training Manual*, Human Sciences Press, New York.
De'Ath, E. (1983) Teaching parenting skills. *Journal of Family Therapy*, 5, 321–35.
Gordon, T. (1970) *Parent Effectiveness Training (PET)*, Peter H. Wyden, New York.
Rutter, M. *et al.* (1983) Parenting in two generations, In, Madge, N. (ed.), *Families at Risk*, Heinemann Educational, London.

PEAK EXPERIENCES

Maslow, A.H. (1962) *Towards a Psychology of Being*, Nosstrand, Princeton.
— (1971) *The Farther Reaches of Human Nature*, Penguin, Harmondsworth.

PERSONAL CONSTRUCT THEORY

Beail, N. (ed.) (1985) *Repertory Grid Technique and Personal Constructs*, Croom Helm, Beckenham.
Bannister, D. and Fransella, F. (1980) *Inquiring Man*, 2nd edn, Penguin, Harmondsworth.
Fransella, F. and Bannister, D. (1977) *A Manual for Repertory Grid Technique*, Academic Press, London.
Kelly, G.A. (1955) *The Psychology of Personal Constructs*, W.W. Norton, New York.
— (1963) *A Theory of Personality*, W.W. Norton, New York.

PERSONALITY DISORDER

DSM III-R (1987) *Diagnosis and Statistical Manual of Mental Disorders*. 3rd end, American Psychiatrics Association, Washington.

PERSON-CENTRED THERAPY

Hart, J.T. and Tomlinson, T.M. (eds) (1970) *New Directions in Client-Centred Therapy*, Houghton Mifflin, New York.
Mearns, D. and Thorne, B. (1988) *Person-Centred Counselling in Action*, Sage, London.
Mitchell, K.M. *et al.* (1977) A reappraisal of accurate empathy, non-possessive warmth and genuineness. In, Gurman, A.S. and Razin, A.M. (eds), *Effective Psychotherapy*, Pergamon, New York.
Rogers, C.R. (1942) *Counselling and Psychotherapy*, Constable, London.
— (1951) *Client-Centred Therapy: Its Current Practice, Implications and Theory*, 1st edn.), Constable, London.
— (1961) *On Becoming a Person: A Therapist's View of Psychotherapy*, Constable, London.
— (1977) *Personal Power: Inner Strength and its Revolutionary Impact*, Constable, London.
— (1980) *A Way of Being*, Houghton Mifflin, Boston.
— and Dymond, R. (eds) (1954) *Psychotherapy and Personality Change*, University of Chicago Press, Chicago.
Thorne, B. (1985) *The Quality of Tenderness*, Norwich Centre Publications, Norwich.
Troemel-Ploetz, S. (1980) I'd come to you for therapy; Interpretation, redefinition and paradox in Rogerian

therapy. *Psychotherapy: Theory, Research and Practice*, 17, 246–57.

Truax, C.B. and Mitchell, K.M. (1971) Research on certain therapist interpersonal skills in relation to process and outcome, In, Bergin, A.E. and Garfield, S.L. (eds) *Handbook of Psychotherapy and Behaviour Change*, Wiley, New York.

Wexler, D.A. and Rice, L.N. (eds) (1974) *Innovations in Client Centred Therapy*, Wiley, New York.

PERSONA

Jung, Carl G. (1958) *The Collected Works – Psychological Types*, vol. 6, Routledge and Kegan Paul, London.

PHENOMENOLOGY

Keen, E. (1982) *A Primer in Phenomenological Psychology*, Holt, Rinehart and Winston, New York.

Maddi, S. and Costa, P. (1972) *Humanism in Personology: Allport, Maslow, and Murray*, Aldine, Chicago.

POST-TRAUMATIC STRESS DISORDER (PTSD)

Bleich, A., Siegel, B., Garb, R. and Lerer, B. (1986) Post traumatic stress disorder following combat exposure: Clinical features and psychopharmacological treatment. *British Journal of Psychiatry*, 149, 365.

Cohen, N. (1989) Lockerbie's other victims. *The Independent*, Feb. 8, 15.

Cunningham, V. (1988) Herald disaster – from the shop floor. *Counselling*, (British Association for Counselling), August: 1–6

Eth, S., Pynoos, R.S. (eds) (1985) *Post-Traumatic Stress Disorder in Children*. American Psychiatric Press, Washington, DC.

Figley, C.R. (ed.) (1985) *Trauma and its Wake: The Study and Treatment of Post-Traumatic Stress Disorder*, Brunner/Mazel, New York.

Frankl, V. (1959) *From Death Camp to Existentialism*, Beacon Press, New York.

Hodgkinson, P.E. (1988) Psychological after-effects of transportation disaster. *Medicine, Science and the Law*, 28(4), 304–9.

— (1989) Technological diaster – survival and bereavement. *Social Sciences and Medicine*, 29(3), 351–6.

Horowitz, M.J. (1974) Stress response syndromes: character style and brief psychotherapy. *Archives of General Psychiatry*, 31, 768.

— Wilner, N. and Alvarez, W. (1980) Signs and symptoms of post-traumatic stress disorder. *Archives of General Psychiatry*, 37, 85.

Kinzie, J.D., Fredrickson, R.H., Ben, R., Fleck, J. and Karl, W. (1984) Post-traumatic stress disorder among survivors of Cambodian concentration camps. *American Journal of Psychiatry*, 141, 645.

Kluznik, J.C., Speed, N., Valkenburg, C.V. and Magraw, R. (1986) Forty-year follow-up of United States prisoners of war. *American Journal of Psychiatry*, 143, 1443.

Kolb, L.C. (1983) Return of the repressed: Delayed stress reaction to war. *Journal of the American Psychoanalytic Association*, 11, 531.

Kolb, van der B.A. (1987) *Psychological Trauma*, American Psychiatric Press, Washington DC.

Lifton, R.J. (1979) *The Broken Connection*, Simon and Schuster, New York.

McCann, I.L., Sakheim, D.K. and Abrahamson, D.J. (1988) Trauma and victimisation: A model of psychological adaptation. *The Counselling Psychologist*, 16(4), October.

McFarlane, A.C. (1988) The aetiology

of post-traumatic stress disorders following a natural diaster. *British Journal of Psychiatry*, 152, 116.

Scrignar, C.B. (1984) *Post-Traumatic Stress Disorder*, Praeger, New York.

Shore, J.H. (ed.) (1986) *Disaster Stress Studies: New Methods and Findings*, American Psychiatric Press, Washington, DC.

Wilson, J.P., Harel, A. and Kahana, B. (1988) *Human Adaptation to Extreme Stress: From the Holocaust to Vietnam*, Plenum Press, New York.

Woodruff, I. (1989) Major incident: Impact on staff. *Hospital Chaplain*, June, 12–17.

Wright, M. (1990) Planning a trauma counselling service. *Counselling* (British Association for Counselling), August.

PRECONSCIOUS

Freud, S. (1915) The unconscious, *Standard Edition*, vol. 14, Hogarth Press, London.

PREJUDICE

Adorno, T.W., Frenkel-Brunswick, E., Levinson, D.J. and Stanford, R.N. (eds) (1950) *The Authoritarian Personality*, Harper, New York.

Allport, G.W. (1954) *The Nature of Prejudice*, Addison-Wesley, Cambridge, Mass.

Sherif, M. (1967) *In Common Predicament: Social Psychology of Intergroup Conflict and Cooperation*, Houghton Mifflin, Boston.

Tajfel, H. (1981) *Human Groups and Social Categories: Studies in Social Psychology*, Cambridge University Press, Cambridge.

PRESENTING PROBLEM

Davison, E.H. (1965) *Social Casework*, Bailliere, Tindall and Cox, London.

PRIMAL THERAPY

Janov, A. (1970) *The Primal Scream*, New York, Putnam.

—— (1971) *the Anatomy of Mental Illness*, Putnam, New York.

—— and Holden, E.M. (eds) (1975) *Primal Man: The New Consciousness*, Crowell, New York.

Kovel, J. (1978) *A Complete Guide to Therapy*, Penguin, Harmondsworth.

Rosen, R. (1978) *Psychobabble*, Wildwood House, London.

Prochaska, J.O. (1979) *Systems of Psychotherapy*. Dorsey Press. Homewood, Ill.

PROBLEM-SOLVING INTERVENTIONS

Blechman, E.A. (1974) The family contract game: A tool to teach interpersonal problem-solving. *Family Coordinator*, 23, 269–81.

Dewey, J. (1933) *How We Think*, D.C. Heath, New York.

D'Zurilla, T.J. and Goldfried, M.R. (1971) Problem-solving and behavioural modification. *Journal of Abnormal Psychology*, 78, 107–26.

Earley, L.C. and Rutledge, P.B. (1980) A nine-step problem-solving model. *The 1980 Annual Handbook for Group Facilitators*, University Associates, San Diego, Calif.

Haley, J. (1976) *Problem-Solving Therapy*, Jossey-Bass, San Francisco.

Spier, M.S. (1973) Kurt Lewin's 'Force Field Analysis'. *The 1973 Annual Handbook for Group Facilitators*. University Associates, San Diego, Calif.

Spivack, G., Platt, J.J. and Shure, M.D. (1976) *The Problem-Solving Approach to Adjustment*, Jossey-Bass, San Francisco.

PROVOCATIVE THERAPY

Farelly, F. and Brandsman, J. (1974) *Provocative Therapy*, Meta Publications, Cupertino, Calif.

PSYCHE

Jung, Carl G. (1958) *The Collected Works – Psychological Types*, vol. 6, Routledge and Kegan Paul, London.

PSYCHIC PAIN

Lader, M.H. (1981) *Focus on Depression*, Bencard, Middlesex.
Lewis, C.S. (1957) *The Problem of Pain*, Fontana, London.
—— (1961) *A Grief Observed*, Faber and Faber, London.

PSYCHOANALYSIS

Balint, M. (1952) *Primary Love and Psychoanalytic Technique*, Tavistock, London.
Brenner, C.(1973) *An Elementary Textbook of Psychoanalysis*, International Universities Press, New York.
Brown, J.A.C. (1961) *Freud and the Post-Freudians*, Penguin, Harmondsworth.
Eysenck, H. and Wilson, G. (eds) (1973) *The Experimental Study of Freudian Theories*, Methuen, London.
Farrell, B.A. (1981) *The Standing of Psychoanalysis*, OUP, Oxford.
Fisher, S. and Greenberg, R.P. (1977) *The Scientific Credibility of Freud's Theories and Therapy*, Harvester Press, New York.
Freud, S. (1913) New introductory lectures on psychoanalysis, *Standard Edition*, vol. 22, Hogarth Press, London.
—— (1901) The psychopathology of everyday life, *Standard Edition*, vol. 6, Hogarth Press, London.
Gabriel, Y. (1983) *Freud and Society*, Routledge and Kegan Paul, London.
Kernberg, G.S. (1976) *Internal World and External Reality*, Jason Aronson, New York.
Klein, G.S. (1976) *Psychoanalytic Theory: An Exploration of Essentials*, International Universities Press, New York.
Kline, P. (1972) *Fact and Fantasy in Freudian Theory*, Methuen, London.
Kohut, H. (1977) *The Restoration of the Self*, International Universities Press, New York.
McGuire, W. (ed.) (1974) *The Freud/Jung Letters*, Routledge and Kegan Paul, London.
Rycroft, C. (ed.) (1968) *Psychoanalysis Observed*, Penguin, Harmondsworth.
Sandler, J., Dare, C. and Holder, A. (1972) Frames of reference in psychoanalytic psychology III: A note on the basic assumptions. *British Journal of Medical Psychology*, 45, 143–7.
Schafer, R. (1976) *A New Language for Psychoanalysis*, Yale University Press, New Haven, Conn.
Will, D. (1980) Psychoanalysis as a human science. *British Journal of Medical Psychology*, 53, 201–11.
Wollheim, R. (ed.) (1974) *Philosophers on Freud*, Jason Aronson, New York.

PSYCHOBIOGRAM

Duhl, F.J. (1981) The use of the chronological chart in general systems family therapy. *Journal of Marital and Family Therapy*, 7, 361–71.
Meyer, A. (1919) The life chart and the obligation of specifying positive data in psychopathological diagnosis, In, *Contributions to Medical and Biological Research*, Paul B. Hoeber, New York.
Winters, E.E. (ed.) (1952) *The Collected Works of Adolf Meyer*, vol. IV, Johns Hopkins University Press, Baltimore.

PSYCHOBIOLOGY

Meyer, A. (1948–1952) *Collected Papers*

of Adolf Meyer, 4 vols. Johns Hopkins University Press, Baltimore.
— (1957) *Psychobiology: A Science of Man*. Charles C. Thomas, Springfield, Ill.

PSYCHODRAMA

Moreno, J.L. and Ennis, J.M. (1950) *Hypnodrama and Psychodrama*, Beacon House, Boston.
Greenberg, I.A. (ed.) (1974) *Psychodrama Theory and Therapy*, Behavioural Publications, New York.

PSYCHOSYNTHESIS

Assagioli, R. (1965) *Psychosynthesis: A Manual of Principles and Techniques*, Turnstone Press, Wellingborough.
— (1969) *Symbols of Transpersonal Experiences*, PRF Issue 11. Institute of Psychosynthesis, London.
— (1974) *The Act of Will*, Wildwood House, London.
— (1976) *Transpersonal Inspiration and Psychological Mountain Climbing*, PRF Issue No. 36. Institute of Psychosynthesis, London.
— (1983) *Psychosynthesis Typology*, Institute of Psychosynthesis, London.
Crampton, M. (1974) *A Historical Survey of Mental Imagery Techniques in Psychotherapy*, Quebec Centre of Psychosynthesis, Montreal.
Desoille, R. (1966) *The Directed Daydream*, PRF Issue No. 18, Institute of Psychosynthesis, London.
Ferrucci, P. (1982) *What We May Be*, Turnstone Press, Wellingborough.

RANKIAN DIALECTIC

Rank, O. (1912) *The Incest Motive in Poetry and Saga*, Hogarth Press, London.
— (1914) *The Myth of the Birth of the Hero*, Nervous and Mental Disease Publishing, New York.
— (1929) *The Trauma of Birth*, London: K. Paul Tench, Trubner and Co. (1979) Harper and Row.
— (1932) *Art and Artist*, Harper and Row, New York.

RAPPORT

Clinebell, H.J. (1966) *Basic Types of Pastoral Counselling*, Abingdon, Nashville.
Rogers, C.R. (1967) *On Becoming a Person*, Constable, London.

RATIONAL EMOTIVE THERAPY (RET)

De Guiseppe, R. *et al.* (1977) Outcome studies of rational emotive therapy. *Counselling Psychologist*, 7, 43–50.
Eschenroeder, C. (1982) How rational is rational emotive therapy? A critical appraisal. *Cognitive Therapy and Research*, 6, 381–91.
Ellis, A. (1957) *How to Live With a Neurotic*, Crown publishers, New York.
— (1977) *Reason and Emotion in Psychotherapy*, Citadel, Secauces, New Jersey.
— (1989) *Why Some Therapies Don't Work*, Prometheus Books, New York.
— and Harper, R.A. (1975) *A New Guide to Rational Living*, Prentice-Hall, Englewood Cliffs, New Jersey.

REALITY THERAPY

Glasser, W. (1980) *What Are You Doing Now*, Harper and Row, New York.
— (1961) *Mental Health or Mental Illness*, Harper and Row, New York.
— (1976) *Positive Addiction*, Harper and Row, New York.
— (1981) *Stations of the Mind*, Harper and Row, New York.
— (1965) *Reality Therapy*, Harper and Row, New York.
Powers, W.T. (1973) *Behaviour: The Control of Perception*, Aldine, Chicago.

REASSURANCE

Clinebell, H.J. (1966) *Basic Types of Pastoral Counselling*, Abingdon, Nashville.
Foskett, J. (1984) *Meaning in Madness*, SPCK, London.
Jacobs, M. (1982) *Still Small Voice*, SPCK, London.

REBIRTHING

Kovel, J. (1978) *A Complete Guide to Therapy*, Penguin, Harmondsworth.
Leboyer, F. (1975) *Birth Without Violence*, Knopf, New York.
Orr, L. and Ray, S. (1977) *Rebirthing in the New Age*, Celestial Arts, Millbrae, Calif.

REDUNDANCY COUNSELLING

Board de, R. (1983) *Counselling People at Work*, Gower, Aldershot.
Briggs Myers, I. (1980) *Gifts Differing*, Consulting Psychologists Press, Palo Alto, Calif.
British Association for Counselling (1983) *Redundancy and Unemployment*, BAC, Rugby.
Burrows, G. (1985) *Redundancy Counselling for Managers*, Institute of Personnel Management, London.
Harrison, R. (1973) Towards a strategy for helping redundant and retiring managers. *Management Education and Development*, 4(2), 77–85.
Hartley, J. and Cooper, C.L. (1976) Redundancy: A psychological problem? *Personnel Review*, Summer, 44–8.
Milne, A. (1982) Crisis counselling in industry. *Personnel Executive*, 1(7), January, 29–32.
Weatherley, M.J. (1982) Counselling in career self-management courses for the mature executive. *British Journal of Guidance and Counselling*, 10(1), 88–96.
Webb, S. (1984) *Guidelines for the Redundant Manager*, British Institute of Management, London.

RE-EVALUATION COUNSELLING

Evison, R. and Horobin, R. (1979) *How to Change Yourself and Your World*, Co-counselling Phoenix, Sheffield.
Heron, J. (1973) *Re-evaluation Counselling: A Theoretical Review*, Human Potential Research, Guildford, Surrey.
—— (1977) *Catharsis in Human Development*, University of Surrey, Guildford.
—— (1989) *The Facilitator's Handbook*, Kogan Page, New Jersey.
Jackins, H. (1965) *The Human Side of Human Beings: The Theory of Re-evaluation Counselling*, Rational Island Press, Seattle.
Proctor, B. (1978) *Counselling Shop*, Burnett Books, London.
Southgate, J. and Randall, R. (1978) *The Barefoot Psychoanalyst*, AKHPC, London.

REFERENCE GROUP

Merton, R.K. (1957) *Social Theory and Social Structure*, Free Press, New York.
—— and Kitt, A.S. (1950) Contributions to the theory of reference group behaviour, In, Merton, R.K. and Lazarfield, P.F. (eds) *Continuities in Social Research: Studies in the Scope and Method of the American Soldier*, Free Press, New York.

REFERRAL

Clinebell, H.J. (1966) *Basic Types of Pastoral Counselling*, Abingdon, Nashville.
Jacobs, M. (1982) *Still Small Voice*, SPCK, London.
Kennedy, E. (1977) *On Becoming a Counsellor*, Gill and MacMillan, Dublin.

REFRAMING

Bandler, R. and Grinder, J. (1982) *Reframing*, Real People Press, Moab, Utah.

Minuchin, S. and Fischman, H.S. (1981) *Family Therapy Techniques*, Harvard University Press, Cambridge, Mass.

Watzlawick, P. *et al*. (1974) *Change: Principles of Problem Formation and Problem Resolution*. W.W. Norton, New York.

REICH, WILHELM

Reich, W. (1949) *Character Analysis*, Farar, Straus and Young, New York.

REPERTORY GRID

Beail, N. (ed.) (1985) *Repertory Grid Technique and Personal Constructs*, Croom Helm, Beckenham.

Bannister, D. and Fransella, F. (1980) *Inquiring Man*, 2nd edn, Penguin, Harmondsworth.

Fransella, F. and Bannister, D. (1977) *A Manual for Repertory Grid Technique*, Academic Press, London.

Kelly, G.A. (1955) *The Psychology of Personal Constructs*, W.W. Norton, New York.

—— (1963) *A Theory of Personality*, W.W. Norton, New York.

Slater, P. (1977) *Explorations of Intrapersonal Space*, Wiley, London.

Watson, J.P. (1970) A repertory grid method of studying groups. *British Journal of Psychiatry*, 117, 309–18.

REPRESSION

Freud, S. (1914) On the history of the psychoanalytic movement, *Standard Edition*, vol. 14, Hogarth Press, London.

—— (1915) Repression, *Standard Edition*, vol. 14, Hogarth Press, London.

Myerson, P.G. (1977) Therapeutic dilemmas relevant to the lifting of repression. *International Journal of Psychoanalysis*, 58, 453–62.

RELATIONSHIP PRINCIPLES

Biestek, F.P. (1957) *The Casework Relationship*, George Allen and Unwin, London.

Friedman, M. (1972) *Touchstones of Reality*, E.P. Dutton, New York.

Rogers, C.R. (1980) *A Way of Being*, Houghton Mifflin, Boston.

—— (1961) *On Becoming a Person*, Houghton Mifflin, Boston.

RESISTANCE

Bandura, A. (1969) *Principles of Behaviour Modification*, Holt, Rinehart and Winston, New York.

Freud, S. (1926) Inhibitions, symptoms and anxiety, *Standard Edition*, vol. 20, Hogarth Press, London.

Karp, H.B. (1988) A positive approach to resistance, The *1988 Annual: Developing Human Resources*, University Associates, San Diego, Calif.

Rabkin, R. (1977) *Strategic Psychotherapy*, Basic Books, New York.

Rosenthall, L. (1980) Resistance in group psychotherapy, In, Volberg, L. and Arunsen, M. (eds), *Group and Family Therapy*, Brunner/Mazel, New York.

Wachtel, P.L. (ed.) (1982) *Resistance: Psychodynamic and Behavioural Approaches*, Plenum Press, New York.

SCAPEGOATING

Ackerman, N.W. (1964) Prejudicial scapegoating and neutralising forces in the family group. *International Journal of Social Psychiatry*, 2, 90.

Scheildlinger, S. (1982) On scapegoating in group psychotherapy. *International Journal of Group Psychotherapy*, 32, 131–42.

Speck, R.V. (1965) The transfer of illness phenomenon in schizophrenic families, In Friedman, A.S. *et al.* *(eds), Psychotherapy for the Whole Family*, Springer, New York.

SELF-ACTUALIZATION

Goldstein, K. (1934) *The Organism*, Beacon Press.

Heine, R.W. (eds) (1963) *Concepts of Personality*, Aldine Atherton, Chicago.

Maslow, A.H. (1954) *Motivation and Personality*, Harper and Row, New York.

Rogers, C.R. (1951) *Client-Centred Therapy*, Constable, London.

Symonds, A. (1980) The stress of self-realisation. *American Journal of Psychoanalysis*, 40, 293–300.

SELF-ACTUALIZING THERAPY

Brammer, L.M. and Shostram, E.L. (1977) *Therapeutic Psychology: Fundamentals of Actualising Counselling and Therapy*, 3rd edn, Prentice-Hall, Englewood Cliffs, New Jersey.

Maslow, A.H. (1954) *Motivation and Personality*, Harper and Row, New York.

Shostram, E.L. (1976) *Actualising Assessment Battery*, Edits, San Diego.

—— (1976) *Actualising Therapy: Foundations for a Scientific Ethic*, Edits, San Diego.

Shostram, E.L. (1963) *Personal Orientation Inventory*, Edits, San Diego.

SELF-AWARENESS

Duval, S. and Wicklund, R.A. (1972)*A Theory of Objective Self-awareness*, Academic Press, London.

Eastcott, J. (1978) *The Silent Path*, Rider, London.

Fenigstein, A., Scheier, M.F. and Buss, A.H. (1975) Public and private self consciousness: Assessment and theory, *Journal of Consulting and Clinical Psychology*, 43, 522–7.

Ferucci, P. (1979) *What We May Be*. Turnstone Press, Wellingborough.

Grof, S. (1979) *Realms of the Human Unconscious*, Souvenir Press, London.

Kleinke, C.L. (1978) *Self-perception: The Psychology of Personal Awareness*, W.H. Freeman, San Francisco.

Rowan, J. (1983) *The Reality Game*, Routledge and Kegan Paul, London.

Wicklund, R.A. and Frey, D.(1980) Self-awareness theory: when the self makes a difference, In, Wegner, D.M. and Vallacher, R.R. (eds), *The Self in Social Psychology*, OUP, Oxford.

SELF-CONCEPT

Allport, G. (1965) *Pattern and Growth in Personality*, Holt, Rinehart and Winston, New York.

Gergen, K. (1961) *The Concept of Self*, Holt, Rinehart and Winston, New York.

Mead, G.H. (1934) *Mind, Self and Society*, University of Chicago Press, Chicago.

SELF-DISCLOSURE

Bierman, R. (1969) Dimensions for interpersonal facilitation in psychotherapy and child development. *Psychological Bulletin*, 72, 338–72.

Cozby, P.C. (1973) Self-disclosure: A literature review. *Psychological Bulletin*, 79, 73–91.

Dies, R.R. (1973) Group therapist self-disclosure: An evaluation by client. *Journal of Counselling Psychology*, 20, 344–8.

Johnson, D.W. and Noonan, M.P. (1972) The effects of acceptance and

reciprocation of self-disclosures on the development of trust. *Journal of Counselling Psychology*, 19, 411–16.
Jourard, S.M. and Friedman, R. (1970) Experimenter-subject 'distance' and self-disclosure. *Journal of Personality and Social Psychology*, 15, 278–82.
—— (1971) *The Transparent Self*, Van Nostrand Reinhold, Toronto.
Kaslow, F. *et al.* (1979) Family therapist authenticity as a key factor in outcome. *International Journal Therapy*, 1, 184–99.
Mowrer, O.H. (1964) Freudianism, behaviour therapy and 'self-disclosure'. *Behaviour Research and Therapy*, 1, 321–37.
Weiner, W.F. (1978) *Therapist Disclosure*, Butterworth, Boston.

SELF-ESTEEM

Becker, J. (1979) Vulnerable self-esteem as a predisposing factor in depressive disorders, In, Depue, R. (ed.) *The Psychopathology of Depressive Disorders: Implications For the Effects of Stress*. Academic Press, New York.
Brisset, D. (1972) Towards a clarification of self-esteem. *Psychiatry*, 35, 255–63.
Brown, G.W. *et al.* (1986) Social support, self-esteem and depression. *Psychological Medicine*, 16, 813–31.
Coopersmith, S. (1967) *The Antecedents of Self-esteem*. W.H. Freeman, San Francisco.
The Lancet, (Editorial) 22 October 1988 (2), 943–4.
Lowry, R.J. (ed.) (1973) *Dominance, Self-esteem, Self-Actualisation: Germinal Papers of A.H. Maslow*, Brooks/Cole, Monterey, Calif.
Maslow, A.H. (1937) Dominance feeling, behaviour and status, *Psychological Review*, 44, 404–29. Reprinted in: Wells, L. and Marwell, G. (1976) *Self-esteem: Its Conceptualisation and Measurement*, Sage, Beverly Hills.
Robson, P.J. (1988) Self-esteem – a psychiatric view, *British Journal of Psychiatry*, 153, 6–15.

SELF-FULFILLING PROPHECY

Merton, R.K. (1949) *Social Theory and Social Structure*, Free Press, Glencoe.

SELF-HYPNOSIS

Cheek, D.B. and Le Cron, L. (1968) *Clinical Hypnotherapy*, Grune and Stratton, New York.
Le Cron, L. (1970) *Self-Hypnosis*, New American Library, New York.
Morris, F. (1974) *Self-Hypnosis in Two Days*, Intergalactic, Berkeley.

SHADOW

Franz, K.L. von (1974) *Shadow and Evil in Fairy Tales*, Spring Publications, Zurich.
Jung, C.G. (1946) The fight with the shadow, *Collected Works*, vol. 10, Routledge and Kegan Paul, London.
—— (1951) Aion, *Collected Works*, vol. 9, Princeton University Press, Princeton, New Jersey.
Wickes, F.G. (1988) *The Inner World of Man*, Sigo Press, Boston.

SILENCE

Bengler, B. (1938) On the resistance situation: The patient is silent. *Psychoanalytic Review*, 25, 170.
Biestek, F. (1961) *The Casework Relationship*, George Allen and Unwin, London.
Breunlin, D.C. and Southgate, P. (1978) An interactional approach to dysfunctional silencing in family therapy. *Family Process*, 17, 207–16.

Buber, M. (1958) *I and Thou*, T. and T. Clark, Edinburgh.
Ferreira, A.J. (1973) On silence. *American Journal of Psychotherapy*, 18, 109–15.
Khan, M.R. (1963) Silence as communication. *Bulletin of the Menninger Clinic*, 27, 299–310.
Nacht, S. (1964) Silence as an integrative factor. *International Journal of Psycho-Analysis*, 45, 300–10.
Zeligs, M.A. (1961) The psychology of silence. *Journal of the American Psychoanalytic Association*, 9, 7–43.
Zuk, G.H. (1965) On the pathology of silencing strategies. *Family Process*, 4, 32–49.

SINGLE-SESSION THERAPY

Bloom, B.L. (1981) Focused single session therapy: Initial development and evaluation, In, Budman, S. (ed.), *Forms of Brief Therapy*, Guilford Press, New York.
Cummings, N.A. (1977) Prolonged (ideal) versus short-term (realistic) psychotherapy. *Professional Psychology*, 8, 491–501.
Malan, D.H. (1976) *The Frontier of Brief Psychotherapy*, Plenum Press, New York.
Rockwell, W. *et al*. (1982) Single-session psychotherapy. *American Journal of Psychotherapy*, 36, 32–40.
Silverman, W.H. and Beech, R.P. (1979) Are drop outs drop outs? *Journal of Community Psychology*, 7, 236–242.

SIX-CATEGORY INTERVENTION
(*See also*: References under Re-evaluation counselling)

Heron, J. (1972) *Experience and Method*, Human Potential Research Project, Guildford, Surrey.
—— (1973) *Experiential Training Techniques*, Human Potential Research Project, Guildford, Surrey.
—— (1974) *Reciprocal Training Manual*, Human Potential Research Project, Guildford, Surrey.
—— (1975) *Six Category Intervention Analysis*. Human Potential Research Project, Guildford, Surrey.
Jackins, H. (1970) *Fundamentals of Co-counselling Manual*, Rational Island Press, Seattle.

SOCIAL THERAPY

Arthur, R.J. (1977) *An Introduction to Social Psychiatry*, Penguin, Harmondsworth.
Canter, D. and Canter, S. (1979) *Designing for Therapeutic Environments*, John Wiley, Chichester.
Edelson, M. (1970) *Sociotherapy and Psychotherapy*, Chicago University Press, Chicago.
Jones, M. (1953) *The Therapeutic Community*, Penguin, Harmondsworth.
—— (1968) *Beyond the Therapeutic Community*, Penguin, Harmondsworth.
Scott, R.D. and Starr, I. (1981) A 24-hour family-oriented psychiatric and crisis service. *Journal of Family Therapy*, 3, 177–86.

SOCIOGRAM

Moreno, J.L. (ed.) (1960) *The Sociometry Reader*, Free Press of Glencoe, Glencoe, Ill.

STRESS MANAGEMENT

Anderson, J.L. and Cohen, M. (1978) *The West Point Fitness and Diet Book*, Avon Books, New York.
Brown, B. (1977) *Stress and the Art of*

Biofeedback, Harper and Row, New York.

Cooper, C.L., Sloan, S.J., Williams, S. (1988) *Occupational Stress Indicator*, NFER, Nelson, Windsor.

Cooper, K.H. (1977) *The Aerobic Way*, M. Evans, New York.

Corbin, C. (1980) *Nutrition*, Holt, Rinehart and Winston, New York.

Davis, M., Robbins, E. and McKay, M. (1982) *The Relaxation and Stress Reduction Workbook*, New Harbinger Publications, Oakland, Calif.

Friedman, M. (1969) *Pathogenesis of Coronary Artery Disease*, McGraw Hill, New York.

Gale, B. (1979) *The Wonderful World of Walking*, William Morrow, New York.

Goodstadt, B. and Hjelle, L.A. (1973) Power to the powerless: Locus of control and the use of power. *Journal of Personality and Social Psychology*, 8, 155–156.

Greenwald, H. (1973) *Direct Decision Therapy*, Edits, Calif.

Holmes, T.H. and Rahe, R.H. (1967) The social readjustment rating scale. *Journal of Psychosomatic Research*, 11, 213–18.

Jenkins, C.D. (1971) Psychologic and social precursors of coronary disease. *New England Journal of Medicine*, 284, 309.

Junin, R.A. (1980) *Mega-Nutrition: The New Prescription for Maximum Health, Energy and Longevity*, McGraw Hill, New York.

Karlins, M., Karlins, A. and Lewis, M. (1972) *Biofeedback: Turning on the Powers of Your Mind*, Lippincott, New York.

Lakein, A. (1973) *How to Get Control of Your Time and Your Life*, Signet, New York.

Livingstone-Booth, A. (1985) *Stressmanship*, Severn House Publishers, London.

Peale, N.V. (1953) *The Power of Positive Thinking*, Cedar/Heinemann, London.

Ramacharaka, Yogi, (1905) *Science of Breath*, Yogi Publication Society, Chicago.

Rotter, J.B. (1966) Generalised expectancies for internal versus external control of reinforcement. *Psychological Monographs: General and Applied*, 80(1), Whole No. 609.

Saraswati, Swami, J. (1976)*Yoga, Tantra and Meditation*, Ballantine, New York.

Selye, H. (1957) *The Stress of Life*, Longman Green, London.

Sorenson, J. (1981) *Aerobic Dancing*, Rawson Way, New York.

Spreads, C. (1978) *Breathing – the ABCs*, Harper and Row, New York.

Thomas, G.S. (1981) *Exercise and Health: Evidence and Implications*, Oelger, Shlager, Gunn and Hain, New York.

Winters, E.E. (ed.) (1952) *The Collected Papers of Adolf Meyer*, vol. IV, The John Hopkins University Press, Baltimore.

Wolff, H.G. (1953) *Stress and Disease*, Charles C. Thomas, Springfield, Ill.

SUICIDE

Dublin, L.I. (1963) *Suicide*, Ronald Press, New York.

Durkheim, E. (1951) *Suicide*, (brought up to date in Jack P. Gibbs and Walter T. Martin (1964) *Status Integration and Suicide*, University of Oregon Books, Eugene, Oregon.

Varah, C. (1965) *The Samaritans: To Help Those Tempted to Suicide*, MacMillan, New York.

SUPERIORITY COMPLEX

Adler, A. (1937) *Understanding Human Nature*, George Allen and Unwin, London.
— (1956) *The Individual Psychology of Alfred Adler*, Ansbacher, H.L. and Ansbacher, R.R. (eds) Basic Books, New York.

SUPERVISION

British Association for Counselling (1987) *Supervision*, Spring issue of the News-Letter of the Counselling at Work Division.
Halmos, P. (1965) *The Faith of the Counsellors*, Constable, London.
Marteau, L. (1976) *Ethical Standards in Counselling*. British Association for Counselling.

SUPPORTIVE PSYCHOTHERAPY

Bloch, S. (1977) Supportive psychotherapy. *British Journal of Hospital Medicine*, 18, 63–67.
— (1979) *Introduction to the Psychotherapies*, OUP, Oxford.
Brandwin, M.A. *et al.* (1976) The continuing care clinic: Outpatient treatment of the chronically ill. *Psychiatry*, 39, 103–17.
MacLeod, J. and Middleman, F. (1962) Wednesday afternoon clinic: A supportive care programme. *Archives of General Psychiatry*, 6, 56–65.
Peplau, L.A. and Perlman, D. (eds.) (1982) *Loneliness: A Source Book of Current Theory, Research and Therapy*, Wiley, New York.
Wolberg, L.R. (1967) *The Technique of Psychotherapy*, 2nd edn, vol. 1, Grune and Stratton, New York.

SYMBOLS AND SYMBOLISM

Cirlot, J.E. (1962) *A Dictionary of Symbols*, Routledge and Kegan Paul, London.
Freud, S. (1900) The interpretation of dreams, *Standard Edition*, vols. 4 and 5, Hogarth Press, London.
Jones, E. (1916) The theory of symbolism, In, *Papers on Psychoanalysis*, Bailliére Tindall and Cox, London.
Jung, C.G. (1962) *Commentary on the Secret of the Golden Flower*, Routledge and Kegan Paul, London.
— (1969) *Man and his Symbols*, Doubleday, Garden City.
Klein, M. (1930) The importance of symbol formation in the development of the ego, In, *Contributions to Psychoanalysis*, Hogarth Press, London.
Milner, M. (1955) The role of illusion in symbol formation, In, Klein, M. *et al.* (eds), *New Directions in Psychoanalysis*, Karnac, Maresfield Reprints, London.
Segal, H. (1957) Notes on symbol formation, In, *The Work of Hannah Segal*, Jason Aronson, New York.

SYSTEMATIC DESENSITIZATION

Eysenck, H.J. and Rachman , S. (1965) *The Causes and Cures of Neurosis*, Pergamon, London.
Jacobson, E. (1938) *Progressive Relaxation*, Chicago University Press, Chicago.
Paul, G.L. (1969) Outcome of systematic desensitization, In, Franks, C.M. (ed.), *Behaviour Therapy: Appraisal and Status*, McGraw-Hill, New York.
Rachman, S. (1976) Systematic desensitisation. *Psychological Bulletin*,67, 93–103.
Wolpe, J. (1958) *Psychotherapy by Reciprocal Inhibition*, Stanford University Press, Stanford, Calif.
— (1962) Isolation of a conditioning

procedure as the crucial psychotherapeutic factor. *Journal of Nervous and Mental Diseases*, 134, 316.
—— (1974) *The Practice of Behaviour Therapy*, 2nd edn, Pergamon, New York.

TAVISTOCK METHOD

Astrachan, B.M. (1975) The Tavistock model of laboratory training. In, Benne, K.D., Bradford, L.P., Gibb, J.R. and Lippitt, R.O. (eds), *The Laboratory Method of Changing and Learning: Theory and Application*, Science and Behaviour Books, Palo Alto, Calif.
Banet, A.G. and Hayden, C. (1977) A Tavistock Primer, *The 1977 Annual Handbook for Group Facilitators*, University Asociates, San Diego, Calif.
Rioch, M.J. (1970) The work of Wilfred R. Bion on groups. *Psychiatry*, 33, 56–66.

TELEPHONE COUNSELLING

CEPEC, N16 (1.87C) (1987) *Notes On The Use Of The Telephone In Counselling*, London.
Kennedy, E. (1981) *Crisis Counselling: The Essential Guide for Nonprofessional Counsellors*, Gill and Macmillan, Dublin.

TOUCH

Kaplan, L. (1979) *Oneness and Separateness*, Johnathan Cape, London.
Lowen, A. (1971) *The Language of the Body*, Collier Books.

TRANSACTIONAL ANALYSIS

Anderson, J.P. (1973) A Transactional Primer, *The 1973 Handbook for Group Facilitators*, University Associates, San Diego, Calif.
Avary, B. (1980) Ego states: Manifestations of psychic organs. *Transactional Analysis Journal*, 10(4), 291–4.
Barnes, G. (1961) *Transactional Analysis after Eric Berne*, Harper and Row, New York.
Berne, E. (1957) *Layman's Guide to Psychiatry and Psychoanalysis*, Simon and Schuster, New York.
—— (1961) *Transactional Analysis in Psychotherapy*, Grove Press, New York.
—— (1964) *Games People Play*, Grove Press, New York.
—— (1964) *Principles of Group Treatment*, Oxford University Press, New York.
—— (1970) Case example, In, *Sex in Human Loving*, Simon and Schuster, New York.
—— (1972) *What Do You Say After You Say Hello?*, Grove Press, New York.
Dusay, J. (1975) Case example, In, Kaplan H. and Sadock, B. (eds), *Comprehensive Group Psychotherapy*, Williams and Wilkins, Baltimore.
Harris, T.A. (1969) *I'm OK –You're OK*, Harper and Row, New York.
James, M. (1975) *The OK Boss*, Addison-Wesley, Reading, Mass.
Jongeward, D. and Scott, D. (1973) Case example, In, *Affirmative Action for Women*, Addison-Wesley, Reading, Mass.
Karpman, S.B. (1968) Fairy tales and script drama analysis. *Transactional Analysis Bulletin*, 7(26), 39–43.
Pareek, U. (1984) Interpersonal styles: The SPIRO instrument, *Handbook for Group Facilitators*, University Associates, San Diego, Calif.
Pitman, E. (1984) *Transactional Analysis*, Routledge and Kegan Paul, London.
Savorgnan, J.A. (1979) Social design of the parental ego state. *Transactional Analysis Journal*, 9(2), 147.

Schiff, C. (1974) *Scripts People Live*, Grove Press, New York.

Stewart, I. and Joines, V. (1987) *T.A. Today*, Lifespace Publishing, Nottingham.

TRANSFERENCE

Blanck, L. and Blanck, R. (1979) *Ego Psychology II: Psychoanalytic Developmental Psychology*, Columbia University Press, New York.

Freud, S. (1915) Observations on transference love, *Standard Edition*, vol. 12, Hogarth Press, London.

—— (1922) *Introductory Lectures on Psychoanalysis*, George Allen and Unwin, London.

Gill, M. (1982) *Analysis of Transference*, vols. 1 and 2, International Universities Press, New York.

Heinmann, D. (1956) Dynamics of transference interpretations. *International Journal of Psychoanalysis*, 37, 303–10.

Jacobs, M. (1988) *Psychodynamic Counselling in Action*, Sage, London.

Jung, C.G. (1946) *The Psychology of the Transference*, Routledge and Kegan Paul, London.

Klein, M. (1952) The origins of transference, In, *Envy and Gratitude and Other Works*, Hogarth Press, London.

Lower, R.B. (1973) An experimental examination of transference. *Archives of General Psychiatry*, 29, 738–41.

Luborsky, L. and Spence, D.A. (1971) Initiative research on psychoanalytic therapy. In, Bergin, A.E. and Garfield, S.L. (eds), *Handbook of Psychotherapy and Behaviour Change*, Wiley, New York.

Patterson, C.H. (1985) *The Therapeutic Relationship: Foundations for an Eclectic Psychotherapy*, Brooks/Cole, Monterey, Calif.

Rogers, C.R. (1951, reprint 1981) *Client-Centred Therapy*, Constable, London.

Sandler, J. *et al.* (1970) Basic psychoanalytic concepts III: Transference. *British Journal of Psychiatry*, 116, 667–72.

Watkins, C.E. (1989) Transference phenomena in the counselling situation, In, Dryden W. (ed.), *Key Issues for Counselling in Action*. Sage, London. Originally in *Personnel and Guidance Journal* (1983), 62, 206–10.

TRANSPERSONAL PSYCHOLOGY

Hendricks, G. and Weinhold, B . (1982) *Transpersonal Approaches to Counselling and Psychotherapy*, Love Publishing, Denver.

Maslow, A.H. (1964) *Toward a Psychology of Being*, Van Nostrand, Princeton, New Jersey.

—— (1971) *The Farther Reaches of Human Nature*, Viking Press, New York.

Pearce, J. (1974) *Exploring the Crack in the Cosmic Egg: Split Minds and Metarealities*, Julian Press, New York.

Pelletier, K. and Garfield, C. (1976) *Consciousness East and West*, Harper Colophon, New York.

Rowan, J. (1983) *The Reality Game*, Routledge and Kegan Paul, London.

Tart, C. (1969) *Altered States of Consciousness*, Wiley, New York.

—— (1975) *Transpersonal Psychologies*, Harper and Row, New York.

—— (1983) *Transpersonal Psychologies*. Psychological Processes, California.

Walsh, R. and Vaughan, F. (1980) *Beyond Ego: Transpersonal Dimensions in Psychology*, J.P. Tarcher, Los Angeles.

TRUST

Bowlby, J. (1969) *Attachment and Loss*,

vol. 1, *Attachment*, Penguin, Harmondsworth.
—— (1973) *Attachment and Loss*, vol. 2, *Separation*, Penguin, Harmondsworth.
—— (1980) *Attachment and Loss*, vol. 3, *Loss*, Penguin, Harmondsworth.
—— (1975) Attachment theory, separation anxiety and mourning, In, Hamburg, D.A. and Brodie, H. (eds) *American Handbook of Psychiatry*, vol. 6, Basic Books, New York.
Chartier, M.R. (1991) Trust-orientation profile, *The 1991 Annual: Developing Human Resources*, University Associates, San Diego, Calif.
Erikson, Erik H. (1963) *Childhood and Society*, 2nd edn, Norton, New York.
Gibb, J.R. (1978) *Trust: A New View of Personal and Organisational Development*, Guild of Tutors Press, Los Angeles.
Giffin, K. and Barnes, R.E. (1976) *Trusting Me, Trusting You*, Charles, E. Merrill, Westerville, Ohio.
Johnson, D.W. (1986) *Reaching Out: Interpersonal Effectiveness and Self-actualisation*, 3rd edn, Prentice-Hall, Englewood Cliffs, New Jersey.

UNCONSCIOUS

Ellenberger, H.F. (1970) *The Discovery of the Unconscious*, Allen Lane, London.
Freud, S. (1900) The interpretation of dreams, *Standard Edition*, vols. 4 and 5, Hogarth Press, London.
—— (1912) A note on the unconscious in psychoanalysis, *Standard Edition*, vol. 12, Hogarth Press, London.
Jung, Carl, G. (1954) *The Collected Works – The practice of psychotherapy*, vol. 16, Routledge and Kegan Paul, London.

UNCONDITIONAL POSITIVE REGARD

Gurman, A. (1977) The patient's perception of the therapeutic relationship, In, *Effective Psychotherapy*, Pergamon, New York.
Mitchell, K.M. *et al.* (1977) A reappraisal of accurate empathy, nonpossessive warmth and genuineness, In, Gurman, A.S. and Razin, A.M. (eds), *Effective Psychotherapy*, Pergamon, New York.
Rogers, C.R. (1967) *The Therapeutic Relationship and its Impact*, Greenwood Press, Westport, Conn.
Schmitt, J.P. (1980) Unconditional positive regard: The hidden paradox. *Psychotherapy: Theory, Research and Practice*, 17, 237–43.
Troemel-Ploetz, S. (1980) 'I'd come to you for therapy'; Interpretation, redefinition and paradox in Rogerian Therapy. *Psychotherapy: Theory, Research and Practice*, 17, 246–57.
Truax, C.B. and Mitchell, K.M. (1971) Research on certain therapist interpersonal skills in relation to process and outcome, In, Bergin, A.E. and Garfield, S.L. (eds), *Handbook of Psychotherapy and Behaviour Change*, Wiley, New York.

VALUES

Hall, B. and Smith M. (1972) *Value Clarification as a Learning Process: A Search into the Choices, Commitments and Celebrations of Modern Man*, Pualist Press, New York.
Oliver, J.E. (1985) The personal value statement: An experiential learning instrument, *The 1985 Annual: Developing Human Resources*, University Associates, San Diego, Calif.

Rao, T.V. (1991) Managerial work-values scale, *The 1991 Annual: Developing Human Resources*, University Associates, San Diego, Calif.

Rokeach, M. (1973) *The Nature of Human Values*, Free Press, New York.

Smith, M. (1973) Some implications of value clarification for organisation development, *The 1973 Annual Handbook for Group Facilitators*, University Associates, San Diego, Calif.

Spranger, E. (1929) *Types of Men*, P.J.W. Pignors, (ed. and trans.), Stechert–Hafner, New York.

WILL THERAPY

Karpf, F.B. (1953) *The Psychology and Psychotherapy of Otto Rank*, Greenwood Press, Conn.

Rank, O. (1936) *Will Therapy*, Knopf, New York.

WINNICOTT, DONALD W.

Winnicott, D.W. (1948) *Collected Papers: Through Paediatrics to Psychoanalysis*, Hogarth Press, London.

—— (1965) *The Maturation Process and the Facilitating Environment*, Hogarth Press and Institute of Psychoanalysis, London.

—— (1964) *The Child, the Family and the Outside World*, Penguin, Harmondsworth.

—— (1971) *Playing and Reality*, Tavistock, London.

WORD ASSOCIATION TEST

Jung, C.G. (1969) *Studies in Word Association*, Routledge and Kegan Paul, London.

WORKING THROUGH

Freud, S. (1914) Remembering, repeating and working through, *Standard Edition*, vol. 12, Hogarth Press, London.

Greenson, R.R. (1967) *The Technique and Practice of Psychoanalysis*, vol. 1, International University Press, New York.

Novery, S. (1962) The principle of working through in psychoanalysis. *Journal of the American Psychoanalytic Association*, 10, 658–76.

WOUNDED HEALER

Guggenbuhl-Craig, A. (1971) *Power in the Helping Professions*, Spring Publications, New York.

Jung, C.G. (1951) Fundamental questions of psychotherapy, *Collected Works*, vol. 15, Routledge and Kegan Paul, London.

Meier, C.A. (1967) *Ancient Incubation and Modern Psychotherapy*, North Western University Press, Evanston.

Z-PROCESS ATTACHMENT THERAPY

Zaslow, R.W. (1970) *Resistance to Growth and Attachment*, San Jose State University Press, Calif.

—— (1981) Z-process attachment therapy, In, Corsini, R.J. (ed.) *Handbook of Innovative Therapies*, Wiley, New York.

—— and Mental, M. (1977) *Rage, Resistance and Holding*, San Jose State University Press, Calif.

Authors, with subjects

Index to subjects

Index to entries

The main entry is in **bold type**